Hobart Years

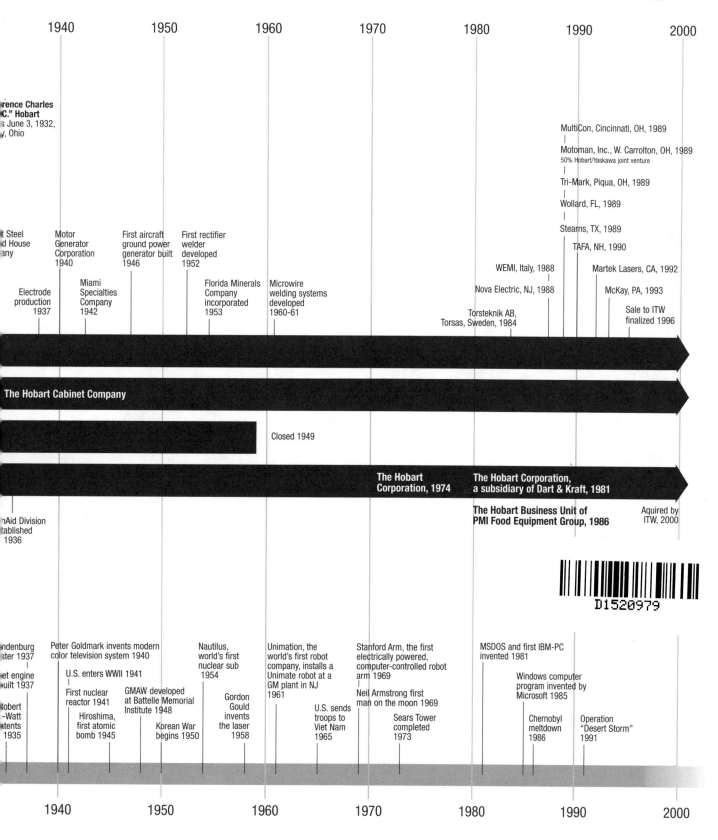

1940	1950	1960	1970	1980	1990	2000

rence Charles
C." Hobart
s June 3, 1932,
y, Ohio

MultiCon, Cincinnati, OH, 1989

Motoman, Inc., W. Carrolton, OH, 1989
50% Hobart/Yaskawa joint venture

Tri-Mark, Piqua, OH, 1989

Wollard, FL, 1989

Stearns, TX, 1989

TAFA, NH, 1990

t Steel
d House
any

Motor
Generator
Corporation
1940

First aircraft
ground power
generator built
1946

First rectifier
welder
developed
1952

WEMI, Italy, 1988

Martek Lasers, CA, 1992

Nova Electric, NJ, 1988

McKay, PA, 1993

Electrode
production
1937

Miami
Specialties
Company
1942

Florida Minerals
Company
incorporated
1953

Microwire
welding systems
developed
1960-61

Torsteknik AB,
Torsas, Sweden, 1984

Sale to ITW
finalized 1996

The Hobart Cabinet Company

Closed 1949

The Hobart
Corporation, 1974

The Hobart Corporation,
a subsidiary of Dart & Kraft, 1981

nAid Division
tablished
1936

**The Hobart Business Unit of
PMI Food Equipment Group, 1986**

Aquired by
ITW, 2000

D1520979

ndenburg
ster 1937

Peter Goldmark invents modern
color television system 1940

Nautilus,
world's first
nuclear sub
1954

Unimation, the
world's first robot
company, installs a
Unimate robot at a
GM plant in NJ
1961

Stanford Arm, the first
electrically powered,
computer-controlled robot
arm 1969

MSDOS and first IBM-PC
invented 1981

et engine
uilt 1937

U.S. enters WWII 1941

Windows computer
program invented by
Microsoft 1985

lobert
-Watt
tents
1935

First nuclear
reactor 1941

GMAW developed
at Battelle Memorial
Institute 1948

Gordon
Gould
invents
the laser
1958

Neil Armstrong first
man on the moon 1969

U.S. sends
troops to
Viet Nam
1965

Sears Tower
completed
1973

Chernobyl
meltdown
1986

Operation
"Desert Storm"
1991

Hiroshima,
first atomic
bomb 1945

Korean War
begins 1950

1940	1950	1960	1970	1980	1990	2000

THE INDUSTRIAL
HOBARTS

Peter C. Hobart

Michael W. Williams

This book is dedicated to our thousands of friends, customers, and associates worldwide (what today are often called "stakeholders") in an attempt to put a one-hundred-year perspective on the history, technology, culture, and philosophy of an industrial family and to serve future generations as a historical document as to the origins of the American Industrial Revolution, in a few words, an American allegory.

My associate, Michael Williams, is an accomplished historian and teacher, who provided writing talent, objectivity, factual insight and material, and the vernacular of today's world.

Peter C. Hobart

Cover design and page layout by Robert J. Hora

Copyright © 2004 by Peter C. Hobart and Michael W. Williams

The Donning Company Publishers
184 Business Park Drive, Suite 206
Virginia Beach, VA 23462

Steve Mull, General Manager
Ed Williams, Project Director

Library of Congress Cataloging-in-Publication Data

Hobart, Peter C.
    The Hobart industrialists / by Peter C. Hobart and Michael W. Williams.
        p.   cm.
    Includes bibliographical references and index.
    ISBN 1-57864-263-9 (hard cover : alk. paper) — ISBN 1-57864-264-7 (soft
cover : alk. paper)
1. Hobart Brothers Company—History. 2. Welding equipment industry—United
States—History. 3. Electric generators—United States—History. 4. Aerospace
engineering—United States—Equipment and supplies—History. 5. Welding—
United States—Automation—History. 6. Welding—Study and teaching—History.
7. Hobart family. I. Williams, Michael W. II. Title.
    TK4660.H5316 2004
    338.7'67152'09771—dc22
                                2004006332

Printed in the USA by Walsworth Publishing Company

Contents

(Contents)

Foreword

by Jeffrey D. Weber

The Hobart family entered the fabric of American life in 1633 when Edmund Hobart, a sixty-three-year-old minister, sailed from England to the Massachusetts Bay Colony. Enthusiastic exercise of the New World's relative intellectual freedom culminated in the rise of the Hobart industrial enterprise that has defined the family for the past one-hundred-plus years. This effort was launched in 1886 when Clarence Charles Hobart left Middletown (Ohio) Edison and formed his own business, the Hobart Electric Manufacturing Company, to produce improved versions of Edison bipolar generators needed by local paper mills. This first factory with the Hobart name burned in 1890, but it was the progenitor of several other family businesses that ultimately specialized in food processing equipment, cabinetry, steel housing, battery chargers, ground power units and, finally, the broad line of Hobart welding equipment and consumables that are known to welding users worldwide.

What makes the chronicle of "The Industrial Hobarts" unique is that the story of this one family parallels the growth of manufacturing in America. More than this, it reflects the history of our nation as a whole, of our people, as we labored and struggled through the emergence of the automobile and aviation, two world wars, the devastating Great Depression, many bouts of social upheaval, and trying times when we have all had to pull together for the common good.

I write these words on September 11, 2003, a national day of mourning exactly two years after the terrorist attacks that had such dire and heartbreaking consequences in New York City, rural Pennsylvania, and Washington, D.C. In doing so, I am reminded of how these tragic events and their aftermath exemplify the unique American spirit—the selfless, industrious, morally straight, and unflaggingly tough spirit that has carried us through good times and bad, and has established the United States as an industrial world power unparalleled in human history. The Hobart clan represents embodiment of this spirit, and their story serves as allegory for the development of American industry.

As milestones in this industrial history, it's easy to start by saying that Edward A. Hobart built his first arc welder in 1925, and that the company's famous welder training facility opened in 1930. However, there are other fascinating stories, all revealed in the book you are holding, that explain how the family businesses got to where

they are today and how they neatly fit into a historical context in the tumultuous twentieth century. Following are some examples of the important and engaging stories told in this comprehensive volume:

The results of an experimental foray into construction of prefabricated, welded steel houses in the 1930s. While this line of manufacturing was ultimately abandoned, production methods developed by the company were crucial to handling huge government orders during World War II.

The development of wide-scale welding electrode production. Starting with a 1934 patent, Hobart Brothers developed a covered electrode line that matched the high quality standards of European products and was generally considered superior to any electrode then produced in the United States.

The story of how a mysterious telegram from the U.S. War Department in 1940 resulted in a whopping order for five thousand motor generators for the Army Signal Corps, sparking a frenzy of self-funded wartime expansion at Hobart Brothers.

Hobart's critical role in supplying equipment for construction of 4,600 cargo ships during the 1940s, including 2,710 10,000-ton Liberty Ships for the war effort.

The use of Hobart welders for building safer all-welded battle tanks during the war, as well as truck-mounted machine shops employed in the field to put damaged weapons and vehicles back into service.

The design and construction of a 6,000-seat winter sports arena in Troy, Ohio. The building was also used as an important entertainment venue, hosting such notable performers as Elvis Presley.

The company's post–World War II struggle to remain profitable without large government orders, and the ultimate development of much-needed ground power units for commercial aircraft.

How Hobart engineers applied their electrical ingenuity to deliver power for the Distant Early Warning, or DEW, line of arctic radar stations designed to ward off nuclear attack across the top of the globe.

Development of a high-deposition electroslag welding system that was used to build the core structure for the twin towers of the World Trade Center in New York City.

How Hobart Brothers became a major supplier for the 4,800-mile natural gas pipeline network running from

Alaska's North Slope and Canadian arctic oilfields to the "Lower 48."

Beyond this, you will read how Hobart Brothers was affected by the 1979 nuclear accident at Three Mile Island, by the 1980s slump in the U.S. auto industry, and by various plans to internationalize the business.

First, though, allow me a few paragraphs to describe Hobart Brothers' influence on the development of American industry and infrastructure. Throughout the thirty years or so I have been involved in construction and manufacturing journalism, the Hobart name has been prominent in all areas of the business. It's been, quite literally, hard to miss. For nearly sixty years, a constantly changing stream of Hobart Brothers advertisements occupied the page-one spot in the *Welding Journal*, monthly magazine of the American Welding Society, my present employer. Earlier, when I occupied editorial spots with *Welding Engineer* and *The Welding Distributor* magazines Hobart was there, as well—as a major advertiser, as a supplier of editorial features, and as a key player in the business news we reported in each issue.

Hobart Brothers has also contributed significantly to leadership of the American Welding Society, which is the industry's primary technical and support association. William H. Hobart served on the Board of AWS from 1963–1965. Serving as elected presidents of AWS were J. H. Blankenbuehler (1962–63), a Hobart design engineer, and Howard B. Cary (1980–81), president of the Hobart Institute of Welding Technology. In addition, Glenn M. Nally, former Hobart Director of Marketing Communications, served as chair of the AWS *Welding Journal* Committee for sixteen years, from 1978 through 1994, and he was twice elected to serve on the AWS Board as director-at-large, 1990–1996. Another former president of the Hobart Institute, Ray Shook, currently serves the American Welding Society in its top staff position as executive director.

Other Hobart Brothers personnel have served in leadership roles on a number of AWS Technical Committees and as members of the Welding Handbook Committee. Publishing ventures from the Hobart staff have included numerous influential articles in the *Welding Journal*, ranging from training and computer topics to a cover story titled "Welded Sculpture: A Truly American

Art Form," by Peter C. Hobart (January 1996). Of course, Howard Cary's book, *Modern Welding Technology* (first published in 1979, and followed by four subsequent editions), has become a classic text for both beginning and advanced welding studies.

Over the years, the Hobart name has been a mainstay of the welding industry overseas, as well. Hobart Brothers was a regular exhibitor at the giant Essen Welding Fair in Germany before many American welding equipment companies even thought about going international. A partnership with Swiss filler metal manufacturer Oerlikon in the late 1980s drew much attention throughout the welding world. The link-up increased recognition and use of Oerlikon stainless steel electrodes in the United States and also opened the door for sales of a specially designed line of Hobart inverter power sources in Europe.

Like many American businesses, Hobart Brothers had some adapting to do in the 1990s, in this case related to major changes in upper management, to acquisition by a larger corporate entity, and to unstable and often unfavorable economic conditions. But, the events related in this book are much more than a story of individual corporate growth and travail. Instead, they provide a personalized view of the rise of industrialism in America, the turbulent political climate of the past century, and the social and economic challenges faced by all Americans. As documented here, the lives of the various members of the Hobart clan reflect the views of twentieth-century Americans from all walks of life. In their enthusiasms, their politics, and their responses to historical events, the Hobarts represent everyman, and their stories are bracingly familiar to nearly all of us.

As you read this book, you can't fail to recognize the struggles America has undertaken as a nation, and to feel justifiable pride in becoming one of the world's leading economic, cultural, and military powers. The venerable Hobart family is our own—as are their successes, their failures and their perseverance. Their history is a classic American tale, one in which we have all played a role.

Jeffrey D. Weber
Publisher Emeritus, *Welding Journal*
American Welding Society
Miami, Florida

Introduction

Dark clouds were dropping a torrential rain on Troy, Ohio, the afternoon of November 8, 2000, as about two dozen people, some with umbrellas furled but still dripping, gathered in the lobby of the Hobart Center for County Government for the building's formal dedication. The crowd chuckled when County Board President Richard Adams said that the governor apologized for his absence but had been called away to Florida to help count votes. For the first time in over a century the U.S. presidential election was still in doubt a day after polls had closed due to disputed ballots and George W. Bush's razor-thin margin of victory in Florida. However, the dedication itself was about certainties, not doubts.

The Hobart family had been part of the Troy business community since 1895 when the Troy Land Improvement Committee invited Clarence Charles Hobart, known as "C. C.," to move his electrical manufacturing company to town. Today two of C. C.'s grandsons, William and Peter Hobart, were here to help dedicate their company's former headquarters for its new life as a center for Miami County services. William explained that the building had been erected during World War II under a "certificate of necessity" to obtain the needed steel. Hobart Brothers Company had been building welders and electrical generators in vast quantities for the war effort. After the company was sold in 1996 to Illinois Tool Works (ITW), the office building was no longer needed, and a national drug store chain began eyeing the prime Main Street location. "They didn't know what they were getting into," said William, "when they planned to tear down something [C. C.'s son] Edward Hobart built." Many in the audience nodded at the double meaning in Hobart's remark. Not only did his uncle and longtime company president Edward Hobart build things to last, the Hobart family valued its heritage and was not about to let a part of it be torn down.

The Hobarts' sense of self-awareness, duty, and dedication to community has a long history in America. In 1633 Edmund Hobart, a sixty-three-year-old Protestant minister, decided that the Massachusetts Bay Colony would be a more fertile ground for his brand of nonconformist religion than the England of Charles I. He landed in Charlestown, just north of Boston with his wife Margaret and three of their children. Later that year he was joined by two of his married sons, Edmund Jr. and Thomas. The Reverend Peter Hobart, another son, sailed from England in 1635 and joined the growing Hobart clan in America. Peter had a wife named Elizabeth and four children of his own. He had graduated from Cambridge University with a master's degree, taught school and been pastor of a church in Haverhill, County Norfolk, where he became known as a Puritan.[1]

In September 1635 the entire Hobart clan moved across Boston Bay to a new settlement on its south shore known as Bare Cove. They renamed it Hingham after Edmund's birthplace in Norfolk County, England.[2] Peter had seven more children by his first wife after he came to America. A year after Elizabeth died in 1645, he married Rebecca Peck and had seven more children and continued to serve as the pastor of Hingham's church until his own death, probably from smallpox, in 1678.[3] Three years later townspeople erected the Old Ship Church, which still stands today. In the graveyard near the church many Hobarts are buried alongside the members of other promising founding families, such as the Lincolns. Peter placed a high value on education, and five of his sons, four of whom became ministers, were educated at Harvard.[4]

Gershom Hobart, the youngest son of Peter and his first wife, was one of these ministers. He married Sarah Aldis in 1675 and moved to Groton, Massachusetts, to become pastor as the town rebuilt after it had been burned in a war with the Narragansetts. His eldest grandson, Shebuel Hobart Jr. married Esther Parker, and in 1751 moved his growing family twelve miles north across the provincial boundary to Hollis, New Hampshire.[5] Three of Shebuel Jr.'s sons joined the struggle for American independence. Jonas and Isaac fought at Bunker Hill where the eighteen-year-old Isaac was killed by a British bayonet. Inspired by the sacrifice of his older brother, Solomon, the youngest of ten children, served two short stints in the militia in 1777 and 1778 and then joined the New Hampshire Continental line for twenty months of active duty.

Shortly after he returned home from war, Solomon Hobart married Abigail Brooks. In October 1804 the Hobarts set out from Hollis, New Hampshire, for northern Vermont. Solomon's eighty-eight-year-old widowed father and an unmarried sister joined his wife and their six children on the trek to Westford in Chittenden County, fourteen miles northeast of Burlington. His father proudly recorded in the family Bible that they completed the two-week journey "without damage or loss of anything only

The Troy Land Improvement Committee invited C. C. Hobart to move his electrical manufacturing company to this undeveloped piece of land on the west side of town, 1890.

an ox."[6] Eventually, Solomon acquired four hundred acres of land in the area before he died in 1849 at the age of eighty-eight.[7]

C. C. Hobart's grandfather was Solomon's eldest child Jonas. Jonas Hobart saw military duty during the War of 1812 in the 2nd Regiment of the Vermont militia, where he attained the rank of captain, a title he carried all his life. He married Sarah Faxon and bought a farm adjoining his father's where they raised five boys and four girls. Jonas served as deacon of the Baptist Church in Westford for fifty-five years until his death in 1880. Both of C. C. Hobart's paternal grandparents lived into their nineties.

Charles Hobart, C. C.'s father, was born March 28, 1816, the sixth child and youngest son of Sarah and Jonas. Among Charles' brothers were a minister, two farmers, and a merchant, but he chose to earn his living as a carpenter who built homes and churches. In contrast to his parents' nearly seventy years of marriage, Charles was widowed twice. C. C. was the fourth child of Charles and his second wife, Parthenia Adeline Sabine. Trained as a lawyer and instilled with a strong Protestant work ethic, C. C. Hobart would set out for the West and eventually put down roots in the rich soil of southwest Ohio and become the first in his family to earn a living in industry. He took his place among a new generation of self-trained engineers and entrepreneurs whose fertile imaginations transformed the Cornbelt into America's industrial heartland.

Growing up in Troy, Ohio, near the epicenter of the American industrial crescent between Chicago and Pittsburgh, the Hobarts were taught to "do it yourself!" Asking questions, learning how things worked, playing hard, and striving to be the best were values reinforced at home, in school, and in the community. Building models of trains, planes, boats, and cars was encouraged. One Troy school superintendent taught, at his choice and with great enthusiasm, a manual training course, where students learned the basics of carpentry, machining, and plumb-

ing. Science teachers were revered, and students looked forward to classes in the laboratory. Sports activities, especially the team sports of football, basketball, and baseball, reinforced the idea that teamwork was an essential pattern for life. The flat Midwest builds its castles in its imagination. Young people were encouraged to be resourceful, to let their minds wander, to dream, but to stay put in one place and concentrate on invention to make the world a better place. Time to think as well as freedom from want, fear, prejudice, and too great a reverence for tradition all helped their creative minds.

Later generations of Hobarts grew up as "living trademark" persons. The Hobart name opened doors and built high expectations as well. They had opportunities to study, to travel, and to work with world leaders in business, high tech industry, and government. Their perspective widened even as ground under them began to shift. In recent decades, the social values and economic conditions of the industrial heartland underwent such rapid transformation that the certainties of the America in which they grew up seemed like half-remembered dreams.

As the millennium and this familiar Industrial Age come to a close, and we enter the unknown Information Age, we find it appropriate to provide a book about a family of industrialists who were intimately involved with the Industrial Age in Ohio, in America, and the world. It was a glorious era that realized its full potential in America and provided a foundation for the future. For those who lived the experience, it was extremely exhilarating, challenging, and life fulfilling. Hopefully, future generations will find similar fulfillment in their lives. This book is written for all of those who want to draw from the past to inspire their future, and for those who made the past worthwhile, especially those people of the Hobart companies, the people who made them what they were by contributing their thoughts, their work, and their lives. Here then is one small statement for posterity, a milestone in history. ❧

CHAPTER 1

A Young Man Reinvents Himself

The dread sound of a fire bell in the night roused Clarence C. Hobart from his sleep. It was just past one o'clock in the morning of April 30, 1890, when the bell a block away atop City Hall began to clang. A sickly orange glow flickered in the east. Hobart ran to the back of his frame house and pushed aside a curtain. Flames were licking from the windows of a two-story brick factory building, the building occupied by the Hobart Electric Company. Hobart sprinted back to his bedroom and began pulling on his clothes with the haste of a man who knew his business was grossly underinsured. His wife, Lou Ella, sprang up in bed, alarmed. She was four months pregnant. Edward, their sixteen-month-old son, cried in the room next door. The responsibilities of the moment crowded in on Clarence Hobart as he hurried to his factory to see what he could do.

By the time he crossed the alley, the entire twelve-man fire department of Middletown, Ohio, had arrived on the scene. With the building fully involved in flames, there was little they and their horse-drawn pumper could do but contain the blaze. Hobart did not have time to collect his thoughts and ponder his next move. A reporter from the *Middletown Signal* was soon on the scene asking him questions. Hobart confessed that he only had $200 worth of insurance but that the building contained about $3,800 in equipment and material, including a $1,100 dynamo, which had been assembled yesterday and scheduled for delivery to a twine factory later that day. Noting this ill-timed coincidence, the fire two years before at this site, and Hobart's role in the ongoing dispute among advocates of gas lighting, Brush arc lights and Edison's generators, the reporter claimed the fire "was thought by many to be the work of an incendiary." More importantly, despite the blow, Hobart did not hesitate to declare to the reporter his intention to rebuild.[1]

For Clarence C. Hobart or "C. C.," as he was known to family and friends, starting over was nothing new. He had changed plans, changed residences, and changed careers several times in his thirty-five years of life. However, by now he knew, with even more certainty than after the fire two years before, that electricity was the energy source of the future, and that his future lay in the building of electrical equipment.

Clarence Charles Hobart was born on September 30, 1854. He was the fourth child of Charles and Parthenia Hobart who lived in the small town of Westford, Vermont, where Charles earned a living as a carpenter who built homes and churches. In September 1854 Franklin Pierce was president of the United States. That fall a man named Lincoln challenged Illinois Senator Stephen Douglas for his support of the Kansas-Nebraska Act, claiming it would spread slavery into northern territories. The Civil War lay less than seven years in the future. An Englishman named Darwin was hard at work on a book he would publish five years later as *The Origin of Species*. The telegraph, the steamship, and the railroad were revolutionizing the world Clarence Hobart's parents had known. However, the first wave of the Industrial Revolution was already cresting. The era dominated by coal, iron, and steam, an era when most innovations came from Great Britain, would soon be overwhelmed by a second more powerful wave led by oil, steel, electricity, and inventions from America. In five years Edwin Drake would strike oil in Titusville, Pennsylvania, with the world's first oil well. Charles Bessemer was already perfecting the process that would make steel an economically viable building material. In that same autumn of 1854 Thomas Edison, a seven-year-old boy, would overhear his teacher tell a school official that Thomas was "addled" and not worth keeping in school.[2] People born in the preindustrial world had trouble understanding the builders of the new era. He would not realize it until he was almost thirty years old, but Clarence Hobart would become a builder of the new industrial age.

The first event that rocked the tiny world of young Clarence was the death of his mother ten days shy of his second birthday. Charles did not let his four children go motherless for long. Widowed for a second time by the death of Parthenia, he now wed twenty-two-year-old Margaret Defoe of Weybridge, Vermont. Margaret would be

Clarence Charles Hobart's undergraduate college training took place in Hamilton, New York, at Madison University, later to be renamed Colgate University. As an undergraduate, he joined the Delta Upsilon Fraternity whose badge he wears in this photo. One of his undergraduate fraternity brothers, Charles Evans Hughes, went on to become governor of New York, U.S. vice president, secretary of state, and chief justice of the U.S. Supreme Court. Clarence also had an interest in law following graduation in 1877, and enrolled in the University of Chicago Law School, then moved on to the University of Iowa in Iowa City where he completed his law degree and was admitted to the bar in 1881.

the only mother Clarence remembered. She had three children of her own by Charles, but only one, a girl named Frances, survived to adulthood.[3]

Clarence grew up in the foothills of the Green Mountains. Mount Mansfield, the tallest peak in the range, stands just ten miles southeast of his birthplace. Westford stretched along Brown's River, a small tributary of the Lamoille River, which flows into Lake Champlain. An iron forge aided the town's early growth until the local source of ore ran out. Residents switched first to raising sheep and eventually dairy farming. Later in life C. C. Hobart often remarked, "Vermont had nothing to offer except scenery, marble, and maple syrup."[4] In fact he was born into a community already in decline from its peak population of 1,458 recorded in the 1850 census. Westford lost over 100 citizens per decade in the last half of the nineteenth century. The Hobarts joined this exodus. All of Charles' children left Westford and three left Vermont.[5]

After grade school, the children all attended the New Hampton Institute in nearby Fairfax, Vermont. Their maternal grandfather, Alvah Sabin, ran the school as its president. Young Clarence or "Clem," as he was called by some close family members, also acquired a practical education in carpentry by helping his father build homes.[6] He grew into a tall lanky youth with a broad forehead, long ears, a hawk nose, and a strong angular chin. His eyes glinted with a wry sense of humor.

Charles C. Hobart, circa 1890

In 1874 he followed his older brother Alvah to Madison University in Hamilton, New York. The Baptist Education Society of New York had established the school in 1817. During its early decades it was primarily a seminary for training ministers. Hobart arrived while the school was undergoing a transition. The freshman class that entered two years after his was the first in which students enrolled in the college division outnumbered those entering the seminary, and it was also the first class with a female student. In 1890 Madison was renamed Colgate University to honor the family of soap manufacturers who had served as benefactors and trustees of the school.[7]

Nearly everyone who knew C. C. Hobart remarked about the extraordinary care and concern he bestowed upon animals of all kinds. This was not simply the result of being raised on a farm; most of Hobart's contemporaries were raised on farms. One of C. C.'s instructors at Colgate was Dr.

Walter R. Brooks who has been described as a Baptist St. Francis of Assisi who saw the lowliest plants and animals as his brothers. Dr. Brooks' preferred laboratory was the great outdoors and he took his students on extended field trips lasting up to four days. As a teacher, he was no medieval throwback. Brooks both regarded and taught evolution as God's method.[8]

One reason why Colgate University in the 1870s was remarkably free of the conflicts between religion and science which would later plague American education was its president, Ebenezer Dodge. Dodge was a staunch believer in academic freedom for both faculty and students and he practiced this philosophy by refusing to censor the student newspaper. In the classroom he taught all seniors a course in Christian Ethics. Although he stoutly professed the views of the Baptist theologian he was, Dodge encouraged free discussion in his course and urged his students to examine all ideas.[9] Throughout his life, C. C. Hobart exhibited the capacity to evaluate an idea on its own merits, caring little what person or group had first advanced it or what label it had acquired before it came to him.

The first sign that C. C. Hobart would set out in new directions was his decision to become a lawyer upon graduating from Colgate in 1877. Hobart's ancestors had been farmers, ministers, colonialists, and soldiers. None of his forbears had pursued a degree in law. Hobart taught school for a year in Vermont and saved enough money to head west by train and enroll in the University of Chicago Law School. The University of Chicago was another school affiliated with the Baptist Church, but, by the time Hobart arrived, the school had fallen on hard times and would fold in 1886, only to be revived and reinvigorated in the 1890s by that most famous of Baptist businessmen, John D. Rockefeller. Hobart spent just a year in Chicago before heading further west to continue his studies in law at the University of Iowa in Iowa City.

Iowa had established the first law school west of the Mississippi and it incorporated several innovations that may have attracted the twenty-six-year-old Hobart. Instruction was in the new and controversial case method style in which professors led students in analyzing recent legal decisions. Within a few decades this teaching strategy would dominate American law schools. The Iowa law school broke other barriers as well. Mary Humphrey Had-

The Hobart siblings (left to right) in birth order: Alvah Sabin Hobart, Ida D. Hobart,
Julia A. Hobart, and C. C. Hobart, the children of Charles and Parthenia Hobart

dock, an 1875 graduate, became the first woman to practice law before a U.S. Federal Court. In 1879 the Iowa School of Law graduated its first black and its first foreign student, a Burmese.[10] Hobart completed his law degree in 1881 and was admitted to the bar.

Clarence returned home to Vermont but soon determined he could not earn a living as a lawyer in the place of his birth. Either heeding the siren call of Horace Greeley that his future lay in the West or seeking to capitalize on contacts made at the University of Iowa, Hobart set out by rail for St. Louis, the gateway city of the West. Disaster struck in Pittsburgh, where his money was either lost or stolen. Here Hobart faced the first of several crossroads. Rather than turn back halfway to his goal, the able-bodied young man hired on as a deckhand on a barge headed down the Ohio. He would work his way to St. Louis. However, fate had another twist in store. By the time the barge reached

Cincinnati, the Army Corps of Engineers had ordered all traffic off the river due to flooding.

Forced ashore, Hobart walked to Cincinnati's downtown YMCA and took a room, which, along with one meal a day, was his free for up to three days. He answered an insurance company ad in the local paper for a claims adjustor, legal experience preferred.[11] Clarence was hired on the spot. Besides the need to earn money, there was a second reason to extend his stay in Cincinnati. His older brother Alvah had become a minister and married after graduating from Colgate and was now pastor of the Mount Auburn Baptist Church in Cincinnati.[12]

Hobart found Cincinnati already well stocked with lawyers, but his travels on behalf of the insurance company took him twenty-five miles north to the town of Middletown, and it was here that C. C. decided to hang out his shingle. Clients did not exactly flood in to the tall

The building that housed the first Hobart Electric Company in Middletown, Ohio, as seen in the 1950s.

ness disrupted the sleep patterns of people and animals. Finally, the arc lamps cost the city far more than gaslights had. Their current consumed its carbon rods in a night, requiring daily replacement.[15] In September 1883 three businessmen returned impressed from a Cincinnati experiment in the Edison method of incandescent lighting and urged the Middletown City Council to adopt it. The council agreed in part because the Edison bid was $1,000 a year less than that of the Brush group. Soon the Middletown Edison Electric Illuminating Company began constructing a plant on Water Street behind the U.S. Hotel on Main Street.[16]

Hobart had become fascinated with electricity and, wanting to learn more, he applied for employment at the new Edison plant. Thanks to his bookkeeping experience, he was given the job of superintendent which involved measuring the monthly use of electrical power in order to bill customers. However, in 1884 there were no meters to read. In order to take a reading C. C. had to measure the amount of metal deposited on a copper plate by the electrical current passing through a solution.[17] With the generation of electrical power in its infancy, Hobart could not have found a better opportunity for educating himself than the job he had just landed. The U.S. Hotel became the first building in town to be wired for electric lights. Several other businesses followed suit, but homeowners did not want their walls marred by ugly wiring and stuck to kerosene or gas.[18]

In the spring of 1884 Edison himself came to Middletown to supervise the installation of his latest invention, a friction control of the electrical current known as a rheostat. By connecting a knob to resistor coils Edison could adjust the resistance in the circuit and control the speed of electric motors or the brightness of the light.[19] This device may have been installed in Middletown to provide the local Edison company with yet another argument to throw in the faces of investors of the gaslight and Brush arc light companies still angry over being usurped by the upstart incandescent firm. The twenty-nine-year-old Hobart relished the opportunity to meet the great inventor who was just seven years his sen-

young man with the New England accent, so Hobart also built homes by day, like his father, and kept books for a paper mill by night to make ends meet.[13]

Soon after he arrived Middletown was embroiled in a public controversy over the issue of city lighting. Since 1871 its streets had been lit by the dim flickering glow of gaslights, but all that changed in the summer of 1882 when Charles Brush of Euclid, Ohio, secured a contract to install his electric arc lights. Residents gawked as workers erected a tapering 210-foot-high iron pole in the center of town. Carefully, they hoisted up a carriage of eight arc lamps with a thirty-two-thousand-candlepower capacity and wired the tower for action. On a dark night in August most of Middletown's five thousand citizens gathered to watch the lamps blaze forth like an anchored sun. The light could be seen almost ten miles away, and residents soon regarded it as a beacon advertising their progressive community and promoting its growth. Furthermore, the arc lamps were lit every night, whereas the gas company had always cut the light on moonlit nights.[14]

Though brilliant, the Brush arc lights did have their drawbacks. Areas blocked by buildings and trees were thrown into dark shadows. This problem was somewhat alleviated by erecting five two-thousand-candlepower units on shorter poles and a pair of streetlights. The open arcs fizzed and sputtered, sometimes showering passers-by with sparks. The stark bright-

❧

Hobart found Cincinnati already well stocked with lawyers.

❧

ior. By now he was convinced he had found his calling. Always a good student, electricity provided a whole new world for Hobart to explore. It was also a world that presented a myriad of opportunities to employ his talent for working with his hands. Finally, Hobart had to apply all his lawyerly powers of persuasion in order to convince potential customers to adopt this new source of power.

The success of Middletown Edison was far from assured. Incandescent streetlights were steady and dependable but, at thirty-two candlepower each, only slightly brighter than the old gaslights. Controversy raged at City Council meetings where the mayor proposed the choice of a lighting company be submitted to the voters, but the Council awarded the contract to Edison. The incandescent streetlights, it was argued, were softer, safer, and cleaner, but many townspeople hankered for the heady glare of arc lights, and the dogged advocates of gaslight refused to surrender as well. After two years of being bombarded by weekly editorials in the *Middletown Signal*, City Council reversed itself and gave the lighting contract back to the arc light company. Middletown Edison now had to survive on private business.[20] Besides uncertainty over the future of his employer, there was a second reason C. C. Hobart began to entertain thoughts of striking out on his own. He was in love.

The object of his affections was Lou Ella Jones, the youngest daughter of Edward and Emma Taylor Jones. Edward Jones was one of Middletown's most prominent citizens, having settled there at age twenty-five in 1836 after leaving his hometown of Weston, Massachusetts. He had worked his way up to managing and then owning the largest meatpacking company in Middletown. In 1843 he married Emma Taylor who had been born in Bedfordshire, England, and had come to Middletown from New Jersey just one year before. Wartime demand helped make Jones the wealthiest man in town toward the end of the Civil War. However, the expanding rail network led to a steady centralization of meatpacking in the "Porkopolis" of Cincinnati. Three years after a damaging fire in 1876, Jones left the meatpacking business to focus on his other investments, banking in particular. Jones had also served on the local School Board, and he and his family were active in the First Baptist Church.[21]

Hobart may have reminded Jones of his younger self, also a New Englander who had come to Middletown and built homes during summers, the slow season for meatpacking. Lou Ella's father had little more than memories of being physically active. In late January of 1884 he had

Always a good student, electricity provided a whole new world for Hobart to explore.

suffered a massive stroke that left him paralyzed. He recovered very slowly and never completely. During her courtship with C. C., Lou Ella helped her mother and her oldest sister Maria care for her invalid father in their home. She married Clarence Hobart on June 16, 1886, just a few days after her twenty-fourth birthday.[22]

The same year Hobart walked down the aisle to marry Lou Ella Jones he also left Edison to start his own business. He never regretted either decision. While still at Middletown Edison, Hobart had done all he could to continue his practical education in electrical engineering. He picked the brain of an Edison technician in town to do repairs, and Lou Ella assisted by copying the winding data on a variety of Edison machines.[23] When Hobart had first watched the Edison dynamos being installed, he had noted they were run by steam engines just like those he had seen in the paper mills around Middletown. Hobart was well aware that the risk of fire plagued paper mills and that, up to now, the sun was the only safe form of light available to the mills. He was convinced that electric incandescent bulbs were the safest artificial form of light on the market and that paper mills could generate their own power cheaply by attaching direct current dynamos to existing steam engines or even water wheels. At one point C. C. had worked out a deal with the Champion Paper Mill in nearby Franklin to lease the needed electrical equipment through the insurance company Hobart had once worked for, and the cost of the lease would be partially offset by lower insurance rates. At the last second the insurance company balked. This convinced Hobart to set up his own business to exploit a market he knew was there.[24]

Paper mills were the chief engine of Middletown's remarkable growth in the 1880s. Its seven mills and two paper bag factories employed about five hundred people and produced four boxcar loads of paper daily.[25] Despite their need for a safer form of lighting, mill owners were reluctant to buy any electrical equipment outright. For one, electrical power was new and there was a good deal of fear about working with electricity even if a little verbal instruction could dispel basic ignorance.[26] Secondly, since the technology was new and evolving rapidly, owners were loathe to invest in a light source that could become obsolete within a few years or even months. Hobart overcame this hesitation by renting the electrical equipment he installed, charging one dollar a month per light for the service.[27] Thus, he began a practice he characterized in a favorite aphorism, "The best way to make money is to help someone else make money."[28]

C. C. Hobart found that he loved to tinker with electrical equipment. He became convinced that he could manufacture improved versions of the Edison bipolar generators that would be less expensive and better adapted to the needs of his customers. Rather than going through the complex process to secure a patent and facing a possible court battle with Edison's formidable lawyers, Hobart simply secured an agreement that permitted him to purchase Edison No. 2 armatures and construct generators which incorporated his own modifications.[29] Dynamos turn mechanical energy into electrical power. By reversing the current they consume electrical power and can be used as motors to drive belts and operate machinery. Soon paper mills and other businesses throughout the Miami Valley were paying to have Hobart generators installed.

Christmas Day of 1888 was an especially joyous holiday for the Hobarts. Lou Ella gave birth to their first child, a son they named Edward Alvah. Just as his father had done, Clarence named his first boy after the child's maternal grandfather. His middle name honored Clarence's maternal grandfather and his brother. C. C. adopted a playful tone as he scribbled a note to his brother on company letterhead. "Edward Alvah Hobart put in his appearance at 10 PM this Christmas night. Weighs 12 pounds. Lacks 99 points of being good looking."[30]

By the spring of 1890 business was brisk and the young couple learned they were expecting a second child. Little seemed to stand in the way of the growth of Hobart's business or family until a fire bell broke the calm of an April night.

As Hobart took stock the morning after the fire, he found several things for which to be thankful. No one had been hurt, and the precious drawings, designs, and technical data in his office were unscathed. Despite rumors of arson, C. C. later told his son Edward that he believed the fire was caused by spontaneous combustion of improperly disposed oily rags.[31] Yes, it was embarrassing for a former insurance agent to be caught underinsured, for the advocate of electrical lighting as a way to reduce the risk of fire to have his plant burned down. However, Hobart knew that his credit was good and the reputation of his products was strong. His in-laws, the Jones family, were willing to help. Rebuilding meant assuming a heavy burden of debt, but the booming economy braced his optimism. The young man who had reinvented himself in response to adversity had become a thirty-five-year old husband and father whose path in life had just been confirmed by adversity. ❧

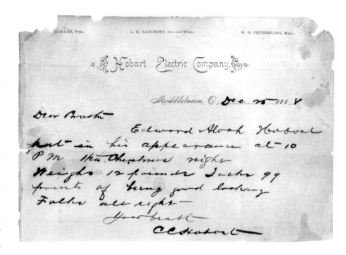

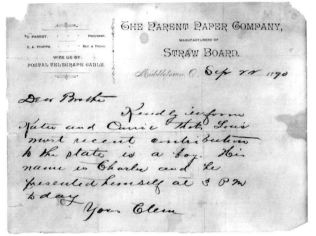

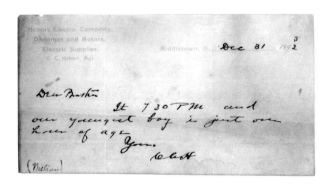

C. C. Hobart's letters announcing the birth of the Three Industrial Hobarts (1888, 1890, and 1892).

CHAPTER 2

A New Business Moves to Troy

As a new factory for the Hobart Electric Company rose from the ashes, C. C. Hobart became a father for a second time on September 22, 1890. "Lou's latest contribution to the state," as C. C. told his brother, was a second son, named Charles Clarence after Hobart's father and himself.[1] In reversing his first and middle names and duplicating his initials, Hobart created a fertile source of confusion for the future. For now, Hobart's future appeared firmly rooted in Middletown, but within five years he would decide to leave that city.

In the early 1890s Hobart employed a mostly male workforce of about twenty-five people.[2] One employee, Charles Barkelew, sought employment at Hobart a few days after he graduated from high school in 1892. His starting wage was three dollars a week for a sixty-hour week, 6:30 a.m. to 5:30 p.m. with an hour off for lunch Monday through Saturday. Within three years he was earning eight dollars a week.[3] The company manufactured electric light dynamos, electric bells and burglar alarms, annunciators for homes and hotels, and electric light plants "installed com-

C. C. Hobart (top row, third from left) and employees of the Hobart Electric Manufacturing Company. Top row, left to right: Louis Sherman, Walter Coles, C. C. Hobart, and William Anderson. Middle row, left to right: Eli Rose, Calvin Beach, Willis Icker, Ida Rhodes, Tom Taylor, unidentified, Iva Boyer, and Tom Gudgeon. Bottom row, left to right: Eli Rose's son, Otto Sherman, Charles Bushfield, Emma Kipp, Girtie Jay, Bertha Siler, and Stella Bayes (Courtesy of Troy Historical Society)

plete." Hobart also served as an agent for Westinghouse steam engines and Babcock and Wilcox steam boilers.[4] C. C.'s sparsely furnished office was located on the second floor of the Leibee Block above a bank on the corner of Third and Main Streets. His home was less than a block south on the east side of Main Street and diagonally behind it was the rebuilt factory facing Wall Street.[5]

Hobart was an energetic and physically active man. With his long strides it did not take much time for him to cover the distances between home, office, and shop. Each workday morning "he would come out of the rear door of his home on a run and turn a hand spring when he was about halfway down the yard." As he approached his shop a warning was passed to those in need of one, "Here comes C. C. Better get busy."[6]

By now the reputation and market of Hobart Electric had expanded far beyond Middletown and the Miami Valley. The company installed light plants as far afield as a paper mill in Whippany, New Jersey, and an ice plant in New Orleans. Since the electrical industry was so new and the need for orders to retire debt so great, on the job training was the norm at Hobart. Barkelew was once called into C. C.'s office at three in the afternoon and told he would be on the six o'clock train for Cincinnati in order to get to French Lick, Indiana, and put in a bid for an annunciator system for a hundred-room annex to a resort hotel near the mineral springs. When Barkelew replied he had never seen the inside of an annunciator before, Hobart promised him printed material to read on the train. The hotel owner accepted the bid, and Barkelew stayed to install the system himself.[7] A job at Hobart was a constant learning experience.

The Hobarts were active in the local community beyond their role in its economic life. C. C. served as treasurer of the First Baptist Church.[8] Lou Ella's younger brother, Frank Jones, became first president of the Rambler's Club, designed for "married folk" who wished to acquire knowledge and promote travel around the world. The Hobarts were charter members, and C. C. read an essay on Niagara Falls at the club's first meeting.[9] With his love for exercise, it is no surprise that Hobart was caught up in the bicycling craze that swept

. . . the reputation and market of Hobart Electric had expanded far beyond Middletown and the Miami Valley.

America in the 1890s. One of his favorites was a bike he had custom made in Dayton at the Wright Cycle Shop.[10]

Another way C. C. made his presence known in Middletown was by intervening on behalf of animals. Those who mistreated their animals or neglected their care were apt to be verbally chided by Hobart. If someone left his horse out in the snow without a blanket, he would return to find a note from C. C. pinned to the horse's bridle.[11] Hobart's concern for his fellow creatures was not limited to domesticated animals. Once Hobart Electric was constructing a power line between the Gardner and Tytus paper mills. Three-foot holes were dug for the poles which were raised the next morning after borrowing the necessary equipment from the telephone company. The first pole had been raised about halfway when C. C. spotted a frog in the hole. "Nothing would do but lower the pole and help the frog out." Just a couple poles later the process had to be repeated when he found a rat that he coaxed out of its hole with difficulty.[12] No animal would be harmed if C. C. could prevent it.

Hobart was the first person in Middletown to own a recording machine. It was a Tainter-Bell Graphophone, an early rival to Edison's phonograph and a target of one of his patent suits. Hobart used it in his office as a dictation device, recording a message whenever he wished and having a secretary type it up later. Hobart pointed out that the recording itself could be mailed to other businessmen if they had a machine to play it. C. C. also had a more novel use for the Graphophone. He told a reporter he sometimes took it home. He sang lullabies into it, and then let "the machine play papa's sweet voice to the baby, thus putting the baby to sleep with little trouble."[13] By December 31, 1892, C. C. had another subject on whom to try this early electrical parenting aid when his wife gave birth to their third son, William Harrison.

Though 1893 began happily with the arrival of Clarence and Lou Ella's own New Year baby, it would soon turn sour as America's twenty-year economic expansion began to unravel. Farm commodity prices dropped, the U.S. gold reserve dwindled, and, after several large financial firms and railroads declared bankruptcy in the spring, stock prices on Wall Street

C. C. Hobart had a lifelong love of animals.

plunged. Soon journalists had a name for it, the Panic of 1893. Manufacturers were among the last to feel the pinch, but unemployment climbed steadily as more and more companies closed their doors. Several paper mills in the Miami Valley went under, and Hobart Electric's lighting contracts went with them. New orders dried up. Leasing fees went unpaid and had to be written off.

Misery peaked in 1894. Several "armies" of the unemployed marched on Washington to demand reform to help the estimated one in five workers who were jobless.[14] Finances were so tight that C. C. decided to send his wife and three sons to spend the summer of 1894 in Cambridge, Vermont, with Grandpa and Grandma Hobart.[15] While the boys enjoyed the cool shade on the big front porch of the comfortable home their grandfather had built, the nation's industrial cities sweltered with unrest. President Cleveland sent federal troops to Chicago to confront striking Pullman employees and railroad workers. Middletown escaped such conflict, but Hobart soon had another loss to confront. A small office he had built in the vacant lot behind his home and next to his factory caught fire and was destroyed. This building was never rebuilt.[16]

As C. C. Hobart well knew, adversity and opportunity often spring from the same seed. Forty miles to the north along the banks of the same Miami River that meandered past Middletown lay the town of Troy, Ohio. This county-seat community was also suffering in the depression when a group of local investors decided to do something about it. J. W. Davis, G. S. Long, E. H. McKnight, Joseph Schauer, George W. Scott, A. G. Stouder, and Frank T. Worman incorporated on December 8, 1894, to form the Troy Land Improvement Company with $25,000 in capital stock. Their stated purpose was "inducing valuable industries to locate here to increase the manufacturing wealth and population of our city and to direct a fresh stream of money into the channels of trade."[17] In order to further this plan, the company bought a 110-acre farm for $22,000 from J. W. McKaig in March 1895. It was level ground just beyond the Cincinnati, Hamilton and Dayton railroad line on the western edge of Troy, a good site for factories. Troy City Council agreed to build gutters and sidewalks for three existing streets on the property and do likewise for four new streets. In return, Troy Land Improvement promised to attract new businesses which would employ at least two hundred workers for five years or pay back the city's expected costs in road improve-

ments. In July, the former McKaig tract was divided into two hundred lots and put on sale for $217 each. With money from these sales, the investors also began constructing two new factory buildings, one a two-story brick structure totaling fifteen thousand square feet and a smaller frame building of five thousand square feet.[18] Now all Troy needed were some tenants.

The Hobart Electric Manufacturing Company, circa 1895

The man who was the first to see the Hobart Electric Company as a likely prospect was E. H. McKnight. McKnight had once managed the Troy Gas Light and Coke Company and in 1889 he became a director of Troy Electric Light & Power, which gradually lit Troy with Thompson-Houston arc lamps as the contracts for other forms of lighting expired. In 1891 he organized a company to provide electric light in Bowling Green, Ohio.[19] By June 1894 McKnight had checked into the U.S. Hotel in Middletown armed with a proposal to end that city's long feud over street lighting. His company would employ arc lamps of lower candlepower suspended on poles a shorter distance above the street. He was in for a long siege. Finally, in November his proposal was submitted to voters and won 2,301 to 1,276, securing a ten-year contract.[20]

Since McKnight's quarters at the U.S. Hotel were nearly across the street from the Hobart residence and the world of electrical engineering in 1894 Middletown was not exactly large, it's likely these two came in contact. One of the last things McKnight did before moving his family to Middletown was to invest in the Troy Land Improvement Company. Hobart may have known an invitation to Troy was coming long before A. G. Stouder formally proffered it.[21] The offer was hard to pass up: a new and much larger two-story brick factory, access to a key north-south rail line, and finally, a bonus of $10,000 if his company could meet one condition—employ at least sixty people.[22] This requirement was a tall order, for the Hobart Electric Manufacturing Company, as it now was known, had never employed half that number. On the balance, now was the best time to move. His sons were approaching school age, C. C. had just purchased equipment at a bargain from a bankrupt Cincinnati firm, and a powerful group of "Trojans" had a vested interest in the success of any company they brought to town.[23] Hobart decided to accept the offer.

The Hobarts moved to Troy in the waning days of summer, 1895. Troy had a population of around five thousand, about a third smaller than Middletown, but there were many similarities. In both cities the Miami River takes a major bend north of the downtown area. In Middletown it curves to the west, in Troy to the east. C. C. bought a house on Water Street, one block closer to the river than he had lived in Middletown. Both towns had a similar ethnic mix with most residents born in America but descended from immigrants from the British Isles or Germany along with some French and a small African American element. In Troy most blacks lived north of the river in a district known as Ninevah. With no soot belching from paper mills, the air in Troy was cleaner. A breeze from the east carried the sweetish smell of mash cooking at the Hayner Distillery. Troy had a well-defined downtown clustered around Public Square, a large four-cornered widening of the intersection of Main and Market Streets. In 1895 a bandstand occupied the center of the Square. Two blocks west rose the beautiful Miami County Courthouse, a domed limestone Neoclassical structure completed just seven years earlier. Standing 185 feet above the street a statue of Justice topped the dome and looked out over the church steeples of Troy. Trojans joked that Justice had turned her back on Piqua, a larger city eight miles north which had periodically vied with Troy for the county seat. The construction of the new courthouse had marked Troy's final victory.[24]

The Miami County Courthouse

By the end of September C. C. was moving equipment into his new factory on Pennsylvania Avenue. The arrival of Hobart's company in Troy was somewhat overshadowed when Troy Land Improvement landed an even bigger fish. The McKinnon Dash Company, reputed to be the world's largest maker of dashboards for carriages and buggies, announced it was relocating its Columbus factory in exchange for a huge two-story brick building at the corner of Olive and Pennsylvania. Once this plant was in operation

Herbert L. Johnston, C. C. Hobart's partner in the Hobart Electrical Manufacturing Company and later shareholder and officer of Hobart Manufacturing

in the spring of 1896, McKinnon Dash became Troy's largest employer with a payroll of 225 people.[25] Hobart enticed his more valuable Middletown employees to come to Troy by offering to nearly double their pay.[26] However, in order to fill out the required 60-person payroll, Hobart hired teenagers, including many females. These low-wage youngsters were kept busy uncrating equipment, pulling out nails to save the wood, and sweeping out the plant.[27]

Hobart may have had the cleanest factory in town, but the pace of work was distressingly slow. He did install two dynamos, six motors, and lights at Piqua Rolling Mills and a 150-light system at the Troy Bending Company, but it was difficult to maintain a payroll for 50 people.[28] Not only was the nation's economic recovery lethargic, but Hobart also faced local competition from the Ohio Specialty Manufacturing Company which made rheostats, dynamo brushes, and installed electrical wiring in homes.[29] Unable to maintain the required payroll, Hobart never saw most of the expected $10,000 bonus from Troy Land Improvement.[30]

In 1897 James L. Orr, one of C. C.'s partners, precipitated a crisis when he left the company and moved to Toledo.[31] Hobart did not have to think hard about whom he wanted as a new partner. Earlier E. H. McKnight had introduced him to Herbert L. Johnston, a graduate of Ohio State University's electrical engineering program. Johnston had moved to Troy to become superintendent of the interurban trolley line McKnight had established between Piqua and Troy.[32] On July 14, 1897, Hobart composed a lawyerly proposition, the heart of which offered to sell Johnston a half interest in:

. . . the business of the Hobart Electric Mfg. Co. for the sum of seven thousand dollars ($7,000) to be paid as follows: $2,500 cash and the balance in nine (9) $500 notes payable one every six months without interest. . . .

Furthermore, to sweeten the deal, not only would Johnston be entitled to half the stock and half the profits once articles of incorporation had been agreed upon, but:

. . . C. C. Hobart shall give H. L. Johnston receipts for one half of all money C. C. Hobart draws out of the firm business in excess of what Johnston draws and said receipts shall be accepted for their face value in payment upon said notes. . . .[33]

Johnston accepted this generous offer, and on July 20, 1897, the Hobart Electric Manufacturing Company was formally incorporated by means of a handwritten document that contained three articles of incorporation and five signatures. Besides Hobart and Johnston, Johnston's two brothers and Hobart's wife Lou Ella signed the articles as well as a separate page that waived publication of the opening of books for subscription of stock.[34] From these modest beginnings would grow a multimillion-dollar international corporation manufacturing a line of goods which neither Hobart nor Johnston had yet envisioned.

Who was this young man C. C. Hobart was so eager to secure as a partner? Herbert L. Johnston was born May 11, 1869, in Washington, Indiana. The son of a Presbyterian minister, Johnston grew up in several Indiana towns as his father's appointments shifted. He was living in Cincinnati when he graduated from Woodward High School in 1888 and chose to enter the University of Cincinnati. After one year he transferred to Ohio State in Columbus and enrolled in its pioneering electrical engineering program. Johnston was an outstanding student at Ohio State where, despite his short stature, he quarterbacked its first football squad to earn a letter. In 1892, the year he graduated with a bachelor of science degree, he also won the university's annual oratorical contest with a speech entitled "The Unity of Man," which he billed as a study of socialism and individualism and their reconciliation through accepting the principles of

Christ. Upon graduation, he was hired by General Electric and went to work in Cincinnati before McKnight recruited him for the interurban job in Troy.[35]

Though just fifteen years younger than Hobart, Johnston belonged to the second generation of electrical engineers who were college-educated in their technical field in contrast to self-taught entrepreneurs like Edison and Hobart. A fellow graduate of Ohio State's electrical engineering program was Charles F. Kettering who went to Dayton and a distinguished career as an inventor and executive with the National Cash Register Company, Delco, and General Motors. Photographs show Johnston as a bespectacled man with a sober even somber look, but he also possessed the kind of wit which could keep a Rotary luncheon "in an uproar of laughter." A stalwart member of the First Presbyterian Church of Troy where he taught Sunday school, Johnston was a man of few vices. He did enjoy a good cigar and on occasion would escape on a summer's day to catch a Cincinnati Reds game.[36]

The addition of Johnston did not create an immediate turnaround in the fortunes of the company which struggled through the remaining years of the nineteenth century. At one point Hobart Electric was down to a paltry nine employees.[37] But the Hobarts had begun to put down roots in Troy. C. C.'s three sons, Edward, Charles, and William, were all now attending elementary school. Lou Ella had become part of Troy's social scene after hosting a fashionable "at home" in January 1898.[38] There was both hope and uncertainty for the new century about to dawn. ❧

There were two interurban companies serving Troy in 1909. One ran from Piqua to Troy and Dayton, Ohio. The second ran from Troy to Springfield, Ohio.
(Photo courtesy of Keith Bader)

CHAPTER 3

The Entrepreneur Tackles New Problems

C. Hobart and his neighbors got their first glimpse of the new century on May 27, 1900, when George Lorimer of Piqua endured the bumps and jolts of a gravel road to drive his new automobile to Troy. He drove past the fairgrounds, along the river, then east along Main, turned north onto Cherry Street and parked his car with self-conscious irony in front of a livery stable. Trojans crowded around to see their first horse-less carriage. Within a few decades the automobile would put several of Troy's largest companies out of business as the car replaced the horse as a means of transportation.[1] In two and a half years the Dayton bicycle mechanics who had counted Hobart among their customers would be soaring above the dunes of North Carolina on the world's first powered flights. Orville and Wilbur Wright would return to Dayton and quietly over the next five years develop a truly practical airplane.

Living along the rail line that connected Dayton to Detroit, C. C. Hobart and his sons were well placed to participate in the transportation revolution touched off by the advent of the automobile and the airplane. In fact, in 1900 Hobart received a very valuable idea from one of his customers in Detroit. Although this idea had nothing to do with transportation, it too would spark another revolution, the application of electrical power to the preparation of food, in both the food service industry and at home.

The Detroit customer was using a belt to attach a Hobart motor to the flywheel of a hand-operated coffee mill. This application intrigued Hobart and Johnston who found they could efficiently attach coffee grinders to their two-horsepower motors and sell the new contraption for little more than what they had charged for the motor alone. Besides selling one to the customer in Detroit, they also convinced two Troy gro-

Electric coffee mill
(Photo courtesy of Hobart Manufacturing Company)

cers to buy new electric coffee mills. Soon, they began adding a wood cabinet to conceal the motor. The world's first electrical food processor was now complete.[2] Since a price list from this era pegs the two-horsepower Hobart motor at $94, an electric coffee grinder complete with cabinet had to cost over $100.[3] This was a hefty investment for a corner grocer in the first years of the twentieth century. This time instead of attracting customers by leasing the equipment, Hobart decided to sell the new appliance through time payments. That way the buyer could use profits from the new coffee mill to help defray its cost. Hobart had already used this form of consumer credit to sell dynamos and motors.[4] Within a short time the new product line showed promise.

Once again, both Hobart and his company had reached a crossroads. Sales of direct current (DC) dynamos were declining. By now, alternating current (AC), pioneered by Westinghouse, had emerged victorious in "the war of the currents." AC systems used high voltage to transport current over greater distances with less power loss than DC. Transformers stepped down the voltage for local use.[5] When the two rival lighting giants, Edison and Thompson-Houston, merged in 1892 to form General Electric, the reorganized power company began converting local subsidiaries to alternating current. As factories and commercial buildings tapped into wide-reaching AC power grids, the market for DC lighting generators dried up. This process accelerated once the economy achieved full recovery around 1900.

Hobart Electric Manufacturing Company was building dynamos and motors ranging from two to thirty kilowatts. The largest machines weighed over two tons and could

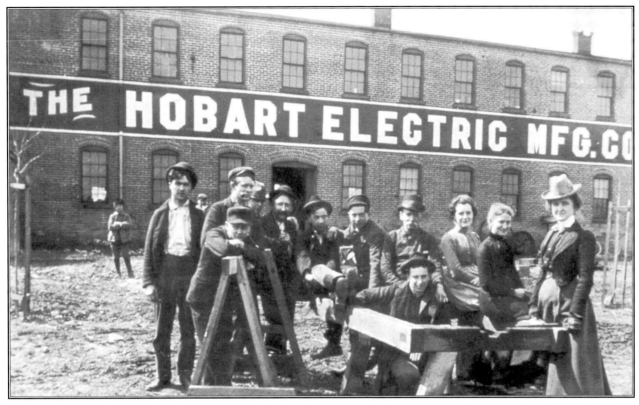

Factory employees in front of the new building of the Hobart Electric Manufacturing Company, Troy, Ohio, in the 1890s.
Left to right: Byron Cruikshank, Ote Lane, Roy Wescoe, Otho Sherman, Pone Wescoe, Charlie Statler, Charlie Harrison,
Bertha Siler, Emma Kipp, Ida Rhodes. Seated: Charlie Bushfield

generate forty-three horsepower or current for up to five hundred arc or incandescent lights. In addition, the company also produced automatic elevator controls, start boxes, rheostats, circuit breakers, wire brushes, and a variety of other electrical supplies.[6] Increasingly, sales tended to be for small labor-saving motors. The question was: should the company specialize within this healthy segment of the business and focus on creating a full line of electrical food processing equipment to expand on the success of the powered coffee mill? Such a course would require more capital to develop new products, secure patent protection, and create marketing campaigns.

Johnston was more enthusiastic about this proposed change of direction than Hobart. As a first step, three new investors became partners in December 1903: Augustus G. Stouder, one of the guiding forces behind the Troy Land Improvement Company; Edwin E. Edgar; and W. E. Bowyer. This influx of cash

Hobart dynamo 30kW, 1890s

more than tripled the company's capital stock from $30,000 to $100,000.[7]

At some point in the next two months C. C. Hobart made a surprising decision. He no longer wanted to be part of the company with its new structure and direction. The reasons why are not entirely clear. Although the food processing idea looked promising, it may not have excited his interest or, as Rachel Hobart later quipped, "He wanted to get out of the kitchen." If so, it would not be the last time a Hobart walked away from a profitable product line simply because the technology involved bored him. A second consideration may have been Hobart's desire to fund the college education of his three sons. Edward, his oldest, had just turned fifteen. Education had been a strong family tradition, and C. C.'s father had seen that all his children went on to higher education. What may have been the most crucial factor behind Hobart's decision to leave was that the restructured company no longer fit his personal business style. Not only was his control diluted, but his independence would be curtailed. That would require quite an adjustment for someone who had owned and operated his own business for the past eighteen years and who had to deal with, at most, a single partner. C. C. Hobart was a classic example of what one scholar called an "engineer-entrepreneur," one of the men who owned and operated the first generation of electrical companies.[8] By now most had been bought out, bankrupted, or absorbed into the research labs of large corporations. Approaching his fiftieth birthday, Hobart chose to once again strike out on his own.

First, he made a bid to buy his old company outright. Hobart wrote a price on a slip of paper, while Johnston and the three new partners did likewise. Whoever had the high bid would buy out the low bidder.[9] It is unlikely that C. C. expected to prevail in a blind bid against four investors, rather he hoped to secure a good price for his share of the company, and that is exactly what happened. On March 1, 1904, Stouder became president of the restructured Hobart Electric Manufacturing Company, while Herbert L. Johnston became its vice president. Another investor, J. M. Spencer, joined the company in 1905. In turn, these three men would be at the helm of the company for the next forty years.[10]

No great acrimony accompanied Hobart's parting. During this transition, he and Stouder served together on a committee to find a new location for the Troy Club's house.[11] Years later Hobart and Johnston could needle each other and laugh about their early years in Troy as partners.[12] The new owners retained the Hobart name; an eighteen-year reputation as a producer of quality electrical power equipment was too valuable to be discarded.

Soon the company began building electric meat grinders, for which Johnston received a patent in 1905.[13] Meat grinders served America's growing appetite for hamburgers. The following year Johnston invented a peanut butter machine, capitalizing on the popularity of one of George Washington Carver's new uses for the peanut.[14] President Theodore Roosevelt and Congress gave Hobart Manufacturing an inadvertent boost by passing the Pure Food and Drug Act in 1906. Sanitary preparation of food was no longer just a point to tout in advertising; it was the law.

After C. C. Hobart, A. G. Stouder was the new president of Hobart Manufacturing Company.

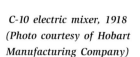

C-10 electric mixer, 1918 (Photo courtesy of Hobart Manufacturing Company)

One day in 1908 Johnston watched a sweaty baker use an old iron spoon and his hands of questionable cleanliness to mix bread dough. Johnston knew there had to be a faster, easier, and more sanitary way. Over the next six years Johnston tested and rejected four models before creating a durable design for a line of electric commercial mixers, ranging up to eighty quarts in size.[15] The mixers became a signature product for the company.

By 1910 sales had grown to the point where the company's directors decided to open foreign sales offices in Toronto, Canada and London, England.[16] Within a short time exports comprised about 10 percent of total sales, and Hobart Manufacturing was exporting more goods than any other Troy firm.[17] Gross sales topped $1 million in 1913, the year "Electric" was dropped from the company name. The Hobart Manufacturing Company had established itself on a course of steady growth that eventually made it a Fortune 500 corporation.[18]

C. C. Hobart could not stay out of the daily tussle of the business world for long. Besides, the man had electricity in his veins. During the years he had promoted electric lighting, Hobart recognized that a major hindrance to sales was the sheer ugliness of early incandescent systems. Factories did not mind bare bulbs hanging from wires that trailed across ceilings and walls, but in private homes, hotels, restaurants, and theaters, any building where aesthetics mattered, the lack of attractive lighting fixtures was a serious drawback. Not normally one to use harsh language, C. C. remarked that indoor electric lighting often "looked like hell!"[19] In contrast, gaslights and kerosene lamps came in a wide variety of appealing designs.

Hobart decided that he could remedy this problem by designing and producing attractive fixtures for electric lights. In September 1904 he and four new partners founded the American Fixture and Manufacturing Company, capitalized at $20,000.[20] Hobart realized that wiring could be hidden within hollow metal fixtures just as gaslights concealed gas-carrying tubes. The glare of bare bulbs could be softened behind frosted or colored glass. Multiple bulbs

The Hobart Electric Manufacturing Company Sales Convention, First Island on the Miami River, 1911

could be mounted in one fixture to light a large area. Soon his new company was turning out a number of designs fit to grace the decor of the finest Victorian homes of the era. Apart from selling the fixtures he made, Hobart also returned to installing home electric systems, a field Hobart Manufacturing had abandoned when it adopted food service equipment as its main product line.

Most sales were regional. Homeowners were slow to convert to electricity. Installing hidden electrical wiring in existing homes could be expensive and time consuming. Besides, gas could be used for cooking as well as lighting and was a marked advance over dirty coal or wood burning stoves.[21] Since the design principles were the same and the demand remained high, Hobart marketed gaslight fixtures as well.[22] Although sales of lighting fixtures proved disappointing, a second business opportunity unexpectedly presented itself to Hobart at this time. This new product line grew out of the fact that C. C. had never stopped practicing the carpentry skills his father had taught him as a boy.

Being creatively self-reliant and frugal, Hobart had been in the habit of making his own desks, file cabinets, storage bins, and parts cabinets. Often he constructed these from scrap wood taken from shipping crates. He took old chalk boxes and fashioned them into drawers. The tool cabinets and office furniture he built were both rugged and custom-made to fit his needs. It was not unusual for a fellow businessman to admire a particular piece and ask Hobart to build a similar item for him. By 1906 C. C. Hobart decided that the potential market for such work was great enough that he added office and storage furniture to his new company's product line.[23]

One thing the new company needed was a physical plant large enough to accommodate the work. Hobart remedied this by leasing part of a complex of buildings on West Water Street known as the Brewery. It had served as a brewery in fact as well as name for over twenty years until Jacob Henne moved his operations to a larger building in the early 1890s.[24] Still known in Troy as the Brewery, this old factory above the banks of the Miami River would serve as the main site for Hobart family businesses for almost twenty years.

One factor that hamstrung the growth of lighting fixture sales was the lack of a national distribution network, no chain of showrooms or stores to market the lights. Sears, Roebuck and Company and Montgomery Ward sold goods by mailing catalogues to potential customers. The cost of that kind of operation would have been prohibitive for a small businessman like C. C. Hobart. However,

Motor-driven DC generator at Hobart Electric-Manufacturing (Themco)

he thought, the target customer for office furniture and parts cabinets would be other businesses, other factories and workshops. From eighteen years of installing small power plants in businesses all over the eastern half of the country, Hobart had quite a list of names and addresses. These were just the sort of businesses which would find Hobart workplace furniture most useful and could be targeted in a campaign of direct mail advertising.[25] Hobart may also have been inspired by the success of Troy's Hayner Distillery, which used direct mail to target the thirsty in states and counties voted dry in order to sell them, quite legally, mail order alcohol. By 1906 Bill Hayner had begun to amass his second million dollars.[26] C. C. found that direct mail worked at selling Hobart cabinetry as well.

Once his new company was on a steady footing, Hobart liked to spend time tinkering in his electrical laboratory. He still hoped to find new applications for DC dynamos and motors. For a time it appeared electric cars would capture a good chunk of the automobile market, but by 1910 the gas-powered internal combustion engine had emerged the clear victor. Sometimes C. C.'s sons helped him in the lab and he looked forward to the time when their educations would be completed and they could join the company.

With her three sons all now in school, Lou Ella had more time to pursue her own interests. She joined the Troy Altrurian Club, which met every Wednesday afternoon from September through May. Founded in 1894, the women's club took its name from that of an ideal citizen portrayed in a William Dean Howells short story. The club was nonsectarian and nonpolitical, requiring that its members possess culture, character, and charity.[27] Many meetings were devoted to studying the "life, art, folklore, history, politics and literature of all nations, both ancient and modern." Visitors were welcome, guest speakers were frequent, and musical presentations were often part of the weekly program. Members conducted symposiums and debates on questions of the day, new sciences, problems of social science, and economics and current events.[28] Lou Ella and her fellow Altrurians did not limit their activities to self-improvement. They also sought to better their community in concrete ways, especially in the fields of education, conservation, and public health. One ongoing effort was raising funds to secure a new location, more access,

Lou Ella Hobart in front of the house on W. Franklin

and improved resources for the Troy Public Library. Lou Ella Hobart served a term as president in 1908–09 and several years thereafter on the club's executive board as a trustee.[29] Later, two of her daughters-in-law would join the club as well.[30]

The summer of 1914 was a time of transition for the Hobarts. Both Edward and Charles had completed their college degrees, and William had just one more year of studies ahead of him. C. C.'s company had grown to occupy all the former brewery. Earlier, he had opened a branch of the American Fixture and Manufacturing Company in downtown Piqua, a slightly larger market than Troy.[31] Now he decided to split the company. On July 30 he sold the electrical contracting and fixture manufacturing portions of the business along with the name and the Piqua location to Forrest Stephens and Ben Gibbs, two of his younger partners. He announced the formation of a new family-owned firm to be known as Hobart Brothers, which would assume the dynamo, motor, and cabinet making portions of the old business. Hobart Brothers would take over the Brewery site, while American Fixture moved to leased space on the Public Square.[32]

It looked like Hobart finally had an opportunity to apply his skill with DC power to the automobile. In Dayton, Charles Kettering had invented the electric self-starter, and the first production model it appeared in was the 1913 Cadillac. But there was yet another reason why C. C. wanted to clear the decks in the summer of 1914. He had decided to run for Congress. ❧

CHAPTER 4

A Progressive Runs for Congress

Most people who contemplate a career in law have some interest in politics. C. C. Hobart was no exception. Furthermore, he grew up in an era of intense party rivalry and high voter turnout. Although Hobart practiced law but briefly, he had experienced the impact of government on his business career. The prolonged dispute over street lighting in Middletown demonstrated that political connections often meant more than technical merit in awarding public contracts. The cooperation of Troy's City Council helped Troy Land Improvement assemble the package of incentives that secured Hobart's relocation to that city. Finally, C. C. had seen that his own involvement could make a difference when he helped found humane societies in Middletown and Troy. He had also served a term on Troy's Board of Public Affairs early in the century when the city paved its first streets and installed its first sewers.[1]

Like many other college-educated, middle class businessmen of his generation, Hobart identified with the loosely defined group of reformers known as progressives. Progressives, who could be found in both major parties, were optimists that believed the application of scientific principles to government and social institutions could produce a society which was healthy, prosperous, and just. One progressive in particular had captured Hobart's imagination, Theodore Roosevelt. Soldier, statesman, conservationist, and reformer, Teddy Roosevelt was the most dynamic public figure of his era. He was also the first man of Hobart's generation, the generation which came of age after the Civil War, to become President. However, Roosevelt and many progressive Republicans were disappointed in the presidential record of his hand-picked successor William Howard Taft, so in 1912 "TR" threw his

Miami County residents had a choice of four candidates for Congress in 1914.

hat in the ring once again. Roosevelt and his supporters felt railroaded by the conservative party leadership at the Republican Convention when the unseating of many Roosevelt delegates led to the renomination of Taft. In August the new Progressive Party nominated Roosevelt for president. Accepting the honor, he bellowed, "I'm feeling like a Bull Moose!"[2]

Soon after the convention, C. C. Hobart, J. W. Means, W. E. Prill, and J. Harrison Smith placed an ad in the Troy newspapers inviting "all Progressives irrespective of former party affiliation" to attend the first meeting of the Miami County Progressive Party at 2:30 p.m. August 29 in the County Courthouse's Grange Hall.[3] The forty people who came selected Hobart among the fifteen delegates sent to the state convention in Columbus the following week. Significantly, Benjamin French, a black, was chosen as secretary at the meeting. The state convention nominated a full slate of candidates, all former Republicans, for statewide offices. However, Miami County Progressives did not follow suit. Revealing their Republican origins and agreeing with the *Miami Union* that a Progressive county ticket would "only hand the Democrats a victory by plurality," they endorsed the local Republican candidates including Dr. R. M. Hughey, the nominee for the U.S. House of Representatives.[4] Though he played a major role in getting the local Progressive Party started, Hobart did not sit on its executive or finance committees for the 1912 election.[5]

Progressives made a strong effort to demonstrate they were not merely the supporters of a renegade Republican named Roosevelt. Large ads in the Troy newspapers trumpeted the Progressive Party Platform: an old age pension, a minimum wage of a dollar a day for all women, and "a tariff for the masses" and not just the upper classes. It declared that the Republican and Democratic parties "were one and the same—both controlled by bosses who prey on the public. Supporters were invited to 'buy hay for the Bull Moose'," which had become the new party's totem.[6]

In November Roosevelt did make a strong showing, but not strong enough. He finished second in the popular vote to Democrat Woodrow Wilson. Ohio's Taft was a disappointing third, while Eugene Debs, the socialist from Indiana, received nearly a million votes. In Troy, most voters stayed with the old line parties, and all Progressive candidates, even the Bull Moose himself, finished third in each of Troy's four wards.[7] The defeat widened the rift between Republicans and Progressives in Ohio. C. C. and his fellow Progressives were unwilling to throw in the towel and resolved to field a full ticket of candidates in 1914.

After two years to think it over, the sixty-year-old C. C. Hobart decided to become one of those candidates. On August 27, 1914, the central committee of the Miami County Progressives met in Grange Hall to agree on a platform and a slate of local candidates. Hobart headed the list as the Progressive choice for Representative to Congress

Theodore Roosevelt

from Ohio's Fourth District. C. C. had no illusions as to the odds against him. Two weeks earlier in Ohio's first direct primary, Democratic and Republican candidates for governor polled well over 400,000 votes, whereas James R. Garfield, the Progressive nominee and son of the late president, received seven thousand votes in his unopposed bid.[8] The main benefit Ohio Progressives hoped to derive in running for office in 1914 was to advance their issues. Hobart announced the resolutions adopted by the county party: "women's suffrage, the prohibition of the manufacture of liquor as a beverage, pensions, opposed Panama Canal tolls, favored shorter hours of labor, opposed child labor, set the seal of approval on a minimum wage, good roads and moral reform."[9]

There was little question that regulation of alcohol would be the most heated issue before Ohioans in 1914. Two alcohol-related state constitutional amendments were on the ballot, thanks to the citizen initiative, a Progressive reform which, along with the direct primary, had been incorporated in Ohio's new constitution in 1912. One proposed amendment called for the local option, which allowed local jurisdictions to decide how to regulate alcohol. The prohibition amendment would ban the manufacture and sale of alcohol as a beverage. Liquor interests or "wets" supported the local option as the lesser of two

evils, as did Democrats. Progressives, including C. C., squarely favored prohibition. Republicans quibbled.[10] Another factor that made prohibition a particularly divisive issue in Troy was its threat to the survival of the Hayner Distillery, not only a major employer but also the largest buyer of grain from Miami County farmers.[11]

In September Hobart spoke at a rally of over one hundred people for the Troy Temperance Auxiliary held at the First Baptist Church.[12] Johnston, Hobart's former partner, also took an active role in the prohibition movement, chairing a Troy meeting of the Women's Christian Temperance Union the day before the election.[13] Like many businessmen, they saw the effects of alcoholism in employee absenteeism, poor productivity, and accidents on the job. However, Hobart did not make an all-out effort in his own behalf. Records show he spent all of $20 on his own campaign.[14] Furthermore, he did not speak at Progressive Party rallies when gubernatorial candidate Garfield made a campaign swing through Hobart's district the third week of October.[15]

Election Day 1914 brought nothing but disappointment to Ohio Progressives. The prohibition and women's suffrage amendments were both defeated, and none of the Party's state or congressional candidates finished better than third in their respective races. Ohio voters adopted the local option on alcohol by a narrow margin. Republican J. Edward Russell was the surprise winner in the Fourth Congressional District over Democrat N. W. Cunningham 25,096 votes to 24,114. Samuel Newman, the Socialist candidate, was third with 1,737 votes while C. C. Hobart came in fourth with 1,400.[16]

Despite the last place finish, C. C. had reason to be proud of the results in light of the campaign he mounted. Over a third of Hobart's vote came from his home county. In Troy itself he captured 10 percent of the votes cast for Congress, which doubled the percentage Progressive candidates for governor and U.S. senator had received.[17] Those who actually knew Hobart were most likely to honor him with their votes, even in a year when they figured his party did not have a chance.

Teddy Roosevelt was thoroughly disgusted with the results of the 1914 election. In a letter to journalist William Allen White, he wrote, ". . . the dog returned to its vomit. Not only did the people wish to beat all reform leaders but they wished to beat the reform legislation."[18] Progressives around the country were discouraged. However, rabid Roosevelt supporters still hoped their hero would enter the fray once more in 1916 and contest the Republican nomination for president. Meanwhile, the "Great War" raged across Europe for two years and drew TR's attention away from domestic reform.

On June 10, 1916, C. C. Hobart sat in Grange Hall with a group of Roosevelt Progressives and listened as a clerk read a telegram from Teddy addressed to Progressives around the country. Roosevelt announced he would decline the nomination of any party for president and advised his supporters to unite behind the Republican nominee and the vital issue of preparedness.[19] A few days later Republicans nominated Charles Evans Hughes, a Supreme Court justice from New York. A couple days later on June 19, Hobart fired off a two-page typed letter to Colonel Roosevelt, Oyster Bay, New York. In it he first alluded to press reports of Roosevelt's pleurisy and told what he had taken to counter the pain—"The only pain like it since I experienced at the auditorium when your telegram was read." C. C. then asserted that "Progressives were not numerous in the district four years ago. A large number of Republicans and not a few Democrats would be enthusiastic Progressives this time if you headed the ticket. Hobart noted that he knew Charles Evans Hughes since both attended Colgate at the same time and joined the same fraternity. What followed was a fine example of damning with faint praise. C. C. and his college friends did not "recall any proposal looking to the general welfare that he [Hughes] had advocated. None of us recall that Mr. Hughes ever used many big swear words. We have no doubt that he attends church with regularity."

Without Roosevelt in the race, Hobart predicted that many Progressives would vote for President Wilson rather than "lean toward" a Republican Party where the same old bosses "still occupy the front seats." Furthermore, in Ohio Democrat former Governor Cox was viewed as more progressive than his Republican opponent Willis.[20] This letter demonstrates that C. C. Hobart was no mere dabbler in politics but an astute and well-informed observer. As he predicted, both Wilson and Cox won in the elections of November 1916.

One year later, after the United States had entered what is now called the First World War, the editor compiling a history of Troy asked Hobart to contribute his personal story to the book. C. C.'s response began with some characteristic tongue in cheek humor. "I am told that the side of Mount Mansfield, the highest peak of the Green

The Progressive Party held meetings in the Grange Hall of the Miami County Courthouse.

Mountain range, broke from its rocky base and slid down with a crash the day I was born. There were other disturbances. Unfortunately at that time records were not kept. The memory of people differ. . . ."[21]

In a slightly more serious vein, Hobart went on to encapsulate many of his fundamental social and political beliefs:

If you want to say anything good about me, you might say that as long as the Republican Party stood for splendid principles, I was a Republican. When the party stopped standing for anything in particular, I found delightful company among Progressives. Some are finding something congenial among the Democrats, and some among the Socialists. At the present time I am part Republican, part Democrat, and part Socialist. I wish the war had never occurred. The thought of the awful suffering and loss of life is too much even to contemplate. Above everything, however, is my desire to see the nation that wants to live by plundering, and that is indifferent to suffering, crushed.

Another strong desire is to see men out from under the baneful influence of liquor. Still another desire with me is to see that all the people have equal rights and equal use of the land and of all things, that the Maker of the universe intended for all, and not for a select few.

Still another desire with me is that the nations as well as the individuals shall recognize fully their obligations to each other, and shall strive not for selfish ends, but to do justice. Then I have also a desire that every man, woman, and child should know what a good thing it is to have the affection of a good dog.[22]

Clearly, Hobart was a man whose political involvement was a means by which to promote the principles that guided his business and personal life. He did not desire a career in politics, nor was he devoted to the success of a particular party. Prohibition of liquor, women's suffrage, humane treatment of animals, and attempting to reduce the inequities in American life were the consistent issues which propelled C. C. Hobart into the political arena. Shortly after the end of World War I, the required number of states ratified prohibition and women's right to vote as the Eighteenth and Nineteenth Amendments to the U.S. Constitution. As he approached age seventy, Hobart could look back and claim, if not complete success, progress. ❧

CHAPTER 5

Three Sons Come of Age

C. Hobart's three sons were just six, four, and two years of age when the family moved from Middletown, Ohio, to Troy in September 1895. Although frequent visits to Middletown kept the boys in touch with their Jones relatives, only Edward, the oldest, had vivid memories of living there. He recalled "the black, belching smokestacks of the Sorg Paper Company" and his house "with a wrought iron fence around it." He credited his mother with giving him his "commercial sense," keeping his feet on the ground, and teaching him "how to keenly appraise worthwhile things in people." From C. C. "came imagination, day dreaming, and a retiring shyness. . . ."[1]

In Troy, Edward, Charles, and William always lived in homes near the Miami River, and they spent much of their time in it, on it, or around it. Edward built a tree house thirty-five feet up in a huge sycamore on the river's north bank. At one time he rigged a pulley to bring lunch over on a rope from the Hobart home on the south bank by Market Street Bridge. The boys tied a rope to the sycamore so they could jump off a derrick platform and swing out high above the river. Edward's "commercial sense was working" when he put a Boat House on the river and began charging a few cents for food and a swim. "You loaded up with your clothes on below the Hobart home. . . ." While swimmers undressed in the Boat House, it was poled downriver to an appropriate swimming spot known as Indian Cellar. They dove off the end of the boat, swam, and got dressed back inside. Then the boat was poled up to a low dam and food was served.[2] During winters the Hobart boys skated on the frozen river and played shinney with their friends.

Shinney was a primitive form of hockey played with sticks and a can.[3]

Due to the distances involved, the boys saw their Hobart relatives less frequently but stayed in touch by letter. When he was nine, Edward wrote Grandpa Hobart, "I am fixing a wagon that has a thing to guide with and a thing to push with something like a handcar as you can see on that other piece of paper." The budding designer included a pencil drawing.[4] Later, he attached a sail to his wagon and rode it around Court House Square on windy days. Another letter to Grandpa told of "a club that gives plays just from Shakespear [sic]." Admission for children was three cents while "grown people" paid five. Edward was the ghost in Hamlet in the first production, but in the Merchant of Venice he played Shylock.[5] Shortly after Edward entered high school, he wrote Grandma Hobart that he had "been working in my shop down in the cellar a good part of the time," and that "Papa" had just bought a new set of tools for the downstairs lab.[6]

Edward was a good student and "usually ranked first in the grades unless Elfreda Drake beat him to it. . . ."[7] During summer breaks from high school, C. C. put him to work in his company, but Edward did not relish electrical contracting jobs. He disliked climbing through dusty attics to string wires. During one particularly tough job that involved cutting into ten-inch oak beams above an old Troy hotel to lay wires, conduits, and insulating tubes, a sweating Edward resolved to do all it took to avoid such work and devote time to the lab experiments he enjoyed.[8] In 1908 he enrolled in the electrical engineering program at the Ohio State University in Columbus.

From left: Charles, William, and Edward Hobart, circa 1900

Left to right: Charles, Edward, and William Hobart, circa 1910

As his last weeks of high school drew to a close, Edward pooled his money with his brothers Charles and William and bought an old electric car from Dr. Senior for $75. The car was steered by a lever instead of a wheel and had been one of the first two automobiles owned by Trojans. The car no longer ran because its battery plates were heavily sulfated. The boys had to borrow a horse to tow it home. Then Edward checked out a three-inch-thick tome by E. J. Wade on storage batteries and went to work. First, he dismantled the old battery and made a bronze mold from the old plates to cast new ones. Edward machined the mold at Troy Sunshade, another company owned by his father's former partners. He cast plates by pouring a lead antimony alloy into the heated mold and later coated the plates with a lead oxide paste. Once the sulfuric acid electrolyte was added to the rebuilt case, the battery began to generate current. A few weeks before he left for college, Edward and his brothers were proudly tooling around Public Square in their used electric car.[9]

Reluctantly, Edward left the auto in the hands of Charles and William when he left for his freshman year at Ohio State in the fall of 1908. Soon he began to receive letters detailing the fun his brothers were having with the car and their high school buddies. One favorite antic involved Charles driving around Public Square towing twenty or more roller skating friends who clung to a rope tied to the car. This stunt always attracted a crowd.[10] On Sunday afternoons Charles and William were fond of taking a five-pound box of chocolates with them as they called on their lady friends and took them for short spins in the car.[11] Each night the car needed to have its batteries recharged, and Edward had built a battery charger for this purpose. When hooked up for recharging, the battery gave off highly explosive hydrogen gas, therefore the battery cover had to be left open to let the gas escape. Both Charles and William were aware of this but one night they forgot. The next morning when they started the car a spark touched off a loud explosion that blew out the back

A car similar in style to the Hobart boys' electric car on the Public Square in Troy, Ohio, circa 1902

of the car and destroyed the battery. Luckily, no one was hurt, but that was the end of the electric car. Charles and William neglected to inform Edward who did not learn about the mishap until he returned home for Christmas break.[12]

Ohio State was one of the first American universities to establish an electrical engineering program. At first a concentration within the Department of Physics, it became an independent department with its own building by 1896. By 1903 the program had grown to the point where over 42 percent of Ohio State engineering students were majoring in electrical engineering. Professor Francis C. Caldwell, department chairman during Edward's years at Ohio State, founded a campus radio station in 1910.[13] Edward's favorite classes were the ones in electrical design taught by Professor John H. Hunt. In carrying out design experiments, he often found himself teamed with a classmate from Greenville, Ohio, named Orval H. Menke.[14] Together they built a dynamometer to measure the mechanical power produced by various types of small motors. They incorporated this research in the senior thesis they coauthored entitled "Small Single Phase Power Motors."[15]

Edward excelled at Ohio State and completed his bachelor's degree in electrical engineering in 1912. He also found time to work on the Senior Social Committee and joined Eta Kappa Nu, the national electrical engineering fraternity, as well as the Institute of American Electrical Engineers.[16] Most of Edward's fellow graduates interviewed with companies such as American Telegraph and Telephone, General Electric, and Westinghouse. Menke, in fact,

accepted a position with AT&T. However, Edward chose to return to Troy and work in the lab alongside his father.[17]

Shortly after his graduation, Edward designed and built a one-kilowatt 110-volt DC generator, using just a ten-inch lathe, a drill press, and some hand tools. Belted to a gasoline engine, it provided current for lighting. He and his father sold a few generators of this design.[18] C. C. and his oldest son began to plan for the day when all three boys and their father could organize a new company based on a new line of products.

According to William, his older brother Charles "was smaller than Edward or William but athletic—baseball, tennis, and all the outdoor sports."[19] Of all three Hobart brothers, Charles had perhaps the greatest love for the outdoors. He would arise before dawn on fall mornings and set off in a canoe to go duck hunting on the Miami River. Charles could dress and clean his kill, change clothes, and walk to Edwards High School in time for morning classes. He was an avid fisherman as well as an athlete who played varsity football, basketball, and baseball his senior year. When working for his dad on summer breaks, he tended to gravitate toward the cabinetry shop.[20]

After Charles graduated from high school in 1909, he attended Denison University, a small Baptist college in Granville, Ohio, just east of Columbus. In early September 1912 he and his mother traveled east by train to Washington, D.C., Philadelphia, New York, and Boston. One purpose of the trip was to decide whether Charles would transfer to the University of Pennsylvania or Pratt Institute in Brooklyn.[21] Charles chose Pratt's two-year program in applied electricity. He also continued his athletic pursuits and played varsity basketball at Pratt.[22]

Pratt's course of study was unusual for its time. Apart from a thorough grounding in mathematics, physics, and chemistry, each trimester in the first year included a class in mechanical drawing and a variety of "shop-work" courses, from carpentry to foundry work. Except for more math and electrical drawing, the second year was almost entirely devoted to hands-on work with electrical systems.[23] Pratt's 1911–12 catalog states ". . .the training is of so practical a nature and is so closely related to commercial work that the graduate cannot fail to find profitable employment for which he has become fitted."[24] By the time he earned his two-year certificate in the spring of 1913, Charles was fit to join his father and brother in their electrical company.

C. C.'s youngest son, William Harrison, was the tallest and most handsome of the Hobart boys. A good athlete, he played football all four years of high school and was a co-captain his senior year.[25] William saw himself as "a lover of things inside."[26] He enjoyed photography, art, poetry, cooking, gardening, and music and became quite adept at playing the popular tunes of the day on the piano. He even accompanied silent movies at a Troy theater with his piano playing.[27]

If Edward was most at home in the lab, and Charles in the great outdoors, William was charming and gregarious and felt more comfortable in social settings than his two older brothers. He followed Charles to Denison where he took a full schedule the first two years with many of his courses in the natural sciences. William completed just two classes his third year before transferring to the Wharton School of Business at the University of Pennsylvania for the 1914–15 school year.[28] Rather than enroll for a second year at Wharton, William returned to Troy to take his place in the Hobart Brothers Company, which his father and older brothers had been operating for nearly a year.

While Charles and William were still away at college and C. C. and Lou Ella were visiting New York, Troy and the entire Miami Valley experienced their worst flood in recorded history. Twenty-four-year-old Edward was alone in the home on East Water Street during the torrential rains that lasted throughout Easter weekend. On the night of Monday, March 24, 1913, Edward worked at the shop until midnight, helping his father's partners secure all they could from the coming flood. He awoke at 4:00 a.m. and within an hour the call went out that a reservoir upriver had broken. Quickly, Edward hauled furniture and rugs upstairs. "No water came into our cellar until it got in the cellar window, then it came in with a rush. I got up some of the flowers and fruit, but the cans and bottles are still floating."[29] North of the river in a sec-

Troy scenes from the 1913 Flood

tion of town known as Ninevah, a black family, Reuben Jones with his wife and child, had been forced to take refuge in a tree. The first man who rowed toward them had his boat swept up by the current and dragged under the Market Street Bridge, which he clung to before being rescued. Edward watched as a trolley conductor and another man paddled to the tree. As the conductor, who had climbed into the tree, lowered in the last refugee the boat overturned, and the other four were swept downriver under the bridge and drowned.[30]

Edward waded into the two feet of icy water in the street and joined the makeshift rescue operations. He and a barber named Ed Knapp secured a steel boat and rescued four families from attics and second-floor windows. They used a clothesline to bring one elderly woman into the boat. "We got about thirteen people out altogether. None were in real danger of their lives, but they were scared." Edward observed, "It was mostly young men and the bums of the town [including one prison inmate] that really helped most in the boats."[31] By afternoon they were ferrying food and provisions to people safe in their second stories amid the strange sights of destruction: drowned horses, massive tangles of driftwood, and a piano lodged in a backyard.

The worst flooding in Troy was directly south of where the river began its eastward bend. The rampaging waters had taken the path of least resistance between the bed of the old Miami-Erie Canal and the ridge west of town. Fourteen Trojans drowned and two died of exposure.[32] The loss of life and property were much worse to the south in Dayton.

Edward helped rig a machine at the *Miami Union* newspaper offices to get the local phone service running again. He reported that only Ben Gibb's room and the machine shop got wet at the American Fixture factory. "There will be lots of Motors to dry out."[33] Despite the disaster, there is an unmistakable tone of exhilaration in

The Brewery on West Water Street served as the Hobart factory circa 1915. Left door: George Welsh, Lulu Weatherhead, Josephine Collins, Mrs. Hawley, Clara Weatherhead, Ed Johnson. Right door: Thelma Campbell, Miss McMath, Maude Erter, Maino Bridges, Ruth Smith, Helen Anagnost, Minna Bader. Standing, left to right: Dewey Smock, Cy Grass, William. Tooley, Jess Shilling, George Aregood, Cal Beach, Curley Leblond, Ed McCool, Tom Collins, Tom Price, Charlie Pemberton, Earl Galbreath, William Hobart, Edward Hobart, Charles Hobart. Seated, left to right: Harry Brown, Bill Smock, James Brown, Earl Carl, Wib Davis, Jump Boldy, Fred Ricker, Cris Kirsch, Lowell Arthur, Cliff Covault, Ted Johnson, August Lamka, unidentified, Stanford Mapes

Edward's account. He seemed to thrive on the activity and responsibility thrust upon him by the flood. Confidently he wrote his mother, "You and Pop had better stay your visit out, as everything is alright here. . . ."[34]

World War I had just begun when C. C. split his company in the summer of 1914. The war would have several unforeseen consequences for the three Hobart brothers and the new company named for them. The most immediate consequences were positive. The economy of neutral America thrived during the early years of the war as agriculture and industry geared up to supply the demands of the warring powers. The previous summer Ford had introduced the first modern assembly line for automobile production, which enabled him to lower the price of a new Model T to $360, putting a car within reach for all

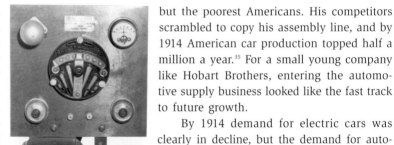

The first Hobart battery charger, 1915

but the poorest Americans. His competitors scrambled to copy his assembly line, and by 1914 American car production topped half a million a year.[35] For a small young company like Hobart Brothers, entering the automotive supply business looked like the fast track to future growth.

By 1914 demand for electric cars was clearly in decline, but the demand for automotive battery chargers was on the rise. Most early automobiles had headlamps that burned acetylene gas, a system pioneered by the Prestolite Company. Now many new cars, still started by being hand-cranked, were equipped with electrical lighting whose batteries needed frequent recharging. Charles Kettering's new electric self-starter was in fact just one component of an ingenious system in which the running car engine converted mechanical energy to the electrical current needed to recharge the battery used for starting and lights.[36] At first, C. C. and his sons were concerned that Kettering's new system would ruin the market for automotive battery charging. They soon learned that between leaving their lights on or starting their cars on cold mornings when the battery's chemical reaction was less efficient, people still had plenty of need to recharge their car batteries.[37]

Edward, who increasingly came to be called by his initials—E. A., purchased and then disassembled a two-horsepower, three-phase Westinghouse electric motor. He installed an armature which was long enough to carry the rotor of a generator as well. When all the parts were reassembled he had a single unit 110-volt motor generator that could be used as a battery charger.[38] Previous battery chargers Hobart Brothers had used had been belted to a separate power source.[39]

Troy residents brought in batteries that needed recharging which then were connected together in series to the charger. The process had several inefficiencies. One had to wait until a sufficient number of batteries were present so, connected in series, their combined voltage capacity equalled that of the charger. One bad battery with an open cell could prevent the whole set of batteries from charging properly. In addition, charging itself could take up to sixteen hours. Despite these shortcomings, Hobart Brothers did a brisk business in battery charging, and tables and benches in the shop were often filled with long lines of batteries in their clunky wooden cases wired up to a charger.[40]

Hobart Brothers decided to begin manufacturing battery chargers for sale to filling stations and auto repair shops. When William joined his brothers at the company in the summer of 1915, C. C. divided responsibilities between his three sons. E. A. became chief engineer, Charles took charge of finances, and William assumed responsibility for sales. A photograph taken at about this time shows thirty-seven employees and the three Hobart brothers standing in front of the former brewery plant on Water Street. Everyone walked to work or rode their bicycles, which they left propped against the side of the building.[41] Whatever the appearance, this no frills operation was growing.

On March 24, 1917, Hobart Brothers Company was formally incorporated by the State of Ohio, capitalized at $100,000. C. C., Lou Ella, and their three sons were the incorporators who held all stock in the new firm. As the *Miami Union* put it, "Mr. Hobart is old at the manufacturing game, having had a long experience, while the sons, all three of whom have completed college courses, have brought to the business technical and business knowledge through which the business has steadily grown." The company also announced it intended to lease and remodel a Henne brewery warehouse on West Main Street in order to relocate the cabinet portion of the business there and allow the electrical end of the company to expand at the Water Street site.[42]

Welcoming employees back from World War I. Standing at far left is C. C. Hobart; second from left is W. H.; third from left is Orval Menke, E. A.'s former college roommate. E. A. is fifth from left, and Charles is kneeling in front of him. Earl Galbreath in a military cap is shown holding the flag at left. Circa 1918

Exactly two weeks later Congress gave President Woodrow Wilson the declaration of war on Germany for which he had called. The United States had entered the Great War. In May 1917, Congress passed the Selective Service Act, which made males between the ages of twenty and thirty eligible for the military draft. That included a good portion of Hobart Brothers employees as well as the company's three young executives. A draft board in Cincinnati classified E. A. as 3-K, for "high class specialists—essential for industrial mobilization of the country." Charles was declared 3-L, an "essential head of a necessary manufacturing concern." William, however, not yet twenty-five years of age and lacking the technical degrees his brothers had, received a classification of 1-A.[43] Rather than waiting to be conscripted, William decided to enlist in the Navy, but, before the process was completed, the Army drafted him. Once the confusion was sorted out, William found himself at boot camp dressed in Army khaki.

The deferments E. A. and Charles received were due in part to the war work Hobart Brothers had become engaged in. The company produced electrical generator sets for battleship intercoms used to direct gunfire.[44] The cabinet shop was also filling government orders under a subcontract arrangement.[45] Across town, Hobart Manufacturing was even more heavily involved in the war effort. Its mixers had become standard equipment on all U.S. Navy vessels. In addition, the company made parts for shell casings, gun carriages, and electrical equipment for aircraft.[46]

Rachel Hobart

In light of all the war work underway in Troy factories and the explosive efforts of a highly publicized and very real German sabotage network on the East Coast, Troy residents could be excused for suspecting the worst when a fire broke out in the Hobart Brothers plant on Water Street before 3:00 a.m. April 1, 1918. The fire did an estimated $20,000 in damage, destroying a frame annex to the rear of the building and partly gutting some brick portions. Water caused more damage. Early accounts contained conflicting reports of people awakened by barking dogs and a car speeding away shortly before the fire was reported. "Crossed wires" was the police theory, but Fire Chief Landry thought the "building was fired by some unknown person, possibly a German sympathizer. . . ," but C. C. had been through this before and had a more sober explanation. Clearly, the fire had begun in the testing department in or near a stove used to heat soldering irons. C. C. thought that employees working late may have left embers smoldering which were reignited by increased gas pressure overnight, and that eventually the metal sheathing could not prevent the woodwork from catching fire. This time Hobart had $22,000 in insurance to cover the buildings, but it would not pay for all the damage since the loss was not total. C. C. predicted the fire would delay completing the Navy contract by at least sixty days.[47]

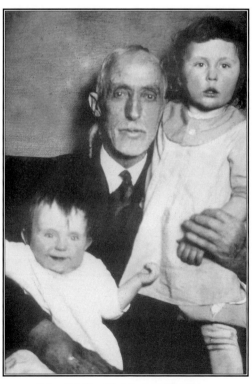

John Cahill with his granddaughters Lucia and Marcia Hobart, circa 1924

Sparks of more than one kind were flying around Hobart Brothers in the spring of 1918. Two of the brothers were in love—with the same woman. Sibling rivalry is found in nearly all families, and, among the three Hobart boys, it was usually Charles and William who were butting heads, from the athletic fields to the more subtle competition of courting. From high school on they had dated several of the same Troy girls. Charles felt that his younger brother had either stolen some of his girlfriends or had dated them after a break up just to spite Charles. At last Charles found a lovely young woman in Piqua by the name of Rachel Cahill. Their courtship may have even advanced to a proposal of marriage in which Charles was turned down.[48] Before William left for the Army, he began to date Miss Cahill. It soon became clear that this was not spite; it was serious.

Rachel Ellen Cahill was born March 4, 1894, to Cora and John Maxwell Cahill. Her father had been born in Albany, New York, in 1857 and learned textile manufacturing in Lawrence, Massachusetts. He moved to Piqua in the mid 1880s to take a position with the F. Gray Company, which fashioned woolens, flannels, jeans, and blankets, including standard blankets for the military and for Pullman sleeping cars.[49] Cahill married Cora Gray, daughter of a doctor and niece of the man who owned the textile mill. Rachel was their only surviving child. She had had a brother who was stillborn and a younger brother who died after just seventeen months.[50] Rachel's mother suffered from tuberculosis, and her father took her west, first to Las Vegas and then to Albuquerque in the hope that the dry climate would improve her condition. Cahill left her in the care of a physician and nurse in Albuquerque when business required him to be in Piqua. While the nine-year old Rachel was visiting Albuquerque with her aunt in August 1903, her mother succumbed to tuberculosis.[51]

In 1899 John Cahill and three partners had organized the Piqua Underwear Company. After selling his interest in that firm, he served for several years as manager of Piqua Hosiery, famous for producing the nation's first "commercially practical drop-seat union suit", popularly known as BVD's.[52] Shortly after his wife's death, Cahill left Rachel in the care of his two sisters-in-law and ventured west to buy land, including a piece of land near Bartlesville, Oklahoma. The textile manager was going to try his hand at drilling for oil. After a couple years and several dry holes, he, like many others, sold his claim to a local banker by the name of Frank Phillips. Later, Phillips struck oil on the Cahill claim, which added yet another stream to the river of Oklahoma crude he used to create Phillips Petroleum.[53]

Father and daughter returned to their comfortable red brick home on Ash Street just west of downtown Piqua. Rachel attended Piqua High School where she served as secretary of the class of 1912 and treasurer of the Girls Athletic Association. An appropriate quotation accompanied the yearbook photo of each graduating senior. Miss Cahill's was the enviable: "None knew her but to love her/ None named her but to praise," paraphrased from American poet Fitz-Greene Halleck.[54] John Cahill wanted the finest education for his daughter, so he sent her to Smith College in Northampton, Massachusetts.

Rachel may have not yet been engaged to William before he left for boot camp in May 1918, but she did join the Hobarts for a reunion with his mother's family, the Jones clan, in Middletown that summer when Willam was able to join them on a weekend pass. In June William moved on to Officer Candidate School at Camp Taylor, Kentucky. Less than a week after he was promoted to sergeant, the Army decided it already had enough officers to win the war and gave William an honorable discharge.[55] He was back at work at Hobart Brothers in Troy long before word came of the armistice, which ended the war November 11, 1918. Hobart Brothers employees joined in the nearly hour-long parade of Troy workers to celebrate what President Wilson had called "the war to end all wars."[56]

The following year William and Rachel exchanged vows in a quiet ceremony before their immediate families

C. C. Hobart and Lou Ella Hobart, 1920

on October 4 in Cincinnati at Mount Auburn Baptist Church, once the church of William's Uncle Alvah and now pastored by Reverend H. T. Crane, a Hobart family friend from Middletown days. After a wedding supper at the Gibson House, the young couple left for an extended honeymoon trip through the east. Before the holiday season they returned home and moved into the Hobart family residence on West Franklin Street in Troy.

As the Hobarts prepared to ring in the 1920s, C. C. could look back on the busy past decade with pride. He had helped found the Miami County Progressive Party and experienced or at least endured a run for Congress. His company and his hometown had weathered a disastrous flood, and now the locally financed Miami Conservancy District was at work, building a network of dams and levees to prevent such floods in the future. He had watched his sons complete their college education and join him in incorporating a new company they could truly call their own. Hobart Brothers' future growth was hitched to America's love for the automobile, a love that was sure to grow now that the country had emerged victorious from war. And now, his youngest son had taken a wife. At age sixty-five, C. C. could look forward to grandchildren. ❧

CHAPTER 6

Hobart Brothers Charges into the Twenties

By 1920 the automobile was already beginning to transform America. In 1914, the year Hobart Brothers was founded, American factories turned out half a million automobiles. Just five years later car manufacturers had tripled their production.[1] Perhaps more importantly, the electric self-starter was becoming standard equipment on American cars. Even Henry Ford, the champion of low-cost bare-bones transportation, grudgingly consented to include the feature on all closed-cab Model T's in 1919.[2] Now women and even the elderly could enjoy the independence of driving a motor car without the aid of a man willing to risk a broken arm or a sprained wrist in order to crank a cold engine into life. America entered the 1920s with 10 million registered cars and trucks. By 1929 that number had exploded to over 26 million, enough vehicles to furnish one for every five Americans.[3] Hobart Brothers endeavored to serve this growing market with battery chargers and an expanding line of car service products.

One problem with charging batteries in series was that it took fifteen to sixteen hours to completely charge a standard auto battery. That meant the customer had to either keep rotating a pair of batteries in and out of his car or be without use of his car for an entire day. The Exide Battery Company pioneered the idea of charging batteries connected in parallel instead of in series. Batteries took a tapered charge, absorbing the bulk of the charge at the start of the cycle and gradually tapering off toward the end. Though it cut charging time in half, this method presented a new challenge for the compound wound generators of the day. Should anything happen to make the battery current come back through the compounding, the generator would reverse its rotation, speed up, and ruin the generator.[4]

E. A. always enjoyed a technical challenge and immediately set to work to correct this problem. At first he thought a voltage regulator would be the answer, but, after a good deal of trial and error, he hit upon the unique idea of a diverter pole. E. A. designed a generator which had the compounding field wound around a small auxiliary pole instead of around the main field. Batteries connected in parallel could discharge into this diverter pole, which E. A. called "a magnetic by-pass," and prevent disastrous reversal of the main field that "generally results in damage to the machine and batteries".[5] Now batteries could be recharged in half the time without the risk of a reversal in current. E. A. obtained his first patent for this invention, and the diverter pole became a standard item discussed in manuals of electrical engineering around the world.[6] Eventually, E. A. secured thirty-five separate patents, a stream of technical innovation that was to prove vital to the growth of Hobart Brothers and established its creative character.

William, now known within the company as "W. H.," began marketing these improved "constant potential" battery chargers to garages and service stations around the country and abroad. Hobart Brothers manufactured five different models of chargers. Three chargers, ranging from five hundred watts to two kilowatts, could charge from eight to thirty-two six volt car batteries and were designed to operate on either direct or alternating current. The largest of these generators had a shipping weight of six hundred pounds. The company also offered a belted charger for use where either part time or no electric current was available. Belted to a one-horsepower motor, it could recharge up to eight car batteries. Finally, they produced a larger belted generator which could charge fourteen car batteries or, like one of C. C.'s old products, power up to fifty lights or charge the batteries on railroad cars.[7]

C. C. Hobart and his three boys, W. H., E. A., and Charles, building the company and new products, circa 1920.

Charles had already successfully used direct mail to promote Hobart products made by the cabinet division, so W. H. followed suit and began compiling a mailing list of service stations and car repair shops that soon numbered in the thousands. W. H. supplemented this campaign by placing ads in trade magazines, such as *Popular Mechanics* and *Popular Science*. To promote the new chargers, he employed a marketing tool C. C. had used twenty years earlier that was now becoming widespread in the 1920's, installment credit. The smallest charger could be purchased for "$15.00 cash and ten monthly payments [of] $20.00." Advertisements claimed a battery could be charged at a cost of twelve to fifteen cents for electrical current. If the "autoists" paid seventy-five cents to $1.50 per battery, the shop or service station could clear a profit of at least $4.80 on each capacity run. In a busy shop, earnings would easily

pay for the machine. "HB chargers last for years. . . . Long service with quick, clean, permanent profits. . . . No burn-outs or expensive renewals." If easy terms, quick profits, and reliable equipment failed to entice the skeptical car shop owner, W. H.'s breezy ad copy provided a further clincher, "a money back guarantee." Direct mail order blanks guaranteed that all equipment could be returned within ten days of its arrival "for any reason whatsoever" for a full refund. "Order now—you run no risk."[8] Many did. Eventually, more than six thousand garages nation-wide bought Hobart Brothers chargers.[9]

Territory closer to home was covered in a different manner. W. H. hired salesmen who had their own cars and instructed them to load them up with battery chargers and drive around stopping at every filling station, battery shop, or garage to give demonstrations and make direct sales right on the spot. These were

Clayton Jenkins demonstrates the
Hobart eight-hour battery charger.

Hobart car washing system, circa 1928

This dramatic photo was used to promote
Hobart air compressors.

salesmen, not technicians. Their demonstrations reinforced advertising claims that "No electrical knowledge [was] necessary to install or operate."[10] One of W. H.'s summer sales incentives likened his staff to heroes of the late war and "regretted" they could not be rewarded by having a medal pinned to their chests and a kiss on both cheeks, but he could offer a handsome $30 walrus handbag to the man who sold the most chargers by August 31.[11]

During the 1920s Hobart Brothers expanded its product line to include a variety of electrical equipment designed to service automobiles. These included air compressors, automatic car washers, several grinders and motors, paint sprayers, and electrical test equipment. E. A. had little trouble turning his engineering skill with electrical motor generators into other practical applications for work on automobiles. He and his design team secured seven more patents for designs and inventions related to automotive service equipment.[12] E. A. encouraged his small team of engineers to tinker and experiment. "Even if it doesn't work or make money," he told them, "You learn something."[13]

This expansion of the company's product line was not a planned diversification, but a series of projects with disparate causes. Salesmen in the field reported that service stations needed a dependable source of compressed air for filling the pneumatic tires that had become standard on all motor vehicles. Many shops had amateurish contraptions using belts or chains to connect a motor to an air pump. They were inefficient and took up a lot of space. E. A. began experimenting with a motor and air pump mounted in a single portable housing. By creating a silent, spiral bevel gear transmission, similar to those that were replacing chain drives on automobiles themselves, he increased the efficiency and decreased the noise of the compressor. The new compressor became an immediate hit with auto shops, and variations of the design sold for industrial applications as well.[14]

Another need of service stations was testing equipment in order to pinpoint the source of a problem in an automobile's electrical system: starting, ignition, and lighting. Many small garages had to bring cars to an electrical

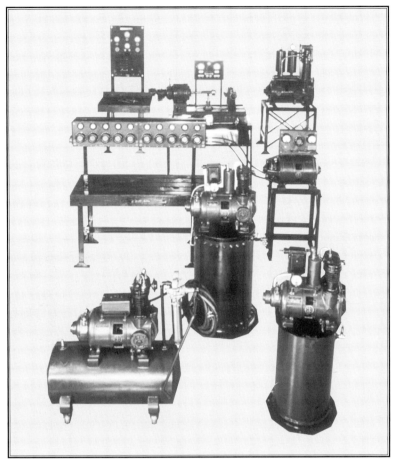

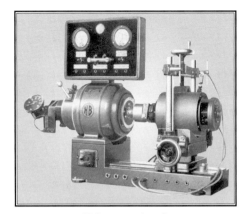

Hobart test bench

Hobart automotive service equipment

specialty shop to diagnose such problems because the testing equipment was too expensive for them to afford. For service stations in small towns and rural areas, this often meant a trip to a large city costing extra time and money. Hobart Brothers developed electrical test benches that sold for $200 to $400 less than models previously on the market.[15]

Like many manufacturers of the era, Hobart Brothers took pride in its independence. When the company needed something for the plant, it made its own. Both C. C. and E. A. in particular wanted to be beholden to no one and believed the knowledge gained in building their own equipment was worth the time and labor it took. On occasion these efforts had unintended benefits in the form of new marketable products. Hobart engineers began adapting their compressors for use in spray painting with the new quick drying lacquers developed by the automobile industry. Employees tested and tweaked the paint sprayers as they used them to paint their own factory buildings and equipment. Soon Hobart Brothers had developed a line of high-

pressure lacquer sprayers driven by either electrical or gasoline motors. Both body shops and industrial finishers became eager customers for the paint sprayers.[16]

One effect of the high-gloss lacquer finishes and rainbow of colors aggressively marketed by General Motors under Alfred Sloan was that drivers took more pride in their car's appearance. Car washes began to spring up all over America. However, America's obsession with speed and efficiency created a demand for automatic car washes. Even car washes that employed people using old-fashioned elbow grease wanted an automatic system for underbody cleaning. Soon a variety of high-pressure water pumps were under observation around the Hobart Brothers plant engaged in practical work. A reciprocating pump designed by E. A. proved the most efficient, was duly patented, and became the basis of the HB "duplex double-action car washer." The new car washer sold so well that within three years of its introduction it was second only to the battery chargers in sales.[17]

The first Main Street factory, circa 1925, a former warehouse, with the new factory being constructed at the right.

The growth in demand for its automotive product line led to the decision in 1925 to build a modern three-story brick factory at the northwest corner of West Main and Adams Streets, the first major facility Hobart Brothers built instead of buying or leasing an existing structure. Rather than subcontract construction of the plant, the company took a characteristically do-it-yourself approach and created a construction department to design and build the plant. C. C. relished the chance to supervise a project that dwarfed the homes he had built in Middletown. A special challenge was building the plant over the old bed of the Miami-Erie canal, including one of its locks.[18] When complete, the new factory with its clean lines, gold-colored brick, and huge windows resembled the efficient buildings of the National Cash Register Company in Dayton.

In order to showcase their products, Hobart Brothers built a model service station on the northeast corner of West Main and Elm next to their new factory. Nearly all the equipment in use at the station was designed and built in the factory next door. The station provided an ideal location to demonstrate Hobart Brothers products to both visiting buyers and passing motorists.[19] Many out-of-state travelers frequented the station since both West Main and North Elm Streets were part of the Dixie Highway's route through Troy. Completed in 1923, the Dixie Highway was the first paved two-lane road to connect Ontario, Canada, with Miami, Florida.[20]

The expansion the Hobarts undertook in the 1920s was extended to their families as well. On August 26, 1920, Rachel Hobart gave birth to her and W. H.'s first child, Marcia Cahill Hobart. Marcia was the first grandchild for sixty-six-year-old C. C. and his fifty-four-year-old wife Lou Ella as well as the first Hobart born in Troy. A second daughter, Lucia Gray, was born April 20, 1922. Before the children arrived W. H. and Rachel had moved out of the Hobart home on West Franklin just a block east to 203 West Franklin on the corner of Plum Street.

E. A. set up his own household in 1921. Many years later W. H. mused, "Edward might have married Ramona Bangs and had thousands of children," . . . [or] . . . "owned all the foundries in this section of Ohio had he persisted . . . with another damsel. He also might have been married to one of the biggest shoplifters in this section of the world, but Edward didn't."[21] Instead, Edward married Martha Jane Lantis, a "charming brunette" from Cincinnati. Martha was a 1920 graduate of the University of Cincinnati where she had majored in political science and been an active member of the Tri Delta Sorority. E. A. met Martha when she came to Troy each summer to visit the family of her uncle, Charles Tobey. Tobey owned a drugstore in Troy and lived just down the street from E. A.'s parents. The young couple had a fashionably 1920s wedding in the bride's Price Hill home in Cincinnati. Martha wore a wedding-and-going-away suit of navy crepe topped by a blue feather turban as she and Edward exchanged vows in a sunroom decked in roses, palms, and ferns. After a buffet luncheon, the newlyweds motored off on a trip to New York, Washington, and the Greenbrier in West Virginia.[22]

Manufacturing battery chargers about 1925

The Hobart factory at Main and Adams Streets, circa 1926

The Hobart model service station, circa 1928, was located on a stretch of West Main Street that was also a segment of the Dixie Highway. The station showcased Hobart Brothers' automotive service products.

After their return, Mr. and Mrs. E. A. Hobart moved into a brick and stucco home at 217 West Franklin. It did not take the new householders long to get used to their neighbors.[23] To one side lived Martha's Uncle Charles and Aunt Ella, on the other side W. H. and Rachel Hobart. In fact, the whole Troy branch of the Hobart clan lived on West Franklin throughout the 1920s. Each workday morning E. A., Charles, and W. H. came to give their mother a kiss before heading off to work. C. C. followed the same routine but first filled the pockets of his coat with birdseed and dog treats before climbing aboard his bike and pedaling three blocks to the plant on Water Street. Knowing an easy mark, a stray dog or two would begin trailing C. C. before he got very far. His feathered friends waited for him outside the factory. On many days and certainly on Fridays Lou followed her husband and sons to work, for she was still the official treasurer for Hobart Brothers and signed everyone's paychecks.[24]

Early in the morning of Sunday, June 8, 1924, C. C. and Lou Ella experienced a little more excitement than they desired. Troy was in the midst of a series of spectacular electrical storms accompanied by torrential rain that raised the Miami River to the highest recorded level since the flood of 1913. C. C.'s letter explaining what happened was printed in the next day's *Troy Daily News*.

About 6 a.m. there came a clap of thunder. It occurred to me that the lightning accompanying that peal must have hit something close by. . . . Lightning had never hit our house before. I was not alarmed this time. I dropped off to sleep.

About 7 a.m. friend wife observed there was smoke in the room. I jumped up, opened the door into the hall. A wall of smoke, black and dense was in front. . . . The phone was at the farther end of the hall. Friend wife started to make a dash for the phone. No human being could have gotten to that phone and back again alive. With language more forcible than polite, Mrs. Hobart was persuaded to not make the dash.[25]

C. C. and Lou Ella were "penned" in their second-story bedroom fifteen feet above the ground. Smoke poured into the room around the door. "Our windows were open, but the smoke didn't seem to want to leave. It grew thicker." C. C. considered several means of escape. He could tie a sheet around Lou and lower her down but was not sure the sheet would hold. "My wife has pride and I knew she would not specially relish being let down from the second-story window that way."

Instead, C. C. decided to yell to his neighbors for help. Not possessed of a strong voice, he elected to call

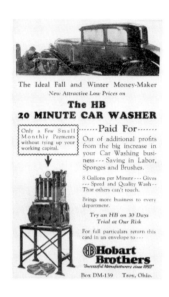

his neighbors by name ". . . and leave it to them to earn a Carnegie medal for getting a ladder up and calling the Fire Department." No one answered. So he abandoned restraint and began to bellow "Fire!" as the smoke grew thicker. "At this point something providential happened." A fireman walking home from his night shift heard his cries and soon had a ladder against the building. "It was like an elopement," C. C. observed, "With its thrill only of a different sort." Another article reported $1,500 in damage to C. C. Hobart's home, not including smoke damage.[26]

The purpose of C. C.'s letter, however, was not to entertain his fellow Trojans but to provide them with a pointed lesson about fire safety. "It is no funny thing to be in a dilemma when you must either go up in smoke or jump and break your legs. . . . Let us each study our homes and make sure that we have a safe and sure means of escape from the building if it caught fire. . . . Be sure you have a workable plan. If you have children, by all means provide for their safety."

Also, C. C. could not resist the opportunity to dispel the myth that "crossed wires" caused many house fires. He asserted that properly grounded electrical wires were

C. C. could not resist the opportunity to dispel the myth that "crossed wires" caused many house fires.

usually as good a protection as lightning rods but that the fire in the Hobart home did not burn out a single fuse. "Our lights have burned as serenely since the fire as before."[27]

One month later C. C. had much happier cause to write a letter, the birth of William Harrison Hobart Jr. on July 5, 1924. "This is the first time I ever wrote a Grandson of mine. Your arrival is timely. I had almost despaired of having a Grandson." He commiserated with the infant boy over the confusion he knew would ensue from being named for his father. ". . . there has lately been 10,000 mistakes or misunderstandings all growing out of their being two C. C. Hobarts." He informed young William that he was placing a small sum in a local building and loan in his name. "That you may be thoughtfully wise and good is the ardent wish of your Grandfather. Your Grandmother furnishes half the deposit and joins in what I have to say."[28]

C. C. Hobart would not have long to bask in the glow of his first grandson's birth before disharmony between his own three sons would force him to reorganize the Hobart Brothers Company in the interest of family unity.

43

CHAPTER 7

The Maverick Charts His Own Course

Left to right: E. A., Charles, and William Hobart

In 1946, after C. C. Hobart's sons had established a charitable foundation in his name, longtime company patent attorney Harry Toulmin, Jr., observed:

The curious thing is that your Father left to his three sons, one each of his three principal characteristics: To Edward he left his electrical and mechanical ability; To Charles he left his deep-seated sense of justice and intolerance of being pushed into an unjust situation; To William he left his sense of adaptability and salesmanship to varying commercial conditions and appreciation of coming markets.

I wonder if he did not sense this when he told you boys to stick together. He was a wise man and he understood that rarely does God in his infinite wisdom have the laws of inheritance and the laws of heredity follow the same channel.[1]

There is no denying the accuracy of Toulmin's observations, but they also contain a pair of ironies, the first of which helps explain the second. Both Edward (E. A.) and William (W. H.) were able to employ their inherited talents in their respective roles at Hobart Brothers, E. A. in engineering and manufacturing, W. H. in marketing and sales. On the other hand, Charles met with nothing but frustration in his allotted role of directing company finances. Though he would later prove to be an imaginative entrepreneur in his own right, finances were never his strong suit. Increasingly, Charles bristled at the injustice of his brothers who plunged into new and often costly ventures in design and marketing before consulting him on sound financing.

The second irony is that despite C. C.'s advice to "stick together" discord between the brothers would reach the point where C. C. himself found it necessary to divide

Hobart Brothers in order to keep the peace. Trouble began when W. H. brought his bride home in November 1919 to live with his parents and brothers in the family home on West Franklin Street. Two single and highly competitive male siblings could hardly be expected to enjoy living in close proximity to their youngest brother and his beautiful new bride. For Charles, who had once dated the future Mrs. Rachel Hobart, it was particularly difficult.

Conflict between Charles and his brothers did not end when they entered the shop door. Apart from disagreements over expenditures, there was the thorny issue of corporate income taxes. Charles had some very definite ideas about the income tax, which had only been in effect since 1913. He believed that the federal government intended all corporations and individuals to pay the full, established rate. Charles viewed all deductions for meals, travel, and other business expenses as cheating.[2] They also greatly complicated his job, and, as the company's chief financial officer, Charles would have to justify the deductions if the company faced an audit. To add to the friction between brothers, it was W. H. in his role as head of sales and marketing who was submitting most business deductions to Charles. However, Charles did not take his unorthodox stand on income taxes merely to provoke a fight. He held to it the rest of his life.[3]

Sometime in the early 1920s Charles made it clear to his father that he could not continue as financial director of the Hobart Brothers Company. Twice before C. C. had sold off all or part of his shares in a business in order to create a company he could pass on intact to his three sons. Now he would have to divide that company in order to keep his family together. Charles expressed an interest in the cabinet portion of the business, and, if a split had to be made, at least the cabinet product line was quite independent of battery chargers and automotive servicing equipment. Yet the company was still so small and interdependent that such a split would take time. Personnel, facilities, and use of machine tools were all intertwined, and complete independence had to be postponed until the new factory was completed in early 1926.

Another concern for C. C. was to be financially fair to his sons in dividing the business. Ironically, he had to take care in giving Charles his portion in order to prevent him from getting gouged by income taxes. After Charles had apparently rejected a $45,000 settlement in September 1924, C. C. proposed to pay Charles a salary of

Charles expressed an interest in the cabinet portion of the business.

$20,000 for 1924 in the form of a $4,000 factory building on Water Street, the $8,000 cabinet business and $8,000 in bonds. He would pay Charles a salary for 1925 of $20,000, entirely in bonds, on January 1. As for the final $10,000 in the $50,000 proposal, C. C. told Charles, "You are to exchange your common stock for preferred stock share for share. There will be no gain or loss and no tax on this transaction." C. C. pointed out that under this proposal Charles' taxes for the two years would total $2,240, whereas a straight exchange of Charles's common stock for the total assets of the cabinet portion in one year would result in a tax of $3,230. To allay Charles' concerns about paying one's fair share of taxes C. C. pointed out that the company had already paid a 12.5 percent tax on its profits. "The tax is really being paid twice, once when the profit is made by the company, and once when you receive what is really yours."[4] Charles accepted the offer.

Some have said that when it came to major business transactions C. C. Hobart was better at making friends than making money. What is indisputable is that whenever he divested himself from a business his former partners left amicably and the resulting company proved viable in the marketplace. Hobart Manufacturing grew into an international Fortune 500 corporation. The American Fixture and Manufacturing Company lasted until 1949. Finally, the Hobart Cabinet Company is still owned by Charles' sons and one of his grandsons is the current president.[5]

The long transition to a separate cabinet company did not proceed entirely without trouble. For a time relations between Charles and W. H. were strained to the point where E. A. had to serve as an intermediary when the feuding pair wished to communicate.[6] On one memo from December 1926 a Hobart Brothers official grumbled about a printing of sales sheets for the cabinet company, ". . . we are doing this as sheer charity out of our own pockets. . . ."[7] Eventually, the brothers and their respective companies found ways in which they could cooperate. In the long run the three Hobart brothers discovered that granting Charles the independence to run his own business proved the best means to enable them to "stick together" as a family.

At the time Charles took control of the company in 1926 Hobart Cabinet had a product line of twenty-five different models and sizes, ranging from a two-shelf section with a shipping weight of 60 pounds to a stock and accessory bin that weighed 275 pounds. Customers paid between $6 to $41 for individual catalog pieces and more for custom made equipment.[8] Most products were of rugged "semi-steel construction" with the cabinet's framework and drawer fronts made of wood finished in golden or light oak fitted with brass plates to hold labels. To reduce weight the cabinets and files had sheet steel backs and most drawers had steel sides and bottoms with wrought steel combination pulls and card holders. Universal stock sections finished in olive green were interchangeable and allowed customers to combine drawers, bins, and shelving in any design they wanted as well as add or rearrange pieces with simple bolt and wing nut fasteners.[9]

Charles found it liberating to be on his own, and he made two key decisions to accelerate the growth of Hobart Cabinet. First, he began to construct all-steel cabinets joined by resistance spot welding, which had first been used in the automotive industry. The plunge in the economy following the 1929 stock market crash left America with an excess of steel-making capacity. The price of steel plummeted. Besides being inexpensive, steel cabinetry was durable and lightweight. The second key ingredient was Charles' faith in direct-mail marketing. Charles' father and brothers had always relied on direct mail to generate a

portion of their sales, but none had used this method on the scale Charles did in order to promote the new line of all steel cabinets.

Hobart Cabinet had inherited quite a list of customers of electrical and automotive products from Hobart Brothers Company. Charles expanded from this base and mailed catalogs to hundreds of businesses around the country. He multiplied contacts at low cost by sending postcards introducing the company to potential customers and notifying existing customers of new products and special offers. Women were hired and paid per card to address hundreds of such postcards. In one two-month period nearly a million pieces were mailed out. Hobart Cabinet generated such a flow of mail that Troy had to construct a new first-class post office in 1932.[10]

As the volume of orders grew, Charles' manufacturing facility, the former Henne Brewery on West Water Street, became cramped. He decided to acquire a large warehouse on East Water Street and move manufacturing there and convert the building on West Water Street into offices.[11] Hobart Cabinet now had direct access to the main north-south rail line through Troy, which lay just west of the new factory. The warehouse had once been the bottling plant for the Hayner Distillery, a company that foundered during National Prohibition.

Charles loved to travel and explore nature. He canoed through the north woods of Minnesota, visited mines in Colorado and California and learned how to pan for gold. He hired Native American guides for hunting and fishing trips in Washington and Oregon. One day in August 1931 Charles was eating dinner outdoors on the upper deck of a boat headed across Lake Erie from Detroit to Buffalo when he spotted a lovely young woman a few tables away that he knew he had to meet. Midway through dinner she unexpectedly left before he had a chance to say a word. Fortunately, the next day he found her in the same tour group at Niagara Falls and introduced himself over lunch. Her name was Rachel Elizabeth Russell. A twenty-three-year-old graduate of Wichita State University, she taught physical education in Eldorado, Kansas. She declined Charles' offer to buy her lunch and told him she was headed for Poughkeepsie, New York, to visit her brother and sister-in-law before returning home.

A Maverick's Maverick

Charles Hobart earned a reputation for successfully achieving goals by single-minded determination that some folks called just plain "stubbornness".

So, it was almost predictable that when Sewell Avery, CEO of Montgomery Ward in Chicago, Illinois stood up to President Franklin D. Roosevelt during the 1930's and 1940's, then refused to comply with a National War Labor Board's ruling in 1944 and was forcibly carried out of his office by two U. S. Army soldiers, Avery instantly became a sainted hero to Charles Hobart.

An enlarged, framed photo of that event was enshrined on the wall behind Hobart's own desk chair from that time on.

The Hobart Cabinet Company, 1945

Unwilling to leave it at that, Charles went to her Buffalo hotel and tipped the desk clerk to let him see her registration. Charles copied her address and sent Miss Russell a letter saying he would soon be in Kansas City on a business trip and asking her to meet him there. She agreed and after they met in Kansas City he drove her back to Eldorado and met her parents. The pair corresponded and decided to get married in St. Louis December 19, 1931, after school let out for the holidays. Charles and Rachel honeymooned in Florida and also took a boat to Havana.

When Charles returned to Ohio he introduced his new bride to the Hobart family in Troy who did not even know he was getting married. A minor crisis ensued when W. H.'s wife Rachel discovered there were now two Mrs. Rachel Hobart's in Troy, but Charles' wife graciously agreed to go by her middle name Elizabeth.[12] The new couple set up house at 119 South Cherry Street.

Hobart Cabinet defied the Depression with its growth in the 1930s, but it did not escape that old nemesis that had struck each Hobart company: fire. On the afternoon of May 29, 1934, sparks from an air compressor ignited flammables in the third-floor paint room of the "new" factory on East Water Street. Flames quickly spread to the fourth floor and sent a dense pall of smoke billowing into the sky. Both Troy fire engines were soon on the scene, but water from their hoses had little effect. By 4:30 units from Piqua, West Milton, and Covington had arrived. Employee William Leach had returned to retrieve his coat and got trapped on the fourth floor. He appeared at a window and yelled for help. A ladder was raised and Fireman Roy Ross scrambled to the top rung but could only reach the windowsill with his hand. Overcome by smoke, Leach swayed backwards. Ross grabbed his ankle to keep him from falling into the flames,

❧

When Charles returned to Ohio he introduced his new bride to the Hobart family in Troy who did not even know he was getting married.

❧

but Leach pitched violently forward, tore out of Ross' grip and plunged to his death.[13]

Employees pulled as many cabinets and tools out of the first two floors as they could and then several turned to help fight the fire. Burning debris blown by a north wind set fire to the attic of one home on East Main and burned two garages to the ground. In six hours firemen expended nearly a million gallons of water to douse the blaze. The building itself was a total loss. Charles estimated that his company lost $20,000 in raw materials and inventory, $10,000 in machinery and equipment, and $15,000 in the building, which was actually in his mother's name. A portion of the plant was under separate ownership and had been leased to a fruit wholesaler.

Before the fire had been extinguished Hobart Cabinet began phoning orders to replace lost materials. Two days after the fire Charles announced the company would function at two-thirds capacity and expected to resume full operation in one week. Double shifts began that day at the old West Water Street plant. He also secured space from Hobart Brothers to carry out painting and crating. None of the workers from the destroyed plant would be laid off.[14]

Charles decided to rebuild across Water Street on the north side where the company was already using a portion of another former Hayner facility. This structure was gradually rebuilt in sections as a modern concrete factory with large windows. The first part, from the railroad tracks to the present day entrance, was completed by the end of 1935. This space was doubled in 1936 by adding on to the east. Hobart Cabinet built a second floor in 1937.[15] Now the company had enough space to move all manufacturing out of the old plant on West Water Street. It was an extraordinary feat for a company to survive a disastrous fire and within three years not only rebuild but expand its facilities and employment, all in the midst of the Great Depression. As Hobart Cabinet hit its stride in the late 1930s it employed about 250 people making it one of the largest businesses in Troy.[16] A variety of factors were at work: good products, a flood of direct mail advertising, a quality workforce, timely help from E. A. and W. H. at Hobart Brothers, and the drive and imagination of the cabinet company's owner and president, Charles C. Hobart.

Not every project that sprang from Charles' fertile imagination proved a success. In the garage of his home on Cherry Street he and a couple friends began assembling prototypes of an electrical refrigerator. Once they were working on a compressor when it sprang a leak and they had to abandon the garage to escape the sulfur dioxide gas. No one was hurt, but the gas leak killed many of Charles' shrubs and wiped out his neighbor's garden. After considerably more tinkering, Hobart Cabinet began producing "Crystal Frost" refrigerators in five- and seven-cubic-foot sizes.[17] They came with a small "ice-making" (freezer) unit on top, a porcelain interior, and three or four metal wire shelves. The regular price for the smaller unit was $120, or customers could rent one for $3 a month and apply half the rental payments toward purchase.[08] A Dayton investor who was supposed to finance and promote the refrigerators pulled out of the project after one year. The company found it had to slash prices to sell the refrigerators and stopped building them after two years with only an oversized punch press to show for its efforts.[19]

After reading a newspaper account that gold flakes had been found in glacial deposits east of Cincinnati, Charles bought a farm outside Owensville, Ohio, in Clermont County. He put his gold-panning skills to work by periodically leading a small crew of factory workers to the farm to use a separating table to mine the gravel of a creek for gold. "After almost two years of part-time work, he obtained enough gold to fill several teeth, nowhere near enough to pay for the operation. He did, however, prove that gold could be found in Ohio."[20]

If one could not find much treasure in nature, perhaps nature could be induced to produce treasure in abundance. Charles purchased a farm north of Troy on Lost Creek and began seeding freshwater clams in an attempt to grow pearls, but the Miami Valley's notoriously unpredictable water table quite literally undermined the

A typical bag
for C. C. Hobart
farm products

experiment. In most years spring floods swept the seeded clams downriver to an unknown fate. Placing the clams where the flow was not strong enough to displace them left them high and dry come summer.[21] Eventually, Charles found a more conventional way to make nature produce.

In 1936 Charles decided to go into fruit farming. His first son, Charles Jr., had been born September 11, 1932, followed by a daughter, Elizabeth Beatrice, on April 11, 1936. In the fall of 1936 Charles moved his growing family to a home on the corner of North Market Street and Staunton Road atop a gentle slope north of the Miami River. Further purchases rounded out the property to just over one hundred acres. The next spring he began planting the first of what would become several thousand fruit trees on five Miami County farms which he acquired over the next few years. Fruit trees were also planted on his brother W. H.'s farm. Charles had several varieties of peaches: Cling, Elberta, and Hale; Transparency, Red, and Golden delicious apples; Bing, Montmorency, and Royal Ann cherries; Bartlett and Seckel pears; Damson plums; apricots; and nectarines. Within a couple years he added flax, wheat, Katahdin potatoes, Spanish melons, and began pressing cider. Charles read up on the latest techniques and had his orchards irrigated. Beginning in 1937 the C. C. Hobart Fruit Farms formally began selling to the public. Charles was a perfectionist who loathed the practice of picking unripe fruit so it would ship well without bruising. He sold only tree-ripened fruit and emphasized that fact in his advertising. Therefore, Hobart fruit did not ship well, but it soon garnered a good reputation for quality in the region. Charles even turned down an offer from Smuckers to buy fallen fruit to make into preserves.[22]

This operation was not purely a venture into gentleman farming. It served a second purpose in evening out the labor supply for the cabinet company. Summer was the slow season for cabinet orders. Employees who would have been idled or let go were instead put to work tending the orchards, picking fruit as well as packing and shipping it. Many workers at Hobart Brothers were also employed during summers on the fruit farms.[23] This allowed the Hobarts to retain an experienced and well-trained pool of labor, while their employees could count on full-time year-round jobs and maintain the company's reputation for secure employment. Since neither company was unionized and unemployment in the late 1930s still ran well over 10 percent, few griped about the arrangement. If anything, the change of pace and outdoor exercise gave a lift to employee morale.

Although Charles believed the federal government was entitled to its full share of income taxes undiluted by business deductions, he positively bristled at government efforts to regulate wages and hours of employment. He fought the requirement to display the terms of the 1938 Fair Labor Standards Act in his factory, eventually showing what he thought of the new law by posting it in the restrooms. A fine and threats of further action finally got the signs out in view of the factory floor.[24]

There was one more mark Charles Hobart left on Troy in the 1930s: he was the man who brought tennis to town in a big way. Charles had been a tennis enthusiast since his college years. Though stocky and unable to cover a lot of ground, he was a good player with quick reflexes who especially enjoyed doubles. In 1937 he had the area's first Har-Tru clay courts installed on his property. These courts were composed of several layers of cinder and clay topped by six inches of the patented blue clay. Although it took much work to maintain the surface, fifteen minutes after a pounding rain the courts would be dry and ready for play. Troy High School used them when the city courts were too wet to play matches.[25]

Professional tennis had begun in the late 1920s, but before 1968 the major international tournaments, like the Olympics, were only open to amateurs. The best players established a reputation by winning Grand Slam tournaments and then turned professional and earned money through exhibitions and matches with other former champions.[26] Charles invited many professionals to Troy to conduct exhibitions on his court. He had bleachers erected on the grassy area west of the court for spectators. There was a net judge stand and an open front tennis house where people could scamper for cover from rain. Elizabeth provided cinnamon rolls and lemonade for refreshments. Hillary McKenna, Ben Gortchakoff, and Joe Whalen were among the nationally known professionals who played on his courts. Many local professionals and amateurs played on them regularly. Some visiting players stayed in Hobart's home while others spent several days in their own trailers parked near the court.

The most famous professional who appeared was Fred Perry, the world's top-rated amateur in the mid-1930s and

Famous English tennis pro Fred Perry was regularly in residence on Charles Hobart's court to play with Charles Hobart and other professionals in the area.

the greatest tennis player England ever produced. Perry had led the team that finally brought the Davis Cup back to England in 1933. He proceeded to win the U.S. Open three of the next four years and Wimbledon three years straight, 1934–36. He turned pro in 1937 and moved to the United States, winning the American professional title in 1938 and 1941. Perry had an exciting style of play, known for hitting a running forehand and charging forward ready to volley if his opponent managed a return. Charles and other local tennis enthusiasts, dressed in the long pants tennis whites of the era, did not just watch the visiting pros but got to play singles and doubles matches with them.[27]

Sunday afternoons during the war years found the Hobart courts hosting an international clientele as Harry Fogelman, the director of physical conditioning at Wright Patterson Air Base near Dayton, brought visiting Allied officers from Great Britain, Canada, Australia, and New Zealand up to Troy to play tennis. Fogelman, who became a good friend of Charles, went to the University of Cincinnati after the war and coached Tony Trabert who won ten Grand Slam tournaments in the 1950s.[28]

In less than twenty years the life of Charles Hobart, the middle son maverick, had undergone a remarkable transformation. In charting a course away from the successful company he had shared with his father and brothers, he had married and started a family, become the proprietor of two successful companies, overcome a tragic fire, and did his part to introduce Troy to the world of tennis and the world to Troy. ❧

CHAPTER 8

Welding Generates a New Future

One day in 1925 E. A. watched with the curiosity and excitement of a boy at Christmas as a machine was uncrated at Hobart Brothers. The package contained an electrical arc welder he had ordered from Cleveland.[1] A few weeks before E. A. had been in Columbus for his induction into Tau Beta Pi, the national engineering honor society. Ohio State had not organized a chapter until 1921, so during the next few years the OSU chapter honored past graduates who had made a mark in the world of engineering by inducting a group each year along with the undergraduates who qualified.[2] In Columbus E. A. spoke with fellow inductee James F. Lincoln who had enrolled in the electrical engineering program at Ohio State five years before E. A. After typhoid fever forced Lincoln to leave OSU during his senior year in 1907, he had gone to work for the Lincoln Electric Company in Cleveland, which had been founded by his older brother John C. Lin-

coln, a noted inventor. In 1914 John handed the business management of the firm over to James to leave himself free to concentrate on the technical side. Just like Hobart Brothers Lincoln Electric had begun by manufacturing dynamos and battery chargers, but what really intrigued E. A. was that in 1909 Lincoln had begun to produce a mobile, variable voltage single operator DC electrical arc welder, the first truly practical arc welder manufactured in America.[3] During World War I demand for electrical arc welders began to soar. With the completion of the roomy new Main Street plant slated for early the following year, Hobart Brothers was looking to expand its product line beyond the automotive area. E. A., as always, was looking for a new technical challenge. Electrical arc welding might prove the ideal find to satisfy both desires.

Shortly after the welder was uncrated, E. A. and Russell Flora tried it out and then began to dismantle it to analyze how it worked. Quickly they saw that it was a fairly simple adaptation of the same kind of DC motor generator that formed the basis of the Hobart Brothers battery chargers. Not only was E. A. convinced he could build a welder of his own, he already had several ideas for improvements.[4] Later that year a Hobart built arc welder joined the Lincoln welder on the shop floor. Workers used both on welding jobs in and around the plant. Soon E. A. noticed that the homemade welder was the one that employees kept in almost constant use. Based on experience, Hobart engineers incorporated a number of modifications into a second

Hobart introduced its new welder featuring an industry first, simplified multi-range current control, along with its full line of shop equipment at trade shows, circa 1928.

The first Hobart arc welder, 1925

tery to produce "a miniature bolt of lightning," a phenomenon which he later termed an "arc."[7] The arc created when electrical current jumped the gap was extremely hot, ten thousand to twenty-thousand degrees Fahrenheit, and could melt metal at once. The electrode, a rod first made of carbon and later of metal, would be connected to a power source along with the metal to be welded. When the welder, the person grasping the rod with an insulated holder, held it a fraction of an inch above the metal pieces to be joined, the current would jump the gap, creating a sustained spark or arc that melted both metal and rod. Metal from the rod flowed into the gap. Cooling solidified the separate pieces into a single homogenous mass.[8]

Practical applications and the first patents for electrical arc welding did not occur until the 1880s. A Frenchman named De Meritens successfully used this method to join lead plates in a storage battery in 1881. A Russian student of his, Nikolai N. Bernardos, refined this procedure and together with fellow Russian Stanislaus Olszewski obtained patents for carbon arc welding from Great Britain in 1885 and the United States in 1887. Three years later American C. L. Coffin from Detroit secured a patent for electrical arc welding with a metal rod.[9]

welder, which was also put to work in the factory.[5] The success of these welders convinced the company to investigate entering the business of manufacturing welding equipment.

Welding in one form or another had been around ever since Bronze Age smiths discovered that separate pieces of some metals could be joined through a process of heating and hammering. By 1000 B.C. Middle Eastern and Mediterranean civilizations had learned to weld iron. Blacksmithing developed during the Middle Ages to the point where complex custom-made suits of armor could be crafted with welded iron. However, it was not until the nineteenth century that modern methods of welding were invented. Acetylene was discovered in 1836, and by the 1890s blowtorches using the heat from an ignited stream of mixed oxygen and acetylene gases were employed for cutting and welding metal.[6]

The first instances of electrical arc welding probably occurred by accident as European scientists experimented with electricity in the late eighteenth century. In 1800 Sir Humphry Davy used two electrodes connected to a bat-

Industrial use of this new technology developed slowly. One reason why was the uncertainty over how to best employ the new invention. The second was the raw and undeveloped state of electrical arc welding itself. The

An early Hobart gasoline engine driven welder, circa 1930

51

Hobart welders, circa 1928

new technology was fraught with problems that masked its potential. Early arc welding units were battery powered and cumbersome. Railroads bought most early welders in America and employed them in their roundhouses and repair sheds. Down time for locomotives and rolling stock meant lost revenue for railroads, therefore, the ability to make fast repairs by welding was attractive. Shipping lines had the same incentive.[10] Welding repairs were rapid but not always reliable. Carbon arc welding sometimes introduced brittle carbon into the weld. The early bare metal electrodes wired to constant voltage welders often produced arcs that overheated and scorched the weld metal.[11] Various refinements came in the first two decades of the twentieth century in the form of coatings for metal electrodes and controls for the electrical current, all designed to produce steady arcs and better welds. Despite progress, arc welding entered its fourth decade with no scientific way to test for unsafe welds. All one could do was eyeball the finished weld and plunk it with a hammer to see if the tone matched that of the parent metal.[12]

C. C. and E. A. Hobart had both read the original patents on arc welding, but outside the world of electrical engineering most Americans had no idea what weld-

ing even was until the United States entered the First World War in 1917. After Congress declared war on April 6 federal authorities boarded the interned German vessels on the East Coast to seize them. They discovered that for the past two months the German crews had been busy wrecking equipment on board in order to render the ships inoperable. Initial reports estimated repairs would take eighteen months to two years. They were wrong. The government desperately needed the over half a million gross tons of potential shipping in the crippled vessels to transport men and material to Europe. Welders went to work and all 109 ships were pressed into service in less than eight months, including the huge liner *Vaterland*. Rechristened the *America*, it became the largest U.S.-flagged troopship used in the war. One of every four doughboys shipped off to France rode in a confiscated German vessel.[13]

Increasingly during the war, industry and government began to see welding not merely as a handy tool for repairs but as a way to both speed and improve production. Welded hulls on submarines could withstand pressure from ocean depths and depth charges better than riveted hulls.[14] Demand for skilled welders far outstripped the supply, and the first specialized schools for welding sprang up. At the height of the fighting in France, the American Expeditionary Force employed more than fourteen hundred full-time welders and clamored for more.[15]

The boom in welding did not end with the war, but in 1918 a ruling by Labor Secretary William Wilson that welding was "a tool rather than a trade" complicated the developing industry. There would be no craft union of welders or agreed upon standards to qualify who could do welding.[16] Nevertheless, the industry began to organize itself in 1919 when the wartime emergency welding committee transformed itself into the American Welding Society (AWS). Although officially welding was not a trade, the AWS soon acquired all the trappings of a trade association: annual meetings, executive directors, a journal, and a headquarters in New York City.[17]

The reasons for E. A.'s interest in welding were obvious. It was a dynamic new industry, filled with both technological challenges and potential for growth. The DC power sources that dominated the arc welding business in the mid-1920s were an outgrowth of the motor generator technology which had been the heart of the Hobart companies ever since C. C. had gone into business in 1885. E. A. felt confident that he and his team of engineers could advance existing technology in ways that would improve the quality of welding and expand its use. What was less clear in 1925 was whether Hobart Brothers could enter the welding field and manufacture and market its products profitably.

Inspired by the success of Frigidaire in Dayton, Hobart Brothers had recently tried building home refrigerators, but refrigerators were not a comfortable fit for the company from a manufacturing or a marketing standpoint. Hobart Brothers had adapted its own air compressors and simply assembled them inside a wooden "icebox" cabinet. Unlike the constant potential battery chargers, there was no technical innovation to tout in advertising or act as a company signature for the refrigerators. More importantly, Hobart Brothers had always been an industrial supplier not a mass marketer of products for the consumer. The company had strayed from C. C.'s advice that "the best way to make money was to help the other guy make money." In the end, Hobart Brothers liquidated the effort by selling its designs and remaining stock to Kelvinator, one of the growing giants in the home appliance industry.[18]

Existing business contacts with gas stations and auto repair shops had been irrelevant in the marketing of refrigerators, but many Hobart Brothers customers were already using welders in their work. The owners of these businesses had faith in the quality and reliability of Hobart Brothers products and could provide a good initial market for its new power sources. W. H. soon became as convinced as E. A.

The Odyssey of E. A. Hobart's Violin

When E. A. Hobart was in high school, he was given the option to write a thesis or construct something of his choice.

He chose to make his own violin which he then taught himself to play and earned a seat in the Troy High School orchestra. Over a period of sixty years, the violin ended up in a closet, unplayed, dusty and its strings broken—until E. A. heard Carl Phillis, supervisor of the Hobart Welding Division play a violin during an Employee Milestone Club Recognition Program.

The entertainment that night was presented entirely by Hobart employees who literally let their hair down putting on a series of amateur night acts patterned after the then popular TV "Gong Show." Carl's group was far from being amateur. They regularly played for special occasions throughout the Miami Valley. E. A. Hobart was very impressed.

The next morning Carl was summoned to Mr. Hobart's office. Carl wondered if he had done something wrong because normally, if Mr. Hobart wanted Carl to do something, Mr. Hobart would leave a hand written note on one of his famous 3 x 5 orange cards at Carl's desk. Mr. Hobart looked at Carl sternly, then broke into a smile and complimented Carl on his Milestone performance the previous night. Then Carl noticed the old violin in front of E. A. which he held up and presented to Carl.

E. A went on to explain the history of the violin and then offered it to Carl saying that it deserved to be played well and asked him if he would restring it—on one condition. The condition was that Carl could keep it as long as he would bring it to Mr. Hobart's home every Friday morning and play it for him during breakfast.

Only Carl knows how many breakfasts the two of them enjoyed together. Upon Mr. Hobart's death, Carl returned the violin to the Hobart estate.

Carl Phillis Sr.

that welding equipment would provide an ideal product line on which to base the future growth of the company.[19]

While Hobart Brothers conducted experiments to help design a commercial welder, the company imported a number of coated electrodes from Europe. Oscar Kjellberg, a Swede, had pioneered the practice of making heavily coated, or fluxed, electrodes under the OK brand. As the coating vaporized during welding, it created a shielding gas that prevented air from entering the weld and making it brittle. There was no question that fluxed electrodes produced better welds, but the early coating processes, such as hand-wrapping or dipping made the electrodes very expensive.[20] Hobart engineers realized there would be a ready market for a welder flexible enough to handle all kinds of electrodes, from the cheapest bare wire to the most sophisticated coated brands.

E. A. designed the new commercial welder with several unique features. It had a single shaft for motor, generator, and exciter. This patented feature made for a compact design which prevented misalignment and reduced friction by cutting the number of bearings in half. The exciter enabled a welder to adjust to different size electrodes, different thicknesses of the material being welded, even different welding positions. Mounting the exciter on the main armature meant it would not loosen up in service. The power source was well-ventilated and provided with a strong fan resulting in "remarkable coolness of operation in continuous, heavy duty service." W. H.'s advertising labeled it a "constant arc" welder to both emphasize its reliable operation and link the new product with the company's successful "constant potential" battery chargers.[21] Also, with its arc welded steel construction, the Hobart machine reinforced the message that manufacturers could use welding to turn out durable products that were lighter and more streamlined than the cast iron or riveted steel competition. The welder

came in both electrical and belt-driven gas powered models. On June 27, 1927, Hobart Brothers successfully tested the first complete welding outfit it had sold.[22] Within the next decade welding equipment would become the mainstay of the business and remain so for more than sixty years.

In 1928 Hobart Brothers added a "unitrol" dial that greatly simplified control of the welder's current. Mounted on a welded steel cabinet atop the welder, the dial was marked with four ranges in amps, electrode sizes, and material thicknesses to greatly simplify current control, especially for beginning welders. Flanked by an ammeter, a voltmeter, and start and stop buttons, the unitrol dial operated like a rheostat to control the welding arc by continuously varying the exciter current. "Simplified Welding" became a key sales slogan and a title for training manuals.[23] Within three years of launching its investigation of arc welding Hobart Brothers had produced a welder flexible enough to handle a wide

Sales literature, circa 1930s

Hobart's 1928 "Unitrol" dial greatly simplified welding.

variety of electrodes and simple enough to be used by operators and companies with limited welding experience. Now the question was, would they sell at a profit?

While W. H. Hobart was still trying to decide if he could light a fire under his salesmen to promote a whole new line of products, smoldering cinders from a first floor hearth lit a fire under him. Smoke from the blaze woke him and Rachel about 6:00 on the frigid morning of December 29, 1925. He fought through the smoke-filled stairwell to reach the phone and call the fire department but then had to exit through the front door. The only two firemen on duty had to pluck Rachel, along with eighteen-month-old William Jr., three-year-old Lucia, five-year-old Marcia, and John Cahill, from second-story windows before the pair could battle the blaze. Rachel's sixty-eight-year-old father jumped from his bedroom window onto the snow-covered shrubbery below. W. H. took his family two doors over to E. A.'s home to escape the sub-zero cold. Snow cover helped contain the fire, but less than two hours into the fight the roof of W. H.'s home collapsed. Oddly, no alarm bell had been rung, and reinforcements had to be called to the scene by phone. By 9:30 the firemen "clad in an armor of ice" were packing up their equipment. Except for a piano and a few other items firemen hauled onto the front porch, the home and its contents were a complete loss, estimated at $40,000. Included in that loss was as much as $1,500 in cash and $4,000 in Liberty Bonds, which Mr. Cahill had kept in his bedroom. Unregistered, the bonds could not be replaced unless physically recovered. In the next two days Trojans managed to salvage $300 worth of Cahill's Liberty Bonds with their serial numbers intact found as far as five blocks away.[24]

Following his father's example, William resolved to rebuild on the same site even though insurance only covered about one-third of the total loss.[25] True to his word, he built a stately red brick Georgian home facing Plum Street. John Cahill continued to live there with his daughter and son-in-law until he died of heart failure at age seventy-six in February 1934.

Late October was a festive time in Troy during the 1920s. In October 1929 the civic celebration of Halloween, scheduled for Monday, October 28, was to have a new and unusual feature—an industrial display. Twenty-one different Troy businesses cooperated to put on a three-day display of the various goods manufactured in Troy. The products would be on public view in the shop windows around Public Square and the downtown area. Those who attended the grand opening on Monday the twenty-eighth would be eligible to win one of seventy-five prizes donated by companies in the exposition.[26] Three Hobart-founded companies were among the participants: Hobart Manufacturing, the closely held maker of food processing equipment; Hobart Cabinet, owned by Charles; and Hobart Brothers, a partnership of C. C. and Lou Ella and their sons, E. A. and W. H.

William Hobart house

The *Troy Daily News* reported a great turnout for the combination Halloween costume parade and opening of the industrial display, noting many who came were both surprised and impressed with the wide variety of goods made right in their home city. The only downbeat note in the whole report was the observation that fewer adults had donned costumes than in recent years. What was truly ghoulish were the front-page stories from the UPI wire service about what was happening on Wall Street. Stocks had taken a frightful tumble Thursday of the previous week, but headlines focused on the minor recoveries on Friday and Monday. Disaster struck on Black Tuesday, the second day of the industrial display in Troy, when investors lost over $10 billion before the stock exchange's closing bell sounded the death knell of the Roaring Twenties.

Few sensed the looming disaster during the next couple of days as employees packed up the products displayed with such pride and confidence, but the hoped for rally on Wall Street never materialized. Within a week concrete signs of a serious downturn appeared. On November 1 a full-page ad from Ford Motor Company proclaimed across the board cuts of up to $200 in the prices of all its new cars. The following day a report admitted that new car sales in Troy, a popular local economic barometer, had suffered a sharp drop in October, from 190 to 150.[27] Despite the assertion that sales were still up for the year, bad news continued to accumulate like falling autumn leaves. The Hobarts, their managers, and their employees would now face their biggest challenge yet, the Great Depression. ❧

CHAPTER 9

A Sales Pitch Creates a Trade School

"Hobart Brothers Company—Successful Manufacturers Since 1893" that familiar slogan adorned nearly every piece of company advertising in the 1920s. Why 1893? C. C. Hobart went into business in 1885. Was 1893 the year he paid off his debts after fire had forced him to borrow to rebuild? Was that the year he stopped modifying Edison armatures and began producing dynamos entirely of his own design? More important than the question of why C. C. approved the slogan is the fact that it was his son W. H. who decided to give it such prominence in the marketing of Hobart Brothers. Before the stock market crash of 1929, the depression of the 1890s was the worst economic disaster in America's collective memory. The slogan served to remind potential customers that the Hobart business had proven its strength in difficult times and survived the Panic of 1893. Once the Great Depression of the 1930s deepened forcing factory after factory to close its doors, the old slogan seemed less reassuring. Although many companies went bankrupt, for the most part, it was not the giants, like General Motors, Dupont, and Sears, that fell. Medium and smaller-sized firms were more likely to succumb to their creditors. Eventually, as sales of welding equipment became the main source of revenue for Hobart Brothers, W. H. phased in the slogan, "One of the World's Largest Builders of Arc Welders."[1] Size was now more reassuring than history. The new slogan also alluded to the fact that in the 1930s Hobart Brothers had begun to look beyond America's shores to seek markets for its goods.

Devising a new slogan was one of the simpler problems W. H. faced in the 1930s. What soon became apparent was that the company's survival in the Great Depression would depend as much upon W. H.'s imaginative marketing as its growth and its entry into the field of welding in the 1920s had depended upon E. A.'s technological innovation.

The timing of Hobart Brothers entry into the welding market proved fortuitous. Just as the welding process was coming of age, the Depression created imperatives for business to cut time and labor in its production methods, to perform maintenance and repair rather than replace worn parts, to salvage and reuse equipment that would have been sent to the scrap heap in better times.[2] This counter-cyclical increase in demand for welding was one of the eternal verities of the welding business. The growth of welding sales in relation to the older product lines gave William a reason to overhaul the company's sales organization.

He established separate sales groups, one to promote the automotive line of battery chargers, air compressors, and other service station equipment, while another group sold welders and accessories. The older product line had a good network of independent distributors, or "jobbers" as they were then called, as well as some who exclusively sold Hobart battery chargers. But many of these distributors were reluctant to become middlemen in the marketing of welding equipment. On the other hand, jobbers who had begun to feature welders often already had close ties with the more established welding manufacturers. W. H. attacked the problem of marketing the new line of welders in three different ways: 1) setting up regional distributors who exclusively sold Hobart welding equipment, 2) offering free training in exchange for the purchase of welders, and 3) using high profile advertising in welding trade publications.[3]

A key man in establishing the new sales network was Wilbur J. Chaffee. Known in the company as "Wib," Chaffee was named sales manager for arc welding equipment shortly after he joined Hobart Brothers in 1925.[4] Chaffee realized that arc welding had almost unlimited potential as a production method and that the only obstacle was

Wilbur J. Chaffee

56

The first classes were held on the third floor of the Hobart factory.

the lack of proper design. Once engineers and architects learned how to apply welding in their designs, Chaffee saw every organization, public or private, which had metal objects to build or machinery to repair as a potential customer. "If it's metal, weld it" became a common line used in the business. This required a staff trained in specialty selling who "sensed the opportunity for large volume sales," not the "order taker type" thumbing through large catalogs. By mid-1930 there were over two hundred direct factory representatives marketing and servicing Hobart Brothers products, whereas independent jobbers and direct mail now accounted for less than 10 percent of sales.[5]

In 1935 W. H. put Chaffee in charge of all Hobart distributors in the United States, Canada, and Mexico.[6] Stocky and bespectacled, with a goatee turning white and a penchant for cigars and white suits, the ebullient Chaffee looked like a Kentucky Colonel and "Kuhnel" became his nickname.[7] Chaffee spent the next ten years crisscrossing the continent promoting Hobart welders and settling territorial squabbles between distributors or "Hobarteers" as

⤫

. . . one to four weeks of free training as a sales incentive for the purchase of one or more welders.

⤫

the company called them. Perhaps Chaffee's greatest stunt was an unscheduled handshake with Britain's King George VI during the monarch's state visit to Montreal in 1939. After the handshake the king invited Chaffee to sit next to him on an outdoor dais even though no one on the dais had any idea who Chaffee was.[8]

One factor that limited the growth of the market for welding equipment was the shortage of trained welders in America. As workers were laid off or had their hours or wages cut, they needed a new marketable skill to get rehired or use in a moonlighting job to help make ends meet. Very few high schools or vocational schools offered welding. W. H. saw an opportunity here. In 1930 he decided to offer from one to four weeks of free training as a sales incentive for the purchase of one or more welders. At first the move was quite tentative. W. H. had Judd Hammond supervise the use of two Hobart Brothers production welders for training. The welders remained on the factory floor and were employed in production when not in use for training. As it turned out, training monopolized the two welders.[9]

Early in 1931 the Sales Department had part of the factory's third floor remodeled for its own use. Four welding booths were built for trainees along with a large sales demonstration room that held one of each of the four Hobart welder models then in production. Besides the need for more space, it had also become clear that Hobart Brothers did not have a master welder to direct the training. Most employees who could weld were largely self-taught and not terribly proficient. They could make the welds needed to produce the goods the company made, but none had experience working with a wide variety of materials and techniques.[10] At that time railroads were still the nation's biggest user of arc welding, so W. H. went to Springfield, Ohio, where New York Central had a division point with extensive repair facilities. There, W. H. met Bob Bercaw, the twenty-eight-year-old welding supervisor for the division. W. H. was impressed by Bercaw's knowledge and skill as a welder and by his ability to articulate what he knew. He convinced Bercaw that he would have a brighter future at Hobart Brothers and hired him as director and chief instructor for the training program.

HOBART TRADE SCHOOL ALUMNI NEWS

BOB BERCAW
Chief Instructor
Hobart Trade School

With more space and a qualified instructor, the company decided to open welding training to anyone willing to pay $10 for a full week of instruction. Soon trainees filled all the booths and regularly spilled over into the demonstration room. The training program that had begun as a sales pitch had taken on a life of its own. In 1932 the State of Ohio granted a nonprofit corporate charter for what now officially became the Hobart Trade School.[11] Low-cost vocational training for adults of all ages in a skill that was in demand met a need that only grew as the Depression dragged on. In 1930 the company had enjoined Chaffee to write a welding manual to help with instruction. With minor changes the manual went through six printings until the advance of technology created the need for a whole new edition in 1935.[12]

Once again in 1937 the need for more space forced the trade school to move, this time to a large self-contained area in the main factory where thirty welding booths were installed. Quality of instruction was one factor that drew students. Bercaw proved to be an inspired choice as director of the welding school. Round-faced and youthful despite a receding hairline, his enthusiasm for welding was infectious. In addition to his teaching duties the company often had Bercaw troubleshoot problems because his welding skill was legendary. Once, during World War II, he and another Hobart representative were sent to a shipyard that had complaints about Hobart electrodes. Bercaw grabbed a few of the allegedly defective electrodes at random and pro-

ceeded to make several perfect welds in a number of positions. It was very quiet after the demonstration until one old shipyard welder said, "You two can't fool me. There's something wrong with those rods—but this guy could stick bare wire in the holder and run a perfect bead."[13]

As an educational institution, the Hobart Trade School was an unqualified success, but it is difficult to quantify how well it met its original goal of expanding sales of Hobart welders. Undoubtedly, the school helped provide a larger and better-trained workforce for businesses who employed welders, especially those firms in the industrial heartland of the Midwest. Thousands of workers learned to weld on Hobart equipment but most would not be in a position to influence buying decisions at their respective companies for many years to come. Hobart Brothers itself hired many former students and sent current employees to the school to improve their skills. Perhaps the greatest benefit the company received from the school was the gratitude and goodwill of graduates whose training had made a positive difference in their lives. As Bercaw once wrote, "The greatest thrill I get is from the former students who write me constantly about the good jobs they have and the interesting experiences they are having."[14] W. H. and E. A. treasured their letters from former students and considered the welding school one of the most important and rewarding chapters of their business career.

Early welding training books created by the Hobart Trade School

The Hobart Trade School was one of the most prominent welded steel buildings in Troy. It was designed and welded entirely by Hobart Brothers Company employees, remaining on N. Elm Street from 1940 to 1958.

The year 1932 was the toughest year of the Depression for Hobart Brothers. Sales held fairly steady, especially for welders, but most equipment was sold on time payment plans and collections were slow as hard-pressed firms fell behind or went delinquent.[15] Then on June 3 C. C. Hobart died at the age of seventy-seven. Although his sons had controlled the daily operations of the company for several years, C. C. still came in to work on his good days. E. A. and W. H. appreciated his ability to arbitrate disputes and the sage counsel he had dispensed, drawing on nearly fifty years of experience in the electrical industry. The founding industrial Hobart would be missed by the whole Troy community. In its front page obituary, the *Troy Daily News* stated "C. C. Hobart was a builder of machines, of factories, and his impress as such will long remain on this and other communities. But he never forgot that men come first in the scheme of things and mechanical and scientific and industrial progress are vain unless they conduce to the happiness of man and to his spiritual advancement."[16] Upon C. C.'s death E. A. assumed the presidency of Hobart Brothers, W. H. became vice president, while their mother Lou Ella remained the treasurer.[17]

Nothing illustrated the success of C. C. Hobart's effort to instill the value of putting people first than the responsibility his sons felt for their employees during the Depression. Although hours sometimes had to be cut, no one was let go for financial reasons. Often, when work was scarce at the plant, employees did upkeep and remodeling work on the Hobart residences. After 1937, work on Charles' fruit farm became another means of keeping workers on at full pay. Rather than resenting the inherent paternalism of this approach, most employees appreciated the job security and felt the company seemed more like a family than a business.[18] One day in 1941, shortly after Jean Collmorgan was hired as a mail clerk, she was startled by what appeared to be a small gray bird's nest gliding just above a row of file cabinets. As she rounded the corner Collmorgan saw the nest was in fact a hair bun atop a short and quite elderly woman clutching a handful of manila folders who passed by with a gingerly yet determined step. Collmorgan went up to an experienced secretary to ask who the lady was. "Oh, that's Mrs. So-and-So. Mr. Hobart told her she'd always have a job here, and that whenever she felt up to it or needed a little extra

During World War II, many of the students were women. Circa 1943

early 1933 that it had sold enough kitchen appliances and commercial food processing equipment in 1932 to post a modest profit of $224,433, enough to pay quarterly dividends totaling a dollar per share for the year.[21] But Troy did not escape the national banking crisis that mounted as Washington prepared to swear in Franklin D. Roosevelt as the new President. On March 1, 1933, the First Troy National Bank, Miami County's strongest financial institution, announced it was restricting withdrawals to just 5 percent of total funds in an account following a day of frantic withdrawals and an all night session by tellers to update account balances.[22]

Roosevelt's first action to combat "fear itself" was to declare a National Bank Holiday to halt the financial hemorrhage and provide time for bank examiners to check books and Congress to initiate legislation to ensure deposits. Every bank in Troy was closed from Monday, March 6, through Tuesday, March 13, but many grocers and merchants extended credit to allow regular customers to obtain what they needed. Trojans breathed a sigh of relief when First Troy National reported that deposits had far exceeded withdrawals when it reopened its doors on March 14.[23]

The nation had turned a crucial corner, but true economic recovery proved to be painfully slow. Like most businessmen, the Hobarts were at first suspicious of the New Deal programs being pumped out of Washington, fearing they would discourage private entrepreneurship and foster dependence on government. However, they came to see the massive Works Progress Administration (WPA) projects to build roads, bridges, public buildings, and massive hydroelectric dams in the west and the Tennessee Valley as a powerful stimulus for the sale of welding equipment.[24]

Before the New Deal era, the only advertising Hobart Brothers had done in national periodicals was modest-sized ads in the classified sections of Popular Mechanics and Popular Science. W. H. believed now was the time to target those in a position to make purchases with a high profile advertising campaign for Hobart welding equipment. He contacted the *Welding Engineer* and offered to trade an idea for keeping their circulation list fresh for the right to stake out page one for a full-page Hobart Brothers ad. His idea was for *Welding Engineer* to have welding distributors provide the periodical with a mailing list of their customers, and *Welding Engineer* would imprint those copies with the

money she could come in and we'd have filing for her to do."[19] Which Mr. Hobart had made the promise was irrelevant. The current generation of owners was as committed as C. C. had been to their employees and to the community of Troy for the generous invitation that had brought their father's company to town back in 1895.

Enlightened self-interest inspired this policy as much as a sense of gratitude and responsibility. E. A. and W. H. expected a lot from their employees who were hired on at a rate of thirty-five cents an hour in 1931.[20] Hobart Brothers had a rather diverse product line for a company of its size. Workers needed the capacity to do several different tasks well, not just one operation in a massive and highly specialized assembly line as could be found in larger factories and companies. Both the automotive service equipment and welding businesses were highly competitive. A company had to be quick on its feet to invent or adopt technological advances to keep its products from being squeezed out of the market. This called for flexibility and initiative on the part of employees. There was sound business sense in the efforts of Hobart Brothers to retain its experienced workers. These efforts were rewarded by an atmosphere of trust and cooperation. In contrast to widespread labor unrest in the 1930s, Hobart Brothers experienced no strikes, no lockouts, and no serious efforts to unionize, a true oasis of calm and prosperity.

In many respects, Troy was more fortunate than most Midwestern communities, which the Depression had struck with more crippling effect. Across town Troy's largest employer, Hobart Manufacturing, announced in

60

distributor's name and address on the back page. *Welding Engineer* bought the idea and, beginning with the March 1934 issue, everyone who opened the magazine found an ad from Hobart Brothers staring up at him from page one.[25] The ads were not free, but for more than sixty years and through a name change to *Welding Design and Fabrication*, no company displaced Hobart Brothers from its page one ad.

The success of the ads in attracting new customers encouraged W. H. to expand the strategy. Page one ads for Hobart Brothers began in the January 1940 issue of *Welding Journal*, and soon the concept was extended to *Industry & Welding* and *Canadian Welder*. W. H. and his staff devoted a good deal of attention to the design of these pages, which varied month to month. Ever since 1928 W. H. had subscribed to *Gebrauchsgraphik*, a respected journal of international advertising art published in Berlin and kept bound copies of the magazine in his office for reference. He was also an avid amateur photographer. The men who appeared in the ads were not models but Hobart managers and employees who had the desired look and had signed the release and pocketed five dollars for their efforts. Eddie Butterfield from Sales with his trademark pipe, Credit Manager David C. (Pete) Jenk-

March 1934 Welding Engineer *cover and ads*

ins, and Byron Lutz from Purchasing were among those who lent their handsome mugs.[26]

The advertising covered a large variety of topics: Hobart Brothers' engineering innovations, the durability and low operating costs of its equipment, its manufacturing facilities, financing options, and the company's service and personnel. Advertising also made an effort to show that company policies were compatible with the goals of the New Deal. "Our sales plans . . . financing the little fellow. Just what the President is trying to get the banks to do." "Our employees operate under the NRA [National Recovery Administration-a voluntary code of fair labor and competition practices], pay increased 10 percent, 30 percent increase in employees."[27]

In 1934, not exactly a banner year for American business, Hobart Brothers earned a profit of over a quarter of a million dollars.[28] C. C.'s boys were doing something right. They now had the confidence to take Hobart Brothers in a new direction. In one sense, they planned to follow in the footsteps of their father and grandfather by becoming homebuilders. In another sense, they were stepping into uncharted territory—the homes would be made entirely of welded steel. ❧

Welding Journal *and ad from January 1940*

CHAPTER 10

The Brothers Build Welded-Steel Houses

Commenting on the Depression, Dayton inventor Charles F. Kettering wrote, "We have an unusual condition in this country where we have an excess of materials, an excess of money, and an excess of men. Now, all that can mean to a primitive mind like mine is that we haven't got any projects."[1] But E. A. and W. H. always seemed to have a project up their sleeves and this time they felt certain they had put their fingers on an honest to goodness need, inexpensive housing.

In 1932 a company survey revealed that half of all Hobart Brothers employees lived outside the city limits of Troy.[2] Those who wanted to move closer to work were frustrated by their inability to find affordable housing in town. Across America the housing industry had all but collapsed, but this collapse led to ferment in the fields of architecture and construction, a ferment that encouraged experimentation. In Europe and North America designers were taking a fresh look at the problem of how to mass-produce modern affordable housing. Some sought to create novel architectural styles that embraced the new building materials of steel, concrete, and insulated glass, while others focused on techniques to reduce the time and cost of building a home.[3] The Hobarts watched these developments unfold in the pages of *Pencil Points*, a monthly architectural magazine to which they had subscribed since 1925. Before their own home-building plans had taken definite shape, they decided to purchase four acres of land south of Main Street across from their plant.[4]

The Chicago World's Fair of 1933–34, billed as "the Century of Progress," clad itself in the latest styles of architecture and promoted steel as a building material. Steel was nearly impervious to fire and vermin and, with its price falling, it became increasingly attractive as a material for home building. Among the model homes W. H. and E. A. saw at the fair, those built by Armco-Ferro, Stran Steel, and General House, used steel as their primary material.[5] However, *Pencil Points'* observer was rather critical of their designs, fearing they would give the public ". . . a confused notion that the strangeness of the house forms in which they [new building materials like steel] are being shown is something essential to the materials employed . . ." and would restrict their adoption.[6] Each of the three steel homes had a flat roof designed for use as a deck. Only the General House, the least attractive of the three, was priced low enough for a mass market. None of the steel homes had been welded together, and each had used concrete or other materials in their basic construction.[7] The two Hobart brothers thought they could do better.

E. A. realized that, as in shipbuilding, large sheets of steel for walls could be assembled rapidly by welding them together. A welded steel home could be constructed in far less time and at lower cost than a comparable brick or wood-sided dwelling. W. H. saw steel welded homes as a new application that could expand the market for Hobart welders. They drew up a plan for a cul-de-sac with ten lots on the land south of Main Street and named the development Hobart Circle. E. A. and W. H. incorporated the Hobart Welded Steel House Company to carry out the venture and began experimenting with home designs.[8]

In the spiral staircases the clean curving line of welded steel reveals its true potential.

A Hobart welded steel house rolls down Main Street past the Hobart factory, 1937.

The first drawings showed a flat roof, which advertising claimed could be transformed into a private skating rink in winter. This failed to elicit an enthusiastic response. Apart from the likely stress on the roof from repeated freezing, expanding, skating, and thawing, rooftop skaters who tripped over the parapet faced a potentially neck-breaking fall. Eventually the flat roof was dropped in favor of a more conventional sloping design, which shed the heavy Midwestern snowfalls and provided space for storage in a small attic.[9] While E. A. sought a replacement for the project's first architect, he himself completed the drawings needed to erect the first prototype home. This home was constructed in parts and welded together on a prepared foundation facing north on West Main Street in 1935.[10]

A descriptive plaque was placed in every steel house describing the original historical model.

A few vacation trips influenced the choices E. A. and W. H. made as their ideas for Hobart Circle evolved toward a more traditional presentation of their novel construction method. In the summer of 1934 W. H. took Rachel, who was expecting, and his son William on a trip to Europe. He visited both England and Germany, the two nations that were the first to experiment with mass housing and steel homes in the 1920s.[11] The following winter E. A. and Martha took a cruise ship to England. Among their snapshots of Stonehenge, Westminster Abbey, and the Tower of London are several photos of a huge development of two-story row houses under construction. A new take on an old theme, the homes had conventional wood frames with brick exteriors, but were fairly spacious with large windows and attractive landscaping.[12]

W. H. also visited Williamsburg, Virginia, where John D. Rockefeller had undertaken America's first large restoration project. In the end, designs from colonial Williamsburg had the greatest influence on the external appearance of most Hobart steel homes, each of which included a plaque inside the entrance describing the eighteenth-century home after which it was modeled.[13] The brothers hoped the reassuringly conventional visual aesthetics of their new homes would help overcome misgivings about their modern building techniques and mate-

Four Hobart welded steel houses under construction in the Main Street Factory

rials. Illustrating the benefits of steel construction, one Hobart model won first prize in *Pencil Points'* Iron Fireman Architectural Competition in 1936 for a fire-safe home of not more than twenty-four thousand cubic feet that included a garage.[14] As W. H. wrote in a brochure, "This practical solution joins together the best of both worlds, old and new."[15]

This effort to literally weld steel into conformity with traditional design probably made the end product more saleable but something was lost as well. The resulting homes tended to mask rather than celebrate their manner of construction. Both interior and exterior steel sheets were painted and finished with a spray composed of silica sand that created the appearance of stucco or of wood made to look like stucco. Yet the precision of the houses' corners and angles, the neatness of the wrought iron accents gave them a machined feel. Nearly every model had a thick belt course completely around the home above the windows of each story. This conformed to eighteenth century Georgian-style architecture and also served to conceal the welding juncture between floors or between one story and the roof.[16] Windows were vertical rectangles with multiple panes, again a Georgian motif. Some two-story models had mansard roofs with dormer windows. Only in the spiral staircases inside the two story models did the clean curving line of welded steel reveal its true potential. The advertising proclaimed, "Not a nail in a Hobart

House," but the external appearance of the homes echoed that proclamation only faintly.

Construction, marketing, and internal modifications of the steel homes were far more innovative. Early in 1937 Hobart Welded Steel House Company decided to commit to complete pre-fabrication of its homes and built an addition behind the Main Street plant for the purpose of both assembling and marketing houses "in the same manner as autos are now displayed and sold in dealer show rooms." E. A. explained that three advantages of this method were that inclement weather could not interfere with construction; efficiency and quality would improve since all needed

A Hobart welded steel house gets final touches at the building site, circa 1935.

A Hobart welded steel house just clears the doorway, circa 1937.

equipment was at hand, and prospective buyers would not have to visualize the home being offered. "Mother can actually see how much closet space there is and father can determine if the den is what he expected it to be."[17] The factory/showroom was large enough to hold four or five steel homes. E. A. did not anticipate any trouble in transporting homes with unitized bodies to the prepared sites. Since the homes were completely arc welded, there were no bolts or screws to be jostled loose as they rode to the site on specially built trucks.

In keeping with the automobile showroom analogy, buyers could order a number of options to customize their homes. Shelving, cabinets, cupboards, staircases, banisters, bookcases, and window moldings were all made of steel and built in the houses according to customer specifications. Several clever space-saving features could be found: an ironing board that folded up inside a wall panel, wheeled basement stairs that could be pushed aside to ease the moving of appliances or furniture. Only in the interior of the Hobart homes did form truly follow function. Customers usually filled their kitchens with the latest appliances by KitchenAid, a division of Hobart Manufacturing in Troy.[18]

Moving the first completely prefabricated steel house from the plant to its site on Hobart Circle was an event.

Moving the first completely prefabricated steel house from the plant to its site on Hobart Circle was an event. "All the women and children came and watched the house on the truck leaving the factory on Main Street. I still remember riding on it and sitting on the windowsill," recalled Nelson Dohm who later worked for Hobart Brothers.[19] E. A. was convinced that within a few years a large percentage of American homes would be manufactured in this manner.[20]

Not everyone at Hobart Brothers shared E. A.'s enthusiasm. "A number of the persons assigned to the welded steel house division felt they were being demoted and some grumbled, some quit. . . ."[21] The impression that the steel homes were a make work project was not entirely in error. After a modest recovery since 1933, the U.S. economy was hit by a sharp recession in 1937. In March of that year Hobart's plant addition and its third house on Hobart Circle accounted for all the building permits issued by the City of Troy apart from a couple garages and room additions.[22] "Ed [Hobart] could see that he needed to keep his best people for when the economy improved. . . ."[23]

The economy also helped dictate the size, shape, and cost of the steel homes. Simple, compact floor plans where

The Cape Cod

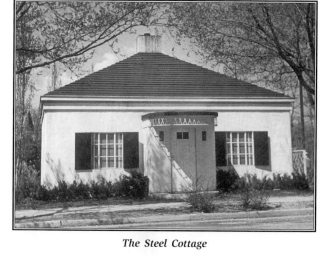

The Steel Cottage

the entire house formed a perfect rectangle accomplished several goals at once. They eased the on site assembly of foundation and house, utilized living space efficiently, and, above all, kept the cost of construction low. A key consideration in the pricing of Hobart steel homes was that Federal Housing Authority (FHA) loan guidelines stated that the total cost of the home should not be more than twice the home buyer's annual income. According to a well-publicized 1935 study, only one in four American families could afford a home that cost over $5,000.[24] The three most popular Hobart models were: a one-story with four rooms, a bath and a cellar for $4,000; a one-and-a-half story with five rooms, a bath, and cellar for $4,700; and a two story with six rooms a bath and cellar for $5,700. Prices included a fully landscaped lot with a walkway. For $300 customers could add a garage.[25] Clearly, the steel homes were priced to sell to a mass market, and Hobart Brothers employees first leased and later purchased all thirteen homes on Hobart Circle and adjoining Hobart Drive.

In 1938 E. A. hired Bill Turner, a nineteen-year-old architectural draftsman from Middletown, Ohio, who had learned his trade working for a group of Chicago architects at Steel Buildings, Inc. Turner had the task of keeping up with E. A., "this whirlwind" who kept making changes in the home designs that had to be recorded properly so they could be repaired or duplicated in the future.

He [E. A.] had no use for paper or paper systems and operated out of his head. He left instructions on 3 x 5 salmon colored cards, and these were ABSOLUTE. They took precedence over anything in the shop! They used to upset the production people something fierce, but it was seldom that Ed had to confront production as to the importance of these cards.[26]

E. A.'s cards were legendary at Hobart Brothers. He would scribble instructions and sometimes diagrams in pencil on the cards and leave them at employee workstations after the plant had closed for the night. Employees

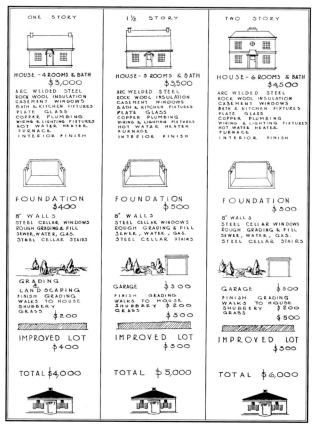

A catalog sheet from the 1930s shows Hobart steel homes were reasonably priced.

The Regency

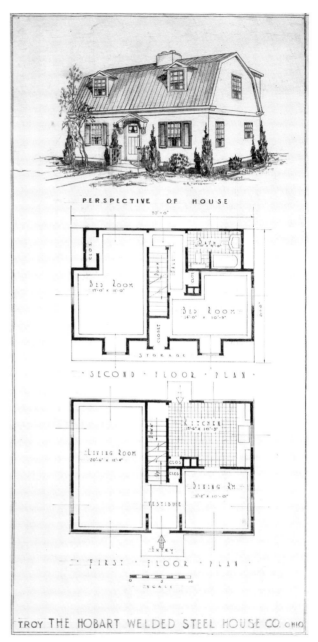

PERSPECTIVE OF HOUSE

A popular floor plan

who received one felt both pride and apprehension. The recipient was proud to be noticed by the company president and regarded as capable of carrying out a top priority job but also apprehensive, knowing E. A.'s high expectations and practice of following up on the cards in just a day or two.[27]

When E. A. Hobart wanted to talk to someone he did not pick up a phone or ask his secretary, he took off on foot and soon was peering over the shoulder of the party in question ready to deliver his message in person. "He had a habit of clearing his throat which helped some, but at the speed Ed moved it didn't help too much."[28] E. A. quickly learned the names of new employees and had key people in every department and at each level of the company he could see to get the real scoop on what was happening.

The people who worked for E. A. had immense respect for him, in part because they felt that he never asked them to do anything he could not do himself. Despite becoming the company's chief executive, E. A. Hobart never stopped being a hands-on engineer. Bill Turner recalled one summer day when he was checking forms at a homesite in the new Edgehill development when a company truck arrived with a concrete mixer to pour the foundation. The driver had just backed into position to pour when the mixer stopped turning. Its clutch had gone out. "Everyone hit the panic button at the same time and nothing was happening" when E. A. drove up in his new Chrysler Imperial. "He was all decked out in a white suit and Panama hat. . . ." No one wanted to be the first to tell him the bad news, but it didn't take E. A. long to figure out he had a full concrete mixer whose porridge would soon turn to stone if it did not start rotating. Someone suggested they find a mechanic to repair the clutch. "There just isn't time for that kind of monkey busi-

ness," E. A. said. With that he grabbed the toolbox out of the truck cab and climbed into the mixer, completely dismantled the clutch and repaired it. Soon after the mixer groaned into motion, and E. A. crawled back out, smeared head to foot with grease and oil. Sheepishly, one of the men said, "Mr. Hobart, you've ruined your white suit." Wiping his hands, E. A. looked at him and replied, "I can afford another one." Then he got into his car and drove away.[29] Such performances were common for a man who was considered a genius by production line welders and fellow engineers alike.

Frisbee home on Hobart Circle

Orval Menke

One reason Hobart had the time to advance technology, establish personal contacts with his workers, and pursue special projects like the steel home was that back in 1918 he had asked Orval Menke, his old college roommate and thesis partner from Ohio State, to come to Troy to supervise production at Hobart Brothers. E. A. could trust Menke to keep the factory running smoothly, while he gathered a small corps of engineers and technicians in his "skunk works" to create product innovations. Patiently, Menke integrated E. A.'s salmon card imperatives into the production process. Looking dapper in his dark suit and trademark black bow tie, Menke presided over formal job interviews at Hobart Brothers for more than forty years.[30]

Earl Galbreath

Earl Galbreath had been with the company even longer than Menke. He had joined Hobart Brothers in 1916, his service interrupted only by a stint in the U.S. Marines during the First World War.[31] Galbreath worked as sales manager under W. H. and later supervised office personnel in a role that paralleled that of Menke's at the

The Hobarts built over thirty steel houses between 1935 and 1941

factory. Upon completion of the Hobart Circle development, the Hobart Steel Welded House Company was reorganized and renamed the Troy Land Improvement Company with Galbreath as its president.[32]

Resurrecting the name of the group that had brought C. C. Hobart to town, Troy Land Improvement tackled a much bigger development project called Edgehill, one hundred acres of farmland that lay just west of Troy's city limits, from the B&O Railroad tracks to Ridge Avenue.[33] W. H., a devoted Anglophile, gave English place names to the streets and cul-de-sacs as they were platted. However, Edgehill was not destined to be an all steel-home development nor would every new homebuyer be a Hobart employee.

The Hobarts built over thirty steel houses between 1935 and 1941, erecting about half of them on sites in Troy. Most of the remainder were sold to buyers in the Dayton area.[34] However, owners began to discover that their steel homes had several problems, most of which were intrinsic to the building material. Instead of breathing, the steel homes sweated. Any drop in temperature or difference in temperature between the air and the home's steel skin caused condensation to form. Humidity made carpets and curtains damp, even moldy. The moisture exacerbated a second problem, which was steel's tendency to rust. Walls, both inside and out, needed frequent painting. E. A. tackled the excess moisture problem by adding a "V" pocket under the windowsill, which funneled condensed water outside through a small tube. Ultimately, an electrical dehumidifier proved the best solution to this problem. Ironically, many owners eventually encased external walls in wood, aluminum, or much later vinyl siding to protect the steel from corrosion, which concealed the home's basic composition even further.[35]

Another set of problems concerned electricity. Radio and later television waves did not penetrate the steel walls, forcing residents to mount antennae outside to pick up signals. During electrical storms parts of the steel houses flickered with the eerie blue-white glow of Saint Elmo's fire. No residents were hurt, but damage to electrical appliances and wiring was frequent. Repairs of hidden wiring and pipes were time-consuming and expensive. A cutting torch had to be used to cut through walls or floors and, once a repair had been made, the hole had to be patched, welded back together and painted with rustproof paint.[36]

Lustron steel homes

Remodeling or even redecorating proved to be a major undertaking. Once a resident had gone through the trouble of bolting a picture to the wall, he did not want to move it. The steel homes, with four inches of insulation in the outside walls as well as built in carpeting or linoleum, proved remarkably good at blocking outdoor noise.[37] Indoors, however, if a child wanted to throw a tantrum by stomping feet or banging walls the steel homes provided a loud and responsive sounding board. ". . . we had a grand piano and when we moved out of the house the floor sprung and gave a great big bong sound, like a great steel spring."[38]

Despite the problems many residents enjoyed their steel homes and the feeling of being a modern housing pioneer. In Hobart Circle, where most residents were young couples with children and all original owners were Hobart employees, a special sense of community developed. For years it was also a showplace that attracted visitors to Troy to see America's first neighborhood of welded steel homes.

The main factor that brought the Hobart's experiment in steel housing to a close was an economic one. The availability of steel at low prices proved to be a passing phenomenon. Demand for steel increased steadily in the late 1930s as the nations of the world geared up for war.

Though expressing America's wish to remain neutral, FDR accelerated the Navy's building program in late 1937. By October 1940 Nazi Germany had already conquered Poland and France, and, with rearmament in full swing, Washington brought allocation of steel under federal control. The last Hobart steel house erected in Troy was the one E. A. built for Martha and himself on Ridge Avenue and completed in 1941.

The Hobart Brothers made one of the first efforts in welded steel housing, but it was by no means the only such effort or even the largest. Shortly after World War II the Lustron Corporation in nearby Columbus, Ohio, jumped into prefabricated steel housing in a big way. Lustron's founder, Carl Strandlund, believed he had solved the corrosion problem by coating his steel wall panels and roof tiles with a layer of porcelain enamel. He did a marvelous job of securing both private and public financing and lining up unions and real estate firms to collaborate on the project. The homes themselves, with their compact rectangular floor plans, bore some resemblance to the Hobart example, but far more of the assembly took place on site instead of in his factory. Soon it became obvious that Lustron had seriously underestimated the complexity of its manufacturing process. The oversold housing project fell far behind schedule then collapsed.[39]

The main factor that brought the Hobart's experiment in steel housing to a close was an economic one.

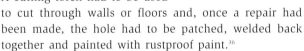

The Hobart experiment in welded steel housing was a useful venture but no roaring success. The project revealed several difficulties with the use of steel as a primary home building material, but E. A. was correct in predicting that the process of prefabricating houses would catch on in America and in Europe. Beyond the lessons in technology, E. A. also learned about the employees assigned to the project. "Those who did well were later rewarded with good paying positions as supervisors when the economy improved as they had passed Ed's attitude and adaptability test."[40] The production methods improvised to build steel houses were a good preparation for the engineers and foremen who would soon be called upon to implement the massive expansion of production needed to meet government orders during World War II. ❧

CHAPTER 11

New Products Blaze a Path Through the Depression

Steel homes were only the largest and most unusual new product that Hobart Brothers produced in an effort to work its way out of the Depression. The company had entered the welding equipment market only two years before the stock market crashed. Therefore, Hobart was still in the process of rounding out its product line in order to compete in each segment of the welding industry. E. A. and his "skunk works" team met this challenge with a burst of creativity, securing twenty patents between 1930 and 1941. By the time the United States entered World War II Hobart Brothers had become the second-largest welding company in America.

Hobart Brothers had always been a company where engineers and engineering were clearly in the driver's seat. E. A. often remarked, "This is my hobby shop. I'm going to have fun."[1] This approach was attractive to other engineers who wanted to tackle challenges and experiment. At times it could also be frustrating to personnel in production, marketing, and finance who often had a very different set of priorities. Typically, E. A. and his engineers would invent a new product or a new technological wrinkle for an established product and then expect W. H. and his sales staff to find or create a market for it while production adjusted to build it and finance scraped together the funds to pay for the whole project. This unorthodox approach worked for many years for three reasons. First, E. A. and W. H. were highly competitive individuals who constantly scanned the business horizon to see what the competition was doing. Secondly, the welding industry itself was still growing and evolving. The field was crowded with competitors, large and small, specialized and broad-based, in gas welding or in electrical arc welding. In this chaotic environment a company could base its growth on quality and innovation and not simply get squashed by competitors with an advantage in price and volume. Finally,

> *The company had entered the welding equipment market only two years before the stock market crashed.*

Hobart Brothers had a talented and highly cohesive workforce that was small enough, averaging two hundred during the 1930s, to be responsive to change.

E. A. never forgot the lessons learned from the controversy over his first patent for the diverter pole employed in Hobart Brothers' "constant potential" battery chargers. E. A. had conceived and sketched out his ideas in early October 1922. By December W. H. had devised a marketing plan and Menke began modifying the production line to produce the new chargers. By the spring of 1923, when Hobart Brothers started shipping the first battery sets it had sold, E. A. found the time to compose a formal application for a patent. He probably had his father C. C., who had a law degree, look over the forms before they were submitted. Who needed a patent lawyer? Everyone knew it took time for the Patent Office to process a claim. In the meanwhile, sales of Hobart Brothers' new line of battery chargers were brisk.

One winter's day early in 1926 E. A.'s face turned red as it always did when angry when he came across a piece of advertising literature from the Rochester Electric Products Corporation. Rochester was touting a device it had just patented that sounded exactly like E. A.'s diverter pole claim, on which the Patent Office had not yet ruled.[2] Though Rochester already had a patent in hand, its application was dated October 22, 1923, several months after Hobart Brothers battery chargers had reached the market.

E. A. reached for the biggest "guns" he knew, Toulmin & Toulmin, a Dayton law firm that specialized in patent law. Harry Toulmin Sr. had represented the Wright Brothers in the landmark international case concerning the first airplane.[3] His son, Harry Toulmin Jr., guided the Hobart Brothers' patent interference case on its nearly three-year course through a hearing and an appeal, winning both times. E. A. tried to get Rochester Electric to

Hobart's multirange dual control provided one thousand welding current settings. This classic Hobart M-300 machine, designed by E. A. Hobart, was produced for nearly fifty years and sold worldwide.

In the 1930s both General Electric and Westinghouse had welding equipment divisions. Linde, a division of Union Carbide, with technology based on German war reparations led America in producing gases and oxy-acetylene welding equipment. Of the firms that specialized in electric arc welding, Cleveland-based Lincoln Electric had the greatest sales volume and perennially provided Hobart Brothers with its toughest head to head competition. As fellow Buckeyes, the two Lincoln brothers and two Hobart brothers squared off for decades in a rivalry that was friendly yet intense. In August 1934 when he heard Hobart Brothers was testing a new remote control for its welders at a Navy shipyard in Virginia, Jim Lincoln fired off a letter full of both bluster and respect:

As man to man, and I hope as friend to friend . . . Lincoln patents have been so much infringed, we have to sue [over remote control]   . . . or else admit that taking out patents is just a bluff.

. . . I would much rather sue somebody else other than yourselves, because I admit I admire the battle you are putting up. . . .[6]

E. A. calmly replied:

I have never seen the mechanism of your telegraphic control. . . . In working out a mechanism which conforms to Navy specifications, I have only used what I have considered to be my own ideas.

Then in a more chatty tone he added that W. H. and his family had just returned from six "wonderful" weeks in Europe. "I trust you also enjoyed your vacation trip in the old country."[7] No lawsuit resulted, but such exchanges between Jim Lincoln and E. A. Hobart were frequent.

Remote control allowed an operator to adjust the current where he worked without having to walk back to the machine. This saved time and reduced the number of inferior welds that resulted from welders who kept on welding instead of interrupting the job to dial up the proper setting for different positions or electrodes.[8] Hobart Brothers further enhanced control in 1938 by increasing the number of ranges on its dual control dial from three to ten. With ten midrange settings, this created a total of one thousand combinations to provide the flexibility to handle a wide variety of electrodes and welding jobs.[9] While improving the quality of its DC-powered welders, Hobart Brothers also streamlined their appearance in accord with

drop its appeal but to no avail.[4] The whole costly experience thoroughly soured him on the idea of patent litigation. "Everyone loses in court but the lawyers," he groused.[5] However, the case forced Hobart Brothers to adopt several strategies that would serve the company well in the decades ahead. E. A. instructed all new engineers to study industry patents. Never again, would E. A. or his engineers apply for a patent without the assistance of Harry Toulmin Jr. to examine and then help expedite the request. Whenever the skunk works explored a new subject for research, E. A. would press Toulmin for copies of relevant patents. The same would happen whenever the company received a letter threatening patent litigation. In general, Hobart Brothers evolved a two-part defensive strategy when it came to patents: be very aware of new technology patented by one's competitors, and stockpile patents on any clear advances obtained by in-house research. If competitors threatened litigation, Hobart could haul out its own patents to do likewise, "trading stock" they were often called. The goal was to get any competitive edge into the marketplace as soon as possible while staying out of court. In the rough and tumble prewar welding industry, waiting for a patent to be approved before putting an improvement into production could prove fatal.

> *E. A. instructed all new engineers to study industry patents.*

the 1930s design trend inspired by the first high-speed passenger trains.[10] The Hobart Manufacturing Company hired noted industrial designer Egmont Arens to redesign its KitchenAid mixer. The streamlined look of the 1937 mixer became an instant classic still in production today.[11]

Beginning in 1932, Hobart Brothers began manufacturing a line of welders powered by gasoline engines instead of electric motors. Internal combustion engines withstood rough handling and outdoor conditions better than DC motor generators and were ideal for customers who wanted mobile welders, especially contractors and pipeliners. Operators with experience on truck, tractor, and automobile engines could handle maintenance and basic repairs on the gas engines. Hobart Brothers purchased Chrysler engines to drive its 200-, 300-, 400-, and 600-ampere welders and a Hercules engine for its 100-ampere welder. The U.S. Army eventually purchased thousands of these gas-powered welders for its mobile machine shops.[12]

Hobart Brothers also targeted the farmer and the handyman entrepreneur by promoting "Build Your Own" welders. A customer could buy a generator only welder and attach it to his own power source, saving from $300

Hobart specialty welder for the railroad industry, circa 1936

to $500 compared to the cost of a complete gas-powered welder. A free booklet, Twelve Rules to Follow if You Have "Build Your Own" Fever, helped those who chose this option to get the job done right.[13] Apart from its main line of five welders powered by either motor generators or gas engines, Hobart Brothers produced some specialty welders. One self-propelled model, looking like a tractor with car tires and a bench seat, could be driven on roads or across fields. Another was designed to run on railway tracks to

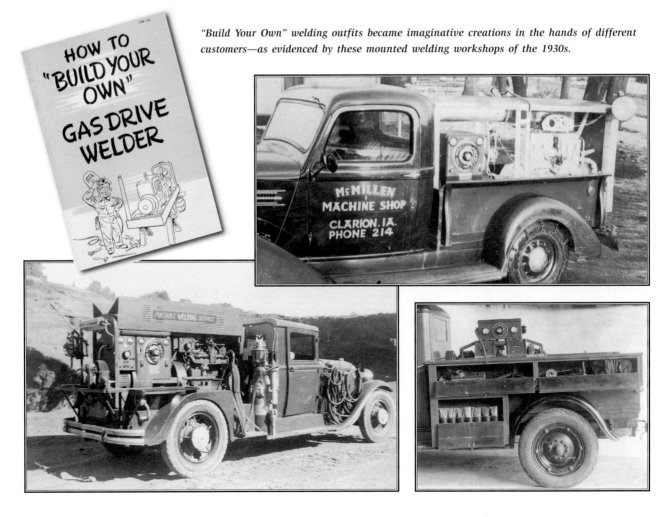

"Build Your Own" welding outfits became imaginative creations in the hands of different customers—as evidenced by these mounted welding workshops of the 1930s.

repair rails and switches.[14] As the government began to increase production of military aircraft in the late 1930s, Hobart engineers created a modified version of its 100-ampere DC welder for higher open circuit voltage and other characteristics to improve its ability to weld aluminum and other lightweight metals and alloys. This model was billed the "Aircraft Special."[15]

In 1929 Niels C. Miller, like C. C. Hobart an electrical tinkerer with no formal training, succeeded in building an AC welder in his basement workshop in Wisconsin. He founded Miller Electric with the goal of supplying farmers with a simple, low cost welder.[16] Actually, AC welding had been invented ten years earlier, but it was not until the early 1930s that designs better able to control its dangerously high open circuit voltage and heavily coated electrodes to stabilize its arc combined to make AC welding commercially viable. When welding manufacturers heard that AC welders had been successfully employed in the construction of Hoover Dam, they began to develop AC welders of their own.[17]

As E. A. and Russ Flora began to explore AC welding they soon realized its potential. Welds made with an AC arc penetrated deeper and deposited weld metal more quickly than DC welders. A transformer could step down the high incoming voltage to a safer level.[18] In 1939 Hobart Brothers began to market its own AC transformer welder with a dual control system that provided thirty steps in a range from twenty to two hundred amperes.[19] This new line of welders would undergo remarkable technological advances in the postwar era.

Hobart's 1939 AC transformer welder reflected the streamlined trend in production design.

Russ Flora at left with E. A. Hobart, 1938

Patents Held by E. A. Hobart

Patent Number	Issue Date	Description
82,889	12/23/30	Design for a Car-Washing Pump
150,358 A	7/27/48	Design for an Electric Welder
1,750,713	3/18/30	Voltage Regulation Winding for Electric Generators
1,771,889	7/29/30	Compressor
1,786,242	12/23/30	Compressor
1,794,291	2/24/31	Brush Support for Electrical Apparatus
1,802,175	8/21/31	Compressor and Tank Unit
1,813,998	8/21/31	Pump
1,825,064	9/29/31	Electric Welder
1,842,173	1/19/32	Tank for Air Compressors
1,907,110	5/2/33	Car Washing Pump
1,956,864	5/1/34	Weld Rod
1,959,674	5/22/34	Control Mechanism for Gas Driven Welder
1,970,854	8/21/34	Means and Method of Control of Electric Welding Circuits
1,994,609	3/19/35	Electric Welding Apparatus
2,049,377	7/28/36	Electric Welder Control
2,130,584	9/20/38	Welder
2,170,861	8/29/39	Electric Apparatus Power Saver
2,176,341	10/17/39	Welding Apparatus
2,197,888	8/23/40	Welder
2,244,063	6/3/41	Tractor Welder
2,328,452	8/31/43	Speed Regulator for Engines
2,396,176	3/5/46	Idling Mechanism for Welding Apparatus
2,457,372 A	12/28/48	Alternating Current Vertical Welder
2,476,373	7/19/49	Combined Welder and Power Plant
2,490,354	12/6/49	Variable Output Welding Transformer
2,490,871 A	12/13/49	Alternating Current Vertical Welder
2,506,787	5/9/50	Electric Control Switch
2,780,356	2/5/57	Apparatus for Separating Minerals from Sand
2,802,981 A	8/13/57	Transformer Welder with Electrically Adjustable Leakage Reactance
2,882,478 A	4/14/59	Method and Apparatus for Welding
2,938,627	5/31/60	Apparatus for Distributing and Separating Ore
2,966,262	12/17/60	Method and Apparatus for Separating Ore
3,000,502	9/19/61	Apparatus for Separating Ore
3,308,265	3/7/67	Filtering Circuit

Compiled by:
Martha A. Baker, Librarian
Hobart Institute of Welding Technology
8/11/04

One major expansion of the Hobart Brothers' welding line in the 1930s, the decision to manufacture electrodes, represented a reversal of the usual pattern of product development within the company. For once it was the marketing and financial people who had to goad the engineers into entering a new field. W. H. and his sales brain trust of Earl Galbreath, Wib Chaffee and Eddie Butterfield had always been fond of using simple analogies to introduce customers to new technology. Now they enlisted one to persuade fellow Hobart executives that Hobart Brothers should produce its own line of electrodes. Which can you sell more of, they asked, razors or razorblades? A well-built welder could be expected to provide ten years of reliable service. One had to wait a long time for repeat business. On the other hand, electrodes were a consumable product that could provide steady income. Furthermore, electrodes could be designed to work with Hobart welders to increase welder sales and enable Hobart Brothers to meet all the welding equipment needs of its clients. Lincoln Electric had been manufacturing electrodes for several years and that gave Lincoln a competitive advantage in landing contracts for welders as well as a tidy source of profits.

E. A. was certainly interested in electrodes. In 1931 he had experimented with a variety of electrode coatings and submitted a patent application for a coated weldrod in October of that year. His application contains a fine description of the process and purpose of coating electrodes. E. A. called for wrapping the weldrod in "a coarse grade of ducking or muslin" and then soaking the rod in a chemical solution composed mainly of sodium silicate:

This chemical acts first as a binder for holding the muslin or fabric in place, and second, it acts as a retarding agent, preventing the rapid burning of the muslin or fabric any further back than the electric arc produced in the process of welding. In fact, the sodium silicate acts as a refractory agent, forming a crater for the arc and allowing the electrode to melt up in the crater and shoot from the crater with some force. The sodium silicate also leaves a glassy slag over the weld itself after it has been finished. The muslin or ducking, being composed of a hydrocarbon in the form of a cellulose, breaks down into carbon monoxide and carbon dioxide and provides an enveloping gas for enclosing the arc.[20]

Both the shielding gas and the slag helped prevent impurities from entering and corroding the weld. E. A. went on to list the advantages of an electrode of this kind:

The covering does not dry and crack under atmospheric and moisture conditions, and rods thus formed can be handled roughly without marring or injuring their qualities. . . .

the shielded arc is smooth and moves evenly. . . . Welding may be produced more rapidly because a higher degree of voltage can be used . . . at the same time a very ductile weld is provided, and one in which there is great tensile strength and rust-resisting qualities.[21]

Despite having a well-written patent application filed in Washington as a form of insurance against the claims of competitors, Hobart Brothers chose to delay moving into the production of electrodes. In May 1934 the Patent Office granted E. A. his patent, but three more years would pass before Hobart Brothers undertook the manufacture of welding rods.

Several factors contributed to this unusual delay. Chief among them were timing, technology, and interest. The years 1932 and 1933 were the darkest of the Depression, not a propitious time to launch a whole new line of products. By the time the economy began to pick up in mid-decade, E. A. and W. H. had diverted their attention to building steel homes.

In the 1930s electrode coating technology was in such a state of flux that Hobart leaders had to be concerned that they could incur heavy costs for capital equipment only to find they had tooled up to produce electrodes which had already become obsolete. New x-ray machines to inspect welds showed that the mineral coated electrodes recently introduced in Europe produced better welds than any coating process then available in the American market.[22] Electrodes for AC welders needed yet another type of coating. Furthermore, electrode manufacturers had entangled themselves in a thorny legal thicket. The A. O. Smith Corporation of Milwaukee had sued Lincoln Electric for infringing its patent for the first American coated electrode. The court ruling in favor of Lincoln made many believe that no electrode patent was enforceable.[23] Welding companies rushed a wide variety of electrode coatings into production and protected their efforts with a flurry of vaguely worded patent applications. It became difficult to assess where real progress was being made let alone determine which company deserved the credit.

Finally, E. A. and the other machine engineers at Hobart Brothers had a decided lack of interest in the kind of manufacturing required to produce filler metals for

. . . electrodes were a consumable product that could provide steady income.

Richard Aufhauser, "Father of the Hobart Filler Metal Line," circa late 1940s

welding. It demanded uniformity and high volume, yet profits would often depend on adroit purchasing of raw materials that were constantly fluctuating in price. Hobart Brothers was accustomed to short production runs of high value added products. Profit depended on sound design, reliability, innovative updates, and even a certain degree of customization. Producing electrodes required a different approach to manufacturing, and many at Hobart Brothers were unsure that the company could adapt and compete successfully in this new field.

Despite apprehensions, the economic arguments in favor of electrode production were compelling. During a 1937 business trip to the Leipzig Trade Fair in Germany, E. A. and W. H. became convinced they needed someone with experience of European methods of electrode coating. Later that year they discovered that one of their customers, the largest American owned steel mill in Mexico, had just built an entire electrode plant in Mexico City under the direction of a recent immigrant named Richard Aufhauser. The Hobarts hired Aufhauser to come to Troy to supervise the establishment of filler metal manufacturing at Hobart Brothers.[24]

Richard Aufhauser was a twenty-five-year-old German Jewish immigrant who had arrived in New York City in 1936 aboard the *Queen Mary* with $35 and a German-built Zundapp motorcycle. A native of Hamburg, Aufhauser had been a student at the University of Hamburg in the summer of 1933 when a group of fellow students clad in Nazi brown shirts invited him to join them at a bonfire of the university's collection of Non-Aryan books and music. Instead, Aufhauser offered to buy the collection they were about to set ablaze. This resulted in Richard's expulsion from college.[25] At the time "he thought Hitler was an anomaly and would get thrown out as soon as everyone realized how crazy he was."[26] Aufhauser went to work for his father who was a professor of chemistry at the University of Berlin and an advisor to shipbuilders in Hamburg. An English cousin of the Aufhausers who owned a metal fabricating company approached them with a problem. The English company had been purchasing coated electrodes from Germany but did not wish to be left high and dry in case of war. Could the Aufhausers determine the composition of the coatings and how they adhered to the wire? The Aufhausers tackled the problem

Hobart Brother's billboard at the entrance to Troy, circa 1930s

and Richard then came to England to set up electrode production for his cousin's firm. Meanwhile, the 1935 Nuremberg Laws had institutionalized German discrimination against Jews. Determined to not return to Germany and unable to extend his work permit in England, Aufhauser decided to go to America in 1936.[27]

One reason why Aufhauser accepted the position at Hobart Brothers was that he liked Troy and believed a small town in the Midwest would be a better place to Americanize himself than New York City with its large German-American community.[28] Under his direction, Hobart Brothers built electrode manufacturing facilities, complete with extrusion presses to coat the rods and ovens to bake the coating on evenly. At first production volume was modest as Aufhauser concentrated on obtaining the extrusion equipment and materials to diversify the product line of Hobart electrodes. By 1940 the company was turning out eighteen types of electrodes. These included a carbon rod, and fifteen varieties of coated electrodes, two of which were designed for use with AC welders.[29] The timing of Hobart Brothers' expansion into electrode manufacturing placed the company in a good position to supply the booming industrial demand for filler metals caused by the U.S. armed forces' rapid increases in weapons and equipment procurement as war clouds gathered in Europe and Asia.

Since the death of her husband C. C. in 1932, Lou Ella Hobart's life had resumed its familiar pattern. As company treasurer she continued to sign payroll checks at Hobart Brothers. She attended the meetings of the three women's clubs to which she belonged and remained active in the First Baptist Church of Troy and served as chair of the distribution committee of the Troy Foundation. Privately, she endeavored to extend financial help to students who wanted to attend college. Lou Ella spent many hours in her backyard flower garden. Considered one of the most beautiful in Troy, it incorporated parts of the abandoned canal bed, which she had turned into lily ponds. She enjoyed visits from her six grandchildren, and her son Charles continued to drive her to Florida for an annual vacation.

In June 1939 Lou Ella joined the multitudes visiting the New York World's Fair. Three days after she returned Lou Ella fell ill and died in her home on June 17, 1939. With the death of Lou Ella, the last of the generation of Hobarts that had grown to adulthood in the nineteenth century had passed away. "All eyes to the future," the recorded narration had intoned as visitors came to the end of the huge City of the Future diorama at the 1939 New York World's Fair.[30] On September 1, 1939, Hitler invaded Poland, and the eyes of the second and third generations of industrial Hobarts were indeed turned to the future. However, it was not the far off future of wonder and imagination presented at the fair, but the immediate uncertainties of tomorrow in a world plunged into war. ❧

By 1940 the company was turning out eighteen types of electrodes.

The Hobart electrode plant on Water Street, circa 1940

76

CHAPTER 12

Hobart Goes to War

Although the United States remained officially neutral, it did not take long for the war to make an impact on Troy. In early October 1939 a German submarine torpedoed a Dutch liner of the Holland-America line in the North Atlantic. Among the cargo sunk was a shipment of mixers, choppers, and grinders from Hobart Manufacturing bound for Amsterdam, the first war loss suffered by a Troy business.[1] However, the most marked effect of the war on the Troy community was a quickening of its economic pulse. The directors of local WPA projects reported a growing number of no shows as their workers found jobs in the private sector.[2] Within a year after the war began the number of people on relief in Miami County dropped below two hundred.[3] The Great Depression was over.

Hobart Brothers helped fuel the job growth in Troy. As a manufacturer of welding equipment and electrical power plants, it occupied a strategic sector of production in a time of accelerated spending on defense. Ships, planes, tanks, and artillery guns could all be made stronger, lighter and assembled more quickly through the use of welding in their manufacture. Men who had been junior officers in the First World War recalled the demand for welding to make rapid repairs and get damaged equipment back into the line. Now, as commanding generals and admirals, they ordered welders for their mobile repair shops. Except to power phone lines and light underground bunkers, electrical generators were rarely seen on or near the battlefields of World War I. Now they were in demand for everything from radar units to artillery firing mechanisms.

Orders for military goods grew slowly at first. Once Germany conquered Poland, the war in Europe settled into stalemate that stretched through the winter of 1939–1940. People began calling it a "phony war" or "sitzkrieg." Under President Roosevelt's urging, Congress had amended its Neutrality Act in November 1939. America could now sell weapons and war materials to belligerents, but such purchases could only be made on a cash and carry basis, and

American vessels were barred from sailing into a wide danger zone that encompassed France, the British Isles, the North Sea, and the Baltic. The most fervid isolationists condemned the revision as un-neutral since the Allied blockade prevented German ships from crossing the Atlantic.[4] The goal was in fact to help the Allies while trying to insulate America from the kind of submarine warfare that had pulled the United States into World War I.

No fervid isolationists were to be found in the Hobart family. Ties of ancestry and cultural heritage further cemented by several visits in the 1930s made the Hobarts passionate supporters of Great Britain. W. H. in particular was a devoted Anglophile as well as a former World War I Army "doughboy." Both he and E. A. had had an opportunity on their tours of Europe to contrast Hitler's Germany with the democracies of France and England. Accompanying their father on a 1937 visit, Marcia and Lucia were drawn to a German street by the tramp of marching feet. As the column swung into view they were astonished to see it was a troop of Hitler Youth, boys and girls their own age, all in uniform marching in lockstep. The memory had a chilling effect.[5]

No fervid isolationists were to be found in the Hobart family.

Most Americans in the Midwest did not sense any threat until Hitler unleashed his war machine in April 1940 and overran Denmark and Norway. A second blitzkrieg exploded across France and the Low Countries in May, conquering in days land that had been fought over for years in the last war. This slashing style of attack spearheaded by mobile armor had been inspired in part by the writings of General Percy Hobart, a distant cousin of the Troy Hobarts. Largely ignored by his superiors in the British Army, Percy Hobart's theories were put into action by German panzer divisions.[6] The dramatic turn of events in the war in Europe loosened the purse strings in Congress, which approved $18 billion in defense spending, but interventionists and isolationists fought a bitter battle over conscription that raged throughout the summer.[7]

As France teetered on the brink of collapse, the executives of Hobart Brothers and Hobart Manufacturing met to confer diplomas and certificates on the graduates of the Hobart Trade School. Johnson West, Company Secretary of Hobart Manufacturing delivered the main speech, an emphatic cry for support of the Allied cause that even urged America to send troops to prevent the fall of Great Britain. He insisted, "Democratic government will not die in 1940."[8] Clearly, the business leaders of Troy did not share the isolationism still prevalent in the American Midwest.

A record number of 115 students graduated from the trade school in 1940, just four fewer than that year's graduating class at Troy High School.[9] In May trade school president Orval Menke had announced plans to expand by erecting a modern two-story building of welded steel construction facing Elm Street on the block between Main and Water Streets, the former site of the Hobart Brothers service garage.[10] The new facility with its curving art deco entrance was ready by late fall and contained fifty-two arc welding booths on the first floor along with twelve stations for oxy-acetylene welding. For the first time the school included the latest testing equipment including x-ray machines for examining welds. After the United States entered the war, the school installed twenty more booths for arc welding and twelve more for gas welding on the second floor, that meant up to seventy-two students at one time could be gaining hands on experience. The school added a second shift at night, and still it operated at capacity throughout the war years.[11] Already students from every state in the union as well as Canada, Mexico, and even the Philippines had learned or sharpened their welding skills at the Troy school.[12]

France did fall to Germany, surrendering on June 22. During the summer, as Britain's Royal Air Force took on the Luftwaffe in the Battle of Britain, WACO, a Troy company that manufactured a popular series of biplanes for civil aviation, began producing trainers for the U.S. Army Air Corps.[13] Encouraged that Great Britain could survive, Congress finally voted to begin America's first peacetime draft in September. That fall the War and Navy Departments in Washington began awarding contracts in earnest as they prepared to arm a military force projected to grow into the millions. However, the attention of many Americans was riveted on the plight of English civilians under the blitz of German bombers, which struck English cities in nightly raids. Radio correspondents like Edward R. Murrow and Robert Trout detailed the story in live broadcasts. Rachel Hobart, W. H.'s wife, helped organize the local

chapter of "Bundles for Britain," a private charity that rolled bandages and collected clothing and toys to send to English civilians injured or displaced by the bombing.[14]

On a cold day in the late fall of 1940 E. A. Hobart received a rather mysterious telegram from the U.S. War Department, telling him to catch the first available train for Chicago and to report to the Blackstone Hotel by 9 a.m. the next day. He followed the directions and found himself the next morning among several other manufacturers of electrical motors listening to a proposal to build five thousand generators, primarily for the Signal Corps and the Ordnance Department of the Army. Military engineers presented specifications for what they needed, but the real challenge lay in the time constraints: a prototype in three and a half weeks, full production underway in six weeks, and the clincher, a detailed bid complete with cost estimates in twenty-four hours. The business executives tried to maintain their poker faces as they absorbed the conditions. Each would have access to materials and a secretary to help prepare their bids, which were due by 9 a.m. the next day.[15]

E. A. returned to his hotel room, took a short nap, showered, and then went to work. Much of his time was spent on the phone planning the bid with key people in Troy. By late that night he and his skunk works team had sketched out a design that met the military specifications. Then E. A. spoke with his people in production and finance to estimate the unit costs to put into the proposal. As the clock crept into the predawn hours the loaned secretary began typing the Hobart Brothers bid. Clutching the finished bid under his arm, E. A. strode to the conference room in the Blackstone Hotel. He glanced at his watch. It was exactly 9:02 a.m. He took a deep breath and opened the door. The Army brass and civilian officials all broke into smiles. E. A. was the only contractor in the room.[16]

Winning the bid for the first large order of generators for the military set off a whirlwind of activity in Troy. Construction began at once on a new three-story factory with eighteen thousand feet of floor space on Water Street. Once completed, the building would be devoted entirely to the manufacture of motor generators. Three Hobart Brothers executives: Orval Menke, Earl Galbreath, and Clayton Jenkins incorporated the Motor Generator Corporation as a separate company designed to be the first profitsharing firm in Troy. Common stock would be sold at $20 a share only to employees of Hobart Brothers or the Motor Generator Corporation. Quarterly dividends would be paid as soon as earnings made them possible.[17] W. H. and E. A. viewed this

E. A. Hobart received a rather mysterious telegram from the U.S. War Department, telling him to catch the first available train for Chicago. . . .

The new three-story factory on Water Street (1) was devoted entirely to the manufacture of motor generators. In the 1950s, Motor Generator Corporation moved across the street into the one-story building (2) in the foreground, circa 1975.

approach as an innovative way to both expand production and create a benefit incentive that would help retain experienced executives and employees at a time when competition for labor was heating up. Although government loans and grants were available, the Hobart brothers disdained them as "handouts" and chose to only use their own capital, bank loans, or employee investments to finance wartime expansion.[18] They wished to remain masters of their own destiny and not get tied to commitments that would restrain their independence.

The same independent streak in their brother Charles had nearly disastrous consequences for the Hobart Cabinet Company. In August 1941 FDR created the Supply Priorities and Allocation Board (SPAB) to control the use of strategic raw materials. Two months later the SPAB ordered a huge increase in the nation's steel production and also moved to restrain the use of steel in non-essential building and construction.[19] Although Charles believed the federal government was entitled to its full share of income taxes undi-

❧

Orval Menke, Earl Galbreath, and Clayton Jenkins incorporated the Motor Generator Corporation as a separate company designed to be the first profit-sharing firm in Troy.

❧

luted by deductions, he was incensed at the idea of government controlling the free flow of raw materials in the market when the nation was still at peace. Charles refused to sign up for the priority system even though he could have still obtained steel for his business at that point. Almost at once railcars loaded with sheets of steel stopped being shunted off the B&O line onto the sidings alongside the Hobart Cabinet Company plant on Water Street. Consuming steel at the rate of a railcar a day, it was not long before Charles exhausted his prime building material.[20]

Hobart Cabinet scrambled to convert production to wood during the war years, but competitors kept making steel office furniture until that use was later designated as non-essential. Orders trickled in for steel cabinetry to be filled after the war was over. As business dwindled Hobart Cabinet lost employees. Many found work at Hobart Brothers or at Troy firms like the Miami Specialty Company, Troy Sunshade, and Hobart Manufacturing, all of which subcontracted government orders secured by Hobart Brothers. During the war years Hobart Cabinet built hundreds of wood tool-boxes for the new employees at Hobart Brothers.[21] Luckily for Charles, the fruit trees he had begun to plant in 1937 were entering their years of peak production, and many cabinet company employees kept busy gathering bountiful harvests during the war years.[22]

Another "victim" of the war effort was Charles' Cadillac. The Caddy was a huge 1936 touring car with a V-16 engine, running boards, and two steel-clad spares mounted alongside the sleek engine compartment. Driving was almost a form of therapy for Charles and he had enjoyed driving his mother to Florida every winter until her death. Often he announced family trips on short notice, giving his wife Elizabeth just a few hours to pack. However, once wartime gasoline rationing took effect, Charles reluctantly parked his Cadillac in a storage shed for the duration.[23]

Whereas the decision to not apply for steel under the government priority plan led to a contraction of Hobart Cabinet, the decision to aggressively pursue government contracts led to unprecedented growth at Hobart Brothers. In 1939 Hobart Brothers employed 232 people. By 1940 it was 280. Employment more than doubled in 1941 to 728 and then nearly doubled again in 1942 to 1,230. During the same period gross sales jumped from $1.6 million in 1939 to over $22 million in 1942.[24] Essentially, the same team of managers that had steered the company through the Depression directed this remarkable expansion.

One recent addition to this team was a man named Glyn Williams. Williams, who had immigrated with his family from Wales when he was seven, was a brilliant young engineer who had first caught the attention of E. A. when he worked one summer at Hobart Brothers between his junior and senior years at Ohio State. Advancing at an accelerated pace, Williams graduated from the electrical engineering program at OSU at age nineteen and went on to earn a master's degree in engineering at Yale.[25] Hobart Brothers hired him in 1938 to design welders.[26] Within two years he was put in charge of production directly under plant manager Menke.[27] Williams worked with employees as well as he worked with the problems of design and engineering. He expected people to do their best but not more than they were

Glyn Williams

capable of doing. Unassuming and anything but intimidating, one family friend said of Williams, "I knew him for a long time before I knew he was smart."[28]

Williams and everyone at Hobart Brothers must have felt as though President Roosevelt were speaking directly to them as a record number of Americans listened to his fireside chat on their radios the evening of December 29, 1940:

. . . I appeal to the owners of plants—to the managers—to the workers—to our own government employees—to put every ounce of effort into producing these munitions swiftly and without stint. . . .

As planes and ships and guns and shells are produced, your government, with its defense experts, can then determine how best to use them to defend this hemisphere. The decision as to how much shall be sent abroad and how much shall remain at home must be made on the basis of overall military necessities.

We must be the great arsenal of democracy. . . .[29]

Within weeks an ambitious piece of legislation, which became known as the Lend Lease Act, was introduced in Congress. America would now attempt to not only rearm itself but also arm every nation whose defense the President deemed essential to the security of the United States.

In February 1941 Hobart Brothers announced it had received another large contract for welders from the War Department's Quartermaster's Corps at Camp Holabird in Baltimore. Dorcey C. Anderson, Hobart Brothers' distributor in Philadelphia, secured the $185,000 contract. E. A. Hobart reported that his plant was working partially on night shifts and turning out one hundred welding units a month.[30] Already Hobart Brothers employees were demonstrating the kind of devotion to work FDR had hoped to engender. Joe Attenweiler, a twenty-year-old testing foreman, was knocked unconscious for several minutes when he touched an ungrounded 650-volt welder. The next morning he was back on the job with "both hands bandaged as big as boxing gloves."[31]

Lowell Mott had just graduated from Miami East High School when he went to work for Hobart Brothers in June 1941.

The Hobart art deco office building, built in 1941, was inspired by Frank Lloyd Wright's Johnson's Wax offices and had a rectangular floor plan around a small courtyard.

His first job was boxing electrodes for thirty-five cents an hour. Continuously, he was bending and lifting loads of metal rods with gloved hands, and brushing glue on cardboard boxes to seal them. After the first week he wondered if he could endure it, but his father encouraged him to stick it out. When Mott began, Richard Aufhauser's electrode operation consisted of just one assembly line running on two shifts. By the time Mott was drafted in 1943 Hobart Brothers had three electrode production lines running on three shifts, and Mott himself had moved on to cutting wire and mixing the coatings. While Mott served as a combat engineer with the Forty-fourth Division in Europe, Hobart Brothers deposited $20 a month in Motor Generator bonds in an account for Mott and for each Hobart employee in the armed forces.[32]

Following the pattern set by Glyn Williams, John Sampson, an electrical engineering student who had just completed his junior year at Ohio State, spent the summer of 1941 working for Hobart Brothers. He found it exhilarating to be plunged into major responsibilities at age twenty-one. His first task was to diagram the electrical system within the factory buildings. The Hobart Brothers plant had undergone such rapid expansion and reorganization that the

company no longer had an accurate blueprint for its wiring and outlets. Next, Sampson was charged with reconfiguring the testing department.[33] This followed the time-honored practice established by C. C. Hobart of training employees by giving them responsibility and seeing what they could do. Summer employment after the junior year became the preferred method of scouting young engineers, primarily from Ohio State. As one senior official later put it, "If they like us and we like them, then after the senior year they are employed by Hobart Brothers Company."[34]

Hobart had assigned Sampson to those two projects because the company's construction department, fresh from building the new trade school and the motor generator factory, was now engaged in another major project, a two-story office building fronting Main Street just east of the main plant. An enclosed second-floor welded-steel walkway with a clock would arch across Adams Street to connect the plant with the new art deco office building. The building had a rectangular floor plan, and featured a small courtyard open to the sky so that offices on the inner ring had windows too. In order to obtain the certificate of necessity needed to build, defense production occupied most of the basement as well as taking over office space in the old plant.[35]

The same day Hobart Brothers announced details of the office building project it also reported that it had received another contract from the U.S. Navy for welders totaling approximately $300,000 and that it was completing delivery on the $2 million generator contract.[36] E. A.'s original unit cost estimate turned out to be off by only ninety-seven cents.[37] However, the headline story for November 27, 1941, concerned the tense negotiations underway in Washington between Japanese and American diplomats. Although the headline writer speculated "Tokyo May Answer U.S. With Attack on Thailand," at that moment a four-carrier strike force of the Imperial Navy was slicing across the Pacific to launch an attack on the U.S. naval base at Pearl Harbor ten days later.[38] Early in the afternoon of Sunday December 7 word began to crackle from radios in Troy reporting the devastating attack. America was at war.

Hobart welders repairing damaged ships at Pearl Harbor.

The next morning Americans returned to work and redoubled their efforts. Security had been a concern for some time at Hobart Brothers, but the onset of hostilities led to tighter measures. Employees had to wear metal photo I.D. buttons at work, and those with more sensitive clearances had their fingerprints on file as well.[39]

Apart from the need to increase the volume and speed of its output, wartime conditions created three special challenges for Hobart Brothers. One was to diversify its product lines to meet the needs of its military and civilian customers. The second was to learn how to pack its products so they could be safely shipped long distances to the Four Corners of the World and resist both rough handling and corrosion. A third was to design welders and generators to endure the climate extremes of a truly global conflict, from the arctic tundra to equatorial jungles.

The rapidly expanding shipyards were a prime customer for Hobart arc welders. Shipyards favored the gas-engine-driven welders, which were produced in 200-, 300-, and 400-amp models. Hobart purchased four-cylinder engines from Willys, the Toledo company that produced the Jeep, for the 200-amp model, and six- and eight-cylinder Chrysler engines to power the larger welders.[40] The massive scale on which shipyards employed these welders outdoors created their own problems. On hot summer days the muffler heat from 600 Hobart welders at the Philadelphia Naval Shipyard was cooking the gas engines' own batteries. The addition of special baffles solved the problem.[41] Welding helped create prodi-

World War II shipyard, Seattle-Tacoma Shipbuilding Corporation, 1944

Hobart welders building Liberty ships for maritime commission.

gies of shipbuilding. American shipyards launched more than 4,600 all-welded cargo ships during the war, including 2,710 10,000-ton Liberty ships, 525 T-2 tankers, and 531 of the larger, faster Victory ships. A Henry Kaiser shipyard set the record by fabricating a Liberty ship in fourteen days, fifteen hours, and thirty minutes.[42] The shipping needed to transport and supply U.S. armed forces in a two-ocean war made victory possible. Colonel Scott Ritchie of the Ordnance Department stated in a 1943 article, "Welding enters into a large percentage of more than 1,700 different weapons . . . furnished to our fighting forces."[43] Welding not only sped production rates, it also helped produce better weapons and vehicles. For example, American tanks built early in the war, like the M-2 Stuart or M-3 Grant were riveted together. In combat even artillery rounds that did not pierce their armor tended to pop rivets that ricocheted inside the tank like

Hobart auxiliary power generator using the E. A. Hobart classic canopy design, for what was known as the Holabird generators.

corn in a popper causing injury or death to the crew. America's first all-welded tank, the M-4 Sherman, became the army's mainstay battle tank.[44] During the war years Hobart Brothers spun off another subsidiary, the Welded Products Company, to manufacture defense items such as frames for the M-5 37-millimeter antiaircraft gun.[45]

The Army Quartermaster Corps at Holabird, Maryland, approached Hobart Brothers with specifications for what amounted to a mobile machine shop, a gas-engine-driven DC welder combined with an AC generator to supply power for a variety of other power tools and/or lights.[46] Soon such Hobart-built units could be found near the front lines mounted on trucks where they could be driven to stricken weapons or vehicles to make them operational once again.

Hobart Brothers produced generators used to operate 37- and 90-millimeter antiaircraft

Hobart power plants operating 90mm antiaircraft guns.

Hobart power plant used to operate 37.5mm guns

guns as well as generators to furnish power for search-lights and radar units.[47] Radar was a new technology at the time. Ohio State brought a visiting instructor to campus in the spring of 1942 to teach its initial course in radar to its graduating class of electrical engineers.[48] Great secrecy shrouded the production of the 5-kilowatt Hobart power units that trundled behind U.S. radar trucks in North Africa, Europe, and the Pacific theater.[49] The biggest generators Hobart Brothers built for the war effort were 5,000-pound 50-kilowatt units designed to provide power for an advanced base. Each unit had to be tested to determine at what distance its electrical field began to interfere with radio signals.[50]

Some trial and error was involved in learning how to pack and ship all this equipment safely. Salt water and salt spray had a particularly corrosive affect on welders and generators shipped overseas. Eventually, silica gel was used to protect moving parts inside the welders, which were then wrapped in cloth and covered in aluminum foil. Gun parts and spark plugs were dipped in rust-resistant paint or enamel and then wrapped in plastic. More daunting than the task of proper packing was the bureaucratic confusion created by a bevy of procurement agencies. Hobart Brothers produced welders and generators for the Ordnance Department, the Signal Corps, the Army Corps of Engineers, the U.S. Navy, and the Bureau of

Hobart welders were standard equipment on mobile Army machine shops.

Hobart welder in the field

Yards and Docks. Each had its own specifications and numbering system that had to be reflected in the name-plates on Hobart products. Needless trouble resulted from the fact that, although many spare parts were inter-changeable, supply officers scanning numbers in a catalog often did not realize this. Also, they tended to order the same number of each spare part, whether it was an item that rarely ever wore out or one that needed periodic replacing, like a filter or battery.[51]

The greatest engineering challenge of Hobart Brothers' wartime effort was the development of equipment, particularly generators, which could withstand great extremes of heat and cold. The military needed lightweight electrical power units that could operate in places like Greenland, the Aleutian Islands, or the Russian front as well as in the tropical rainforests of the South Pacific and the heat and dust of North Africa. Hobart built a climate-control test chamber, one of only two at the time in Ohio, which could subject machinery to temperatures ranging from -60° F to 135° F. Hobart cooperated with Chrysler and Willys to develop carburetors that could deal with temperature extremes. Hobart designed and patented special governors. Another crucial goal was to design generators with the proper acoustical shielding that ran very quietly so they would not betray the presence of a radar station or gun emplacement to the enemy.[52]

One of thousands of Hobart welders and generators going ashore in the Pacific.

Wartime expansion at Hobart Brothers
was entirely financed by private funds and loans:
from 232 employees and $1.6 million in sales in 1939
to 1,230 employees and over $22 million in sales by 1942.

Hobart facilities, 1945

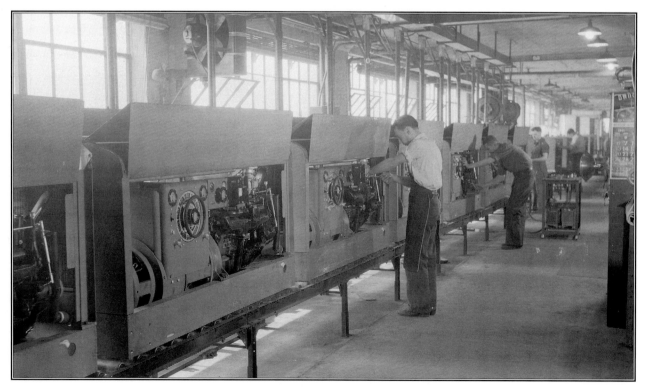

Wartime production of engine-driven welders/power plants

Hobart Main Street Plant, Coil Winding Department, 1940s

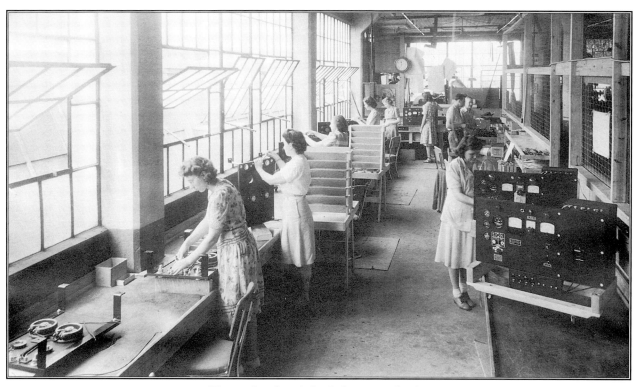

Women played a vital role in war production.

Hobart Brothers Company receives the Army-Navy "E" Award.

Except for the naval victory of Midway, little good news punctuated the first year of the war. One cause for celebration in Troy in the fall of 1942 was the announcement that Hobart Brothers had won an Army-Navy "E" Award for excellence in production. At 3 p.m. on the sunny autumnal afternoon of October 7 a crowd of four thousand gathered in front of the new Hobart Brothers office building draped in red, white, and blue bunting. Flags of all the allied nations flapped atop the building while scores of American flags were planted on the grounds in front of the company headquarters. Several other factories in Troy closed briefly to allow their employees to attend the presentation ceremony along with Hobart Brothers workers. Dayton's WING radio station broadcasted the event live and recorded it for rebroadcast in the evening.

After a color guard from Patterson Field hoisted the red, white, and blue Army-Navy "E" banner Congressman Robert E. Jones and Major Carl Rich of the Cincinnati Army Ordnance district spoke. Rich captured the imperative of making up for lost time which infused the spirit of America's war production effort against the Axis powers:

We must out-produce them, machine for machine, man for man, woman for woman, hour by hour, second by second in order to overtake this backlog of 22 years they have ahead of us.[53]

In his remarks, E. A. Hobart gave credit to the older employees of his company who had taken in and trained over a thousand new men and women and made it possible to increase production tenfold over the past 18 months. "Our production schedules for the next 12 months call for almost double the amount of our present output, which means more ships, more guns, more tanks—quickly!"[54]

Lieutenant Commander R. L. Macy of the Navy Bureau of Aeronautics then presented "E" lapel pins to Lowell Arthur and Bessie Oakes, the male and female

"E" lapel pin

employees with the most years of service at the company. Both Oakes and Arthur, a World War I veteran, spoke expressing their enthusiastic commitment to more production. The whole crowd sang "The Star-Spangled Banner" and "America" to conclude the brisk ceremony that took just half an hour. Putting words into practice, employees returned "immediately afterwards to their machines and work benches. . . ."[55]

Hobart Brothers was one of several Troy industries engaged in war production. Hobart Manufacturing subcontracted generators and antiaircraft gun parts from Hobart Brothers as well as producing telescope mounts and servo units for artillery in addition to the food service equipment it had supplied the military for years.[56] Later, it too became an "E" award recipient. WACO designed and built two thousand gliders for the Army's three airborne divisions.[57] Other manufacturers around the country built thousands more under license, for the wooden gliders rarely survived a combat landing intact enough for reuse. These three companies combined forces with five other Troy defense contractors to pay for a full-page ad each week in the *Troy Daily News* to promote the war effort. Most of these ads urged citizens to "back the attack" by buying war bonds, while others encouraged people to contribute to paper drives and other efforts to conserve raw materials.[58] One of the grimmest ads displayed the photos of thirty-two Trojans killed in combat as of August 1944 along with the reminder that over five thousand men and women from Miami County were currently in the service.[59]

WACO built two thousand gliders for the war effort. (Photo courtesy Richard Graef of the WACO Historical Society)

Chief instructor Bob Bercaw instructs a class of women during World War II.

By 1944 the military's need for manpower and industry's need for labor began to strain the nation's human resources. Women had taken up much of the slack, and "Rosie the Riveter" had her counterpart in "Wanda the Welder," but by December 1944 the shortage of skilled labor had grown so great that forty-seven hundred soldiers "with the necessary skills" were actually furloughed to work in war industries through April 1945.[60] Training

hundreds of new Hobart Brothers employees whose only work experience had been on a farm, in a kitchen, or in a high school classroom to safely handle production machinery and electrical equipment required the undivided attention of the trade school instructors, supervisory staff and veteran workers who did the teaching. Apart from those trained in Troy, Hobart personnel traveled around the country training hundreds of military and civilian service crews how to keep the generators and welders running. "You had one week to keep them from getting killed."[61]

Government policy alternately helped and hindered the efforts of E. A. and W. H. to manage their company in a manner that was both rational and profitable. In 1943 the federal government authorized Hobart Brothers to take over the Miami Specialties Company, an old Troy firm that manufactured frames and trailers, truck canopies, and automotive chassis because its entire production capacity was required for the wheeled hauling frames that made gas-driven welders and generators mobile.[62] On the negative side, federal procurement officials had the right to renegotiate "pricing adjustments" in their defense contracts to reflect changes in the cost and availability of labor and key commodities and assure fair payment for contractors in all regions of the country. Most adjustments tended to be down rather than up.[63] While this undoubtedly saved taxpayers money and ensured "more bang for the buck," it often sliced heavily into the expected profits of war industries. For example, in 1942 renegotiation cut gross sales for the Motor Generator Corporation from just over $4.6 million to $3.9 million, lowering profits by $120,000.[64] Therefore, a Hobart Brothers 300-amp gas-engine-driven welder sold for $995 in 1942, whereas a comparable but less advanced 1934 model had been priced at $1,400 in the midst of the Depression.[65] High wartime tax rates including a special tax on excess profits ensured that a large chunk of corporate earnings were funneled back to Washington, and, beginning in 1943, all working Americans saw payroll deductions taken directly from their wages and salaries.[66] Despite these obstacles, there was money to be made, but the widely held view that any company engaged in war work could simply muddle along and still rake in huge profits was a myth.

The physical challenge of long hours and multiple shifts competed with the concerns of recruiting, training, and accounting. During the war years it was not unusual to see managers and foremen at Hobart Brothers stretched out on couches set up in hallways and break rooms of the office building and factories. When crucial deadlines neared, key personnel would virtually take up residence on site heading home Saturday night to spend an exhausted Sunday with their families.[67] If an equipment problem occurred or a bottleneck in supplies developed, Byron Lutz in purchasing secured priority tickets on the crowded railroads. Sometimes even a four-star general could not have bumped a Hobart troubleshooter.[68] After several years of working up to eighty hours a week, Marion Centliver, a member of E. A.'s "skunk

Atop the Hobart factory building, Rachel Cahill Hobart is one of the volunteers searching the sky for enemy aircraft from the lookout post.

works" team who had built the prototype for the generator contract, was down to 118 pounds. His doctor told him, "Get out of it for a while or you won't last."[69]

The philosophy at Hobart Brothers for maintaining morale combined fair wages and working conditions with an effort to keep employees informed about the impact of their work on the war effort. The War Labor Board and the Fair Employment Practices Commission, established to enforce FDR's executive order prohibiting racial discrimination in hiring for defense work, heard no complaints against Hobart Brothers.[70] On D-Day, June 6, 1944, news bulletins on the Allied invasion of France were relayed to employees throughout the day over the plant's public address system.[71] Thereafter, the company continued the practice whenever major events occurred in the war. Part of the success of the D-Day invasion and the bitter fighting for Normandy was attributed to the tanks of British General Percy Hobart's Seventy-ninth Armored Division. Hobart had modified his tanks, nicknamed "funnies," to land amphibiously, clear minefields, throw flames, and rip through the underbrush of the Norman hedgerows.[72]

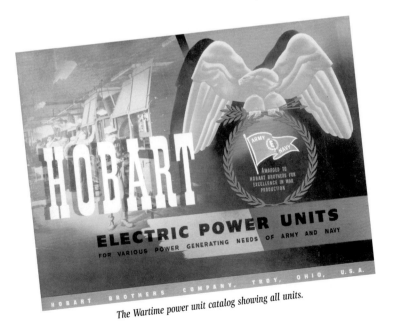

The Wartime power unit catalog showing all units.

❦

World War II marked a proud achievement for everyone at Hobart Brothers and a turning point in the history of the company.

❦

On May 8, 1945, Hobart employees listened to President Truman's live broadcast announcing Germany's surrender. Factories blew their whistles and churches rang their bells, but reactions were restrained. Workers were told they could take the rest of the day off, but most chose to stay on the job.[73] One sign of normalcy returned to Troy five days later when the City Council voted to go off War Time and return to "slow" or Eastern Standard Time.[74] The first report that the United States had dropped an atomic bomb on the Japanese city of Hiroshima did not make the top headline in Troy. Only two days later did the scope of destruction and the significance of the new weapon become clear. Upon news that a second bomb had been dropped on Nagasaki, rumors that the war would soon end ran rampant.[75] When the Japanese surrender was finally announced at 6 p.m. Tuesday, August 14, Troy "cut loose." People rushed out into the warm evening and began honking their car horns to add to the pealing of church bells. Many headed downtown to Public Square which soon became packed with cars that circled the square in slow motion, crammed with people laughing and waving and blaring their horns.[76] C. C. Hobart would have been proud to learn that Troy City Council had prepared for this celebration the previous fall by passing an ordinance that suspended all liquor sales for twenty-four hours from the moment victory was declared.[77]

World War II marked a proud achievement for everyone at Hobart Brothers and a turning point in the history of the company. A small Ohio manufacturer of welders and battery chargers had transformed itself into a key defense contractor with a national market and international name recognition, thanks to lend-lease exports and military use of its equipment in regions across the world. It had produced over one hundred thousand welders and fifty thousand generators along with many tons of electrodes during the war years. Employment had sextupled and gross sales had jumped from less than two million into the tens of millions.[78] However, E. A. and W. H. Hobart recognized the challenges they would face in the postwar transition. As early as April 1943 W. H. had ordered a report projecting market changes and sales policies for after the war.[79] Scores of Hobart employees were returning home from the service at the same time the government was canceling billions of dollars in defense contracts every week. The next few years would require the same foresight and imagination Hobart management had displayed in meeting the challenge of war.

From Where the Bugles Blow!
News From Former Weldors Now Serving in the Armed Forces

HOBART WELDERS IN ACTION OVERSEAS

Weldors of the 36th Naval Construction Battalion (CB's) with One of their Hobart Gas Engine Drive Arc Welders

Dear Sir:

We, the weldors of the 36th Naval Construction Battalion, thought you would be interested to know that we have used Hobart Arc Welders back in the States and are now using your welders overseas. Would like to have you publish the picture in your *Arc Welding News*, some of our former buddies may recognize us. Reading from left to right, the weldors are – M. J. Loebig, Iowa; J. W. Pollard, Michigan; "Slim" Gesduel, California; J. C. Raef, Indiana; H. A. McCalley, Texas; J. Berger, Texas.

Keep sending Hobart *Arc Welding News* to us!

M. J. Loebig, S/P 1st Class U.S.N.R., 36th Naval Const. Batt.
C/o Navy Fleet Post Office, San Fransisco, California

The same day the war ended word also reached Troy that two Trojans had been reported missing in action in the sinking of the U.S.S. *Indianapolis*. One of the two men, Gunner's Mate David C. Metcalf, age thirty, was a former Hobart Brothers employee.[80] Ironically, the heavy cruiser *Indianapolis* had just completed its mission delivering the Hiroshima atomic bomb to a B-29 base on the island of Tinian when it was torpedoed. The deaths of Metcalf and his fellow sailors were a sobering reminder of the real costs of war.

CHAPTER 13

Civic Pride Renews the Face of Troy

One reason why America was isolated and unprepared for World War II was the belief that greedy munitions makers had pushed the country into the First World War. Although that belief was mistaken, E. A. and W. H. Hobart were sensitive to possible charges of war profiteering and gathered an array of statistics detailing how the dramatic wartime expansion of Hobart Brothers had been financed entirely with private funds.[1] At the same time they were frustrated by the combination of renegotiation and high income taxes that sent most locally earned profits to Washington. For some time they had been depositing funds in the Troy Foundation, which had been established in 1924 by Augustus Stouder, longtime president of Hobart Manufacturing and their father's former partner. In the fall of 1942 Hobart attorney L. H. Shipman Sr. suggested, "Why not operate a foundation of your own?"[2]

Ever since C. C. Hobart had died in 1932 all three Hobart brothers had talked about doing something in their father's memory that would express his deep gratitude to the whole Troy community for the opportunity it had given him. They heartily endorsed the idea of a foundation in the name of C. C. Hobart and asked Shipman to draw up the articles of incorporation. On December 8, 1942, the State of Ohio recognized the C. C. Hobart Foundation established to collect and disperse funds "for charitable, benevolent, philanthropic, and/or educational purposes, so long as such purposes are of public character. . . ."[3] The IRS granted the foundation tax exempt status in November 1943.[4] Between the money the Troy Foundation allowed the Hobarts to transfer and the funds deposited during the last two years of the war, the C. C. Hobart Foundation was off to a substantial start.[5]

As early as the summer of 1945, with the war effort beginning to wind down, E. A. had William Van Ausdal, head of the company's construction division, begin to

C. C. Hobart for whom the foundation was named, circa 1930

sketch out plans for an indoor sports arena for Troy. Both E. A. and W. H. had been impressed when they visited the winter sports arena in Hershey, Pennsylvania. Built in 1936 with funds from the Hershey Company, a chocolate maker, the beautiful facility was well-managed and hosted the kind of sporting and entertainment events that drew a regional audience and made it an economic success.[6] Knowing Troy was larger than Hershey and Dayton, the nearest urban center, was larger than Harrisburg, Pennsylvania, the Hobart brothers believed the same kind of arena could prove successful here.

A public project sidelined their efforts for a time. Ohio had passed a law that permitted local communities to levy a property tax for up to one mill for up to ten years in order to build a monument or facility as a war memorial. However, the law required a 65 percent majority vote in order to pass such a levy. Miami County commissioners decided to put an issue on the November 1946 ballot asking for the maximum allowed in order to erect a memorial building on the Miami County Fairground just north of Troy. The facility would include a five-thousand-seat auditorium and gym, banquet facilities for up to one thousand and offices for the use of community organizations and veterans.[7] Except for Troy itself, support for the memorial proved tepid, and the issue fell short of even a simple majority by more than three hundred votes.[8]

"It was our thought, after seeing the results of the election," wrote E. A., "that we could do better than that. . . ."[9] Three weeks after the levy failed E. A. and W. H. launched a three-day blitz to present their proposal for a comprehensive park and recreational plan for the city of Troy. On day one E. A. spoke before the Young Business Men's Club and outlined plans for a seven-thousand-seat all-welded-steel memorial football stadium with modern amenities and extensive parking to be erected on the

The bold vision for the citizens of Troy

grounds of the current nine-hole municipal golf course across the Miami River north of downtown Troy.[10] Day two the Rotary Club heard details on the projected new eighteen-hole municipal golf course to be built just downriver of the present course on land currently owned by the Miami Conservancy District.[11] Finally, before the Kiwanis Club on day three E. A. rolled out the centerpiece of the ambitious project, a five-thousand-seat winter sports arena whose construction would be entirely financed by the C. C. Hobart Foundation. The plan also called for the construction of tennis courts and converting the grounds of the current football stadium into baseball and softball fields. As could be expected with any Hobart Brothers project, the presentations were illustrated with detailed floor plans and drawings of the proposed facilities. Financing the public portion of the plan would require a twenty-year one-mill levy.[12]

Enthusiasm for the proposal was immediate.[13] The bold vision of the recreational plan provided a needed shot in the arm for Troy in the wake of the levy defeat and the economic difficulties of converting to a peacetime economy. The whole week of the plan's announcement Ohio was hit by partial blackouts due to an ongoing coal miners' strike.[14] Lending credence to the new proposal was a recreation project for Hobart Brothers employees already nearing completion. The company had purchased a sixteen-acre

tact of land along a bend of the river where it shifted course from south to southeast just north of Troy. Van Ausdal's crew dug a channel to form a lagoon leading to a two-story boathouse with facilities for launching, storing, and servicing boats.[15] Reminiscent of a concept for the steel homes, the flat roof of the boathouse would be decked out in Japanese lanterns and used for evening parties in the summer.[16] A footbridge connected the boathouse to "Treasure Island" where picnic facilities and a lighted baseball diamond were built. Welfare, Incorporated, an employee-run operation funded by profits from Hobart Brothers company cafeterias, snack carts, and vending machines ran the boathouse and Treasure Island and used the facilities for picnics, parties, and dances.[17]

All three Hobart boys had spent much of their boyhood on or along the river, swimming, fishing, and boating in the summer, ice skating in the winter. In one sense, the recreational plan represented an effort to share with the community the idyllic athletic and social activities that had enriched their youth. It also reflected two broader trends, one national and one regional: the desire to enjoy life after the sacrifices demanded by depression and war and a turn back to the rivers of the Miami Valley three decades after the devastating flood of 1913. Much of the land needed for the proposal was owned by the Miami Conservancy District, which had constructed a series of dams and levees

The Boathouse, circa 1950

and prohibited most business and residential development adjoining the rivers. Arthur Morgan, the chief engineer who designed the flood control system, and E. A. Hobart were both members of the Dayton Engineer's Club. Morgan now had nearly thirty years of records showing how superbly the network of dams had tamed the rivers and knew that much conservancy land was safe for recreational development.[18] E. A., an eye-witness to the danger and the potential of the rivers, was appointed to be one of the three directors of the Miami Conservancy District.[19]

The Troy City Council and the same coalition of businesses that had promoted the local war effort rallied behind the comprehensive recreational plan, urging Trojans to vote yes on the special bond issue needed to fund it.[20] The decision of the C. C. Hobart Foundation to donate an ice arena served as a catalyst for other individuals and groups to contribute to the cause. An anonymous donor secured the services of noted golf course architect Donald Ross to design the new Troy course to rival the ones he had laid out in Dayton and Columbus.[21] Orval Menke donated a removable basketball floor, while other Trojans provided shatterproof backboards, an electrical scoreboard, and other equipment to outfit the proposed arena.[22] The groundswell of support led to an overwhelming victory at the polls. On March 4, 1947, the bond issue won 3,519 to 466. The 88.3 percent approval rate marked the highest favorable vote Trojans had ever given a ballot issue.[23]

The positive response of the community was most gratifying to E. A., W. H., and everyone connected with the project from the beginning. A series of groundbreakings punctuated 1947 and 1948 as the construction of each facility got underway. Trojans watched with pride as their new recreational centers began to take shape. The facilities not only held bright promise for the future, they also provided a real and much-appreciated immediate benefit—returning veterans could find jobs in Troy.

As the breakneck pace of wartime production slowed in 1945, the Hobart brothers found time to reflect on the past as well as to plan for the future. They began to compile information for a small book on the C. C. Hobart

E. A. Hobart's first all-welded-stainless "submarine" at the boathouse

94

Foundation which was the first attempt to tell the story of the industrial Hobarts. Their uncle, the Reverend Alvah Hobart, had already composed a family genealogy tracing Hobart history in America back to 1633. E. A. and W. H. returned to Middletown and poked around the sites of old paper mills hoping to recover one of their father's early generators. They found the home C. C. had built and his second factory still standing, but any remaining generators had probably been scrapped during the war.[24] Their efforts produced an illustrated thirty-five-page hardbound booklet that described the C. C. Hobart Foundation and the three Troy companies their father had founded, Hobart Manufacturing, Hobart Brothers, and Hobart Cabinet.[25]

The project to build a boathouse and lagoon involved the Hobarts in a broader perspective researching the history of Troy itself. In order to dig a channel for the lagoon workers had to move a huge boulder known as "Trojan Rock," reputed to be the 1797 landing spot where John Knoop led a surveying team who were the first whites to see the area.[26] The following spring Knoop, his brother Benjamin, Henry Garard, Benjamin Hamlet, and John Tilders returned with their families to establish a settlement.[27] With the approach of Troy's sesquicentennial in 1948, E. A. and W. H. decided to put together a book celebrating Troy's history. Finally published in 1950, *Troy of Yesterday, Today, and Tomorrow* represented the combined efforts of twenty-three Trojans, the historical societies of Troy and Miami County, and the Public Relations Department of Hobart Brothers Company. It contained a chronologically arranged collection of photographs, illustrations, and text about people, events, institutions, and businesses from Troy's history as well as plans and sketches for future facilities.

In the course of their research, E. A. and W. H. became convinced that Overfield Tavern, the most prominent building in the early history of Troy, was still standing at the northeast corner of Water and Mulberry Streets. They

The Overfield Tavern

believed that hidden beneath a sheathing of outdoor siding and plastered inner walls were the squared off hand-hewn logs of a two-story tavern built in 1808 by Benjamin Overfield. Ever the hands-on engineer who preferred to test any hypothesis himself, E. A. took a detour past the suspected historic site on his drive home from work each night. One dusky evening he noticed the residents were away so he parked, grabbed a brace and bit he kept in the car, hopped out and walked up to the house. He drilled a small hole through the siding and struck solid wood, maybe a stud. He moved a foot to the side and drilled another hole—again, solid wood. One more time in another spot, his drill chewed through the siding—solid wood again. Excited, he immediately went to tell W. H. the good news. Soon after the brothers purchased the home from the owner and ". . . could hardly wait for the ink to dry on the sales contract before they took off for the building with crowbars in hand to tear off some of the siding."[28]

The Hobarts had in fact rediscovered the Overfield Tavern where Benjamin Overfield had fed and provided overnight lodging to many a guest between 1808 and his death in 1831. As the largest dwelling in Troy, the tavern had also served as a temporary courthouse until 1811 and as a jail for a while after that. Among its more famous guests the tavern counted Arthur St. Clair, former Revolutionary War general and first governor of the Northwest Territory, and General William Henry Harrison, victor at the Battle of Tippecanoe and later the ninth president of the United States. The Overfield family sold the home in 1834, and, through many resales and remodelings as a private residence, the building's origins were forgotten. In 1949 the C. C. Hobart Foundation formally began the task of restoring the tavern and transforming it into Troy's first historical museum. E. A. supervised restoration of the outside of the tavern while W. H. oversaw restoration of its interior. It became the headquarters of the Troy Historical Society and was used to display the local artifacts collected

The Hobart Arena on the Great Miami River

by W. H., E. A., and other Trojans. In 1966 the Historical Society opened Overfield Tavern to the general public, while the Hobart Foundation retained ownership and responsibility for its upkeep.[29]

While engaged in restoring a home from the past, the Hobarts returned to their prewar project of providing homes for the future in Troy. All over America housing development had been curtailed by the need to divert materials and manpower to war production. Huge population shifts had occurred during the war. These factors coupled with returning veterans who were marrying and beginning families created an unprecedented demand for new housing. In 1945 they began to plat out a large development north of Main Street and west of Ridge Avenue, which they named Westbrook after a small stream that flowed through the area before emptying into the Great Miami River. In contrast to Hobart Circle and Edgehill, modest developments built in the 1930s that totaled thirty-four acres and 116 homes, Westbrook contained three hundred acres and would eventually hold 1,000 homes.[30]

On the eastern edge of Westbrook E. A. and W. H. set aside a large tract of land just west of a rail line as an industrial park for the future expansion of Hobart Brothers Company. The streets immediately west of the

future industrial park were slated to become tree-lined boulevards to create a greenbelt between industrial and residential properties. This planning reflected the garden communities the Hobarts had admired on their trips to England in the 1930s.[31] W. H. acknowledged this connection by bestowing English place names, like Dorset, Sussex, and Chelsea, on all the new residential streets in Westbrook. Here, Troy Land Improvement, instead of constructing homes itself as it had done with the steel homes in the 1930s, sold lots to individual home buyers who then contracted with a builder. This provided Westbrook with a diversity of styles and models in contrast to the cookie cutter sameness of some housing developments of the era. The area south of Westbrook on the opposite side of Main Street was developed as the Southbrook Shopping Center, now known as the Trojan Village.

As the 1940s drew to a close the first two pieces of Troy's comprehensive recreational plan reached completion. About 150 local golfers tested the new eighteen-hole Miami Shores municipal course on Saturday April 22, 1949, when it opened for play. Formal dedication of the course and clubhouse followed in August. In September of the same year the ten-thousand-seat welded-steel Memorial Stadium opened with a special pre-season scrimmage fea-

The Hobart Arena under construction

Basketball at the Hobart Arena, circa 1950

turing high school football teams from Troy, Piqua, Sidney, and Greenville.[32] Thereafter the stadium served as the impressive home turf of the Troy Trojans.

By the end of January 1950 Van Ausdal's construction crews had completed enough of the winter sports arena to host basketball games. Eager sports fans packed the six-thousand-seat arena on February 2 to see the new facility and formed the largest crowd to date to watch a regular season high school basketball game in Ohio. A majority of area Class A schools voted to hold the district tournament at the new Hobart Arena instead of the old Fairgrounds Coliseum in Dayton. Attendance at the tourney topped twenty-two thousand. Shortly after the final whistle sounded, work-

ers began laying nearly eleven miles of pipe needed to freeze the surface for ice skating. Laying the concrete surface above the pipes was a delicate operation that required a twenty-four-hour continuous pouring.[33]

That following summer the board of park commissioners signed a two-year renewable contract with Pat Thurkettle to bring "top-flight entertainment" to the arena in exchange for a weekly rental fee and 20 percent of the gross receipts from concessions. Thurkettle agreed to leave open the dates for Troy's home basketball games as well as the county and district tournaments. He secured a performance by Holiday on Ice for Hobart Arena's grand opening and dedication on September 7, 1950.[34]

Southbrook Shopping Center

W. H. and E. A. Hobart present the "key" to Hobart Arena to Mayor Kerr of the City of Troy.

Troy Daily News *got peppered with ads.*

Edward, William, and Charles Hobart skating at the opening ceremony of the Hobart Arena, 1950.

unique event in sports history, professional hockey's only two-site doubleheader. The Bruins shut out their arch rivals, the Cincinnati Mohawks, 3-0 in an afternoon match in Troy and then lost the nightcap in Cincinnati 5-3. In the off-season several hockey players found work at Hobart Brothers and a few, like former goalie Guy Leclerc, enjoyed a long career in the company.[38] The Troy Skating Club, founded in 1954, nurtured eight professional skaters and several international skating judges and officials. Two future U.S. Olympians trained at Hobart Arena, including Peter Oppegard who along with partner Jill Watson won a bronze medal in pairs skating at the 1988 Olympics in Calgary.[39]

Eventually, bigger newer facilities in nearby Dayton drew the headline entertainers and professional hockey teams toward their larger market, but the arena and the comprehensive recreational plan of which it was a part remained valuable resources for the Miami Valley, resources nearly unmatched for a city of Troy's size. The bold vision E. A. and W. H. Hobart presented to Troy in the fall of 1946 not only changed the face of Troy but improved its quality of life and rewarded its citizens for their hard work in overcoming the challenges of war and depression. ❧

Charles, the middle Hobart son, had to feel left out of the hoopla while the *Troy Daily News* got peppered with ads from both individuals and businesses thanking "Ed and Bill Hobart" for the gift of the arena and a local Boy Scout troops collected over forty-five-hundred signatures of Troy residents who wished to extend the same thanks. However, on the arena's opening night all three Hobart boys strapped on skates and took a spin across the fresh unmarked ice in front of the huge opening night crowd. They had come a long way in the half-century since they had first skated across the frozen Great Miami River in Troy. In memory of their father C. C. Hobart, E. A. officially handed over the building to the citizens of Troy by giving Mayor Paul W. Kerr a huge golden key.[35]

At the time of its dedication Hobart Arena was one of the finest winter sports facilities in America, ranking eleventh in size between arenas in Providence and Pittsburgh.[36] For many years it would be the top indoor arena for sports and entertainment within a wide area bounded by Toledo, Columbus, Cincinnati, and Indianapolis. Entertainers like Gene Autry, Victor Borge, Ray Charles, the Harlem Globetrotters, Roy Rogers and Dale Evans, and Elvis Presley drew large crowds from the whole region.[37] For seven seasons in the 1950s, the International Hockey League's Troy Bruins, an independent farm team for the NHL, made Hobart Arena its home. On January 25, 1953, the Troy Bruins took part in a

The Hobart Arena was renovated in 2001 through the efforts of Robert and Lucia Bravo.

CHAPTER 14

A Third Generation Joins the Company

"Be at your best." That was the personal motto of Rachel Cahill Hobart. As a precept for herself and for her children it was a much more ambitious goal than to simply do one's best. Though short and petite, Rachel was a strong-willed woman who took an active role in the Troy community as soon as she came to town as Mrs. W. H. Hobart in the fall of 1919. In addition to joining the Altrurian Club, where her mother-in-law Lou Ella was a longtime member, she was one of the founding organizers of the Miami County Women's League of Voters and also helped begin the Girl Scouts in Troy.[1] As she grew older Rachel Hobart's ankles gave her trouble, but that did not hamper her mobility because she did her own driving. Peter Jenkins, a childhood friend of her youngest son Peter, recalled the petite Mrs. Hobart dressed in a floppy wide-brimmed hat climbing behind the wheel of a traditional long black Cadillac to drive him and Peter up to William Sr.'s farm north of town at breakneck speed. He wondered how she could see over the hood.[2] However, Rachel Hobart focused most of her considerable energy on her roles as a wife and mother.

Rachel saw herself as a homemaker not a housewife, and as a progressive homemaker she prided herself on setting high standards. Despite their college educations, W. H. and his two brothers remained true to their roots, more at home tinkering in a lab or outdoors or on an athletic field than in a drawing room. Their wives tackled the job of adding a level of polish and sophistication.[3] Rachel did not share her husband's taste for popular music. She insisted that her children receive formal lessons and an emphasis on the classics. Rachel fostered an appreciation for all the arts and encouraged her children to become patrons of the arts, "the Medici of the Miami Valley" as she often quipped. Although W. H's parents were Baptists and Rachel had been raised as a Methodist, the young married couple began attending the Episcopal Church in Troy in the late 1920's after both Rachel and her son William had pulled through serious illnesses and the death of a fourth child named Philip shortly after his birth.[4]

Rachel and W. H. shared a love for reading, entertaining, and travel. They read the latest books on a variety of topics as well as countless magazines, were excellent hosts, and traveled widely with their children. Favorite places to visit included Sea Island, Georgia in the spring, and in the summer Higgins Lake, Michigan, Saratoga Springs, New York, and the Greenbrier resort in West Virginia. In the summer of 1934 W. H. and Rachel, who was expecting their fifth child, took ten-year-old William Jr. along on their first trip to Europe. W. H., whose hobbies included antiques, gardening, and photography, loved Europe and brought his daughters Marcia and Lucia there the following summer while Rachel stayed home with the baby, Peter Cahill, who had been born in December 1934.[5]

W. H. and Rachel entertained often and tried to make each visit to their home on Plum St. an elegant occasion to be remembered. Although they had domestic help, both enjoyed cooking and W. H. was an adept mixologist. Dinners were both hearty and delectable. Some nights there would be dancing in the third-floor ballroom or the traditional game of bridge.[6]

Rachel read to her children often and took a keen interest in their education. All four children had their elementary education at Troy's public schools where their father was elected to several terms on the school board. Rachel visited several different prep schools in the east with her daughters before choosing Westover in Waterbury, Connecticut, for Marcia and Miss Hall's in Pittsfield, Massachusetts, for Lucia. For a while Marcia had dreams of attending a photography school in Chicago and becoming a photojournalist like Margaret Bourke-White, but her father considered photography a fine hobby for a woman but not a proper career. Instead she continued her studies at Pine Manor Junior College after a poor score on a French test kept her from entering Smith, her mother's alma mater.[7] Marcia had a keen interest in Hobart Brothers. W. H. sometimes showed Wib Chaffee letters from his daughter that criticized members of his staff as "old fogeys." "Isn't it too bad she isn't a boy?" W. H. would remark.[8]

Tall and athletic, Marcia enjoyed her time at Pine Manor and became a champion golfer. In 1939 she began dating Bill Howell, a business student at Ohio State who was working during the summer for Hobart Manufacturing. Howell, a handsome barrel-chested man with a deep voice, was a swimmer on the Ohio State 400-meter freestyle relay team which won the 1939 NCAA Championship.[9] He graduated from OSU in 1940 with a bachelor's degree in social administration and went to work full time in sales for Hobart Manufacturing.[10] Though an only child raised in Hamilton, Ohio, William Busser Howell already had a connection to the Troy area. His maternal grandfather owned a business in Piqua.[11] Shortly after Howell gave Marcia his Beta Theta Pi fraternity ring, she decided to force the issue by asking Howell when he wanted to have the wedding. The couple married August 2, 1941, in Troy and honeymooned in Walloon Lake, Michigan.[12]

Bill Howell was an extrovert. With his gregariousness and domineering personality, he naturally gravitated toward sales.[13] After his marriage he left Hobart Manufacturing for Hobart Brothers. Being an OSU alumnus gave Howell an immediate connection with E. A. and the other Buckeye grads in the company. Following three wartime years in the Navy, mostly at the Naval Shipyard near Seattle, Howell returned to Hobart Brothers and worked under Dick Sherwood.[14] After lucrative government contracts dried up with the end of the war, Howell found that Hobart Brothers sales were overly dependent upon mail order and set to work with extensive travels to build a strong national network of distributors.

Marcia provided a counterbalance to her husband's impulsive nature. Although she did not play a direct role in the company, Marcia helped her husband by serving as a gracious hostess to many visiting customers, salesmen and vendors. The couple struck up lasting friendships with other couples from distributors and customers around the country, interweaving their work and social lives as was common for their generation. Lucia, their first child was born in December 1943 and four more followed in the next seventeen years. During that time Marcia stayed with her children at home, but, once they were older, she accompanied her husband on many sales trips, conventions, and welding shows.[15] She also became the first woman appointed to the Board of the C. C. Hobart Foundation.[16]

Lucia Hobart was an excellent student and intellectual who attended Smith College as had her mother. She chose to major in sociology at Smith because that field encompassed so many other subjects and examined how they interacted in the real world.[17] While at Smith, Lucia met Robert Barrett Bravo, who was a student at nearby Amherst College. Bravo had attended Sidwell Friends prep school in Washington, D.C., where his father held several appointed positions in Franklin Roosevelt's administration. After graduating from Amherst, Bravo joined the Naval Reserve and trained to become a pilot in Squantum, Massachusetts.[18] He was sent to Pensacola, Florida, where he learned to fly PBY "Catalinas." The Catalina was a graceful-looking but lumbering two-engine flying boat that carried a crew of four or five men. With a range of over two thousand miles, its primary missions were reconnaissance and air-sea rescue.[19] Lucia and Robert got engaged in the summer of 1943 and married the following January shortly after Lucia graduated from Smith. With his tall stature, dark hair, and high forehead, Bravo cut a dashing figure in his ensign's uniform.

The young couple spent the next several months in Kokomo, Indiana, where Bravo served as a flight instructor. Then he was sent to a naval air station on the West Coast near Oak Harbor, Washington, on Whidby Island which guarded the entrance to Puget Sound. Lucia found the medical facilities on the island a bit primitive and returned to Troy to give birth to their first daughter, Hylton on July 1, 1945. Bravo managed to obtain leave to see his new baby and just four months later received his discharge from the Navy. Bravo's education and life experience sparked a great interest in international affairs and he went to Washington, D.C., to seek a job as a diplomat for the State Department. Unfortunately, the State Department was awash with job applications, most from former military men. He was told that what the department really needed was people with business experience and that perhaps he could try again after he had acquired some.[20]

Lucia and Bravo returned to Troy where Lucia's father was delighted to welcome Bravo into Hobart Brothers. W. H. put Bravo on a series of two-month rotations that gave him experience working with each division of the company before settling into a job in sales.[21] Soon Bravo's experience as a pilot and his interest in international affairs would prove to be valuable assets for the company.

William Jr. attended Troy City Schools through his sophomore year of high school. During the summers young William continued his education at Hobart Brothers by learning to weld, working in the factory, and stuffing envelopes with direct mail ads for his father. He and his parents visited different prep schools in the East before his parents chose Hotchkiss, located in Lakeville, Connecticut, in the northwest corner of the state. Hotchkiss was an all-male boarding school with a traditional English approach to education. Hotchkiss had been established to prepare students for Yale, and that is where William moved on to college in the summer of 1943.[22]

Before leaving for Yale, William and his father took a car trip together and drove up to the Gaspe' peninsula in Quebec. Knowing the draft would likely cut short his college career, William Jr. resolved to try and enter the Navy, but, just like his father during the First World War, he ended up in the Army instead. The war effort had kicked into high gear by the summer of 1943 and dominated even the ivied grounds of Yale. Captain Glenn Miller was encamped there with his Army Air Corps band.

The Army in its inscrutable wisdom sent William to an Infantry Replacement Training Center (IRTC) and assigned him to a heavy weapons company, where he spent his days lugging around machine guns or mortars. Within a short time toting these heavy weights injured a nerve in his arm and he was reassigned to Atlanta to train as a medical technician.[23] The injury may have saved his life. Infantry replacements in World War II were moved to the front lines in one's and two's to fill out units that had suffered heavy casualties. Surrounded by strangers instead of boot camp buddies, they were more likely to become casualties themselves.[24] One of William's good friends from his IRTC was killed immediately upon landing by a land mine at Anzio.

For the rest of the war William served as a medical technician at Northington General Hospital in Tuscaloosa, Alabama, where he did lab procedures and also worked directly with quadriplegics, paraplegics, and psychological cases suffering from what was then called "battle fatigue." The experience made him seriously consider a career in medicine. Above all, the time he spent in the Army gave him a deeper appreciation for the values instilled by his parents, to live by the Golden Rule, to treat everyone the same. He met many good people in the Army, men who had grown up in places and circumstances as far removed from his own as he could imagine. The people William Jr. met in the Army reaffirmed what his father had told him about never prejudging anyone, "Let people show what they can do."[26]

William returned to Yale in the fall of 1946 as an economics business major. He joined the Trumbull Residential College and lived in its gray granite English Gothic cloister patterned after King's College Cambridge and played on its squash team among a number of other activities. One of the organizations William joined while at Yale was the Dixwell Group, composed of New Haven residents and Yale students working to improve race relations, which were in ferment all over America following the war.[27] Determined to make up for lost time, William accelerated and completed his bachelor's degree in March 1950 in order to move on to Penn's Wharton School of Business to earn a master's in business administration by June of 1951. He completed six years of school in four and a half years in order to begin again at Hobart Brothers.[28]

William Jr. returned to Troy where he was given a variety of financial projects by his father and then assigned to the Advertising Department. One interesting job involved putting together promotional films for two of Hobart Brothers'

newest operations: supplying ground power units for aircraft and mining operations in Florida to secure rutile for coating electrodes. E. A. and W. H. allowed W. H.'s sons and sons-in-law to follow their own interests once they joined the company rather than try to groom them for a particular job.[29] William Jr.'s talents led him in the direction of administration and finance. By 1954 he had been named assistant secretary-treasurer of Hobart Brothers.[30]

Socially, William Jr. found that many of his friends in Troy had married or moved away during his time in the service and while away at college. Therefore, he started to go to Dayton where he made some new friends. After several years he met an attractive young lady named Julia DeCamp at a dance. She was home on break from Tufts University. William knew after he drove her home that night that she was "special." He proposed just three months after they met.[31] The couple married at Christ Episcopal Church in Dayton on March 10, 1956.

Serving as best man at his brother's wedding was twenty-one-year-old Peter Hobart, a junior at Yale. Ten years younger than William and the same age as his new wife Julia, Peter had grown up pretty much as an only child. Like his father and uncles before him, Peter too played on the frozen Miami River with his friends, but the manner of play and equipment used showed how much times had changed. With wartime gas rationing now just a memory, Peter and his friends drove and spun Army surplus jeeps on the frozen river.

After his freshman year at Troy High School, Peter took a summer school session at Hotchkiss so that he could enter the prep school that fall. He found the headmaster who also taught religions to be a bit stern and haughty, but he discovered an affinity in himself for learning foreign languages. In the summer of 1952 between his junior and senior years he and his brother and parents took an ocean liner to Europe, a regular family event every two years in the tradition of the "grand tour." In England and on the continent they rented cars and toured many of the most famous sights that lay west of what people already called the Iron Curtain. Peter was fascinated by the variety of language, culture, and art and the weight of history that lay behind it. World War II and the subsequent Cold War had shocked America out of its isolationist mode and there was a new consensus that America needed to be actively engaged in the world. Notwithstanding the family's industrial heritage, Peter's mother made no secret of her wish that he would enter the diplomatic corps.

Naturally, Peter's father and uncle had other ideas. Like his brother William, Peter learned to do a bit of everything Hobart Brothers was about during his teenage years. Since E. A. and Martha had been unable to have children and E. A.'s brother Charles had a company of his own, there was the hope that W. H.'s two sons could repeat the magic

E. A. and W. H. had created in running Hobart Brothers, with one son handling the technical and engineering side of the business while the other handled finance and marketing. By the time Peter graduated from Hotchkiss it appeared that William Jr. had staked out his father's old role, so Peter entered Yale as an electrical engineering major. Perhaps his lanky six-foot-four frame indicated he had inherited some of his grandfather C. C. Hobart's electrical tinkering genes, but after one year Peter concluded that he could at best become a competent engineer. He certainly did not share E. A.'s passion for engineering.

While at home that summer Peter took a number of courses, including business law, at the University of Dayton and switched his focus to business and economics for his sophomore year at Yale. Finally, in his last two years he decided to major in art history. His mother supported the change, but his unconventional choice raised the eyebrows of the elder male Hobarts. Peter reassured them that he still intended to make a career for himself in the company but that this was what he needed to round out his life. Under the direction of Vincent Scully, one of America's foremost art historians, Peter journeyed to Rome in the summer of 1956 to conduct research on the triumphal arch of Septimius Severus for his honor's thesis.

While in Italy, Peter met Anna Zambon, a cousin of one of his classmates at Hotchkiss and Yale. Anna was utterly unlike any American women he knew. She played guitar and sang and was an intellectual. Her father had been an admiral in the Italian Navy. Following his graduation from Yale in the spring of 1957 Peter faced two years of mandatory military service. Thanks to his education, experience and lingual ability he managed to wrangle an appointment to a U.S. Army counter-intelligence unit based in Verona, Italy. The unit was stocked with Ivy League graduates who were given a snub-nosed .38 caliber pistol, a jeep, and a lot of independence in carrying out their threefold mission: monitor Marshal Tito's forces in neighboring Yugoslavia, guard against threats to U.S. tactical nuclear weapons based in Italy, and keep a watchful eye on the activities of the Italian Communist Party. Peter found the last task neither difficult nor disagreeable as he befriended the local Communist Party chairman, a crippled but congenial man just ten years his senior. Occasional leaves gave Peter a chance to call on Anna Zambon in Milan.

At the end of his military service in 1959 Peter faced a career choice that involved three specific job offers. First, there was the expected path of joining Hobart Brothers, finding his niche and working his way up to an as yet undefined executive position. Secondly, the Central Intelligence Agency offered him a job on frontline of the Cold War. Its reputation as yet unsullied by the Bay of Pigs debacle or subsequent scandals, the CIA was where the action was and a patriotic choice as well. Third, he had an offer from the head of the National Art Gallery in Washington, D.C., to become an understudy. Finally, his mother still hoped he would look into the State Department and become a diplomat. It took some time before Peter definitely chose Hobart Brothers, but he was eventually able to shape his role within the company in a manner that allowed him to also explore the roads not taken.

Charles Hobart married and started his family thirteen years later than W. H. With most of Charles' children being much younger than W. H's, the Hobart cousins did not see a lot of each other growing up. Elizabeth and Charles' oldest son, Charles Jr., did play with Peter, who was two years younger, and the cousins went on a few outings together, such as a summer camp in Colorado.[32] On another camping trip together Uncle Charlie impressed Peter by showing the boys how to pan for gold and then took the flakes they found into town and exchanged them for provisions.

As a teenager Charles Jr. worked in both the office and factory at Hobart Cabinet, although his father would not let him run the punch presses which he considered too dangerous. After graduating from Troy High School in 1950, Charles Jr. went to Denison University, the alma mater of his father and his Uncle William. He started off majoring in his first love, astronomy, but, after a great deal of pressure from E. A. and some from his father, he switched to business administration in the middle of his sophomore year.[33] For young Charles the launch of Sputnik came a few years too late.

Upon graduation in 1954 he went to work for his father at Hobart Cabinet doing payroll and accounts receivable and acting as a liaison between the office, still located in the old Brewery building on West Water Street and the factory on East Water Street.[34] Hobart Cabinet had survived the war years and was back to making steel office furniture and storage bins, but with fifty employees in the mid-1950s it was a shadow of its former self.[35] The Hobart fruit farms were still productive and provided seasonal employment at full factory pay for both cabinet company workers and Hobart Brothers employees during lag times in orders.[36]

Charles's second child and only daughter, Elizabeth, developed mental health problems in her adolescent years. Charles had never been a great believer in doctors and conventional medicine and their inability to solve Elizabeth's problems did nothing to dispel his doubts. After a difficult episode, Charles and his wife Elizabeth decided to commit their daughter to a state mental hospital in Dayton. Within a few years Elizabeth made some improvement and her parents became convinced they could care for her at home. They found to their horror that the primitive manner in which state law handled mental illness would not allow them to care for Elizabeth at home. Charles bristled at this injustice and brought a suit against the State of Ohio to regain custody of his daughter. In a landmark decision, Charles and his wife won their case and brought Elizabeth back to their home in Troy. At times Charles' stubbornness could be frustrating, but at others his refusal to yield in the face of great odds could produce admirable results.[37]

If anyone in the third generation of industrial Hobarts inherited the family genes for electrical tinkering, it was Charles' two middle sons, Edward and Edmund. Born just a year apart in 1940 and 1941, the boys turned a room in the basement of their home into their own "mad scientist's lab." Their Mecca was a government surplus store located just north of Dayton. Thanks to nearby Wright-Patterson Air Force Base and the former Army Signal Corps Supply Center, the surplus store was full of discarded electrical equipment from World War II, German and Japanese equipment as well as Allied. Rewiring and hooking up new power sources, Edward and Edmund brought old circuits back to life. Once a German teletype machine with a radio receiver kicked into action and began typing the coordinates of a ship at sea minus letters from a few keys still frozen in time. One of their experiments proved too successful. They rigged a radar set from a B-17 to a Hobart Brothers battery charger and tried to pick up planes that flew overhead, but the only object they registered on the screen was the fence around their father's tennis court. Then one Saturday morning a blue car pulled up to their home on Staunton Road. An Air Force officer climbed out, rang the bell and asked their mother if she knew of anyone operating radar nearby. At first he refused to believe it was her children until Edward and Edmund showed him their set. Astonished, he read them the riot act, illegal operation of radar was a federal offense, their signal interfered with planes making their approach to Wright-Patterson. He ordered them to dismantle the set at once.[38]

The boys followed orders but not long after that they spotted something at the surplus store that really excited them, a complete tail gun turret off a B-29 bomber, but at $125 it was far beyond their means. They knew their father would not give them that kind of money for something so frivolous, but they knew someone who might. Naturally, Edward and Edmund idolized their uncle E. A. and, like all youngsters, made careful plans as to when and how to ask for a favor. E. A. loved to go to Hobart Arena and sit in the center aisle of the top row and watch the Troy Bruins play hockey. It was at just such a moment that the boys approached him with their plans. Within a couple weeks they had installed the remote-controlled turret in their basement and gotten it to work. Edward and Edmund were the envy of their playmates. They also learned to be skeptical about manufacturer's claims. The turret's Plexiglas was supposed to withstand a .50 caliber bullet, but the boys managed to crack its surface by shooting it with a BB gun pellet.[39] Edward went on to college at the University of Cincinnati, while Edmund began at Ohio State and then finished up at Tri-State University in Angola, Indiana. Both earned bachelor's degrees in electrical engineering and went to work for E. A. at Hobart Brothers.[40]

When his youngest son was born in 1946 Charles named him Jonifer Avery after his personal hero, Sewell Avery, president of Montgomery Ward. In 1944 at the height of the war, Avery had defied a ruling by the War Labor Board, which caused the federal government to temporarily seize control of his company. A large framed photograph of two MP's carrying Avery out of his office occupied a place of honor behind Charles' desk.[41] Jonifer too had enjoyed tinkering in the basement lab. He graduated from Troy High School in 1964 and attended Tri-State University. Later he transferred to Parks College in East St. Louis to focus on his fascination with aircraft and graduated in Air Frame and Power Plant Mechanics, but by the early 1970s he too found work at Hobart Brothers.[42]

Edward and Martha Hobart were disappointed they were unable to have children, but, with a number of nieces and nephews in town and later grandnieces and grandnephews, children were by no means a rare sight in their Ridge Avenue home. Outside the company, E. A., or "Unc" as the next generation called him, still tended toward shyness and lacked the infectious sense of humor that made his brother W. H. an instant hit with children.[43] However, the bottom drawer of E. A.'s desk always had a box of chocolates and any youngster could easily persuade him to slide it open.[44] Unable to resist a gadget that appealed to kids as well, E. A. installed a soda fountain in his family room. Any sign of curiosity about things mechanical could turn this quiet man into a chatty and engaging tutor.[45] Christmas meant a double celebration at Unc and Aunt Martha's since December 25 was E. A.'s birthday as well.

Ice cream parlor in the art deco home of E. A. and Martha Hobart

For many years a neon script "Merry Christmas" light perched above the doorway of E. A.'s home. Though it was only lit during the holidays, he relished the spirit of Christmas year round.

Martha Lantis Hobart was a Presbyterian and a Democrat. She succeeded in converting E. A. to the Presbyterian Church; in fact, he became a trustee and one of its greatest benefactors.[46] But E. A. remained as staunch a Republican as his wife was a Democrat. Elections were apt to provoke lively debates or a quiet but uneasy truce in their Ridge Avenue home.[47] E. A. was a friend and supporter of John Bricker, a fellow OSU graduate and two-term Republican governor and then senator from Ohio. In 1944 Bricker was on the national ticket as Thomas Dewey's vice presidential running mate. His Columbus law firm, Bricker and Eckler, handled legal matters at the state level for Hobart Brothers.[48] Martha had more luck getting E. A. to change his wardrobe than his politics. W. H. had always been a natty dresser, but before his marriage E. A. had not fussed much about clothing. Martha took E. A. to her family's tailor in Cincinnati and saw to it that he was impeccably dressed. Since E. A. was in the habit of ruining his suits during an experiment or an impromptu repair job, he visited the tailor often. Martha was especially close to her oldest niece Marcia. "Aunt Markey," as she was called by her nieces and nephews, was always there to lend a sympathetic ear.[49]

E. A.'s relationship with his brother W. H. was a close tie that overlapped his personal and professional lives. As E. A. approached his sixtieth birthday in 1948, W. H. began writing a history of the company that would have been far more detailed than the 1945 book on the C. C. Hobart Foundation. W. H. never got beyond the first chapter, but what he wrote shows that he and E. A. were proud of what their father had achieved but could still see humor in the humble beginnings of their company. W. H. also began composing a biographical poem about his older brother that was more personal in nature.

Entitled "Edward," the completed portion focuses on their parents, the three brothers, and E. A.'s childhood and schooling. After describing his own hobbies and interests, W. H. continues in his poem "Edward":

William H. Hobart

Executive Vice-president of Hobart Brothers Company, largest manufacturers of one-day battery charging equipment and pioneers in the development of special power devices for automobile service stations and repair shops.

"World-wide recognition came our way when we changed methods"

How new methods built an international business in a bustling Ohio town

DICTATE TO THE DICTAPHONE

Mary Beck—Secretary to Mr. Hobart, says: "My idea of a nightmare is going back to the old days when I constantly had to decipher Mr. Hobart's hastily written notes and he constantly interrupted me to take shorthand dictation. I handle at least twice as much work now, yet it is easier to do and I never seem to be rushed."

but [W. H.] loved to bask
in the sunshine
of Edward's achievements
and used them all
usually breaking
some of them
and always causing trouble.[50]

"Loved to bask" alludes to W. H.'s fondness for sunbathing. He often took to the roof of the office building, taking desk, files, and Dictaphone along to work in the sun. W. H. certainly did not want to see Hobart Brothers dashed to pieces as he had done to some of E. A.'s boyhood contraptions, but, with E. A. childless, the future of the company would be in the hands of W. H.'s children and sons-in-law.

The complementary talents of E. A. and W. H. had produced an effective partnership. Would the next generation of Hobart siblings be able to shoulder the responsibility and continue that tradition? W. H.'s wife Rachel had no doubt that they would. She told her daughter Lucia that Bill Howell was "a born salesman," Robert Bravo "a long-term planner," her son Peter "a front runner," and that William Jr. "a fiscal conservative" was a fine choice to be president. "If those four men get along, they will make a wonderful combination."[51] ❧

CHAPTER 15

Ground Power Takes Off

E. A. Hobart was concerned as he cranked a fresh sheet of paper into his typewriter to put his thoughts into a memo he entitled "What's Ahead for 1946." With his capitals sometimes soaring above their lines, he typed "Past Five Years: Rush—Expand—Not Counting Cost—Sub Contracting . . . Orders 500 and 1000 lots. Government always pushing. Win the War and Get Out Production." Then in a column to the right, "Entering a New Era: Competition. Reduced Sales. One order at a time. Prices shot. 10 percent lower. Purchases are of small machines. Salesmen not satisfied with 15 percent commission. Don't know war time spending is over." The bottom half of the page contained numbers that bore out E. A.'s impressions. Sales for September 1945 were $462,000, $433,000 for October, while estimates for November and December dropped to $300,000 and $200,000. A detailed accounting for October showed a loss of $23,000.[1] How would Hobart Brothers cope with the loss of wartime government orders and at the same time absorb returning servicemen into its labor force?

Building new recreational facilities would occupy the construction teams and some workers could be employed on Charles' fruit farms during the slow summer production months, but these activities did not generate revenue for the company. Wib Chaffee's 1943 memo on postwar markets had pointed to some hopeful trends for welders, electrodes and the welded products line, but it did not say a word about how the massive wartime output of the Motor Generator Corporation could be converted to civilian products.[2] Fortunately, Hobart Brothers received a request to take its

engine generator technology in a new direction, and the company was quick to jump on it.

In the fall of 1945 American Airlines contacted the New York City distributorship of Hobart Brothers, the Gordons, and asked if the Motor Generator Corporation could construct a generator specially designed to start large aircraft engines and operate the plane's electrical systems while it was on the ground. Most aircraft built in the pre-war era had simple twelve-volt DC electrical systems to power an engine starter, lights, and a few instruments. The larger, more complex planes built during the war were equipped with twenty-eight-volt DC systems to start more powerful engines and a growing array of instruments.[3] For example, B-29 bombers had a pressurized cabin, remote-controlled gun turrets, and some carried onboard radar.[4]

Hobart's first ground power unit was built for American Airlines, circa 1946.

These planes were usually serviced by battery carts. For years, American Airlines had used Hobart battery chargers to charge the battery carts, which were then towed out on the tarmac and hooked up to planes when parked at terminal gates. As the electrical needs of aircraft grew, both airlines and the military grew frustrated with the clumsiness and inefficiency of such operations. To avoid maintenance problems associated with batteries, aircraft mechanics often jerry-rigged small industrial gas engines or even arc welding generators to replace battery packs as a ground power source for aircraft.[5] These makeshift solutions saved time when ground crews faced hectic wartime pressures to quickly service large numbers of planes and get them airborne, but these measures created problems of their own, such as couplings that did not fit or arc welding generators with too high a voltage that required two regu-

An Eastern Airlines Lockheed Constellation having its first engine started by a Hobart self-propelled
Ground Power Unit (GPU).

lators to handle the field currents.[6] American hoped that Hobart Brothers, with its expertise in battery chargers and DC generators, could produce the world's first generators custom designed to serve as ground power units for aircraft.

The engineers at the Motor Generator Corporation welcomed the challenge of pioneering a new application for electrical power. The war had made Americans recognize the importance of air power along with the need for and the feasibility of large-scale air passenger travel. Aircraft ground power was a field with real growth potential. The first ground power units were designed to service the four-propeller engine DC-4s. American had ordered DC-4s to replace its aging fleet of two-engine DC-3s only to see the new planes commandeered by the military along with many of its pilots for wartime service in the Air Transport Command (ATC). Now in the fall of 1945 the ATC began returning these planes, which had been designated as C-54s for cargo use, to American and other airlines for conversion into forty-seat passenger aircraft.[7]

John Sampson designed the first Hobart ground power unit, completing the engineering specification in September

John Sampson,
Chief GPU engineer

1946. American Airlines engineers were not sure what the total electrical load would be for lighting, galley, heating or air conditioning the plane, and starting the first engine. Sampson decided to design a 28.5-volt 500-ampere generator coupled to an eight-cylinder in-line Chrysler engine. He selected an engine with enough horsepower to drive a 750-ampere generator in case the plane's systems required more current. When the unit was first tested, the plane's load was only 380 amperes, so the engine size was reduced for future orders.[8] There had been several plane crashes shortly before Sampson came to LaGuardia for the shakedown tests. American's engineers delighted in embellishing the details of the accidents, remarking that if one engine failed at takeoff and the pilot did not "feather" or change the propeller pitch at once the plane was sure to crash. This did nothing to comfort Sampson on his return flight to Troy.

Most early ground power units were gas-engine driven and mounted on a trailer that could be towed out to a plane. The generators operated at 400 Hertz (cycles) developed during the war years to enable a lightweight motor to swing a radar unit quickly enough to track an aircraft. After the ground power unit started one engine,

107

an onboard generator started the rest. The 400-Hertz power reduced the size and weight of the onboard generator.[9] American Airlines ground crews found the new units to be a far more efficient way to handle power demands at airports, and soon other U.S. airlines clamored for Hobart ground power units (GPU's).[10]

Hobart Brothers began producing ground power for a wide variety of aircraft: the older DC-3s and DC-4s, the Lockheed Constellation, the first passenger liner with a pressurized cabin, the Convair 200 and 240, and the DC-6, which not only had a pressurized cabin but air-conditioning as well. Onboard galleys became more extensive.[11] The ground power units had to operate within close tolerances to avoid harming the sensitive electrical systems of the various aircraft. Hobart was famous for its precise power and expanded the power ratings of its units to cover ranges from 4 to 15 kilowatts and 175 to 2,000 amperes. Some units could operate off AC power in a hangar. Others could be placed in a pit or tunnel under the tarmac and covered with a trap door when not in use. To avoid depending on a tug to tow a unit into place, Hobart developed a self-propelled unit which could be driven from plane to plane, saving time and reducing the clutter of vehicles around the aircraft.[12]

Pressurized cabins and improved engines meant faster flights at higher altitudes above the weather which had often made early air travel bumpy and unnerving. Trans-Atlantic flights became routine. As demand for air travel rose steadily, airline executives were receptive when Robert Bravo of Hobart Brothers came calling with a solution for the power demands of their airplanes parked at the crowded terminal gates of expanding airports. Many airline executives had served in the military during the war. As a former Navy pilot, Bravo spoke their language. He soon found that the market for ground power units was not just national but international, as the world followed America's example. Thousands of Hobart Brothers generators and welders had been shipped overseas as lend-lease goods or left behind as surplus by U.S. armed forces in the rush to demobilize and return home. The company began to reap the benefit of the name recognition and reputation for reliability created by its wartime output in the form of orders for ground power units from foreign airlines. Only a couple years after giving up the idea of a State Department career, Bravo found himself dealing with the top officials of dozens of international airlines, many of which were government-owned.[13]

In 1952 Bravo was diagnosed with polio along with more than 57,600 other Americans as the epidemic reached its peak.[14] He still made a few more sales before the disease's progression forced him to take a leave of absence from work. Raised as a Christian Scientist, Bravo avoided medical treatment for several months but was eventually persuaded to seek help from a local doctor whose daughter had polio. Following a visit to a treatment center in Magnetic Springs, Ohio, he began to make a slow recovery, but a year passed before he was able to grip the railing and pull himself up the steps of the office building at Hobart Brothers.[15] Once while Bravo was still convalescing at home and making sales by phone, Lucia heard him shout in exultation. He had just sold a set of ground power units to Egypt Air. Now every airline in the world owned a Hobart GPU.[16] They were so ubiquitous that for many ground crews "the Hobart" became the generic term for any aircraft ground power unit.[17]

Air travel reached a milestone in 1957 when for the first time the number of people traveling between America and Europe by plane exceeded the number who went by boat.[18] The following year Pan Am took delivery of the first Boeing 707 jetliners and began trans-Atlantic jet service with a splash of publicity. In November 1958 officials at Rome's Fiumicino Airport became frantic when they discovered a problem with the Hobart ground power unit that was to service the Pan Am Flight 1, already on its way on a promotional around the world flight that began in New York. They discovered that a Hobart was serving with the U.S. Army in Italy and rushed Peter to the airport to take a look at the unit. Located while on leave, he arrived and took off his jacket and tie hoping the prob-

Pan Am 747 first around the world flights and a Hobart self-propelled GPU

lem was one he could cope with based on the short time he had spent in the plant in Troy that assembled ground power units. Luckily, it was just a reversed wire and he had the unit working in time for the arrival of the Pan Am jet. Peter was bemused at being treated like a hero when he felt sure that an electrician at the airport could have performed the same repair, but he demonstrated the adage that the Hobarts stood behind their products and took note that the name seemed to open more doors overseas than it did in the United States.

As airlines gradually converted their propeller-driven air fleets to jet-powered craft, the requirements for ground power units changed. Forced air began to be used to start jet engines, so ground power units were no longer needed to start engines. However, the larger jetliners had ever more

Precise power static systems for bridges and mobile ground power

elaborate electrical needs to run onboard systems for communication, monitoring controls and instruments, and providing for the comfort of passengers. The notoriously fuel hungry early jets made it very inefficient to operate the plane's own engine-powered auxiliary units until it was time to taxi to the runway.[19]

In building AC power units for the early jets, the company's experience reinforced its traditions of self-reliance and showing confidence in its new young employees. The manufacture of voltage regulators for the new ground

Hobart "Whisper Power" ground power unit for low noise applications

power units had been subcontracted with Cline Electric. When that firm suddenly went bankrupt, Hobart Brothers bought the design and turned to Larry Atterholt on the basis of his five hours of work on magnetic amplifiers during his senior year at Ohio State. The technicians assisting Atterholt were Edward and Edmund Hobart who were still in high school. The team managed to get voltage regulators into production for new GPUs in the summer of 1958.[20]

Complying with customer requests sometimes led to problems. Pan Am decided that it wanted Cummins diesel engines incorporated in its ground power units. Motor Generator built units for Pan Am substituting Cummins engines for the usual Chrysler engines. The units tested fine, but once in service for just a few hours the generator shafts would break. This led to a heated meeting in John Blankenbuehler's office in which an executive from Cummins refused to cooperate on a solution. He pounded the desk, "The problem's on *your* side

109

of the coupling, so you're going to have to fix it!" After the Cummins man strode out of the office E. A. was livid. He called in Roger Frantz, another Ohio State engineer who had joined the company in 1946 after serving three years as a captain in the Air Force. He wanted Frantz to design an "armor plated" generator unit to couple with the Cummins engine. Sure enough, after the rebuilt units ran a while, the Cummins engine shaft would break. E. A. phoned Cummins, "The failure's on your side of the unit now. Let's get together and fix it." The problem was in fact caused by torsional vibration, a phenomenon not well understood at the time. With cooperation, that bug finally got ironed out.[21]

Hobart PoWerMaster® 400Hz solid state frequency converter

Hobart was the first company in the world to manufacture aircraft ground power units, but by the late 1950s several competitors had entered the field, such as Guinault in France in 1949, Streuver in Germany, Houchin in Great Britain, Seiko Denki in Japan, AXA in Denmark in 1954, and Texas-based Stewart and Stevenson in 1958.[22] In order to stay at the top of the industry, Hobart continued to innovate, converting its ground power units to solid state technology in the 1970s and developing the first units to serve the new jumbo jets as well as the supersonic Concorde.[23] Most of the international sales were made by Aviquipo, a specialized international aviation equipment organization. With passenger traffic growing at a rate of 15 to 20 percent a year, Hobart addressed the need to reduce the clutter of vehicles on the tarmac by developing central station systems. A huge Hobart vertical rotating generator unit of 200- or 312-kva size would be installed deep in the bowels of an airport terminal to distribute precise power through transformer stations to gate boxes at the end of its cable tentacles hundreds of feet away. These boxes, located below the passenger bridges used to board airplanes, had safeguard devices to protect the aircraft from damaging variations in voltage and could be tested while the rest of the system remained in operation.[24] Central station systems proved ideal for newly constructed airports and additions and sold well in international markets too. Internationally, and especially

in Europe, the port authorities who owned the airports tended to be the purchasers of ground power units rather than individual airlines as in America.[25] The increased demand for aircraft ground power showed no signs of slowing as the 1970s dawned.

The Soviet Union stunned the world on August 29, 1949, by setting off its first atomic bomb, barely four years after the United States had dropped atomic bombs on Hiroshima and Nagasaki. The sense of security Americans had felt after the defeat of the Axis powers proved to be short lived. Yet it was not until a month after the start of the Korean War in June 1950 that the U.S. military created the Army Antiaircraft Command and began to prepare to defend the country against the threat of Soviet bombers armed with nuclear bombs.[26] As in the past, the U.S. Army Corps of Engineers approached Hobart's Motor Generator Corporation this time with a request to build a 30-kilowatt 400-Hertz generator to power radar sets to establish a picket line to detect Soviet bombers attacking the United States across the North Pole and Canada, the shortest route from the USSR to America.[27] Updating its design from World War II, Hobart engineers created the model that became known as the HG-30C. They were first deployed along what became known as the Pinetree Line, which grew to forty-four continuously manned stations that stretched from the northern tip of British Columbia's Victoria Island in the Pacific throughout southern Canada to Newfoundland in the Atlantic and up the icy coast of Labrador to the northernmost station at Frobisher Bay on Baffin Island. The line became operational in 1954.[28]

Just as the Hobart generators of the Pinetree Line kicked into life, President Eisenhower signed a bill calling for an even more ambitious network of radar stations to

Concord supersonic jet and Hobart truck mounted GPU

guard against a nuclear Pearl Harbor. The Distant Early Warning or "DEW" Line would consist of fifty-eight radar installations to rim the Arctic Circle from the north shore of Alaska across Canada and Greenland to Iceland. Generators for DEW Line radar had to operate under extremely demanding conditions. Only stations a hundred miles or more apart would be manned, therefore equipment had to run reliably with low maintenance and at temperatures as low as -60°F.[29] Hobart's testing room for temperature extremes, the strong performance of its earlier generators for the military, and its proximity to air defense experts at Wright-Patterson Air Force Base combined to secure this important contract. The final strand in the web of early warning radar was the Mid-Canada Line, eight staffed control stations that operated a microwave "fence"

Isonorized trailer mounted GPU

of almost ninety unmanned sites along the 55th parallel.[30] Fears of a "bomber gap" and the launch of Sputnik in 1957 spurred the United States and Canada to complete construction by early 1958. Continuously upgraded, parts of this electronic defense network remained operational throughout the Cold War into the early 1990s.[31]

As the 1950s drew to a close, E. A. Hobart's worries about the future of the Motor Generator Corporation were

a distant memory. The business had opened up a new market for growth in the manufacture of aircraft ground power and renewed Hobart's connection to the defense industry. The search for postwar markets sent Hobart Brothers into extremes of geography and climate. While its generators ran radar installations that probed the frigid skies of the arctic, E. A. had taken up mining and was digging in the sands of sunny Florida. ❧

"Ground power unit for Distant Early Warning or "DEW" Line radar sets

CHAPTER 16

The Quest for Rutile Leads to Florida

E. A. Hobart was married to his job. Typically he could be found on Saturdays and even Sundays in his office poring over paperwork he had not gotten to during the week or wandering the plant and office buildings scribbling with a pencil and dropping off his salmon-colored 3 x 5 card directives at the work stations of chosen employees. Unlike W. H. and Charles, E. A. had few interests outside the company and little desire to travel beyond Troy. However, he was also married to Martha and she liked luxury and a chance to sample some of the society the company's success had made possible. After World War II E. A. and Martha began taking the train to Florida for an annual winter vacation.[1] They stayed at the Breakers in Palm Beach, an Italianate resort hotel built by Henry Flagler that was the favored winter retreat for the rich and famous from the East Coast. Martha enjoyed the warm sun and sophisticated company. E. A. was usually pretty bored.

Normally E. A. had nothing but scorn for professional consultants, but one trusted advisor that he and W. H. listened to was Harry Toulmin, their patent lawyer.[2] Toulmin had authored thirteen books, including one on the Senate War Investigation Committee that had looked into waste and fraud in the war effort.[3] Toulmin had been a non-government representative on that panel which had been judged so effective that its chairman, Harry Truman, was propelled into the vice-presidency and ultimately the White House. Toulmin told the Hobart brothers to use vacation time in Florida to get involved with some project that could benefit their company as well. "Do not expand the Troy plant but go some place else so you don't have all your eggs in one basket." He advised locating a second operation somewhere in the South. "You can't defeat nature by trying to carry at sixty the burdens you carried at fifty. The

wisdom of sixty can be applied most effectively if there are periods of change or rest between periods of activity. . . . I would recommend that whatever is done that a set plan be established by Ed and Bill to devote a substantial period of time away from the plant. This should not be bulked in one vacation or two, but every few weeks there should be a change of scene and a change of pace. A home in some other locality where the complete relaxation can be secured is essential. No fashionable hotel can ever fill that bill."[4]

As luck would have it, the perfect raw material for such a project lay just fifty miles north of the Breakers in the sands of Florida's Atlantic Coast. Just north of Vero Beach lay rich deposits of titanium minerals, one, titanium dioxide (TiO_2), was a key ingredient in white outdoor paint and the whitewalls of tires. While a different compound, rutile ($TiFeO_2$) was one of the best flux coating materials for welding rods. Rutile coating on an electrode stabilizes the welding arc and forms a slag over a weld that both slows its cooling and increases the ductility of the finished weld.[5] Demand for rutile skyrocketed during World War II as the production of welding electrodes topped a billion pounds (500 million kilos) in 1943, a figure that would not be equaled until the 1960s.[6] Before a major effort was made to locate domestic sources, welding rod production returned to normal levels, and the welding industry continued to rely on imported rutile, primarily from Australia. Rutile and ilmenite, a similar mineral, were also becoming more valuable as sources for the metal titanium. Titanium's light weight and ability to resist heat and corrosion made it ideal for use in jet engines and the skin of military aircraft.[7] The market shifted again with the onset of the Korean War in June 1950. The price of rutile shot up as demand for titanium jumped at the same time that military shipping needs in the Pacific

Rutile coating on an electrode stabilizes the welding arc and forms a slag over a weld that both slows its cooling and increases the ductility of the finished weld.

made it problematic to import rutile in bulk from Australia.[8] The U.S. government put rutile on its list of strategic raw materials and began to acquire a stockpile, offering tax breaks or matching funds from the U.S. Bureau of Mines to help develop an American source. These developments combined to force the price of rutile up from about $70 a ton to over $900 a ton.[9] Suddenly, mining a domestic source of rutile became an attractive business proposition.

How did E. A. know there was rutile in Florida waiting to be mined? A fellow Ohioan told him. In Frederick A. Hauck, an

Hobart Brothers Company Vero Beach office and rutile separation plant

entrepreneur-engineer from Cincinnati, E. A. found a truly kindred spirit. Just six years E. A.'s junior, Hauck had been born into a family that had earned millions in brewing and banking. At age twenty-five a doctor had told him his heart would kill him within a year, but the only effect on Hauck was that "he lived each day as if it were created for him."[10] After a successful career in the sale of medical instruments, he took up a new field of interest in mining and bought up the leases of several American mining companies in Mexico during the Depression. The Hauck Exploration Company succeeded in finding silver and copper and later was tapped by the U.S. government to help stockpile strategic minerals for the war effort, including materials used in the Manhattan Project. While walking the Florida beaches on vacation in the late 1940s, Hauck noticed striated bands of dark crystals amid the white sands. He took a mineral light and went exploring at night and observed a fluorescence in the dark bands.[11] Hauck scooped up some samples and sent them to a lab for analysis. Several valuable minerals were present, including zircon, garnet, and monazite, along with rutile and ilmenite, both of which were titanium compounds. Of greatest interest to Hauck was deriving zirconium, a better nuclear shielding material than lead, and hafnium, a metal used in control rods for nuclear reactors.[12]

Hauck learned that the minerals originated in the rocks of the Piedmont region of Georgia and the Carolinas. Over millennia erosion had washed them downriver into the ocean where the tidal action of

waves deposited them ashore in a process "much like panning for gold," the lighter silica sand washing back to sea, the heavier mineral flakes settling on the beach.[13] E. A. was fascinated by what Hauck told him, and the pair tramped up and down the coast discovering some of the best deposits along Sand Ridge, a gentle rise that had once been Florida's ancient shore but was now a mile inland from the Inner Coastal Waterway, locally known as Indian River.[14] Hobart Brothers purchased about thirteen hundred acres of land just north of Vero Beach in an area known as Winter Beach. Ironically, this piece of land lay just west of the Dixie Highway (U.S. 1), the same Dixie Highway that fronted the Hobart Brothers plant in Troy, Ohio.[15]

E. A. avidly studied books on mining to figure out the best means to exploit this move into vertical integration, but the Hobart tradition of self-reliance, the confidence they could do it better on their own, meant this effort to acquire raw materials would not be subcontracted. Van Ausdal's construction crews had finished Hobart Arena and were itching for a fresh challenge. Besides, E. A. had too much fun learning a whole new technology in his sixties to forgo the opportunity. Hobart Brothers built its own all welded steel dredge in Troy, christened it "Little Sandy," and tested it by scouring a channel in the Miami River near the Boathouse. Little Sandy was then disassembled and shipped to Florida aboard seven railcars. Dredging operations commenced in 1953 at Winter Beach under the banner of the newly incorporated Florida Minerals Company.[16]

First, the nearly wild land had to be cleared of dense brush, vegetation, snakes, and alligators. Next, Little Sandy dug its own small lake and used

Fred Hauck

113

"Little Sandy," the prototype rutile mining dredge designed by E. A. Hobart, 1953

"Big Sandy," the biggest industrial dredge for rutile mining designed and patented by E. A. Hobart, circa 1957

its rotary cutting head and suction pump to create a slurry containing about 40 percent water and 60 percent sand and minerals. The dredge dumped the discarded sand to its rear, filling in the lake as it pushed forward. The slurry was pumped through a floating pipeline to pass through a vibrating screen to remove roots and other hard objects that could clog the separator. The wet mill separator took advantage of the higher specific gravity of the desired minerals as it pumped the slurry through a series of troughs that upgraded the mineral concentration of the resulting mixture to about 40 percent. At first, this sand-mineral mix had to be trucked twenty-five miles north to a mineral plant in Melbourne, an expensive step that was eliminated once Florida Minerals built its own dry mill separation plant next to Dixie Highway and the Florida East Coast rail line.[17]

Though the operation employed the latest technology for recovering minerals from sandy coastal land, E. A. believed he could make it more efficient. By 1952 electrode production in Troy had expanded under Henry Bryan and moved into a new plant on Ridge Avenue in the Westbrook subdivision. Shortly after the move, Lowell Mott got to spend "a very enjoyable year" working with E. A. and a small team trying to improve the wet mill separation of minerals destined to be shipped north to coat electrodes. Carrying in his pocket the first rutile nugget recovered from Florida, E. A. devised

Fred Hauck, left, and E. A. Hobart
at Vero Beach, 1950s

a "cow's udder" method of pushing the slurry through a series of funneled plastic troughs in contrast to the patented Dupont free flow or "horsetail" method. E. A. showed Mott how to keep clear records that were signed and dated. He told Mott to test various alignments but to not adjust the diameter of the pipe at the bottom of the funnels, but Mott discovered the slurry flowed better if he cut the pipe diameter. E. A. checked on Mott's progress twice daily and noted the different diameter at once and told him to change it back. Reluctantly, Mott complied but his observations showed the smaller diameter was more efficient. The next day E. A. saw Mott had put the smaller pipes back in place. "Didn't I tell you not to change the diameter?" "Yes, Mr. Hobart, but it works better this way." E. A. watched the assembly in action and slowly a big smile spread across his face. "Low-well, I believe you're right. Keep it your way."[18]

Mott did not think for a minute that he had out-engineered E. A. Hobart. Rather, he felt as though he had passed some kind of test. Mott thought E. A. wanted to see if he had enough independence, enough trust in his own observations and judgment to do research. After his work on the separator project, Mott became an assistant to several directors of electrode research at Hobart Brothers until he became the director himself in 1984.[19] E. A. respected formal education, but he never let the absence of a college degree exclude anyone when he scouted his own employees for talent to work on research projects. Marion Centliver, Perry Filbrun, Marion Oldham, and Harold Stephens, E. A.'s "Experimental" team of researchers, all had only high school educations.[20]

By the summer of 1953 the new wet mill separator was put to work in Florida and E. A. submitted his design for a patent, which was granted in early 1957.[21] At first the new separator floated on a set of pontoons behind Little Sandy. Fed by a floating pipeline, it upgraded the slurry to a concentration of 64 percent minerals and handled a bigger volume at faster speeds than the old equipment. One limiting factor was the need to make costly repairs to the rotating head of the dredge.[22] E. A. began work on a new dredge design in Troy. This larger design, dubbed Big Sandy, would incorporate the new separator and replace the conventional rotating head with a series of link buckets whose cutting lips were hard surfaced with Hobart Tufanhard 600. This huge new unit could handle four hundred tons of sand an hour and cut as deep as thirty feet below the surface of the water. As with the first dredge, Big Sandy was designed and welded together in Troy and tested on the Miami River before being disassembled and shipped south by rail, requiring twenty railcars for the move.[23]

Though he was now approaching seventy, E. A. Hobart never ceased being a hands-on engineer. Eager to test the twin engines on his new dredge and dressed in his customary gray suit and black Navy-issue shoes, he positioned himself behind the big rig where he could read the gauge while the dredge lay tied up to the shore of the Miami River. Each engine was supposed to generate three thousand pounds of thrust. When he gave the signal, the pilot gunned the engines to full throttle. Big Sandy quickly

Hobart Landing in the early stages of its construction

The Vero Beach Boat House

yanked its mooring lines taut and as it did the rear of the dredge bucked and shot back a plume of water that struck E. A. in the chest and sent him sprawling backward onto the muddy riverbank. The pilot cut the engines and a pair of employees scrambled to the aid of their sixty-nine-year-old CEO. A mud-spattered E. A. just grinned at them and shouted, "They got to six thousand pounds!"[24]

By 1958 Florida Mineral was the third largest U.S. producer of titanium behind Dupont and National Lead.[25] The Vero Beach mining operation supplied all the rutile Hobart Brothers required and even sold extensively to its competitors in the field of filler metals for welding. For fifteen years it was the nation's leading domestic producer of welding grade rutile.[26] Norm Van Ausdal served as president of the mining subsidiary while Sterling Dangler was its superintendent of operations with thirty to forty full-time employees in Indian River County.[27] Fred Hauck's Cincinnati-based Consolidated Minerals Processing purchased zircon to refine for the Atomic Energy Commission.[28] Hauck had E. A. appointed to Consolidated Minerals' Board of Directors, a position he held the rest of his life.[29]

All three Hobart brothers got involved with mining rutile in Florida. Charles had been a frequent visitor to Miami Beach ever since the 1930s when he had driven his mother down for vacations. Always interested in mining, his imagination was fired by the depositing of minerals on the shore in a natural process that resembled panning for gold. Charles was convinced that a similar process would be the most efficient means of extracting commercial grade minerals from the sand, but his natural competitiveness and pride in his role as the "black sheep" of the family kept him from combining efforts with his brothers. Instead he leased a small parcel of land near the Florida Mineral holdings and worked on his own process for extracting minerals. He did succeed in devising a method that worked and proudly secured a patent for it, although it proved impractical for commercial development.[30]

Once the improved dredge and wet mill separator had been developed, E. A. focused his attention on improving the dry staging processes in the plant outside Vero Beach. The mineral concentrate was pumped into the plant and run in suspension over vibrating Dyster tables whose parallel rubber ridges separated material by weight, from the heaviest—monazite, to the lightest—sand. This step upgraded the concentration to about 80 percent. Long

cylindrical rotating kilns then dried the mixture, which was sent through electrostatic separators that exploited the fact that rutile and ilmenite conduct electricity while garnet, monazite, and zircon do not. Finally, the minerals passed over two electromagnetic separators. Ilmenite, which contains iron, clung to the magnet, allowing the rutile to be separated. Likewise, zircon is not magnetic, while monazite and garnet are.[31] Workers then bagged the high-grade minerals for shipment to Hobart Brothers and a variety of corporate customers. Over the next few years E. A. secured three different patents for improvements to equipment and methods for separating ores.[32]

E. A. and W. H. had always envisioned redeveloping the mining grounds for residential use. As Little Sandy chewed its way inland from Indian River its path was cut into channels and lined with seawalls until local authorities informed the company that it needed permits to alter the shoreline. This piece of land became Hobart Landing where vacation homes were built for Hobart Brothers employees. One executive, Byron Lutz, met his future wife in Florida, marrying a daughter of Arthur McKee, the founder of McKee Botanical Gardens.[33] E. A. Hobart built himself a home as well as a boathouse for the recreational use of the community of Ohio transplants.

By early 1959 Florida Mineral was ready to present waterfront home sites for sale to the general public. Millions of tons of sand had been reshaped to form gentle hills interspersed with lakes, roads had been paved, and pine or palm trees would be planted on all purchased lots. To avoid land speculation resulting in unsightly weed-choked vacant parcels, land titles would not be transferred until building had begun. No lot would be smaller than 100 x 140 feet.[34] The timing of the project could not have been better. Indian River County's population more than

E. A.'s home at Vero Beach, Florida

117

doubled during the 1950s as it became a fashionable resort community located midway between the sprawling urban stretch of Miami and Fort Lauderdale and the expanding space facilities at Cape Canaveral.[35] Bill Howell took advantage of the company's mining connection to the area and established a branch sales office for Hobart Brothers welding equipment in Vero Beach to access the growing Florida market.

Dredged artifacts from the Hobart mining site include Spanish doubloons and Arawak Indian arrowheads.

Another byproduct of the mining operation was a large number of archaeological finds. For centuries Native Americans who lived along Florida's East Coast had used the top of Sand Ridge as a trail to link their communities with trade. Later Spanish goods and colonists made their way north and south along the trail. Consequently, the dredges' screens caught many arrowheads and other Indian artifacts along with Spanish coins, including several silver reals (often broken and used as "pieces of eight") and a gold doubloon from 1640.[36] These finds whetted the interest of E. A. and other Hobart people in the fate of the Spanish treasure fleet which had lost ten of its eleven ships off the shore of present-day Indian River County in a hurricane in 1715. Occasional discoveries of coins washed up on the beach had led residents to dub the region the Treasure Coast, as it truly was for Hobart. Hobart workers and vacationers followed and some invested in the projects of Kip Wagner, a building contractor who had moved to Florida from Miamisburg, Ohio, another Miami River town thirty miles south of Troy. Wagner organized Real 8 with seven other partners to salvage coastal wrecks for treasure. In January 1961 they had their first success, locating the wreck of *El Capitana* near the mouth of Sebastian Inlet. More discoveries enhanced the tourist appeal of the Treasure Coast and filled local museums with Spanish silver and gold.

In 1963 the U.S. government removed rutile from its list of strategic raw materials and the price of rutile quickly collapsed from around $900 a ton to about $125 a ton. Matching funds from the Bureau of Mines disappeared as well. Hobart Brothers decided to shut down its

In 1963 the U.S. government removed rutile from its list of strategic raw materials and the price of rutile quickly collapsed from around $900 a ton to about $125 a ton

Florida mining operations the following year when it became apparent that market conditions favored imports and were not going to change. One dredge was sold to Kip Wagner for treasure salvage while other equipment was sold to other domestic and foreign mining operations. Residential development continued for several years, and part of the former mining grounds were transformed into a golf course with numerous water hazards. Grapefruit and orange trees were planted on the property and the company operated one of Indian River County's famed citrus groves for about ten years. This property was later donated to the county for parkland and today is known as Hobart-Kiwanis Park.[37]

The welding industry returned to importing most of its rutile from Australia, South Africa, and India. Today one company still mines rutile, ilmenite, and zircon from the sands of the Florida coast just south of Jacksonville, while some synthetic rutile is produced from ilmenite.[38] Although Hobart's Florida mining operation enjoyed a fairly brief heyday, employees and family members recall it as a great adventure. Many of them established permanent ties to the area, traveling there for annual vacations. Some Hobart Brothers retirees became snowbirds and made Vero Beach their winter home while others chose to live there year round. For E. A. and the engineers and technicians who pioneered and perfected the rutile mining operation it was more than a working vacation, it was an exciting challenge and a rewarding learning experience. ❧

CHAPTER 17

The Technical Center Expands Its Reach

The Hobart Technical Center school, sculpture park and fountain

Although tanks had been the tracked vehicle America mass-produced in the 1940s, bulldozers and power shovels took their place in the 1950s as the country enjoyed a boom in construction, especially in roads and housing. The Westbrook subdivision absorbed much of the new construction in Troy as new Hobart Brothers plants rose on its eastern edge and single-family homes took shape west of a park-like greenbelt. Further west surveyors were marking the course for Interstate 75, a four-lane superhighway designed to replace the old Dixie Highway that ran through town. Hobart executives had decided that the Trade School had outgrown its home on Elm Street and that they would replace it with an eighty-thousand-square-foot facility in their new Westbrook industrial park.[1] In hiring a new director for the expanded school, W. H. Hobart chose Howard Cary, a highly qualified

> ✺
>
> *Hobart Brothers had decided to not merely enlarge its quarters but to redefine the school and the role of its leader*
>
> ✺

engineer who had trained workers and developed systems to weld both tanks and powers shovels.

Cary had grown up in Columbus, Ohio, and attended Ohio State where he graduated as a mechanical engineer in 1942 with a submajor in welding. He went to work for Fisher Body in Flint, Michigan, building Sherman tanks, America's first all-welded body tank. Cary's first task became his life's work, training people and developing technology to weld with speed and precision to make goods where people's lives would depend on the quality of the welds. After serving as a radio technician on a seaplane tender in the Navy, Cary spent two years doing research on gas-shielded welding at the Battelle Institute in Columbus. Then he was hired by Marion Power Shovel, a company that supplied shovels for large construction projects and strip mining.

119

Cary rose through the ranks to become assistant general works manager. He first got to know Hobart Brothers as a customer buying welders and filler metals. Marion Power Shovel consumed two railcar loads of welding rods per month.[2]

The offer to direct the Trade School interested Cary because Hobart Brothers had decided to not merely enlarge its quarters but to redefine the school and the role of its leader. An internal review had reached three conclusions:

1. The arc welding industry was becoming more complex, more technically oriented and sophisticated.

2. Hobart needed to become more aggressive with a more technological leadership to become a more dominant factor in the arc welding business.

3. Hobart Brothers should develop a facility or center which should become the focus of Hobart to promote new developments in arc welding to the welding industry.[3]

Naturally, the school would continue to educate students in the basics of welding, and renowned Chief Instructor Raymond C. Dunlavy would supervise the teaching of the full sixteen-week course of intensive practice and training along with shorter courses that focused on specific skills. However, the rapid advance of welding technology had created a need to educate foremen, supervisors, and even engineers about new processes, procedures, and products. Hobart planned to offer a Welding Technician Certificate for completing an ambitious array of courses in chemistry, physics, mathematics, metallurgy, and welding design. Both the school's staff and course catalogue had to be expanded to meet these goals. Apart from classrooms and welding booths like those found in the former building, the new center would include a 250-seat auditorium, demonstration areas, laboratories, and the latest equipment for weld testing and metalworking.[4]

Ray Dunlavy

W. H. Hobart walked Cary through the just completed but empty building that still smelled of fresh paint. W. H. urged Cary "to make it into a . . . focus point or showroom of Hobart welding products to show them off to the welding industry" to make the tech center the fountain-

"Everybody's friend," Charlie Brown, left, and Howard Cary

head of welding knowledge. He also encouraged Cary to play an active role in the American Welding Society.[5] Another key feature of the renamed Hobart Welding Technical Institute would be the Procedure Lab. For several years a dynamic individual named Charlie Brown had both taught courses at the Trade School and run a demonstration lab, where he had shown Hobart salesmen and independent distributors how to operate and sell new welding equipment. He had also done some troubleshooting on problems brought to him by customers in the field. The new Procedure Lab would expand these valuable services and go several steps further by becoming much more proactive. It would evaluate Hobart equipment from the welder's point of view as well as the equipment of competitors and their advertised claims. The Lab would develop optimum welding procedures needed to meet code requirements. Finally, it would analyze the needs of customers and integrate the talents of Hobart equipment designers and filler metal formulators to create welding systems that would produce the welds the customers desired to the quality standards required.[6] As director of the new Technical Institute, Cary, often referred to as "Mr. Welding," would have responsibilities in the areas of education and research and development as well as a role in customer relations and sales.

The school had been evolving in the years prior to its reorganization in 1958. Thanks to the G.I. Bill and the nation's rapid retooling to manufacture consumer goods, the Hobart Trade School had never experienced a severe drop in enrollment following World War II. By 1947, 90 percent of its students were veterans and, unlike the war years, no women were enrolled. The former G.I.'s, seeking a solid profession that was needed and well paid, made for a rough but colorful student body whose favorite watering hole was the infamous Mr. Bill's, a bar on the northwest corner of the Public Square in Troy. Bob Bercaw had added several pieces of metal cutting equipment along with a tool and die course to train workers for dozens of tool and die firms in nearby Dayton who were subcontracting work for the automotive industry.[7] Bercaw never let anything go to waste and constantly scrounged scrap from the factory to use in student projects.[8] Throughout the Troy community people knew they could bring welding jobs and minor repairs to the Trade School to have them done for free by students eager to apply their new skills.[9] As the ex-G.I.'s returned to the workforce, their places were taken by younger students just out of high school and some who had not even finished high school. Many of these young men were living away from home for the first time in their lives and saw Ray Dunlavy as a father figure and looked to him for guidance both within and beyond the classroom.[10]

When Cary was named director of the expanded institute in September 1958, Bercaw moved on to become Hobart Brothers' roving welding expert as the company sought to expand its international sales. Sales had been the focus of the company's first "Summit Meeting," a term borrowed from the 1955 encounter between Eisenhower and Khrushchev in Geneva. In June 1958 Hobart Brothers hosted a three-day conference in Troy for the directors of the top-100 Hobart distributors as part of a major effort to improve communications and sales. Headed by Dick Sherwood and Bill Howell, the Hobart sales staff introduced new products, gave plant tours of the new Westbrook facilities, and held training sessions and open discussion sessions with distributors. The role of the new technical center was explained and ample time provided for informal socializing and exchange of views. Hobart leaders and distributors, Hobarteers, considered the Summit Meeting such a success that they agreed to hold one every three years.[11]

The Summit Meeting provided a host of challenges for those charged with the technical direction of the company. The five key men involved were Howard Cary, Glynn Williams who was head of engineering, Henry Bryan the chief formulator in charge of filler metal research, company president E. A. Hobart, and John Blankenbuehler an expert on AC power systems who had worked at Westinghouse and was now a special assistant to E. A.[12] For the past several years they had focused on expanding Hobart Brothers' product line of welding machines and consum-

John Blankenbuehler

ables. During the height of wartime production when standardization and high output were emphasized the company had manufactured only three different models of welders. As various experimental welding technologies became practical and began to find a market, Hobart's line of welding power sources expanded to twenty-two various models by 1953.[13]

In the late 1940s E. A. and Russ Flora had designed more powerful AC welders suitable for industrial use.[14] By 1949 Hobart Brothers had added a Tungsten Inert Gas or "TIG" welder, which used an arc from a nonconsumable tungsten electrode shielded by helium or argon gas to join stainless steel or aluminum. In 1953 Hobart brought out its first constant voltage power source for automatic welding.[15] Next, E. A., Blankenbuehler, and Bill Schober combined to design a rectifier welder.[16] Rectifier power sources used a selenium and later a silicon diode to transform alternating current into direct current, which provides a smoother arc for welding.[17] The 1950s were an exciting time as new welding processes and technology came into daily use that revealed their strengths and weaknesses and sorted out the job applications and new materials best suited for each process.

Ray Shook, former director of Hobart Institute of Welding Technology, was named executive director of AWS 2002.

Hobart's technical brain trust realized it lacked the capital and manpower needed to do basic research to invent entirely new welding processes. Research institutes like Battelle and large publicly funded corporations such as General Electric, Westinghouse, and Linde, a division of Union Carbide, did that kind of work. Instead, Hobart Brothers developed the strategy of being a "quick follower." The idea was to rapidly put new technology into a Hobart power source, either through licensing agreements or building in its own improvements that could be patented, and getting it quickly in the hands of Hobart customers.[18] Feedback, both positive and negative, would be channeled through the Procedure Lab where welding design engineers and electrode formulators would be called in to fix problems and incorporate the solutions into new designs and processes. The company may not be the first to roll out an exotic new technology, but its engineers were confident they could create the first integrated welding systems to employ new technology in practical reliable welding equipment, "total arc welding systems."

Peter Hobart and Rudy Mohler

The Technical Institute would play three crucial roles in this strategy. Its staff would serve as Hobart's eyes and ears in attending conferences and welding shows, giving lectures, writing articles, reading and contributing to technical periodicals, and generally keeping abreast of new technology. Secondly, the Procedure Lab would serve as a clearinghouse where customers, distributors, and Hobart engineers would be brought together to solve problems and train people to demonstrate Hobart equipment at national and international trade shows. Finally, the Institute would educate Hobart employees, salesmen, distributors, customers, and the general public in the latest developments in welding technology and their applications.[19] As former students found jobs and fanned out across the country, their positive learning experience in Troy using Hobart equipment could eventually pay dividends as those individuals moved into leadership positions in their respective companies.

The reorganized institute proved to be an unqualified success. By 1963 Hobart Brothers

manufactured a total of 129 different power sources and packages for welding and its sales had grown at a much faster rate than that of the welding industry as a whole.[20] Over the next three decades the technical center would be responsible for many of the innovations incorporated into Hobart welding systems. Its educational functions expanded offering short courses and workshops for those who supervised and evaluated welding, and it hosted national seminars on topics like pipeline construction and welding for railway cars, auto repair, nuclear power plants and submarines. A convivial evening at historic Overfield Tavern with Charlie Brown preparing the steaks was a welcome part of these short courses. The Technical Center developed its own Programmed Audio-Visual Training or "PAT" program as well as a variety of printed instructional materials. Senior Instructor Rudy Mohler wrote most of the training workbooks adapted for the audio-visual format and later published the textbook *Practical Welding Technology*. The Field Training Department brought courses off campus into plants and other sites around the country and eventually around the world. Hobart provided accredited courses for Peace Corps and Job Corps training as well as summer refresher courses for high school vocational instructors. As Hobart Brothers' international sales grew, more foreign students enrolled. Eventually, the Institute was asked to design national

The John H. Blankenbuehler Memorial Library

training programs for the United Kingdom, Netherlands, Italy, Algeria, Saudi Arabia, Indonesia, the Philippines, Colombia, Venezuela, Costa Rica, and Trinidad and it opened branch schools in Amsterdam; Paris; Manila; Sydney, Australia; Woodstock, Ontario; and Mexico City.[21]

During John Blankenbuehler's term as president of the American Welding Society he decided the Hobart Institute should have its own library and presented it with twelve books.[22] From that humble beginning it grew into one of the largest libraries dedicated to welding in the world with over four thousand volumes and an extensive collection of American and international trade and technical journals on welding and metalworking.[23] When Blankenbuehler suddenly passed away in 1964 the library was named in his honor and his catchphrase, "Tell them of the wonderful world of welding," became its motto.

Updating the institute's training equipment and laboratories continued to be a priority. The school was a leader in teaching non-destructive testing procedures in its x-ray laboratory and added ultrasonic and magnetic particle inspection laboratories. There was also a machine shop and equipment for mechanical testing of welds, making the school fully capable of qualifying welders and welding procedures.[24]

Imitation was another key measure of the Technical Institute's success. Lincoln Electric and Miller Electric, both family-owned American competitors of Hobart Brothers, built new technical centers for their companies. For many years Lincoln had run a welding school in the basement of its Euclid, Ohio, plant outside Cleveland, but now built a new structure to house its school and demonstration lab. Miller housed its effort in Appleton, Wisconsin in its new Customer's Technical Service Building. ESAB, a major Swedish competitor, also opened a welding school. The Paton Institute in Kiev, one of the largest technical institutes in the world, patterned its welding program after that of the Hobart Institute as did the welding institutes of Czechoslovakia and several other countries.[25]

The institute in Troy was not the sole effort the Hobarts made to promote welding education. In June 1961 E. A. presented Ohio State University with a two-year graduate fellowship for a student pursuing a master's degree in welding engineering.[26] The C. C. Hobart Foundation would maintain the award. For years Hobart Brothers enjoyed a close relationship with Roy B. McCauley, chairman of OSU's Department of Welding Engineering. Many of McCauley's students interned in Troy during the summer, and Hobart Brothers hired several upon graduation. Counting E. A. himself, thirteen Ohio State engineering graduates worked at Hobart Brothers by the mid-1960s. In 1963 E. A. added four Hobart Brothers Welding Scholarships for undergraduates at Ohio State.

E. A. Hobart, at right, receives an Honorary Doctor of Science degree from his alma mater, The Ohio State University.

Soon the Hobart Technical Center began awarding its own scholarship later named in honor of Ray Dunlevy.[27] In recognition of E. A.'s thirty-five patents and his efforts to advance research and education in the field of welding engineering, The Ohio State University conferred an honorary doctor of science degree upon E. A. Hobart in June 1969. E. A. and his wife Martha also promoted Martha's alma mater, the University of Cincinnati. Each summer they hosted a party at their home for Miami County high school graduates who had enrolled at the University of Cincinnati. Here, future freshmen could meet administrators and faculty members from the university and find new friends or at least valuable car pool rides among local students heading to Cincinnati.[28] Several engineering graduates from Cincinnati also came to work at Hobart Brothers. The Hobart Foundation gave an annual gift to the University of Cincinnati as well as to other schools family members had attended.[29]

Technical Center instructors and Hobart Brothers salesmen agreed that visual aids were an excellent means for gaining the attention of an audience. For the third Hobart Summit Meeting in June 1964 they employed a memorable display to illustrate the theme "Rocket Your Profits—Sell Hobart." For one week a 100-foot-tall, 110-ton Titan II Missile stood on display in the middle of the circular drive in front of the entrance to the Hobart Technology Institute. Officers from Wright-Patterson Air Force Base stood by daily to answer questions.[30] Operational in 1963, the $2.2 million Titan II's armed with atomic warheads were stationed in underground silos and manned by crews trained to fire them on a minute's notice. Titans would provide the nation's main nuclear deterrent for the next twenty-four years.[31] The Titan II also served as the booster rocket for the ten manned space flights of Project Gemini.

Two factors had enabled Hobart Brothers to pull off the coup of the Titan display. The most important was that Hobart's own Chief Engineer Glyn Williams had played a key role on the NASA committee that had designed the rocket. Williams had designed the missile's ground power support system, repeatedly downsizing it.[32] NASA's Kennedy Space Center in Florida was also a customer of Hobart's Vero Beach sales branch.

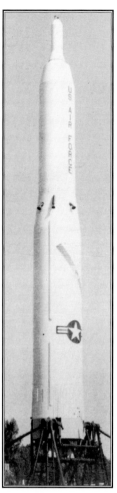

Titan II missile

The impulse to create art seemed worlds away from the cold war concerns of intercontinental ballistic missiles and the space race. In the early 1950s New York City's Museum of Modern Art had bestowed an industrial design award on Hobart's Welded Products Company for its sleek yet functional welding helmets that came in a variety of bright colors to help identify welders on a job. By the 1960s American artists like Alexander Calder and David Smith had employed welding to construct a uniquely American form of sculpture that gradually began to receive world critical acclaim alongside more traditional forms.[33] As the technique gained acceptance, the Hobart Institute set up courses for artists to learn welding or improve their skills. When the Dayton Art Institute received a shipment of broken metal sculptures, it called upon the Technical Center to see if they could be repaired. This was just the sort of new challenge Cary and his instructors enjoyed. The successful repairs strengthened ties between the school and the local art community.

In July 1967 Richard Stankiewicz, known for his welded art sculptures of found objects, was invited to lead a two-week workshop for artists. He repeated the effort the following summer, expanding instruction to three weeks with an optional fourth week. The 1969 workshop was directed by Richard Hunt, an African-

The "family look" with blue, black, and gold colors was unveiled at the 1964 Hobart Summit Meeting.

American artist from Chicago who had recently been featured in a major article in *Life* magazine. Workshop enrollment swelled to twenty-eight, a number that proved too large to be practical. Future enrollment was limited to fifteen, but it became increasingly difficult to find workshop leaders whose skills exceeded those of repeat participants. Troy resident Aka Pereyma, a nationally known artist of Ukrainian origin who had participated in several workshops, assumed the role of workshop coordinator. She now sought to bring resident artists to Troy to present their own work to stimulate discussion and "bridge the gap between the industrial and aesthetic uses of welding" while leaving the improvement of welding skills to the school's own staff. Konstantine Milanados served as the first artist in residence.[34] Both Howard Cary and Peter Hobart became enthusiastic sponsors and collectors of welded sculpture. Eventually, Peter was chosen as chairman of the International Sculpture Committee in Washington, D.C. These classes marked the beginning of the Hobart welded sculpture collection, appropriately located in the industrial park around the Technical Center and making Troy, Ohio the city of welded sculpture.

The year 1967 would mark the fiftieth anniversary of the incorporation of Hobart Brothers, and its fourth Summit Meeting would be an international summit that would

"CONSTRUCTION" by Richard Stankiewicz, 1958, found objects

Richard Stankiewicz

"SPLIT II" by Charles Ginnever, 1973, 1/4" Cor-ten steel

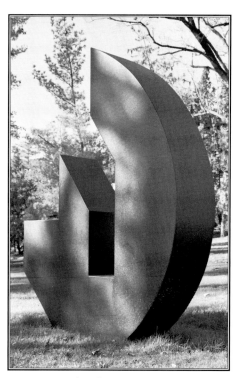

"ECLIPSE" by Aka Pereyma, Cor-ten steel

"SANTA FÉ SUN" by John Henry, aluminum

"WELDICON" by Pino Spagnulo, 1962, mild steel

"TRINITY" by Mike McConnel, 1975, Cor-ten steel

bring the company's growing cadre of foreign distributors to Troy. Hobart leaders hit upon the idea of commissioning a welded sculpture as an appropriate way to commemorate the occasion.[35]

A group of Hobart executives and consulting sculptors selected the bronze welded sculptural fountain design of George Tsutakawa, professor of art at the University of Washington, to be installed in front of the entrance to the Technical Center. Inspired by the totem poles of Native Americans of the Pacific Northwest, Tsutakawa created a pole of five spheres to represent the company's five decades. Coincidentally, the term "totem-polers" was currently being bestowed on Hobart Brothers top-selling distributors. Water tumbled from the spheres and spiraled out toward onlookers from the pinwheel-shaped base designed by David Niland, an architecture professor from the University of Cincinnati and Hobart family friend. Tsutakawa and his partner Jack Uchida, a hydraulics engineer, came to Troy to supervise the sculpture being welded into place. E. A. Hobart pressed the button to start the water flowing before a crowd of employees and dignitaries that included the mayor of Troy and the Director of the Dayton Art Institute.[36] In reviewing the fountain, a *Troy Daily News* editorial noted the interplay of cascading water on the sculpted spheres and that its sound contributed to its effect.[37] Just one month later the City of Troy began accepting designs for the construction of a fountain in the middle of its Public Square.[38]

"UNITY OF MAN" by George Tsutakawa, 1967

The new fountain in front of the Technical Center may have had a calming effect on passers-by, but the Institute itself had clearly energized Hobart Brothers since Cary had taken the helm in its new home less than a decade before. The celebrations that accompanied the company's fiftieth anniversary and first international summit marked a high point in its history. It truly seemed as though the world was beating a path to Troy. Many employees had not fully grasped the company's new place in international markets until its multinational partners came to town.[39] The Technical Center had helped nurture the human contacts and technology that had made this growth possible. Hobart Brothers employees and distributors felt excited to be a part of a company that was at the center of the welding world, the "fountainhead of Welding Knowledge."🕊

127

CHAPTER 18

Hobart Creates the Complete Package

Back in 1926 after the factory on Main Street had been completed, a large steel and glass room adjoining the elevator shaft house was built on the roof of the three-story building. Referred to as "the penthouse," this became the first home of a Hobart Brothers institution, the executive luncheon. Five days a week, E. A., W. H., and the heads of each department ate lunch together and discussed the progress of their business. If someone was out of town or could not make the luncheon, he was expected to send a representative from his department in his stead.[1] Engineers, employees, consultants, distributors, and salesmen were often invited to luncheons to make presentations and discuss proposals, so the number present could vary from seven or eight to as many as twenty. When the new office building was constructed in 1941, E. A. and W. H. designed a well-equipped kitchen adjoining a new executive lunchroom. The luncheon meeting tradition continued for more than half a century and was a key factor in maintaining communication throughout the company and creating synergies among the various departments and their projects and friendly human relations as well.

This concept was extended to all employees with the addition of a company cafeteria. Inspired by the success of a foremen's club at a General Motors plant in Dayton, Hobart instituted a weekly foremen's lunch in a separate meeting room.[2] Many foremen had their problems solved by suggestions from their peers, some of whom found

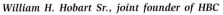

William H. Hobart Sr., joint founder of HBC

themselves making a presentation to the top brass at their next meal.

W. H. supervised the executive luncheons and did all he could to make them an occasion people looked forward to rather than dreaded. He spared no expense in ordering food and hired the best cook he could find. In the early years a woman named Clara, who made splendid cheese soufflés, prepared the meals. After Clara died, Trenton Bell's wife Margie became the new cook.[3] Company officials came home praising the meals they had at Hobart Brothers, and Margie Bell's recipes and services were sought by wives worried that their husbands ate better at work than at home.[4] Dessert always topped off the luncheon. E. A., a noted "sweet tooth," sometimes ate two. When business was not too pressing, W. H. even arranged for entertainment during lunch. On one memorable occasion in the early 1930s they listened to a talented singing quartet of boys still in knee britches, the sons of an African-American barber in Piqua. The young men later gained world renown as the Mills Brothers.[5]

The luncheons grew more interesting in the 1950s as a new generation, W. H.'s sons and sons-in-law, took their place at the table. During their early years with Hobart Brothers Bill Howell, Bob Bravo, and William reported to W. H., who would sometimes respond to their new ideas with the dreaded phrase, "I don't go along with that." More frustrating was W. H.'s tendency to delay and not give a definite answer to a specific proposal. Ocassionally, those in the third generation had to go to E. A. to push W. H. into making a decision. Luncheons gave the young men a chance to take their ideas directly to E. A. and the other executives. Bravo found, "E. A. would give you a definite no, but he also could be persuaded if you had a good plan."[6]

When it came to sales W. H. was most comfortable with the strategies of direct mail and print advertising. These played to his talents and interests. W. H. subscribed to dozens of magazines and pored over them, noting the layout of their ads, their use of photographs and illustrations, even the size and typeface of the printed text.[7] Although gregarious around his family and his old friends from Troy, he was uncomfortable around the many hard-drinking and carousing salesmen of that era.[8] To house visiting customers and distributors Hobart Brothers leased rooms in the office building that W. H. nicknamed "No Eve Arms" because of his rule that no women be permitted to enter.[9] W. H. knew how best to sell through direct mail, print advertising, and trade shows. W. H. believed in the importance of focused trade shows, specifically those of the American Welding Society (AWS) and other industry exhibitions domestically and internationally. Eddie Butterfield had been the key contact person for large government orders. Dick Sherwood was the first to push for sales to large commercial clients like Chicago Bridge and Iron and the big three automobile makers.[10] Bill Howell heartily endorsed that emphasis but strongly believed Hobart Brothers' entire sales network needed to be restructured. By 1953 he had persuaded Hobart executives to go along with his plans. One close observer, Wib Chaffee who had established the first links with welding distributors and now ran international sales for Hobart, considered Howell's reorganization of domestic sales such an important event that he believed 1953 marked the transition from the second to the third generation of Hobarts.[11]

Although the third generation felt that its period of tutelage lasted much longer, Howell's overhaul of sales was clearly the company's most important postwar move since the addition of ground power equipment had reinvigorated the Motor Generator Corporation. Howell increased the number of sales districts and district supervisors to twelve and created a formal statement of policies for supervisors that included salary,

expenses, annual review, and a sales bonus incentive. Aptitude tests became one criterion for selecting district supervisors. To streamline distribution, seven warehouses were set up around the country. District supervisors reported to an assistant for distributor sales.[12]

Howell ran into a stumbling block when he sought to reinstate a reporting system Chaffee had initiated to encourage competition among Hobart distributors. The company's antiquated bookkeeping system did not produce the kind of prompt sales records needed to run such a plan. In one of his first major decisions as the company's assistant secretary-treasurer, William Jr. brought in a data processing staff, and the faster and more varied measurements it provided improved the efficiency of all departments.[13]

Using Chaffee's "horse race" theme, Howell classified distributors from A to E based on the concentration of Hobart equipment in their total sales. Although most distributors fell into the "B" category, they could move into "A" classification by regularly sending personnel to Troy for training. Higher classifications were eligible for bonus discounts and exclusivity on sales in their territory. Each distributor was given a monthly sales quota, and those that exceeded it were listed in percentage order as "Quotabusters" in a monthly newsletter, while the top twenty in total sales volume were ranked in the "Volume Sweepstakes." This system gave recognition to both small and large welding supply distributors. Beginning in 1958 the leaders of A and B class distributors were invited to attend the triennial Summit Meetings in Troy. In 1960 Howell revised the monthly reporting using an airplane theme. Sales quotas were now called "three-point landings" which included sales on filler metals, sales of machines and accessories, and overall sales. Those who met quotas on all three points were eligible for ranking as "Quotabusters." The top twenty listing in total sales continued, but their name was changed to "Totempolers." The top three Quotabusters and Totempolers received awards at the Summit Meetings. Later the company added an award for outstanding international distributor and a "Million Dollar Club" for the highest volume distributors.[14] Distributors or "Hobarteers" kept abreast of the latest sales rankings by reading *Hobarteering*, their monthly newsletter.

When it came to sales W. H. was most comfortable with the strategies of direct mail and print advertising.

Ed Butterfield,
government sales manager

Since 1942 the company had also published a quarterly magazine for customers and distributors called the *Hobart Arc Welding News*, which contained many photographs of Hobart equipment at work, application stories, and usually had a page on the activities and new courses at the welding school. Its first editor Bob Wagner solicited articles from his readers by offering a $200 annual prize to the best story submitted. Later the magazine's name was shortened to *Hobart Welding News* and the second editor Dick Swisher paid from $2 to $25 for each article and imprinted the back cover with the names and addresses of each distributor. There were 284 distributors who sold Hobart equipment by the early 1960s.[15]

Hobart Arc Welding News, *1942*

The magazine's look and mailing list had become dated by 1967 when Cliff Priest hired Glenn Nally to become the new communications director for Hobart Brothers. Nally had worked with the company since 1953 as an employee of the Ralph Dalton and Associates Advertising Agency. Nally had distributors pay twenty-five cents per issue to imprint their name on the back cover and continuously update their mailing list which enabled him to update the magazine to a full color format. Dan Lea was appointed writer-editor-photographer. The publication, renamed *Hobart Weldworld*, became a stylish and informative showcase for Hobart products and their use around the world. In the mid-1970s Nally was asked to redesign the cover and format for the *Welding Journal*, the official trade publication of the American Welding Society. The *Welding Journal* employed Nally's format until 1999.[16]

Multi-wire ®

No marketing organization or advertising campaign can sustain an increase in sales unless there are quality products to sell. In 1960–61 Hobart Brothers brought out its most attractive products to date, the "Complete Package" for its "Microwire" and "Multiwire" semiautomatic welders. The concept was the Procedure Lab's response to customer input on the difficulty of trying to sort through the many new welding processes on the market while purchasing power sources, electrodes, gases, and accessories from a variety of manufacturers, many of whom gave conflicting advice over welding procedures and applications. Sometimes the local distributor contributed to customer frustration by pushing equipment that netted the best profits for itself but did not necessarily work smoothly together or produce the best results for the customer. Hobart addressed these problems by embracing "a single source responsibility for the welding equipment, consumables, accessories, training and service."[17]

Glyn Williams and his team designed matched welding equipment in the first two packages, both of which employed the gas metal arc welding process where an automatically spooled wire electrode is fed through a welding gun that also sprays a shielding gas around the weld in progress.[18] Hobart technicians demonstrated the Microwire package at the National Metal Show in October 1960. The Multiwire welder, an even more versatile machine capable of handling larger diameter wires as well as flux-cored wire for a number of different applications, was introduced at the following year's Summit Meeting. Both were immediate hits. By 1962 automatic packages accounted for more than one third of the gross sales in dollars of Hobart welding equipment.[19] In discussing how to price one of the packages a panel had settled on $1,500 when someone suggested pricing it at $1,492, a figure that would be easy to remember and a dream to market with its

Glenn Nally,
marketing communications
director, 1977

Welding Journal *received a*
new look in the 1970s.

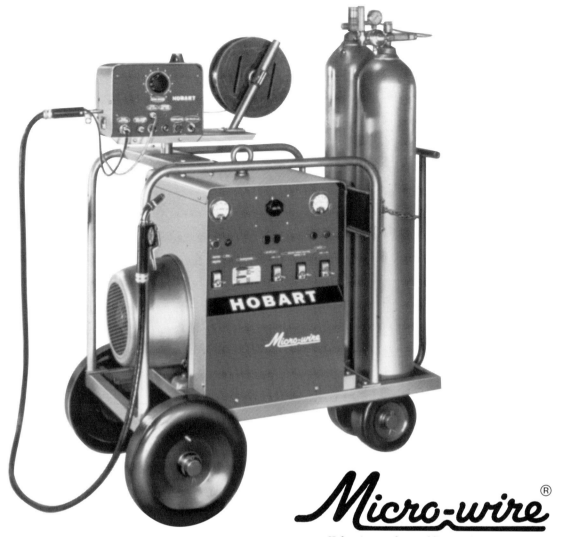

Micro-wire®

*Hobart's complete welding package with
the renowned AGH-27 wire feeder*

implied reference to discovery. To complement these new systems Hobart developed the AGH-27 wire feeder, which became the world's standard for quality wire feeders in CO_2 welding.

The Microwire and Multiwire welding systems sold so well that they created a crisis in the allocation of personnel and resources at Hobart Brothers. The Motor Generator Corporation had been planning a major expansion of its product line. A portion of the Westbrook plant expansion had been tooled up to manufacture civilian versions of the electrical generators it had been producing for years for the military. The plan was to market the generators as auxiliary power sources for hospitals, businesses, and even homes. Adam Callan had been hired away from Onan to direct the mar-

The Microwire and Multiwire welding systems sold so well that they created a crisis in the allocation of personnel and resources at Hobart Brothers.

keting of the new product line. Shortly before production was scheduled to begin in 1965, E. A. cancelled the whole project in order to devote the new plant space to produce welding wire for the hot-selling Microwire and Multiwire systems.[20] Microwire eventually became the generic term for fine wire CO_2 welding. The people at Motor Generator were stunned by the decision.[21] Months later New York City and several East Coast communities experienced a crippling blackout that stimulated the market for auxiliary generators. By the early 1970s the ongoing energy crisis had created quite a lucrative market for small generators, much of it captured by Japanese companies. In hindsight, E. A.'s decision appeared to be one of the few missteps in his entrepreneurial career.

A closer look at the decision reveals that it made perfect sense at the time, but it also reflected the traditions and limitations of the company. For more than three decades welding equipment had been Hobart Brother's bread and butter. Why forgo the opportunity to fill wire orders to begin a risky new product line for a peripheral division of the company? After all, welding wire represented the "razor blades," the consumables that would earn the main profits for the new welding systems. E. A. may have been uncomfortable with the idea of selling generators to a mass market where pricing, distribution, and advertising were paramount compared to the U.S. military where reliability and performance geared to precise specifications guaranteed sales. E. A. may have been bored by the technology of the auxiliary generators whereas the new welding systems marked a step into the challenging field of semiautomatic welding. A rough parallel can be drawn with his father C. C. Hobart's decision to get out of the business of manufacturing food processing equipment. However, the fact that a choice had to be made at all showed that Hobart Brothers was bumping into the limits of private financing. Even if the capital to expand both wire and generator production were available, the labor was simply not there. Manufacturing employment throughout the Miami Valley was reaching a postwar peak in 1965, and Hobart Brothers had to compete with publicly financed and unionized companies like Hobart Manufacturing as well as NCR and General Motors.

William Howell, senior vice president of sales and marketing, played a critical role in establishing a nationwide network of Hobart branch sales offices.

Rutile production was still underway in Florida and the distribution center overseas in Amsterdam had just been turned into a manufacturing facility. E. A.'s company simply lacked the capital or management to build yet another production center somewhere beyond the Miami Valley.

The only places in North America where Hobart equipment was not selling well were regions that lacked a strong independent distributor. In 1963 Howell began to fill in those gaps by setting up the first Hobart Brothers branch for direct sales in Tulsa, Oklahoma, the oil patch. Despite some protests from distributors who feared Hobart branches would cut into their sales, Howell continued the strategy, opening sales and service offices in Boston; Brooklyn; and Buffalo, New York; Vero Beach, Orlando, and Tampa, Florida; Cincinnati; Gary, Indiana; Peoria, Illinois; Philadelphia; St. Louis; New Orleans; Houston; Los Angeles and Oakland, California; and Seattle over the next several years.[22] By carefully establishing and adhering to territorial boundaries with established independent distributors, Howell smoothed their ruffled feathers and presided over a growth in sales that put Hobart in a position to challenge Lincoln Electric for the top spot among American welding firms. Overtaking Lincoln was an ambition everyone at Hobart Brothers shared. In the midst of this all-out competition, another patent dispute erupted with Lincoln, but E. A. and Jim Lincoln worked out a compromise that kept their companies out of court. As part of the deal, the pair of rivals and fellow Ohio State Buckeyes

The Hobart Tulsa Branch

The Hobart Los Angeles Branch

agreed to exchange visits to their respective plants, so E. A. journeyed to Cleveland to walk through Lincoln Electrics works, and Jim Lincoln came to Troy and toured the Hobart plants.[23] Both men enjoyed the same kind of celebrity status and awkward geniality as an American or Soviet head of state being hosted by its superpower adversary. It was the last time E. A. saw Jim Lincoln alive. Lincoln passed away in 1965, but the rivalry lived on.

Despite the advances in technology and the surge in sales, there was a shadow over Hobart Brothers in the mid-1960s. The generation that had led the company through depression and war was aging and beginning to falter. Starting in 1960 W. H. suffered a series of small strokes that made it difficult for him to speak. His son William and Margaret Stratton, his longtime secretary, were still able to communicate with him by asking questions and deciphering his replies.[24] William continued to assume more of his father's responsibilities. W. H. spent less time at the office, but his sense of humor never deserted him. He could be seen heading home with items he had ordered for his grandchildren stuffed in a canvas bag that had "Stolen from W. H. Hobart" stenciled on it. As W. H.'s health declined, employees stopped receiving his blue 3 x 5 cards. A counterpoint to his brother's salmon card directives, W. H. often left blue cards that might praise an employee for a job well done, chide him for how he dressed or comported himself at work or in the community, or even dispense advice on child rearing. Employees did not fear hearing from W. H. but often scratched their heads or smiled at his gentle if paternalistic touch.[25] W. H. was a father figure to the Troy

The only places in North America where Hobart equipment was not selling well were regions that lacked a strong independent distributor.

community as well, serving for thirty years on the local School Board during a time of expansion and helped supervise the building of a new elementary school and a new high school. Troy's public library, then located in the former Hayner mansion on West Main Street, was another special concern of W. H.'s to which he donated both books and funds.

To his nineteen grandchildren he was known affectionately as "Dudu," a "load of fun" who played songs for them on the piano and told marvelous tales about local history characters he had invented.[26] Each Christmas he designed original Christmas cards full of witty observations on life and Troy that became cherished possessions. He also composed a letter to his grandchildren, explaining the gift of stock in Hobart subsidiaries he and "Unc" (E. A.) were giving them. The letters sparkled with humor and advice and pointed out that everyone who worked at Hobart Brothers had helped to create this gift and that the stock represented a responsibility that was being handed on to them.

As W. H. lay on his deathbed, his wife Rachel had her arms around two of her grandchildren, Robb and David Howell. "It's your job to carry on the company your grandfather helped build," she whispered to them.[27] It was a message all W. H.'s children and grandchildren heard more than once.

After William Hobart died on February 20, 1965, local newspapers and welding publications listed his public accomplishments and professional associations, but word also trickled out about his anonymous donations, many of which went to or were filtered through Trinity Episcopal Church.[28] At his funeral a poem was read that W. H.

The Hobart St. Louis Branch

The Hobart Peoria Branch

had written in 1939, the year his mother had died, but to his relatives and friends it sounded like Bill Hobart's final words of advice:

Beloved ones don't sorrow or grieve
Over that tired body that you see I have
    left behind . . .
I am a step beyond you, understanding things, . . .
Talk to me in your still moments, unburden your
    thoughts and fears . . .
Remember the first principle of life is to like people
And second is to help them help themselves.
These two principles have built every good thing in
    life.[29]

W. H. had been E. A.'s sounding board when he wanted to talk over a business decision, but there had been few of E. A.'s generation left that he could turn to once his brother fell ill. Orval Menke, E. A.'s old college roommate, had begun to decline about the same time as W. H. The task of running the manufacturing operations of the company soon got beyond him, but no one had the heart to ask him to retire. Like E. A. and Martha, Menke and his wife were childless and the company was his life. For nearly three years Glyn Williams shouldered most of Menke's duties while remaining chief engineer and working on projects for NASA. Despite the strain, Williams had the people skills to keep the factories running smoothly. In 1963 when E. A. decided to hire someone to formally replace Menke, he offered the position to Williams. It was not an easy choice to make, but Williams decided to stay with his first love and remain in engineering.[30] The day after W. H.'s funeral Williams left after work to play handball with two of his friends, Floyd Pansing from Hobart Corporation and Tom Noftle head of employee relations at Hobart Brothers. After changing clothes he told Noftle and Pansing that he didn't feel like playing and that he would stop by Dettmer Hospital on his way home. His friends phoned his doctor, but Williams drove straight home where he collapsed and died of a heart attack. He was just forty-nine years of age.[31]

Having just buried his brother, E. A. was bitter over the loss of Williams. "It's just not fair," he told Glyn's widow Gladys. E. A. had been going to name Williams as a new vice president, and some believed he was grooming Williams to be his successor. Since there were no engineers

W. H. had been E. A.'s sounding board when he wanted to talk over a business decision, but there had been few of E. A.'s generation left that he could turn to once his brother fell ill.

among W. H.'s sons and sons-in-law, E. A. may have wanted to entrust the top job to a fellow engineer. Williams was certainly a man who had gained E. A.'s trust. He had put the twenty-five-year-old Williams in charge of production on the eve of World War II and later appointed him a director of the C. C. Hobart Foundation. Williams had been the only company official in the next generation senior to the Hobart family members and in-laws of the next generation.[32] It now became clear that William Jr. was E. A.'s heir apparent as president.

Orval Menke died just four days after Williams. Like Charles and W. H. Hobart, Menke was a gentleman farmer who had planted orchards and kept bees on a piece of land he owned south of West Main.[33] He bequeathed this land to the City of Troy, which turned it into Menke Park. When his brother and Menke had been ailing, E. A. had turned for a confidante to John Blankenbuehler, a brilliant engineer who held as many patents as E. A. did. Blankenbuehler's 23 years of experience at Westinghouse provided a valuable perspective on how a large corporation had approached its business challenges, but E. A. had lost Blankenbuehler too when he died suddenly in March 1964.[34] Some of E. A.'s contemporaries managed to retire rather than die in harness. The colorful Wib Chaffee left in 1965.[35] Office Manager and Company Secretary Earl Galbreath retired in 1968 along with Eddie Butterfield and longtime Company Treasurer D. C. Jenkins. Nicknamed Pete, Jenkins had also served for 24 years on Troy's City Council and while in that capacity he supervised the operation of Hobart Arena. Combined, the three men had put in over 140 years at Hobart Brothers.[36]

Some seventy-six-year-old men would have been staggered by these losses, but E. A. possessed a remarkable physical constitution and a keen youthfulness of mind. Yet an even more important factor was at work. As his nephew and namesake Edward J. Hobart said, "Essentially, E. A. saw everyone who worked at Hobart Brothers as being part of his family. He wasn't about to let down on that responsibility."[37]

With the departure of confidantes his own age, E. A. turned to a much younger man who had joined the company in 1958. Don Karnes had grown up in Troy where he was a classmate of Peter Hobart and had sometimes done yardwork for Peter's father. Karnes earned his degree in electrical engineering at Wilmington College and interviewed at both Hobart Corporation and Hobart Brothers after graduation. Menke beat Hobart Corporation's offer and secured Karnes' services. After a three-month orientation period, Karnes became a special projects assistant to Blankenbuehler, and in 1963 he was named assistant to the president.

Karnes had come from a family of entrepreneurs and had been very close to his grandfather who had died in 1960. E. A., who was about the same age as Karnes' grandfather, got along well with Karnes from the first and came to use him as a sounding board when he wanted to think aloud to mull over new ideas and make decisions. This often put Karnes in an awkward position with E. A.'s nephews and nephews-in-law who held senior positions in the company but were not as privy to "Unc's" decision-making as this young man in his twenties who was not a family member. Karnes once complained that E. A. was putting him in a tough position with the rest of the family who were starting to resent him. "Don't worry about them," E. A. bristled. "You don't work for them. You work for me. I own this place. As long as you're doing what I want you to do, you have nothing to worry about."[38] Sometimes E. A. appeared to use Karnes as a cat's paw in a way that tended to exaggerate his influence in the eyes of company officers. Executive luncheons often included a lively and sometimes contentious discussion of a proposal and ended with a decision hanging fire. As everyone got up and turned to leave, E. A. would often call out, "Karnes— in my office." Karnes walked past the glowering assembly and followed E. A. out. Sometimes E. A. would discuss the subject raised at the luncheon, occasionally asking for Karnes' input, but he was just as likely to talk about a completely different topic. Bill Howell who had always been close to E. A. was the most angered by Karnes' special access and made no secret of the fact that he planned to fire Karnes as soon as he was no longer under E. A.'s protection. "And don't let the door hit your butt on the way out," he told Karnes.[39]

For a man his age E. A. was unusually focused on the future.

For a man his age E. A. was unusually focused on the future, but as the Christmas season and his own birthday approached, he would mellow, grow nostalgic and occasionally reminisce about the past with Karnes. E. A. often spoke about how his father C. C. had made his way to the Miami Valley and the fits and starts of his early business ventures. E. A. was immensely proud of his father's achievements. He spoke less often about his own early years at Hobart Brothers and what he and his brothers had accomplished. Sometimes he detailed the extraordinary efforts made during the war years. These talks always ended the same way. E. A. would smile and shake his head at the remarkable life he had enjoyed and say, "I just want five more good years."[40]

E. A. continued his paternalistic style of management by walking around. "E. A. still prowls office and factory with a pocket full of salmon pink 3 x 5 cards " Chaffee reported.[41] In fact, employees noticed that E. A. became more gregarious as he grew older. He seemed to be on a first name basis with nearly every employee who had been with the company for more than a couple years. He stopped and chatted for longer spells now and asked questions about wives and children not just the work at hand. E. A. made a conscious effort to assume the role his brother had played in the company and in the family as well. A Hobart official spotted one of E. A.'s cards on his desk in the morning and thought, "Uh oh, that man has been here again," but upon reading it found that E. A. was inquiring about the health of his wife who had been in the hospital.[42] E. A. took over writing the annual Christmas letter on the gift of stock shares to his grandnieces and grandnephews. "Never sell it," he enjoined them. "Make it grow larger."[43] In the 1960s it seemed as though all parts of Hobart Brothers were indeed growing larger, but the one aspect of the company's growth that E. A. found disquieting was what his nephew Peter was doing with the international side of the business.

D. C. Jenkins, longtime Hobart Brothers Company treasurer

135

CHAPTER 19

Hobart International
"The Beginning of Globalization"

In the 1930s E. A. and W. H. Hobart attended the Leipzig Industrial Fair in Germany. While there they had discussions with officials from the Skoda Works, one of the largest industrial firms in Europe. Skoda had been the main armaments manufacturer for the Austro-Hungarian Empire before that nation was dismembered following its defeat in the First World War. Skoda ended up in the newly minted nation of Czechoslovakia. Nothing came of the talks with Skoda until a couple of years later when W. H. received a letter expressing interest in a joint venture. E. A. and W. H. felt a bit insulted. Did the executives at Skoda think the Hobarts were a pair of naïve Americans unaware of world events? In the interim the western powers had caved in to Hitler's demands at Munich to annex the Sudetenland from Czechoslovakia. Six months later Hitler had marched in unopposed and seized the western half of the country including the city of Pilsen, the home of Skoda Works. W. H. replied that the current political situation made any cooperative venture unadvisable. Shortly after the war began the mask was dropped and Skoda was absorbed into the Hermann Goering Works and produced arms for the German war machine until Pilsen was liberated in 1945.[1]

E. A. and W. H. never were enthusiastic about the export trade, and the episode with Skoda seemed to confirm their belief that many foreigners could not be trusted. World War II and the ensuing Cold War made it obvious to just about everyone that welding was strategically vital. As the elder Hobarts understood it, that fact made it foolish to launch a major push for international markets. Why would any nation that wanted to be an industrial or military power allow itself to depend on a foreign welding company? A government always stacked the deck in favor of its domestic

Peter C. Hobart,
1960s vice president international
and president HBI, A.G.

welding industry. The logic of this position was difficult to refute.

For many years Wib Chaffee was the sole Hobart executive who wanted to promote the export business. Even in the days when battery chargers and garage equipment were the company's mainstay, Hobart Brothers had some international sales, mostly to Canada, Mexico, the United Kingdom, and the Netherlands. World War II nearly killed off the company's export business. In 1943 Chaffee discovered that Hobart distributors in nations outside North America had been dismissed with a notice that there would be no equipment for export until after the war. After protesting to W. H. that these contacts should not be lost, Chaffee was told, "Go ahead and be a godfather to the export business." Stepfather may have been a more apt term since international sales were neglected until 1946 when export licenses became easier to obtain.[2] Within a short time Chaffee reestablished a network of international distributors and started to place print ads in export publications.[3] Apart from a few jaunts to Canada, Cuba, and Mexico, the export trade was run by mail entirely from Chaffee's desk, the bottom drawer of which contained a spittoon that the tobacco-chewing and cigar-chomping Chaffee used as a target to punctuate his conversations.

After World War II America began to withdraw into its old isolationism, and most businesses who did not have their own international organizations were forced to use trading companies or export houses, mainly European, to sell their products, especially in the former colonies. Some were able to piggyback on the international gas companies, like Union Carbide, AGA, and L'Air Liquide. Enterprising distributors in a few developing nations handled

Rotterdam distributor of Hobart service station equipment (circled items), 1930s

much of the business. However, large groups, such as Muller and Phipps, Scott and English, and the Danish East Asiatic Group and Dutch Ruhaak Trading Company were the main sources of distribution.

Despite these limitations, exports quickly jumped to three or four times the prewar level, especially with spare parts. Thanks to the tens of thousands of Hobart generators and welders shipped to allies and to every war theater on the globe, the Hobart name had become well known worldwide and its equipment already had a reputation for quality and reliability.[4] Many requests came in simply addressed "Hobart Brothers, Troy, Ohio" taken right off the name-plates on machines. Experiencing health problems in 1956, Chaffee convinced William Jr. to hire a man with export experience to take over foreign sales. Dick Whitlow was put in charge of the Export Department, but the elder Hobart brothers still vetoed many of his proposals to pursue international markets more aggressively. During the year between his graduation from Yale and his induction into the Army, Peter Hobart visited two industrial fairs in Europe and wrote a pair of articles about them in *Welding Engineer*:

The welding exhibits showed a European adherence to manual arc welding and lack of interest in automatic proce-

> *For many years Wib Chaffee was the sole Hobart executive who wanted to promote the export business.*

dures. . . The American welding industry could very profitably enter Western Europe with an offer of technological advances. . . The advent of the European Common Market in the near future with its potential of 160 million people makes serious consideration of this industrial area advisable. . . .[5]

At Hobart Brothers such serious consideration had to wait two more years.

When Peter returned to Troy following his Army service in Italy, he looked at his prospects at Hobart Brothers with a different eye. He saw his brother and brothers-in-law had been given more responsibilities, but they were still under the thumb of E. A. and W. H. Moreover, William, Bravo, and Howell each had ten to fifteen years more experience with the company than Peter had. The way ahead looked crowded with precious little room for independent initiative. Peter decided to follow his interests and his father's advice to write his own job description by creating a role for himself in expanding the international side of the business. First, he brought Anna Zambon to Troy to visit, and the pair soon announced their engagement. Some eyebrows were raised within the family over Peter's marrying an Italian Catholic, but Anna's charm and intelligence won them over.

Peter used the potential tax advantages and flexibility of incorporating a foreign subsidiary of Hobart Brothers to win company executives over to the idea of expanding internationally. Using as a model the Outboard Marine Corporation and the advice of Baker and McKenzie, a rapidly growing international law firm from Chicago, Hobart Brothers, A.G. was incorporated on October 8, 1960, in Zug, Switzerland. However, it placed its main office in Nassau, Bahamas, for its convenient proximity to the company's Florida holdings and Latin American customers. The company's distribution contracts, international warranties, sales conditions, and trademark registrations were a model for globalization of an enterprise. Hobart Brothers was one of the first medium-sized American companies to take such a step. Baker and McKenzie's Lajos Schmidt, who had earned his first law degree in Hungary and ultimately became a freedom fighter against both Nazi's and communists before making his way to America, was the main advisor and reference for Hobart Brothers in the firm.[6]

By March 1961 ownership of Hobart Brothers, A.G. was entirely in the hands of the young quartet of Bravo, Howell, William and Peter Hobart, the first company controlled by the third generation. With Peter serving as president, the company was at first a middleman between Hobart Brothers who manufactured the equipment and the foreign distributors who sold it. Hobart Brothers, A.G. would take half of its commission on sales after distributor discounts and reinvest it in qualified staff, travel, exhibitions, service facilities, and training programs for overseas markets. If warranted, the company would then develop assembly and manufacturing abroad. Using the pattern set by Howell in the United States, Peter appointed regional sales managers to find and train well-qualified new distributors, change poor ones, promote new equipment, and explore possibilities for joint ventures. This created a basic network for intelligence gathering and effective implementing of sales programs.

In the beginning, Hobart Brothers, A.G. had what was called a United Nations approach where every country was considered a potential market. The U.S. government was not yet able to provide economic intel-

Jack Cossman,
vice president european
sales and marketing

Andre Odermatt,
European chief engineer
and plant manager of
Hobart Amsterdam,
president HIWT 2002

ligence, so companies like Hobart Brothers had to develop their own. Within two years qualified regional managers were in place for Canada, Europe, Latin America, the Pacific region, and Africa including the Middle East. Recruiting these managers was extremely difficult. Few Americans at that time wanted to work abroad or possessed the requisite language skills, so primarily European or Latin American businessmen were selected. For example, Jacques Rene "Jack" Cossman, an extremely qualified European welding executive who had worked with a Hobart distributor, was chosen to head a modest office in Amsterdam with just one assistant and a secretary, but in the next few years his territory experienced explosive growth.[7]

An aggressive program to participate in several international trade shows with multi-lingual personnel and literature spurred sales growth for Hobart, A.G.[8] The most important of these shows was the Welding Exhibition in Essen held in the heart of West Germany's industrial Ruhr District. As the first American welding company to exhibit at Essen, the small Hobart Brothers booth on the first floor aroused a great deal of curiosity and many orders. Demonstrations of its new Microwire and Multiwire semi-automatic welding systems drew clusters of observers interested in the technology. Engineers from Thyssen, the largest steel manufacturer in Germany, were amazed at the smooth welding arc and welds produced by the Hobart power source. Some were convinced a special shielding gas was being employed and were skeptical when Hobart's Bob Bercaw told them it was simply industrial grade CO_2. The German engineers hooked up their own gas tank and found the arc was just as smooth as before. They were so impressed that Thyssen agreed to become the exclusive German distributor for Hobart products and sold over a thousand welding packages in the first year.[9]

Andre Odermatt, a young technician from Oerlikon in Switzerland, was also impressed with the "beautifully engineered" Hobart machine he tested while evaluating competitive power sources for Oerlikon. Although he had no idea where Troy, Ohio was, he wanted to work for a company that made such machines and wrote letters of introduction. First, he received a curt reply from E. A. stating, "We don't employ foreigners here," but his letter was also sent on to Peter Hobart who directed Jack Cossman to interview and eventually hire Odermatt in 1964 to design a European line of welders and oversee service and technology for this market. Odermatt was taken aback by the American approach to business. "You will do well," Peter told him, "or we will fire you."[10]

Peter was in a hurry to exploit the jump in sales in the European market by establishing a manufacturing plant on the continent in Amsterdam. Due to the added costs of shipping and import duties, American welders were expensive in Europe, and exporting low value-added goods, such as electrodes and welding wire, was out of the question. A plant located within the European Economic Community could turn out and customize products that were suitable for the different European styles and technical requirements.[11] Only a handful of American manufacturers in other industries were making this move in the 1960s. Holland was a prime location for internationalization.

Based solely on the export of welding machines, Hobart Brothers A.G.'s sales had more than doubled from $2.4 million in 1960 to $5.5 million in 1963.[12] Peter took the next step in 1963 by moving to Amsterdam to supervise the building of the European sales network, overseeing service, warehousing, and ultimately manufacturing facilities as manager of European operations, while in Troy Bravo became vice president for international sales, including aircraft ground power equipment.[13] Peter was accompanied by Bob Bercaw as a technical consultant and E. A.'s "policeman." Hobart, A.G. also established joint manufacturing ventures in Australia and Spain in 1963 and added enough distributors the following year to surpass the 100 mark.[14]

Robert Bravo

Over the next decade. Hobart Brothers, A.G. transformed itself from an international sales network for exported Hobart welding machines to a global enterprise that manufactured most of the welding equipment and consumables it sold locally in the markets served.

Gradually, Peter and his resident international managers developed a strategy to direct this expansion. Wholly owned subsidiaries, usually with manufacturing and training capability, would be established in developed countries that proved to be strong markets. Joint ventures would be sought in industrialized or developing countries with good growth potential. Finally, licensing agreements would be used in developing nations where long-term economic prospects involved more risk.

Peter enjoyed the demands that creating and running an international company made upon him. Extensive travel was essential for all managers to do international business. This was the beginning of globalization based on quality, advanced technology, and worldwide service. He was fascinated by the different cultures he encountered and became fluent in Dutch, French, German, Italian, and Spanish. As a pioneer in global company "hands-on" management, Peter was often called upon to lecture management groups about what was then called "the American Challenge," after the title of a book by J. J. Servan Schreiber, whom he once debated before the Dutch Management Association. Peter had succeeded in creating a role for himself within Hobart Brothers that allowed him to integrate his interests in art and culture, diplomacy, and even intelligence gathering into his life. Free time during his travels was spent visiting art galleries, architectural wonders, and archaeological sites.

As the CEO of a foreign corporation Peter often had to deal with government officials. These meetings as well as the knowledge of economic and military affairs gained in his business travels made Peter a desirable source of information for U.S. intelligence agencies, as was common in those years for international businessmen. Agencies often sent someone to debrief him and other Hobart executives. Peter's intelligence role was not simply a matter of keeping his eyes and ears open. He was also instructed to make use of contacts with people in the Eastern Bloc to make a "sales pitch" for working for or defecting to the West. One incident illustrates the serious nature of this form of Cold War competition. During an industrial conference in Delft, Netherlands Peter made a pitch to a young nuclear scientist from the People's Republic of China who listened impassively in silence. Shortly after this meeting Peter read that the young scientist had jumped or fallen from a second-story window of the Chinese consulate. Consulate employees had then hustled him back into the building where he "died of his wounds" instead of escaping to the West.

Peter realized that the constant travel took a toll on his roles as a husband and father, but his nieces and nephews in Troy were intrigued by his jet-set lifestyle. One nephew saw him as a James Bond kind of figure.[15] After the birth of his son, Peter John, and his daughter, Michelle, he moved his young family to Rome to concen-

Hobart Brothers A.G.'s sales had more than doubled from $2.4 million in 1960 to $5.5 million in 1963.

The Saudi-Hobart facility, 1979

trate on the Southern European, African, and Middle East markets, as well as permitting his wife, Anna, to work at her profession as a psychoanalyst and also because he had come to love Italian culture. Peter's international ventures also provided opportunities for members of the fourth generation of industrial Hobarts to cut their teeth in the family business. Robb Howell, the second-oldest son of Bill and Marcia Howell, was a recent graduate from Ohio State in 1978 when he accepted Peter's invitation to serve as a manager at Saudi Hobart, an electrode factory in Dammam, Saudi Arabia.[16] His sister, Debbie, had already been living abroad in Amsterdam with her husband Josh Kurd who was production manager at the Hobart plant. Kurd was Jack Cossman's stepson and he had met Debbie on a business visit to Troy. The couple married in 1969.[17]

Naturally, the successes of Hobart, A.G. were punctuated by disappointments. ISG, a joint venture with Thyssen to manufacture flux-cored wires in Hamm was closed and moved to southern France in Bellegarde to reduce costs, improve technology, and increase sales. The national sales and service operation in West Germany was reduced to a small regional sales office in Frankfurt directed by Bernard Behlen.[18] Metallogen, managed by Paul Bergmann, was a joint venture established in Germany in 1972 to produce flux-cored wires and electrodes for the specialty maintenance and repair business that proved much more successful. This was the beginning of a major program of diversifi-

cation for the entire company that eventually developed a huge family of maintenance and repair products that moved into high tech lines and was sold mainly on a direct basis. Production in Latin America began in 1965 with a licensing operation in Mexico and a joint venture to manufacture electrodes in Guatemala.[19] These operations proved profitable in the long run, but several other joint ventures and licensed manufacturing deals in Central and South America were short lived. A direct sales and service branch for Great Britain was set up in Leeds under Gene Howard and later Mervyn Roberts, but sales growth in the United Kingdom was sluggish.[20]

Peter was willing to explore a wide variety of locations and financing arrangements to maximize production and distribution. Hobart Schweisstechnik, its distributor in Vienna under Anton Zeifkovits, became a conduit for sales to the USSR and the Soviet Bloc countries of Eastern Europe. Professor Boris Paton, director of the prestigious Paton Institute in Kiev and a good friend of Peter Hobart's, often commented philosophically to Peter and other Hobart executives, "We technicians get along famously and see eye to eye on the world; the only difference is the political scenario, but we shall overcome." When things went wrong with international markets, it generally was the politicians who were the cause. Wars, tariff barriers, currency devaluations, and political upheavals affected profitability more than fluctuations of the business cycle or the inevitable advance of technology.

Saudi electrode, 1979

First Amsterdam factory in Zeeburger Dijk, 1966

The Amsterdam plant brought in more money each year in the late 1960s. At first Hobart's Dutch workforce mainly warehoused inventory and assembled components shipped from Troy but gradually began to manufacture welding equipment designed for the European market, meeting strict European technical standards, having metrical measurements and technical information in the various local languages. In general, European customers favored smaller, lighter more energy efficient machines and hence less expensive than the American models. First, Odermatt designed a European-style wire feeder with a DC motor with speed control, then a welding gun. The machining for prototypes for a small static welder for the European market was subcontracted to Philips, a large Dutch electrical equipment corporation that was also a distributor for Hobart in Holland and Great Britain. After modifications, the RC 150 became Hobart's first power source totally designed and produced overseas for a foreign market.[21] A later model, the RC-226 sold even better, and the Amsterdam plant expanded in 1969 to meet demand. That same year Amsterdam added its own Technical Center modeled on the one in Troy complete with its own Procedure Lab.[22] Richard Boekholt, a professional welding engineer, directed the Amsterdam Technical Center and was later succeeded by his assistant Hans Visser. Boekholt and Visser were experts in welding for nuclear reactors and the railroad industry as well as for heavy plate and shipbuilding, the largest welding market. By 1969 annual sales had topped $11.5 million and Hobart Brothers, A.G. was employing 241 people directly and a further 328 in joint ventures.[23] Sales totals roughly equaled those of its American parent company in the mid-1950s.

Richard Boekholt was the Hobart Brothers International's first technical director.

Hobart's international business faced a rockier road in the 1970s that began with President Nixon's questionable decision to devalue the dollar in August 1971 in an effort to ease America's growing balance of payments deficit. This forced Peter and most international executives of American firms to rethink their entire approach, moving production abroad while still trying to promote exports. To avoid constant currency fluctuations, Hobart Brothers, A.G. switched its financial operations into the more stable Swiss Franc.[24] During the October 1973 Arab-Israeli War, the Organization of Petroleum Exporting Countries (OPEC) embargoed oil shipments to the United States and the Netherlands then, after it lifted the embargo, proceeded to cut production and quadruple the price of crude oil.[25] The ensuing energy crisis created both problems and opportunities for Hobart Brothers, A.G.

In Europe and Japan governments raised taxes on oil products to reduce consumption and therefore dependence on imported oil. In the short term this boosted the welding business as nations spent tax revenue on pipelines, refineries, offshore drilling rigs, and storage facilities and upgraded their mass transit systems to reduce the impact of future oil shocks. Businesses spent money retooling to conserve energy or to develop alternative energy sources. However, higher taxes and higher energy costs led to a condition called stagflation, high inflation combined with high unemployment, throughout the industrialized free world. Stagflation was one of the factors that eroded the welding industry's base, demand from the manufacturing sector. Hobart's world markets outside Japan and the industrialized West were just as skewed by the energy crisis. OPEC countries awash in petrodollars went on a construction binge and also made fitful attempts to establish domestic industries. Whereas the effect on the economies of Third World countries that lacked energy resources was little short of disastrous. The cumulative result was that the profitability of Hobart's international business peaked in 1975, declined slightly the next two years, then dropped precipitously beginning in 1978, but the business cycle of each region had its own unique story.

Hobart Exotherme, Gonesse, France

In 1971 Hobart increased its penetration of the European welding consumables market with the purchase of La Soudure Exotherme, headed by Alfred Molnar, from CGE when that major French electrical company left the welding business. Besides building a new sales and administrative headquarters in the Paris suburb of Gonesse, Hobart also took possession of an aging electrode factory in Bellegarde, under George Cerutti, a former partisan. Under Molnar and later Yves Lanaud, Exotherme updated the factory and expanded by adding flux-cored wire production from the German plant and conducting research on wires and electrodes. Together with the plant and technical center in Amsterdam, the joint venture electrode, flux, and wire factory, Union Tecnicas S.A. in Spain headed by Celso Penche and Luis Eguren, branch offices in England, Austria and West Germany, and a wide network of distributors, Hobart Brothers could now offer total welding systems to the European market much as it did in the U.S.[26] *Hobart Weldworld* produced special issues for the 1973 Essen Welding Show. In the next few years *Weldworld* produced entire foreign language editions for the international market.[27] European sales grew at a double-digit annual rate in the years 1973–1975 before peaking in 1976 at nearly $17 million.[28] At its height Hobart Brothers had perhaps a 40 percent market share in France, Netherlands, Spain, and Sweden and a 25–30 percent market share throughout Western Europe and was beginning to make inroads into Eastern Europe as a result of participating in numerous trade shows in the Soviet Union and other East Bloc countries.[29]

Hobart Pavillion at the 1973 "Schweissen und Schneiden" (Welding and Cutting) Exhibition in Essen

Hobart Brothers International, A.G. in Amsterdam, 1970s

The contribution of Hobart Brothers of Canada was second only to Europe in the growth in profits from international sales. HB Canada began in 1965 with a sales and service office and a rented warehouse in Woodstock, Ontario, managed by Tom Hall. Production of flux-cored welding wire began the following year, and sales started to climb. By 1973 Bill Stephens, former sales executive under Bill Howell, had moved to Woodstock as Managing Director of Hobart Brothers Canada for which a new office and factory complex had just been constructed. Thanks to efficient workers, a first-class management team, a good network of distributors, and large direct sales customers like the automobile factories and National Steel Car, a railroad car maker in Hamilton, Canadian sales exceeded $6 million a year by the mid 1970s.[30]

In 1974 Hobart Brothers, A.G. added the word *International* to its name. Appropriately, the company opened offices in Algeria and Beirut, Lebanon that year and sales to the Middle East more than tripled between 1973 and 1975.[31] In 1975 Hobart hired international welding engineer Patricio Gonzalez from Chile to head all activities in the developing world. Despite the Arab-Israeli conflict, Hobart products sold well, from a rush order of equipment to Israel to repair Soviet tanks captured in the 1973 war to sending a Tech Center instructor to Saudi Arabia to super-

Pat Gonzalez, director of international sales and licensing

vise use of Hobart welding equipment on an oil pipeline.[32] Civil War in Lebanon forced the Beirut office to relocate, first to Kuwait and later to Cyprus. The key managers who helped build these valuable markets for Hobart were Bob Swan, Ib Rasmussen, Bill Hamberg, Peter Payne, Gilles de Carufel, and Brian Spall. Saudi Hobart, a joint venture to manufacture electrodes, opened in 1978.[33] Another key Middle Eastern market was Turkey, where Hobart was the vernacular word for welding. Business was conducted through a strong distributor named Burla and later a direct office and a local licensee for filler metals.

Increased competition and political upheavals undermined Hobart's Middle Eastern markets over the next few years. Iran, where Hobart had a licensee, was shaken by the overthrow of the Shah, and the ensuing hostage crisis virtually closed the country to American exports. Saudi Hobart never received the tariff protection the government had promised. Consequently, foreign producers dumped their excess electrode output in Saudi Arabia at or below Saudi Hobart's production costs.[34]

After the Bahamas and Puerto Rico, Hobart International's sales office for Latin America found a home in Miami, Florida, the growing capital of Latin American business. A second smaller office at the home of Indura, Hobart's key licensee in Santiago, Chile, assisted the sales

Hobart Micro-wire welders on a Mexican pipeline

effort. As before in the 1930s, a wave of political refugees provided Hobart with executive talent. Adolfo Arango, known as "Fofo," was a successful Cuban businessman and Hobart distributor who had at first applauded Fidel Castro's movement to overthrow Fulgencio Batista, Cuba's corrupt dictator. Arango's reward was government confiscation of his company and personal assets. As a final indignity a customs official stripped him of his wedding ring as he boarded the plane that would carry him to exile in America. In 1962 Hobart put Arango in charge of sales for Latin America, and he did an outstanding job of building up a network of distributors, joint ventures, and licensees.[35] His successor was an engineer named Rudy Hernandez, another Cuban expatriot.

Exports to the region flourished in the late 1970s while sales to Europe and the Middle East were dropping. Political instability and recurring bouts of high inflation and devaluation had long made Latin America a volatile region for manufacturing. Hobart used joint ventures or, more commonly, licensed facilities to produce welding consumables in Mexico (Champion-Hobart), Jamaica, El Salvador, Guatemala (Electrodos de Centro America), Honduras, Panama, Colombia, Peru (Soldadoras

>✹

The "Big Pulgada [Inch]," 833-mile natural gas pipeline began in the oil and gas fields of Chiapas

✹<

Andinas), Ecuador with a direct subsidiary, Chile with Indura, Argentina (IKA), and Brazil with the joint venture Troy Soldas to produce welding machines and accessories. Several operations survived for only a short time, but Champion-Hobart in Mexico thrived and also built welding power sources and accessories, some under license and some of their own design. Champion-Hobart enjoyed participating in the huge development of the oil industry in Mexico.[36] One of the most important projects was the "Big *Pulgada* [Inch]," an 833-mile natural gas pipeline that began in the oil and gas fields of Chiapas and stretched north through Mexico's Gulf coast cities of Veracruz and Tampico to feed the growing *maquiladoras* [foreign-owned industries] in northern Mexico and to link up with gas pipelines in Texas. Pemex, the state-owned Mexican energy corporation, employed six different firms to construct various segments of the line, which would be longer than the Alaskan Pipeline. One firm alone employed four hundred automatic and semi-automatic Hobart welding machines, which supervisors nicknamed *Burros de Trabajo* [burros of work].[37]

Many parts of Latin America lacked the income, infrastructure, or training to make use of Hobart's more sophis-

144

ticated equipment. Several efforts were made to introduce advanced welding technology to the region. Bob Bercaw and other Hobart technicians conducted training seminars in several countries, often in close cooperation with vocational schools run by the priests and brothers of the Salesian Order. Robert Bravo worked with the Pan American Development Foundation (PADF), a group whose goals were to promote entrepreneurship, technical skills, and provide small business loans to produce manufactured exports as opposed to traditional commodities like sugar and bananas. Bravo loved this kind of work. As part of the "Tools for Freedom" program, Hobart Brothers donated scores of welders for use in vocational programs in Latin America. Outfitting vocational schools had the added benefit of getting Hobart's "foot in the door" when local economies began to industrialize.[38]

Hobart Brothers International, A.G. always sought to move beyond the old colonial model in which a small number of local elites often sought to preserve the mercantile status quo rather than develop the industrial self-sufficiency to become truly competitive in international markets. Some Third World leaders, such as Algeria's Ben Bella, tried to combat this tendency. Apart from the nuts and bolts of training and employing native-born managers

Joint Venture Champion-Hobart, Mexico

and workers, Hobart also tried to promote the intellectual and economic philosophies that undergirded global free trade. These efforts ranged from Hobart representatives, such as Arango, lecturing against both fascist and communist restraints on freedom, business, travel, and political rights to the support of new institutions of higher learning, such as the University of Francisco Marroquin in Guatemala where rector Manual Ayau was a dear friend and business partner of Peter Hobart. The university and promoted the free market gospel espoused by Austrian School economists Ludwig von Mises and Friedrich Hayek.

Much of Hobart International's efforts in Africa had the same the long-term focus. Peter Hobart wrote in 1968 that purchases financed by the U.S. Agency for International Development (AID):

. . . were the major factor in keeping our sales at their high level in the African market. Due to U.S. legal restrictions no income was derived by this company on aid financed sales, but it was felt from this company's long range point of view that the sales and promotional activities in this part of the world should be performed even on a non-compensatory basis.[39]

Mexican Pipelines under construction with Hobart Micro-wire systems. Contractor for the project was Protexa.

Multiple oscillating electroslag welding of hydraulic press frame in South Africa, 1970s.

An exception to this rule was the more developed economy of South Africa where Hobart had a large market share served by Arc Engineering, its distributor since the 1930s, initiated by Geza Erenyi and his capable management team of Gordon McLeod and Gerd Niterl to serve this wealthy country in developing mining, shipbuilding, pipelines, coal conversion to oil (SASOL), railways, earth moving equipment, and the defense industry. In the 1970s oil wealth made Algeria and Nigeria important markets as well. A licensee in Nigeria became a large producer of welding consumables to that nation.[40] In 1974 Hobart opened a large sales subsidiary in Algeria, with a staff of fifteen to twenty people operating throughout the country, especially the oil, gas, and burgeoning manufacturing industries.

The region of Asia and the Pacific was one where high hopes never reached full realization. A joint venture in Australia that did very well in the mid-1960s had to be closed in early 1972 when the government enacted impossible import restrictions.[41] Japan proved to be a particularly hard market to crack. Despite a few longstanding relationships, Peter always felt like a customer in dealing with Japanese firms. In the early 1960s Hobart was one of the first American companies to open a direct office in Japan with a regional manager and staff under Horace Bowman, a qualified welding expert who spoke fluent Japanese. Mr. Saito, a marketing consultant who edited the progressive *Japanese Welding News*, assisted him. Hobart forged licensing agreements with steel companies in Japan similar to that with Thyssen in Germany until nationalistic rules made the market untenable and forced Japanese products on domestic companies. Although Hobart's share of the Japanese market fell far short of its hopes, its long presence in the country and continued participation in welding shows and seminars would later reap benefits for the company and the Troy community as well. In the early 1960s Peter was introduced to Soichiro Honda and found the path-breaking motorcycle and automobile maker in his "skunk works" wearing a baseball cap. Honda nodded in recognition when he heard the Hobart name and said he wanted to use Hobart products "the best products" in his plants, but Honda was an exception, a maverick who worked outside and beyond the traditional Japanese approach to business.[42] Eventually, a joint venture in robotics with the Japanese firm Yaskawa and the decision of both Honda and Panasonic to locate plants in Troy proved the value of these early contacts.

Bell-Hobart, since 1974 a joint venture in the Philippines, long a major Hobart market, developed into a key producer of welding machines and consumables. In 1976 Mike Connell, a former Jaguar race car driver and experienced welding executive, took over from Robert Van Gils, as sales manager for the region. His office was established in Manila along with a technical school, while a new warehouse in Singapore improved delivery times in the region.[43] Pakistan had a Hobart filler metal licensee since 1968, and another was added in Indonesia in 1976. In 1974 licensed production began in Taiwan and Korea to participate in the economic boom underway in these two "baby tigers." In the 1970s Bill Howell visited Hubei Province in the People's Republic of China on a series of trade missions led by Ohio Governor James Rhodes. With the normalization of relations between the United States and China in January 1979, there were hopes that the biggest tiger of them all could become a market for Hobart Brothers.

*Hobart Korean Licensee
HICO catalog, 1980*

The relationship between Hobart International and its parent company in Troy was not always a smooth one. Though skeptical at first, E. A. was a true entrepreneur who enjoyed seeing someone else's venture prosper. However, he opposed his nephew Peter's decision to leave Troy and move to Europe, and the idea of a businessman wanting to live in Rome completely befuddled him. Most Hobart executives and employees in Troy were excited by the expansion of their business overseas, on which they were regularly updated by illustrated talks

*Peter C. Hobart talking to Dr. Van Der Willigen,
director of Philips of Holland Research Laboratory
and inventor of the CO_2 welding process.*

given by Peter and his regional managers. Hobart employees enjoyed the cachet that being a worldwide enterprise gave their company, but there was a certain degree of rivalry as well. Hobart employees in the United States referred to those in the international side of the business as "the Air Force." Some people in Troy did not want to see Hobart International become too successful. Galbreath once tried to prevent granting a volume discount on a sale of a thousand welders to a South African railroad. As with other American manufacturers, the executives and engineers in Troy were reluctant to modify Hobart equipment to tailor to the needs of foreign customers.[44] When Hobart International acquired its own overseas production facilities, its commission on sales of exported machinery was reduced.

Some of the leaders in Troy believed Peter spent money too freely and was overly generous in the terms he granted for establishing joint ventures and licensing operations. Moreover, there was a basic difference in how Hobart International was viewed by the Troy leadership as opposed to its own executives. Troy saw Hobart International as an extension of its domestic business, a means to better serve its key multinational customers. They also hoped it would become a reliable profit center that could help the overall balance sheet when Hobart had a tough year in the domestic market. On the other hand, Peter Hobart and Jack Cossman wanted to aggressively pursue market share as the best strategy for building profits in the long run and to plow them back into the international

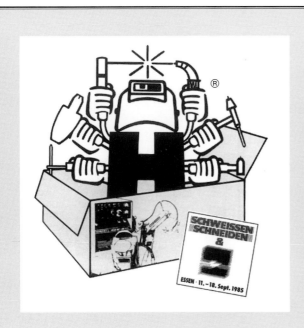

Sparky demonstrates "Out-Of-The-Box" capabilities

Hobart sales personnel at trade shows always liked to show prospects as many live welding demonstrations as possible and the ability to put Hobart products directly to work as they come out of their shipping containers. To highlight both characteristics, Sparky was shown coming out of the box in this trade show literature holding the tools of all the live processes being demonstrated. Up to 17 live demonstrations in welding booths and in theatre presentations were made in trade shows such as the AWS Welding Show in Las Vegas, USA and the Schweissen Und Schneiden International Exhibition in Essen, Germany. Following the trade shows, the same literature was used as direct mailings to customers and prospects in their language.

*French sales literature, 1980s,
for Hobart Motoman robot systems*

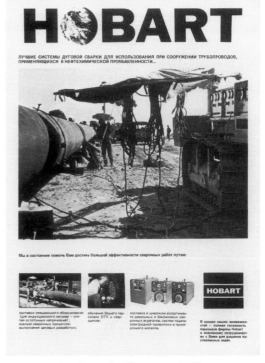

*Russian sales literature, 1980s,
for the Orenburg Pipeline*

German sales literature, 1980s,
for orbital Tube-to-Tubesheet welding system

British sales literature, 1980s,
for shipbuilding

HOBART IN EUROPE

HOBART IN EUROPE

MULTI AXIS COMPUTER CONTROLLED DABBER SYSTEM

The Dabber weld method is used for rebuilding thin edges of costly turbine blades, vanes, knife edge seals, and other components made with Titanium, Inconels, or other Nickel or Cobalt based alloys. The precise control of heat input and deposition allow expensive components which were previously scrapped to be salvaged.

The Dabber method produces a lower heat input to the part offering the benefits of thinner deposits, reduced machining, smaller heat affected zones, and minimal distortion. The same benefits allow the same process to be used in other applications such as rebuilding or hardfacing steel or tool steel alloys with advantageous results.

PLASMA TRANSFERRED ARC/K-10 ROBOT SYSTEM

The Plasma Transferred Arc System uses a powder filler material to deposit metals ranging from Stainless Steels to Cobalt based alloys. The powder is fed through the torch, into an arc, and finally into a weld puddle.

Use of the powder filler material allows for lower dilution levels resulting in a deposit of higher quality than commonly found with deposits of either GTAW or GMAW. Filler material savings with the PTA process can be as great as 50% over wire costs.

The PTA system is mounted on a K-10 robotic manipulator, a six axis articulated arm with repeatabilities of plus or minus 0,1 mm. The articulated arm is inverted, allowing the powder feed to mount to the base of the robot and maintaining a proper powder feed.

The entire system is controlled by an ERC Controller. The controller can maintain the six coordinated axis. It is capable of point-to-point programming/teaching with 2200 steps with 1200 instructions.

HAWCS COMPUTER CONTROLLED WELDING SYSTEM

The Hobart Advanced Welding Control System (HAWCS) is the most advanced weld process control system available today for use in high quality Plasma and Gas Tungsten Arc Welding applications. The controller is used to program and monitor up to 16 analog

outputs such as current, voltage, wire feed speed, gas flow or pressure, and magnetic oscillation.

Each of these outputs are controlled strictly by software, eliminating switches and knobs, to simplify the operation of the system. The software uses EGA color graphics and a touch screen monitor to lead the operator through menu driven screens. Colors are used to assist in the operation.

This eliminates errors by operators in setting up the unit. The software can be programmed to determine if a weld is made within a set range, and to react properly if that range is exceeded. The system can record actual parameters on a time period as short as 100 milliseconds. The HAWCS controller uses an IBM PC-AT platform and can readily be expanded to meet varying requirements.

ORBITAL WELDING HEADS

As part of an ever-expanding offering of ORBITAL equipment, in addition to the existing range of ORBITIG M-heads and 450/550 heads, HOBART BROTHERS COMPANY has acquired the exclusive rights to sell, service and manufacture the complete range of former RTA ORBITAL WELDING SYSTEMS.

Tube-to-tube sheet welding heads

Models 214 and 214.01 have precise centering devices consisting of a locating arm and self centering mandrel with spring loaded ball bearings for the complete range of tube diameters (9.5 mm - 80 mm.)

The welding diameter can easily be adjusted using a vernier screw mechanism. The electrode to work distance is also adjustable by a vernier mechanism or through the Automatic Voltage Control (AVC) on the Model 214.01.

Tube-to-tube welding heads

Specifically designed to weld tubes with minimum radial clearances, the Models 223 and 226 use interchangeable modules. This allows the heads to be used on a variety of applications where joint accessibility is limited, such as tube bundles.

The head is centered on the tube through an adjustable elastic clamping jaw. The clamping jaw is adjustable for all tube diameters within the range of the heads (Model 223: 12 mm. - 51 mm., Model 226: 38 mm. - 108 mm.)

Models 223 and 226 are equipped with a mechanical follower, to maintain arc length or, on the Models 223.01 and 226.01, Automatic Voltage Control (AVC). Torch oscillation is also available on these heads, which make them ideal for multipass welds.

Hobart multilingual literature

Hobart International Management Team, Amsterdam, 1980.
Left to right: Patricio Gonzalez, Peter C. Hobart, Bill Hamberg, Brian Spall, Martin Wognum, Massimo Latronico, Rudy Hernandez,
David Howell, Ermanno Barocco, Andre A. Odermatt, Peter Spillekom, Magnus Wennardt

business. Apart from this difference in perspective, the inherent rivalry among four highly competitive business-men who were also siblings and brothers-in-law was not exactly smoothed over when Peter pointed out in the mid-1970s that Hobart International had earned more profits than its parent company. Some of the frustration Peter felt toward the approach of the Troy leadership spilled over into his annual report for 1976:

Part of our drop in profitability was also the result of higher prices from Hobart Brothers Company who has apparently chosen the policy of higher profits and lower market share which is in direct conflict with that of Hobart Brothers International which is too small to accept a smaller market share.[45]

However, it was larger market forces, not the poli-cies of its parent company that forced Hobart Interna-tional to drastically cut back its European operations in 1979. Stagflation, a sixth straight year of decline in steel production, further OPEC price increases exacerbated by a drop in Middle Eastern oil exports, economic national-ism, and damaging shifts in currency exchange rates com-bined to devastate Hobart's European and world markets and cause the cost of production in Amsterdam to sky-rocket. Thanks to a double digit American inflation rate and the falling dollar, it now cost 25 percent more to man-ufacture a machine in the Netherlands with the strong Dutch Guilder than it did for Troy to build and deliver the same machine to Amsterdam.[46] Following a detailed study by McKinsey and Company consultants, Peter and the Board in Troy decided to shut down manufacturing and reduce Amsterdam to a warehousing, sales and service operation. Odermatt found it painful to dismiss nearly two hundred employees but saw the economic necessity for the move. He was then asked to come to Troy to develop a strategy for manufacturing welding power sources for the international market.[47] The unprofitable German sales branch was closed. Meanwhile, a leftist workers' com-mittee had occupied Union Tecnicas, the electrode, flux and wire-making joint venture in Spain, following a severe recession that had practically bankrupted the entire Spanish welding industry. La Soudure Exotherme with its electrode plant in Bellegarde survived the crisis with a mild restructuring. Bellegarde and Metallogen were the only production facilities Hobart had left in Europe as it entered the 1980s.[48] On the positive side, the reorganization created closer cooperation between Hobart International and its parent company in Troy, including a unified worldwide marketing plan and a return to the original commission on export sales.[49]

A tornado caused extensive damage to the Hobart Brothers of Canada facility in 1979.

While an economic whirlwind was devastating Amsterdam, Hobart Brothers of Canada was struck by an actual tornado. It was about 7 p.m. on Tuesday August 7, 1979, when a tornado ripped through Woodstock, Ontario, killing two, injuring over one hundred, and destroying or damaging millions of dollars in property.[50] Hobart Brothers was three hours into its second shift when the twister tore the roof and parts of two walls off the factory. A janitor had just finished cleaning offices on the second floor when the winds blew them apart and tumbled him down the stairway. Miraculously, no employees were seriously hurt. Despite the missing roof, wire production never ceased at the plant, which had just completed a forty-thousand-square-foot $2 million expansion the year before.[51] Employees manned extruding machines in the open air and covered them with tarps to keep off the rain and dew. Trailers were hauled in for office space. General Manager Clayton "Chic" Bartlett was encouraged by how everyone pulled together in the aftermath of the disaster. The insurer made an upfront payment and Hobart managers, employees, and the building contractor set to work cleaning up and rebuilding.

"You won't make any money *this* year," Peter told Bartlett.

"We'll make money," he promised.

"If you do," said Peter, "I'll throw the biggest champagne party you ever saw." Bartlett got his party. The plant was completely refurbished and rededicated by December, and HB Canada reported a profit of over half a million dollars on gross sales of $11 million for 1979.[52] Ironically, those profits did not go into the ledger for Hobart International because the Canadian subsidiary had been sold to the parent company that year to cover the cost of severance expenses for the employees let go in Europe.[53] HB Canada was now part of the Filler Metals division of Hobart Brothers. Troy hoped to capitalize on the weak Canadian dollar and export part of the Woodstock plant's output.

Though no longer together, both Hobart International and Hobart Brothers of Canada would continue. So it was that Hobart Brothers and many other American firms that expanded aggressively from the 1950s through the 1970s found themselves repositioning for the next challenge. This transition marked the end of the first wave of globalization, in which "global enterprises" included both large and medium-sized firms. Over the years Hobart Brothers operated, directly or through joint ventures or licensees, in twenty-nine different countries.

Most world airlines had already standardized on Hobart ground power equipment. Now Hobart welding products were well established as basic tools for world industry, famous for their advanced technology, high quality, reliability, and serviceability, based upon the original philosophy of the company's founders.

Welding is a basic trade, essential for developing the skills and industries important to help both advanced nations and developing nations move "from swords to plowshares." Hobart's worldwide offering of high quality versatile machines, a complete line of matching filler metals, motion and control devices at all levels of sophistication, backed by a complete parts and service organization, and, most importantly, the "software" of know-how embodied in the Hobart Institute of Welding Technology with its traveling instructors, training aids and publications was a dynamic combination that embodied the best values of America and the company's founders.

Several individuals recruited for the international side of the business earned key management positions with the parent company in Troy. Their success and the perseverance with which Hobart's international employees dealt with the crises of the late 1970s reinforced the longstanding belief at Hobart Brothers that people make a company. ❧

CHAPTER 20

Employees Achieve Many Milestones

"It wasn't like going to work," said Nan Kidder after twenty-eight years at Hobart Brothers. "It was like leaving home at 7:30 and going to your other home."[1] Retirees and veteran employees from Hobart rarely talk about the company for long without mentioning the word *family*, not that it was a family-owned business but that they looked upon their co-workers as family, creating a sense of loyalty. At one time this was by no means unusual in America. In the first half of the twentieth century the Midwest was full of small to medium-sized family owned companies where owners, managers, and employees interacted closely, at work, at play, and at social gatherings. Hobart Brothers was unusual only because this family feeling survived several generations of owners and rapid growth in the company's size and geographic reach. The persistence of this family atmosphere relied on four closely related factors: 1) direct contact between the Hobart family and their employees, 2) the company's formal policies and programs, and 3) the corporate culture that developed at Hobart Brothers, 4) and finally the people themselves with their small-town Midwestern values and work ethic.

Employee memories of C. C. Hobart tend to focus on his eccentricities. The image burned into most minds is that of a tall, bespectacled gentleman in a black derby sitting bolt upright on a bicycle with "longhorn" handle bars adjusted to a nearly vertical position riding sedately to work trailing a complement of dogs eager for the treats he kept in his coat pockets.[2] C. C. had some strict ideas about cleanliness and personal hygiene. He once offered a shop foreman $50 to quit chewing tobacco for thirty days. The foreman failed to kick the habit, and C. C. had the question, "Do you chew tobacco?" stamped onto job application forms. No current employee would be dismissed, but no one who chewed tobacco was to be hired.[3] Since C. C. was already in his sixties when Hobart Brothers was founded, his greatest

Retirees and veteran employees from Hobart rarely talk about the company for long without mentioning the word family . . .

influence was through the values he instilled in his sons. One of the key values he passed down was to keep ownership within the family and work together. Family ownership preserved the independence needed to run the company in the best interests of the family, its employees, and the Troy community. In the mid-1920s while the "new" Hobart Brothers factory was being erected on Main Street, C. C. Hobart was stopped on the street by a widow who was a longtime friend of the family. "Clarence Hobart," she asked, "What's the chance of buying some stock in that Hobart Brothers Company?" C. C. gazed down at her looking somewhat affronted. "Is your name Hobart?" he replied.[4]

Not having to satisfy shareholders with a quarterly balance sheet allowed the Hobarts to provide their employees with an extraordinary degree of job security. All of C. C.'s sons knew their father had been brought to Troy and given a factory building in exchange for providing jobs and that C. C. had lost a bonus because he could not continue to employ as many people as he had projected. Charles, E. A., and W. H. saw a job as a mutual set of obligations. They would provide work, even if economic conditions had curtailed demand for the specific job someone had been hired to do. The three Hobarts also tried to provide their employees with needed help, whether that meant a short-term loan, dental or medical care for a child, or a down payment on a home. In return, what they expected from their employees was loyalty and flexibility. Loyalty meant that complaints and criticisms would be kept within the company family. If an employee did not fear being fired or demoted, he would bring problems to his foreman or to employee relations and get them resolved.[5] But loyalty also meant not trying to form a union. The second generation did not feel that unions were necessary to be treated fairly by the company. They believed that a union would destroy the flexibility they needed from their employees. Rigid union work rules would make it difficult for a small company to respond to changes in the market and stay profitable. Flexibility also undergirded job security at Hobart Brothers and Hobart Cabinet. Employees hired to do factory or office work might find themselves painting the plant, picking fruit on one of Charles' farms, mowing the lawn of a Hobart home, or running errands for the family.[6] The second generation of Hobarts did not observe strict boundaries between home and work. Consequently, employees felt like they knew and worked for the family rather than for a company. That equation was balanced by the interest and concern employees felt the Hobarts had for their families. Benevolent paternalism was very common, not only in Troy, but in the United States at this time and in family-owned companies it seemed to work.

As E. A. roamed the shop floors he often stopped to enquire by name about an employee's wife and children. When he heard of new additions to a family it was typical for him pull that employee aside and say, "It's time you became a homeowner. I'll tell you what I'm going to do." He asked him to find a nice house and get a loan with a payment he could handle, and then E. A. would take care of the down payment. Some employees insisted on paying him back, but E. A. never sought or expected repayment.[7] Sometimes E. A. expressed concern over how employees spent their own money. When he heard Louise Rex was in Las Vegas on vacation he asked other women in the office if she was out there to gamble. No, they assured him, she went to see the shows. "Good," he said, "She works too hard for her money to lose it." The day Rex returned to the switchboard E. A. stopped by to welcome her back from vacation.[8]

This kind of personal concern for employees came naturally to members of the third generation as well. Nan Kidder recalled poring over a reference work with very tiny print finding names and addresses of international businesses for Peter Hobart when his brother William walked by and told her to take a break. "Look off in the distance for a while and rest your eyes."[9] There was nothing extraordinary about such moments, just a consistent manner of seeing employees as individuals and not slots on an organizational chart or expendable units of labor. Executives, managers, and engineers who grew up in Troy with the Hobarts or who came to the company early in their careers shared the same values and treated workers in the same manner.

Longtime distributors, suppliers, and customers became part of the extended Hobart Brothers family.

Longtime distributors, suppliers, and customers became part of the extended Hobart Brothers family as well.

The Roy Smith Company in Detroit was a perennial top-selling distributor and Hobart Brothers' link to the automobile industry. After Roy Smith died and his son Frank inherited the company, E. A. had himself driven up to Detroit to take Frank out to dinner on his birthday just as Frank's father had done. Frank Smith's wife had grown up in Troy next door to Earl Galbreath, and Smith's sons Greg and Steve looked forward to visiting Troy where they often played with Bill and Marcia Howell's children.[10] Bill Howell made sure Frank Smith got tickets to see Elvis Presley and other big name acts that appeared at Hobart Arena. "Our relationship with Hobart Brothers was more like a family relationship than a business partnership," said Steve Smith.[11] H. K. Miller in Chicago was another important longtime distributor of Hobart equipment. After the demise of Saudi Hobart, Robb Howell spent a few years in Chicago working for Vern Miller who had inherited the company from his father.[12] Both Miller and Smith once kept several hundred Hobart power sources for rental use and customarily loaned each other units when demand for rentals soared and ultimately shipped them to Mexico.[13]

More important than occasional personal contact and the family-like concern for employees was the attention that E. A. and other Hobart family members gave to the actual work that rank and file employees did. When E. A. stopped on one of his rambles through the factory to get his hands dirty fixing a machine it was not a parlor trick to boost morale. For one, he genuinely loved making things work and was nearly obsessive about such opportunities. He once spent a half hour on the phone during a Christmas celebration at home patiently explaining to a customer how to get one of the company's "Porta-thaw" machines for defrosting pipes to work. Secondly, each time a Hobart executive gave individual attention to an employee's work he reinforced the dignity of such work by acknowledging its value. Opel Donaldson who assisted Byron Lutz in Purchasing recalled that back when Hobart Brothers had several people doing engineering work who did not have degrees, E. A. himself would come in after she had clocked off and start going through catalogs to order instruments and equipment for them. She pitched in and the two worked together in silence until E. A. noticed the clock and exclaimed, "Oh my, look at the time!" and apologized profusely about making her late for supper. Donaldson took great pride in the time spent working with E. A. and in her becoming one of his "go to" people when he needed information from Purchasing.[14] E. A. and W. H. understood the value in sending their pink and blue cards to hourly employees as well as to managers and engineers. They communicated this attitude to younger generations of Hobarts in private communications where they consistently pointed out that the company and the wealth it produced was not created by their efforts alone but in partnership with the work of their employees.[15] As the third generation gradually took over the helm, the company was growing rapidly, and its larger workforce was separated into divisions. Increasingly, the Hobart leadership relied on company programs and policies to help communicate the values that had been conveyed primarily through personal contact.

Although competitive within Troy, wages and benefits at Hobart Brothers were certainly less than that for comparable work at the plants of General Motors and NCR in Dayton. The company's reputation for job security helped draw workers as did the appeal of Troy itself. Several engineers who interviewed at Hobart Brothers found Troy to be "cleaner and more progressive" than the small Midwestern towns in which they had been raised. Their choice was partly based on the idea that Troy would be a good place to raise children.[16] "You're living in Shangri-La. This is Camelot," said the visiting Roy Bandy, an Englishman who did marketing work for Hobart International, noting Troy's prosperity, the quaint and completely intact factories from the 1920s, and the town's impressive recreational facilities. Even the U.S. State Department liked to bring foreign visitors to Troy to sample its Main Street, U.S.A. qualities.

Family atmosphere, job security, and the appeal of Troy itself were not sufficient to bring in enough people when demand for labor was very high, such as during the war years or the early to mid-1960s. The Motor Generator Company, incorporated as a profitsharing firm for Hobart employees in December 1940, was converted to private ownership shortly after the war. Employees who had bought stock at $20 a share were paid $30 a share, a sizeable gain, especially for returning veterans who had been issued a share per month during their time in the service.[17] Shortly afterward, the company instituted a profitsharing plan. Hobart Brothers would devote 15 percent of its annual pretax profits to accounts for each employee with five or more years service as part of their retirement pension.[18] Later, eligibility for profit sharing was shortened to three years of employment.[19] This program provided a personal incentive for employees to increase the company's profitability.

The HB Reporter,
employee newsletter, 1965

E. A. and W. H. were aware that nothing sows mistrust between owners and employees and fuels calls for union representation at a factory more than a cavalier attitude toward worker safety. In 1942, with their burgeoning and often inexperienced workforce utilizing every inch of space at a wartime pace of three shifts a day, they saw the need to publish a booklet entitled *Plant Safety Rules.* Among the rules explained was the plant floor layout. Bright yellow painted lines marked the purpose for each area: storage, production, etc. Transit lanes were marked for the safe and speedy movement of parts and materials. Careless employees who obstructed a transit lane were sharply reprimanded by foremen and co-workers alike.[20]

The company undertook an even greater safety effort in 1965 in the wake of another major expansion in employment. Representatives from each of Hobart Brothers' twenty-four departments took an eight-week Red Cross course in safety precautions and emergency medical procedures. A total of sixty people received training in order to cover each shift.

Four members of the Troy Emergency Squad employed at Hobart Brothers could provide immediate transportation to local hospitals with their ambulance. Refresher courses and new employee courses were also part of the revised safety plan.[21]

Shortly after being named executive vice president in 1964, William Jr. decided that an in-house publication was needed and stated in its first issue, "The aim—to give a better understanding of where you work and how plans and objectives of the company affect you."[22] The *Hobart Brothers Reporter,* as the new publication was named in a contest, would focus on the employees, social activities, and policy changes within the company itself. The *Reporter* began as a quarterly and later became a bimonthly publication with a separate international edition. William served as its first editor and his niece, Hylton Bravo, became his chief photographer and assistant.

Following the deaths of W. H. Hobart, Glyn Williams, and Orval Menke in 1965, Dick Swisher became the new editor, but William continued to use the *Reporter* as a vehicle to help communicate with employees through frequent open letters. Beginning in 1976, William's editorial took the form of an annual report and answers to questions submitted by employees.[23] Other key executives also wrote editorials in the *Reporter* to explain goals and changes in their areas of responsibility. In addition, the *Reporter* kept employees informed on births, deaths, retirements, promotions, and the fortunes of the company's many sports teams. Awards won by employees, including cash prizes of up to

Scenes from Hobart Brothers Annual Christmas Party and Dance, 1966

Scenes from Hobart Brothers Annual Picnic, 1966

$2,000 for "Top Suggestors," received prominent photo spreads. Naturally, the *Reporter* also promoted the company's many annual social events.[24]

While many large industrial firms began to scale back family-oriented social activities in the 1960s and 1970s, Hobart Brothers expanded its calendar of annual events. The summer picnic had been a big occasion since the postwar years when it began being held at the new facilities on Treasure Island. Softball games, pony rides, live music, and a variety of contests provided entertainment. E. A. had built a diesel-powered steel barge dubbed the *Miami Queen* to ferry up to fifty passengers at a time. Complete with public address system, spotlights, and festoons of party lights, the barge was also rented out for private parties and served as

the judges' stand for boat races held on the river each summer.[25] E. A. also designed a gas-powered train to take children around the park and participate in parades.

December brought the annual Christmas party, which moved from the high school auditorium to Hobart Arena after its completion. This event always included a visit from Santa Claus with treats for the children followed by open skating and a dance in the evening for adults. An open house at the Technical Center to display the company's latest equipment and most modern processes usually kicked off the triennial summits. Major anniversaries of Hobart Brothers' 1917 incorporation meant an extra round of activities, but for the company's fiftieth year celebration in 1967 a new organization and annual event were begun.

William started the Milestone Club to recognize employees with five years of service and those at every ten-year interval thereafter. Personnel Manager Peter Jenkins stated at the first Milestone banquet and induction in January 1967, "A company is only as effective as the people that make it up. . . . We feel that this recognition should not just be a one time event at twenty-five years."[26] Milestone banquets, which were later moved to October, had the added benefit of mixing different generations of employees from various departments in a relaxed social setting. Accompanying the ceremony was a Milestone program booklet that contained photos of all the "advanced class" members with fifteen, twenty-five, thirty-five, or forty-five years of service, candid photos from the company's past, and information about what had been happening in the country and the world in the year each group had joined the company. William gave a presentation on the company's performance and future prospects, and E. A. took part in the actual awarding of Milestone

badges, which were symbolic of the company's history and purpose and outlined in colors that varied depending on the recipient's years of service. Two or three entertainment acts, which could include guest speakers, comedians, magicians, dancers, or musicians, concluded the evening.[27] The Milestone program became a popular annual event at Hobart Brothers.

"The good Lord gave us two ears and one mouth for a reason," said longtime Employee Relations Manager Tom Noftle. "In my job I always tried to listen twice as much as I talked." In an average week, Noftle saw five to ten employees with various problems or complaints. Most could be resolved after he met separately with a foreman or supervisor. In cases where there was a severe conflict or repeated problems, an employee would be moved, sometimes more than once, instead of being fired. "Every dog is entitled to one bite," said Noftle. When an employee did decide to quit or had to be let go, Noftle conducted a lengthy exit interview and shared the information with all relevant supervisory staff. [28]

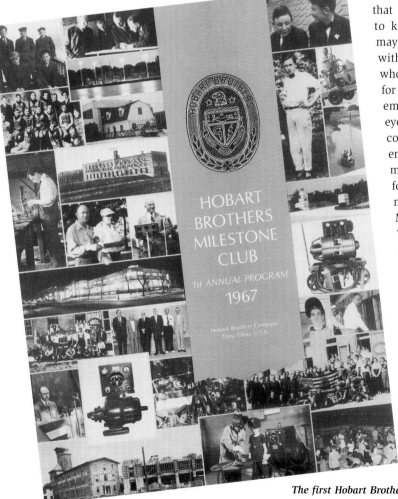

Hobart Brothers' leadership never assumed that wages, benefits, and awards would suffice to keep workers happy. Peter Jenkins, later mayor of Troy, maintained that, "Good morale within a company is a retail business, not a wholesale business." Part of that retail business for him meant knowing almost two thousand employees by name.[29] Management kept its eyes and ears open for problems that a union could exploit, and usually learned from its employees when a serious attempt was being made to unionize Hobart Brothers.[30] Therefore, it came as no surprise when the International Union of Electrical, Radio, and Machine Workers (IUE) held a meeting at the Trojan Inn the night of October 29, 1968, to start a campaign to organize approximately twelve hundred of the production workers at Hobart Brothers. IUE's Harry Shay claimed it was basically a matter of money. "They (Hobart workers) are not participating in the economic boom."[31]

Two days later management responded with a letter from E. A. sent "to all employees and your families," the first salvo in a well-organized campaign to defeat the union. A team made up of E. A. and William Hobart Jr., Paul Whaley, Peter Jenkins, Tom Noftle, Glenn

The first Hobart Brothers Milestone program

Third Annual Hobart Milestone Club banquet. From left to right at the head table: Don Bercaw, Peter Jenkins, Kip Wagner, E. A. Hobart, Fred Hauck, Peter Hobart, William Hobart Jr., and Paul Whaley. Kip Wagner, a former Ohioan who now captained a Florida treasure-hunting company called Real Eight, was guest speaker at this Milestone Club meeting.

Nally, Cliff Priest, and Arthur Donovan spearheaded the campaign. Within three weeks they had set a schedule of twelve subjects to address over a two-month period with posters in the plants and letters mailed home. The culminating effort was a series of meetings on January 13–14, where E. A. and William delivered a slide presentation to all workers eligible to vote on January 16, 1969, to accept or reject IUE representation.[32] The theme the company hit the hardest was Hobart Brothers' fifty-one years with no strikes, work stoppages, or layoffs ". . . even through slow business cycles and recessions."[33] In one sense, the IUE effort was poorly timed. In November a wildcat strike at NCR in Dayton led to a walkout of almost its entire fifteen-thousand-member independent union. The unplanned strike stretched through the holidays and provided ample newspaper clippings and slide photos that Hobart's anti-union team employed to illustrate their argument that unions meant strikes.[34] Within Troy itself, the United Auto Workers had organized the hourly workforces at B. F. Goodrich and at Hobart Manufacturing. Troy's Goodrich workers had struck and Hobart Manufacturing had gone through a strike of three hundred employees at its Greenville, Ohio plant, providing more fodder for the anti-union campaign.[35]

"Good morale within a company is a retail business, not a wholesale business."

Peter Jenkins,
human resource director

The IUE fought back with its own mailings, pointing out that strikes did not take place without a majority vote by the local members and that the IUE did not represent employees at NCR. Further, they alleged that Hobart Brothers could afford a major pay increase and that it kept workers in the dark to hide not paying employees equally for equal work.[36] Following an intense two-month bombardment of charges and counter-charges, Hobart workers rejected IUE representation in a resounding 678 to 367 vote. "We got the hell beat out of us," Shay admitted to reporters.[37]

Six weeks later William announced a set of changes, explaining "the company has been free to proceed with plans that had to be set aside last fall," but the policy shift also addressed criticisms that had found some traction during the attempt to unionize. The most important change was an across the board wage increase achieved by reducing by the forty-five-hour factory work week to forty-two hours with no reduction in pay with a forty-hour week as an eventual goal. The scheduled overtime reflected the high volume of orders and tight labor market of the late 1960s. Also, Hobart's wage structure would be made more transparent by establishing job classifications and wage ranges, but merit pay increases would continue. Finally, the company pledged to pick up additional costs in the insurance program and improve and expand profit sharing.[38] A ninth paid holiday was added in 1970.[39] Hobart Brothers did not face another major attempt to organize a union until the summer of 1978. That effort by the Teamsters was parried with relative ease. Once again the theme was that Hobart employees did not need membership in an outside club to get fair treatment within the company.[40] When William wrote, "They [the Teamsters] only want your money for dues. They don't care about you, your job or the company," the Teamster's own well-publicized scandals in the 1970s provided all the evidence that was needed.[41]

Hobart International operated in several nations where unions were more powerful and often less adversarial than in the United States. Therefore, some subsidiaries as well as many licensees and joint ventures operated with varying union labor rules. Management in Troy only became alarmed when workers at Hobart Brothers of Canada in Woodstock, Ontario, voted to form a union, and a strike that lasted more than two months ensued before a contract got hammered out. However, the union's presence did not prevent HB Canada from becoming one of the company's most profitable divisions during the 1970s and 1980s.[42]

E. A. disliked the term "manager." "You manage assets, not people," he often said. "People are led. You have to pull on the rope, not push it around."[43] E. A. believed in leading by example. Once in the early 1960s E. A. patiently sat listening to an hour-long presentation from a consultant at a luncheon. The topic was control of supplies and inventory. The consultant was appalled that Hobart Brothers did not keep tighter control of its materials. There were too many opportunities for employees to steal. The consultant proposed a more careful accounting of supplies, keeping all materials not in use under lock and key, and the creation of a full-time position to manage the new control system. When he finished E. A. asked what it would cost. The consultant named a large figure. Could he guarantee this system would pay for itself in reducing theft? Wouldn't such a system create a challenge for employees to get around—make it into a game? After the consultant admitted he could not answer those questions, E. A. rejected the plan. He believed that showing a lack of trust in his employees would negate the effort, and that the plan's cost would far exceed what it would save in missing items.[44] As the years went by and younger generations entered the company, lamentably this typical Midwestern trust gradually eroded.

Trust pervaded daily interactions at Hobart Brothers for most of the company's history. This trust was built upon a mutual commitment to the company's future. The Hobart family was obviously in for the long haul. Three

The meaning of the Hobart Milestone Club emblem

The Eagle stands for the company, representing strength, keen vision, and leadership.

The Two Stars stand for the founding brothers of the company, Edward A. Hobart and William H. Hobart.

The Lighted Lamp represents the knowledge necessary to design, produce and sell the company's products. It also stands for the constant search for better ways of doing things.

The Micrometer signifies the aim for accuracy and high quality products.

The Bolt of Lightning stands for the electrical energy used in Hobart products. It also represents the spark necessary to turn ideas into products.

The Scroll lists in Latin, three vital factors in the company's success – knowledge, quality and power.

successive generations had provided leadership at Hobart Brothers and now members of a fourth generation could be seen visiting the office as children and working in the summers as teens. E. A. had of course been present since the company's founding, and, after Russ Flora and Richard Schmueker retired in 1971, he was the sole active link to its first decade.[45]

Decades of continuous employment were the norm at Hobart Brothers rather than the exception. People who had raised a family and put their children through school and then retired with forty to forty-five years of service were inspiring.[46] The company had always been willing to hire relatives of current employees. It was not unusual to see siblings, spouses, or even two or three generations from the same family working at Hobart. With the company's history of providing job security, few feared putting all the family's eggs in one basket. Co-workers often treated each other like family. Mothers brought new babies in to show them off, making sure E. A. got to see them.[47] People would work off the clock to meet an important deadline or to cover for a co-worker who was sick, or missing a few days to attend a wedding or funeral. "They were a great bunch of guys in my engineering group," said Larry Atterholt. "I'd do just about anything for any one of them."[48]

The Midwestern small-town work ethic and native friendliness of Miami Valley workers contributed greatly to the corporate culture. Union organizers alleged that large numbers of German Baptists at Hobart Brothers had been hired because their religious beliefs precluded joining a union.[49] In fact, Orval Menke had come from a German Baptist background, and the "Dunkards" he and others hired were among the most reliable and hard working of employees.

African-Americans had worked at Hobart Brothers since its beginning, but it was only in the late 1960s and early 1970s that blacks began to move into the ranks of

Trenton Bell,
manager of employee and
community relations

management. Chester Baker became supervisor of plant maintenance and security in 1972 when John Boyd retired.[50] Trenton Bell held several management positions in Human Resources. When his son Gordon became a star running back for the University of Michigan, Bell and Bill Howell entertained the office staff with their friendly sports fan rivalry that peaked each year at the time of the Ohio State-Michigan football game.[51] Gordon Bell later worked as a sales manager for Hobart Brothers.

Women too had always been employed at Hobart Brothers, but, as was true of the whole male-dominated welding industry, it was hard to find women in formal leadership roles, even though C. C.'s wife Lou Ella had been the company's first treasurer. Nonetheless, some of the company's most valuable employees were women. Secretaries at Hobart Brothers were true administrative assistants long before the term came into use. Howard Cary often traveled around the world to stay abreast of

Decades of continuous employment were the norm at Hobart Brothers rather than the exception.

developments in welding technology. He was also in great demand as a guest speaker. As Nan Kidder grew into her position as Cary's secretary, she found herself making important decisions when he was away. "Howard never second guessed what I did and that gave me confidence."[52] Jeanne Sargent came to apply for a job just to accompany a friend who did not want to go by herself. Sargent got hired, but her friend did not. By 1965 she had become Robert Bravo's secretary, where her quick memory and cheerful disposition made him the envy of his fellow executives.[53] Since E. A. was customarily first into the office each morning, he had Sargent run various banking errands for him and sometimes stopped by just to chat.[54] Sargent went on to serve as administrative assistant to Kim Packard, president-COO, and the last two chairmen of the Board, William Hobart and Frank Anderson. Both upper management and the Hobart family came to trust her to find the people or information they needed and to convey important messages.

One thing at Hobart Brothers had not changed since C. C.'s days back in Middletown. Employees were often astounded by the responsibilities they had been given and by how they had gone on to do things they had never imagined at the start of their careers. Hired on as a design engineer in 1963, Leo Wildenthaler had not expected the "free hand" he was given. "It gave me a unique feeling of ownership."[55] "Let people show what they can do," was a maxim William inherited from his father W. H. who had probably heard it from C. C.[56] Challenges to develop one's talents combined with the security to learn from mistakes made Hobart Brothers a meaningful place to work. ❧

This cast medallion was created by William Hobart for presentation to distinguished visitors of the company and to deserving employees in recognition for a "Job Well Done."

CHAPTER 21

A New Team Reorganizes for the Seventies

"In business," William Hobart, Jr., liked to say, "Change is the only constant."[1] Hobart Brothers certainly experienced its share of change in the early 1970s as a new generation of executives took control of the firm and reorganized its structure. Many recall this time as a golden era, a time when the company was running on all cylinders. Hobart Brothers' participation in some of the most challenging high profile construction projects in the country and the world provided one visible sign of success, or as the advertising slogan said: "The world of welding is the world of Hobart." The new applications employed were the fruition of seeds planted by the founding of the Technical Center and its integration with the engineering and marketing components of the company. Strong elements of tradition and continuity contributed as well. E. A. still made his presence felt, and the difficult technical projects the firm tackled reflected his "hobby shop" approach of pursuing the interesting and exciting challenges not just the assuredly profitable ones.

William H. Hobart

As he assumed the reins at Hobart, William set out to "professionalize" the company. He did not want the Hobart family to withdraw from managing the business and simply carry out the ownership role as a board of directors. Rather, he intended that every executive position should be filled on the basis of merit and that each position would be open to qualified candidates from within and outside the family, the company, and the Troy community. After all, those were the three concentric circles that defined the Hobart Brothers "family." It was common for individuals within any of those circles to define someone from beyond that circle as an "outsider." William and Peter viewed this as an unhealthy attitude. If Hobart Brothers wanted to be a world-class manufacturer, it could not exclude the wider world from its search for talent.

Some outsiders had been brought in at the management level before but only to fill positions that were new or peripheral to the company. Bob Bercaw and Howard Cary were both Ohioans who worked for customers of Hobart Brothers before they were chosen to direct the welding school. Richard Aufhauser, an immigrant from Germany, was brought in to establish electrode production, but he may have perceived a glass ceiling within the company and left near the end of World War II to join his brothers' import/export firm in New York. Renamed Aufhauser Brothers, modeled after the Hobart moniker, the company eventually manufactured filler metals for copper, silver and specialty alloys.[2] The first outsider hired to lead a major division of the company was Paul Whaley who arrived in 1963 and succeeded Orval Menke as director of manufacturing. Whaley was originally from Syracuse and began his career as a design engineer who moved on to management positions at several companies, most recently as production superintendent for the Appliance Division of General Motors in Dayton.[3] Whaley liked Troy and proved to be a good fit at Hobart Brothers.

Hobart Brothers streamlined its structure in 1967 when four subsidiary corporations, originally begun as profit centers: the Welded Products Company, the Motor Generator Corporation, the Miami Specialty Company, and the Florida Minerals Corporation, were folded back into the parent company. These companies had been created to achieve three goals. First, each divided a separate product line from the welding power sources and consumables, which had become the main business of Hobart Brothers by the late 1930s. During the war years this made it easier to obtain allocations of raw materials. Secondly, they provided opportunities for other family members as well as nonfamily managers to become shareholders while E. A. and W. H. retained ownership of Hobart Brothers itself. Finally, dividing business activities in this manner produced some tax benefits. By 1966 W. H. had died and passed on his shares to his wife and children. Several nonfamily executive shareholders had died or retired, and the company had wrapped up the operations of Florida Mineral. Management sent a letter to employees, distributors, and vendors explaining that as of January 1, 1967, only Hobart Brothers itself and Hobart Brothers, A.G, its international arm, remained as separate entities. The restructuring for "greater efficiency and less red tape" did not result in any loss of jobs.[4]

In a continuing effort to rationalize processes at Hobart Brothers, William established a materials management department in 1971 and brought in Roger Williams to lead it. Williams had an accounting degree from the University of Dayton and had done accounting and industrial production control for two local electrical firms and then served as materials manager for Harris Seybold, an offset printing company. Butting heads with those who did not want to change made the job challenging.[5] Aggressive price competition from Lincoln Electric fueled a push to buy lower cost materials. However, the concept of

"value engineering" had to be fine-tuned before any real savings could be realized. For example, using cheaper steel in a power source led to higher heat loss, which in turn required the use of more magnetic wire and a larger fan, negating the cost savings on the steel.[6]

Worldwide sourcing, now used by a growing number of firms, was the approach Hobart adopted, and it became one

Roger P. Williams, director of materials management and later vice president of Power Systems Division

of the first U.S. companies to purchase large quantities of steel from the Japanese and other sources as foreign steel began to outpace American in both price and quality. Hobart became one of the nation's largest consumers of "green rod," untreated steel rod for the manufacture of electrodes and welding wire. At one point, as the use of green rod mounted into the thousands of tons per month, the company studied the construction of its own modern mini-mill to produce its own steel. The Board of Directors reluctantly rejected this major investment of capital, but the federal government's shifting use of quotas, embargoes, and

duties to protect the faltering domestic steel industry kept Williams on a constant search for economic sources of steel.[7]

During the 1970s, inspired by a progressive French company Poclain, Byron Lutz and Roger Williams organized annual "Suppliers Day" meetings that paralleled those that the company had been hosting for distributors. Suppliers' representatives were provided with a reception and a plant tour that showed how their products were used at Hobart Brothers, and Hobart people in purchasing and materials management solicited suggestions on how to better utilize the parts and materials provided. Goodwill and better communications were the result.

In early January 1972 Hobart Brothers announced a shift in executive titles and responsibilities. E. A. moved into the newly created position of chairman of the Board while his nephew William became president. Bill Howell continued to supervise sales but now also held the position of executive vice president. Robert Bravo was appointed to the new post of vice president for corporate development, responsible for acquisitions and the nonwelding divisions of the company. Peter Hobart became vice president for international operations in addition to his role as president of Hobart Brothers, A.G. Four new vice presidents were created: Paul Whaley, manufacturing; Howard Cary, welding systems; Roger Frantz, engineering; and Byron Lutz, purchasing. Ralph Ehlers retained his title as secretary-treasurer and shortly afterwards was also made a vice president for finance.[8] This reorganization placed the postwar generation

Hobart Porta-Slag welds eight-inch-thick steel plates for hydraulic press.

in clear control of the company. Only Ehlers and Lutz had been with Hobart since the 1930s. For the first time Hobart Brothers had vice presidents who were not family members, and, in Cary and Whaley, men who had been executives for other companies.

E. A. was by no means ready to retire. Alert and spry at eighty-four, he kept abreast of every major project and continued to direct the activities of the facilities engineering department.[9] Frequently, he popped into one of the sprawling plants in Troy to ask questions or chat with workers on the line. By this time he also wore a hearing aid that he constantly kept adjusting to pick up conversations so he would not miss a trick. Later, when his hip was bothering him, he tooled around the factories in a golf cart, which he thoroughly enjoyed since it enabled him to move as quietly as he had in the past but even faster.[10]

The pace of technological change in the welding industry continued to accelerate in the 1970s, and Hobart Brothers was proud to be in the forefront. The electroslag welding process had been invented in the United States in the late 1930s but had seen little use. Engineers at Russia's Paton Institute developed electroslag into a practical method for welding thick pieces of steel in a vertical position and unveiled the achievement at the 1958 World's Fair in Brussels.[11] Naturally, Howard Cary was intrigued, and in the 1960s he was able to investigate in person during visits to the Paton Institute in Kiev, where several of the Russian engineers told Peter Hobart that they had learned to weld during World War II on Hobart Lend Lease machines. The Soviet electroslag process required a good deal of modification and development in order to make it commercially viable in the United States.[12] Hobart Brothers patented its own more practical version called Porta-slag and introduced it to the public at the American Welding Society (AWS) Show in Chicago in 1968.[13] For the next several years Hobart dominated the U.S. market for electroslag welding of heavy metal plate.

Australian-born Andy Axtell, the aggressive manager of the Hobart Brothers sales branch in Newark who was also a director of the New York Port Authority, and his top salesman Joe Golden got the company in on the ground floor of the biggest skyscraper project of the era, the twin towers of the World Trade Center. More accurately, Hobart equipment came in below ground level on the massive excavation to prepare the site. Its diesel engine driven welders welded all joints in the pumping and piping system that pulled seepage out of the site and preventing it from undermining the 3,100-foot wall that held back the Hudson River or from shifting the tubes for the subway, which remained in operation. Hobart welders helped construct the temporary bridge used by massive off-road haulers to carry 1.2 million cubic yards of rock and dirt over the temporary wall to cre-

Base work on the World Trade Center using Hobart engine driven welders

ate twenty-three acres of valuable new land on the southwest edge of Manhattan Island.[14]

The size and complexity of the World Trade Center made it a dream project for both Bill Howell and Howard Cary and a true test for Hobart's total systems approach. Minoru Yamasaki's innovative design for the 110-floor towers did not depend on a complex skeleton of interior columns as earlier skyscrapers had. Instead, supporting columns were only located around the outer wall and within the building core, containing elevators and utilities. This meant that each floor had nearly an acre of unobstructed space that clients could subdivide any way they wanted. This design, the use of high strength steel, and welding to join the members produced economies of about 40 percent compared to older construction styles.[15] The anticipated economies appeared lost when the Port Authority received bids on steel from the U.S. and Bethlehem Steel Companies that exceeded estimates by more than $40 million.[16] Instead, the contract was awarded to dozens of smaller steel companies, such as Atlas Machine and Iron Works of Arlington, Virginia, which supplied the steel for the first six floors of both towers. To construct girders for the building's core Atlas turned to Hobart's new Porta-slag system.[17] Porta-slag's high deposition rate produced time saving ratios of twenty to one to fifty to one compared to older welding processes.[18] Consequently, a large portion of the core structure for the twin towers was Porta-slag welded, despite

"Kangaroo Cranes" at the World Trade Center

❧

. . . biggest skyscraper project of the era, the twin towers of the World Trade Center.

❧

political and competitive interferences in this courageous project.

Another innovation was the use of "Kangaroo Cranes" built by Australia's Favelle Industries. Mounted on the core columns, these cranes had the ability to lift themselves along with the structure. The kangaroos' dual hydraulic systems allowed them to operate at greater speeds than conventional cranes and at capacity even when extended to full reach. The kangaroos lifted three-column wall units up to three stories high and weighing as much as twenty-two tons apiece. These sections were already prewelded to spandrel beams designed to hold the steel

Sears Tower, Chicago (photo by Dan Lea)

decking for floors. Column splices required preheating and sixteen to eighteen passes with stick electrodes or Hobart's FabCO® flux-cored wire for joining.[19] Builders employed nearly every type of Hobart equipment and welding process in the construction of the World Trade Center.

Hobart's role in building the twin towers was featured prominently in the company's advertising for more than a decade.[20] Several executives from the company as well as Dan Lea, the editor for *Hobart Weldworld*, could not pass up the invitation to ride to the top of the advancing towers to view the work in progress. From the dizzying height they watched high steel workers, many of whom were Mohawk Native Americans, walking about with aristocratic calm oblivious to height as they welded the prefabricated floor decking into place. After Trade Center One had been topped off in July 1971 E. A. Hobart ascended it to check out the view from atop the 1,350-foot skeletal structure.[21] He had come a long way from the basement of his father's Water Street home where he had tinkered with electrical equipment seventy years before.

Bill Howell's sales team managed to snag two projects that surpassed the Trade Center in height if not in size and scope. Many of the same welding processes and systems and Hobart equipment models employed in New York would also be used to erect the Sears Tower in Chicago, soon to be the world's tallest building and its second largest office building after the Pentagon.[22] Meanwhile, the world's tallest free-standing structure was being built in Toronto. The 1,815-foot CN Tower, owned by Canadian National Railway, was designed to be a bold showpiece for Canadian industry, a communications tower, and a tourist attraction as well.[23]

Below the 1,100-foot level the tower was a slip-formed concrete spike needing few welds. However, above that point, the Skypod for observation decks and revolving restaurant and the antenna mast required welds that met exacting standards to withstand severe wind pressures at temperatures as low as -20°F. Welds were divided into eight classifications based on the degree of stress they would face. All high-stress welds were ground smooth and subjected to visual and radiographic

New York World Trade Center under construction.

inspection. Ultrasonic and magnetic particle tests were given to some classes of welds. Contractors prefabricated the mast structure in tapered sections and lifted them into place with a Sikorsky Skycrane helicopter. Once assembled in 1975, about four thousand hours of welding and four tons of Hobart's FabCO® 81 flux cored wire had gone into the three-hundred-ton antenna mast that towered above Toronto.[24] The CN Tower became Toronto's signature landmark and still is today.

Submerged arc welding was first patented in 1930 and became widely used during the war years in shipyards and ordnance factories, becoming a basic welding process for medium to heavy plate.[25] A layer of granular flux placed over the weld metal shields the arc. Flux above the arc melts and blends with the molten weld metal and electrode, providing a perfect shielding, which helps to purify and fortify the resulting weld. Since the arc is submerged under granular flux there is no splatter and minimal need for protective gear.[26] Submerged arc also proved to be one of the easiest welding processes to automate in a flat position.

Hobart automatic submerged arc welding units played a key role in several major construction projects in the 1970s. One of these was the Bay Area Rapid Transit System (BART), designed to relieve commuter congestion in California's rapidly growing San Francisco Bay area. BART, the world's first computerized rail system, had many innovative components, including a 3.6 mile double-bore Trans-Bay Tube that would carry BART trains from 75 to 135 feet below the surface of San Francisco Bay. Automatic submerged arc welding sealed the longitudinal seams in each 48 feet wide by 24 feet deep double-barreled tube section.

CN Tower, Toronto

The Bay Area Transit, San Francisco Bay, California

Encased in reinforced concrete, each prefabricated tube section weighing up to ten thousand tons was floated to the drop zone and sunk to its site. Divers then aligned the section with lasers and locked it into place. Next, the water was pumped out, and the new joint was sealed by Micro-wire welding.[27] Political squabbles leading to the redesign of other components delayed the completion of BART, but the Trans-Bay Tube was an immediate hit with thousands of bay area residents who bicycled through it before it was closed for track laying and electrification prior to the initiation of rapid transit service in 1972.[28]

Hobart Micro-Wire Welders on U.S.-Canadian pipeline

The Alaska Pipeline was a prestigious construction project that both captured the imagination of Americans in the 1970s and spotlighted the nation's struggle over its need to develop its natural resources versus its desire to preserve the environment. As usual, engineers tackled the daunting task of attempting to do both. The Prudhoe Bay oil field on Alaska's Arctic north shore had to be connected to an oil terminus port at Valdez eight hundred miles to the south by a four-foot diameter pipe. This pipeline had to cross hundreds of miles of permafrost, three mountain ranges, about 350 rivers and streams, and three earthquake fault zones as well as enable caribou and other migrating animals to cross the line itself.[29] Over permafrost and river crossings, builders had to suspend the pipeline above ground on seventy-eight thousand vertical supports, which supported a steel cross-beam cradling a Teflon-coated shoe assembly that allowed the pipe to move laterally as it expanded and contracted with the fluctuations in temperature. In the Denali earthquake zone, engineers buried the pipeline on a track that allowed the line to move up to five inches vertically and twenty inches laterally. "So when the earth moves, so does the pipeline. Just like a strand of spaghetti," explained the project's chief seismic engineer.[30]

Hobart Brothers hoped to be a major supplier of total arc welding systems for the Alaska pipeline but ran into some snags. The Tulsa-based H. C. Price Company became one major contractor for the pipeline, but pressure from its unionized labor force hoping to maximize employment led it to reject the automatic and semiautomatic welding systems offered by the Hobart direct sales branch in Tulsa.[31]

Hobart built a cold room to test engine drive welders at -50° F.

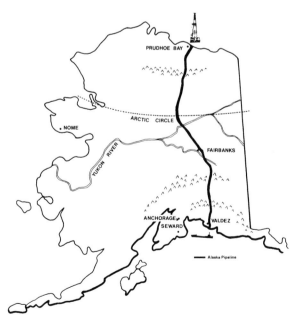

William Howell, senior vice president of sales and marketing, played a critical role in establishing Hobart as a supplier for the Alaska Pipeline and the World Trade Center projects.

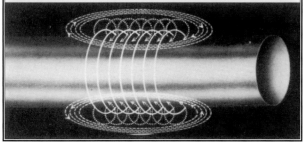

Hobart M-50, 400 hertz induction heating unit and programmer

cracks developing and increases the pipeline's resistance to corrosion and to brittleness due to low temperatures, thus extending its service life.[33] Stress relieving is commonly employed on any critical welded vessel, pipe, or tank expected to carry large volumes of liquids or gases under pressure. The Alaska pipeline required over seventy-one thousand field welds, all of them subjected to x-ray tests.[34]

Prospects improved for Hobart Brothers following an ownership change at Alaska Welding Supply, its local distributor, and a week-long visit to Alaska by Bill Howell in June 1975. Hobart did become a major welding supplier for a larger but less publicized project, a pipeline to carry natural gas from the new gas fields in Alaska and Canada to the energy hungry lower forty-eight states. This network of pipelines, built in three phases between 1980 and 1987, would eventually span 4,805 miles and carry over 2.4 billion cubic feet of gas per day.[35] By this time the speed and efficiency of Hobart's automatic welding systems had won many converts and overcome union opposition. One of the Canadian firms at work on phase one of the line managed to weld an average of eighty-five to ninety joints a day.[36] Development of the oil locked in Canada's extensive tar sands, a project called Syncrude, was another energy venture in which Hobart played a key role.

Hobart had long attempted to become a major supplier to pipeline contractors worldwide, who were using 1930s technology. With Micro-wire welding the opportunity was there, and many international contractors readily adopted this faster, high-quality, lower-cost method, but not in the United States, where the majority of contractors were bogged down in outdated systems imposed by suppliers and unions. With breakthroughs in the off-shore markets of Europe, Australia, and the Middle East and then closer to home in Canada and Mexico, Hobart's famous WWCC-510s mounted on Caterpillar equipment revolutionized this business. Collaboration with H. C. Price, the Fabick Tractor Company, and others, under the guidance of Chief Engineer Gerry Scott and Sales Manager Keith Wogoman, brought this technology to the most difficult of pipeline projects, such as deep-sea pipelines emplaced by lay barges. In fact, Hobart Brothers was a founding member of the International Pipeline and Offshore Contractors Association (IPLOCA). Eventually, Hobart brought semiautomatic pipeline welding to the United States.

Another problem was that it took until the summer of 1975 for Hobart to modify and qualify its power sources for storage and operation at temperatures ranging from 50°F to 70°F below zero.[32] However, Hobart induction heating units for stress relieving were already on the job in Alaska. Hobart's unique 400-Hertz stress-relieving units had been designed and developed by chief engineer Gerry Scott for the U.S. Navy's nuclear submarine program and tested within the factory's cold room to meet the most rigorous standards for work in Alaska. Stress relieving uses heat to reduce the temperature differential between the hot electric arc and the cool base metal and then to gradually cool the welded pipe section at an even rate. This reduces the chance of

Gerry Scott,
chief engineer

Keith Wogoman,
pipeline sales manager

168

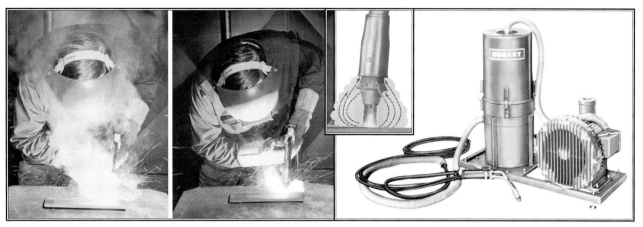

Before and after Hobart smoke exhaust system   *The Hobart smoke exhaust system*

The Clean Air Act of 1970 mandated tougher emissions standards for automobiles beginning in the model year of 1973. American car manufacturers complied by adding catalytic converters to the exhaust systems of their automobiles. These converters, designed to reduce smog-producing hydrocarbons and nitrogen oxides as well as toxic carbon monoxide, had to withstand extreme heat which was best tolerated by 409-grade stainless steel, a notoriously difficult metal to weld. Hobart's Lowell Mott confirmed the faith E. A. had shown in him years before by developing FabLoy®, one of a unique family of alloy tubular wire that could be used to weld the new converters to exhaust assemblies.[37] FabLoy® became a big seller for Filler Metals, which became a separate division of Hobart Brothers in 1977.[38]

Another environmental concern the company addressed in the 1970s was reducing the potentially harmful gases and fumes welders inhaled while welding. Even before the new Occupational Health and Safety Agency (OSHA) created its first guidelines for welding ventilation, Hobart engineers were at work designing a smoke exhaust system. In 1969 the International Lead/Zinc Research Organization, inspired by a British study, had asked the company to develop a system for its continuous wire electrode process. Shortly afterward, Hobart Brothers established a joint research and development program with Caterpillar Corporation whose ambition was "to make the factory as pleasant and safe a place to work as the office."[39] By late 1971 Wade Troyer and Leo Wildenthaler had designed a combination welding gun and exhaust system that used a suction pump to pull smoke particles from a duct just above and around the arc nozzle. A filter trapped particles as small as five microns. Though somewhat bulkier and heavier than a standard welding gun, the built in smoke exhaust system greatly improved the quality of the air the operator breathed and made it easier to

visually monitor the weld in progress.[40] Caterpillar installed more than three thousand of the systems on continuous arc welding stations in its factories and subsidiaries around the world.[41] Hobart often made special units for key customers, such as when it responded to a request from the Buick plant in Flint, Michigan, for a TIG (Tungsten Inert Gas) welder that could blow holes in automobile bodies for the insertion of door handles and other features. Hobart adapted a TIG welder with compressed gas, dubbed the "Holomatic," to perform the application.

Tungsten Inert Gas or "TIG" Welding underwent a revolution in the early 1970s when the application of solid-state circuitry permitted fine-tuning and programming of the TIG welding arc and greatly expanded the possible applications of the method. Following three years of development, Hobart in early 1971 introduced "Cyber-Tig®," a TIG welding system that featured eight different series of increasingly sophisticated programmer modules. The mod-

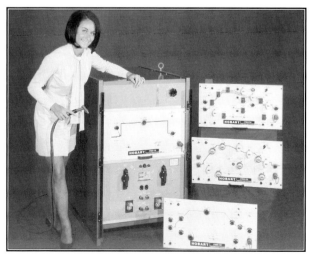

The Hobart multiple program Cyber-Tig®

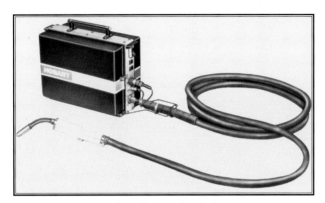

Hobart linear wire feeder

ules could be used interchangeably on either an AC/DC or DC welding power unit.[42] The flexibility of this system made the high-tech applications of modern TIG welding affordable for many more companies.

The 800 series Hobart Cyber-Tig® programmers soon were controlling some of the most sensitive welding jobs in the world: from Rockwell International's hermetically sealed valves and PX Engineering's naphtha heat exchangers for nuclear power plants to Boeing jetfoils for hydrofoil ferry craft.[43] Patented linear wire feeders and boosters, "Porta-wire," now permitted welding on large objects or in tight spaces up to one hundred feet away from the welding wire source, especially on non-ferrous metals.[44] A Hobart Cyber-Tig® CT-300 unit coupled with an 800 series programmer could precision weld two metal flanges on a cathode ray tube for an oscilloscope. Each flange was just thirteen-thousandths of an inch thick. Oscilloscopes are sensitive monitors capable of measuring electrical events as short as a nanosecond.[45]

At the other extreme of the size scale, Cyber-Tig® was instrumental in the construction of a trio of Newport News Shipbuilding liquid natural gas (LNG) tankers, displacing 98,600 metric tons apiece. The cavernous storage chambers of the tankers were lined with interlocking stainless steel "waffle" membranes capable of expanding and contracting when the LNG, cooled to −260°F (−162°C), was loaded and unloaded. The 1.2-millimeter waffle membranes were tacked and fused to a 2 mm thick stainless steel plate base by Cyber-Tig® power sources shielded by Argon gas, resulting in a glittering expandable surface to contain the natural gas.[46]

By the late 1970s new welding processes and refinements of old processes provided a versatility of applications undreamed of in the immediate postwar era. Much of this new construction was part of an effort to improve production and transportation of energy for an American economy that could no longer depend on cheap sources of energy. Double-digit inflation led to a steep climb in interest rates that soon curtailed much of this new construction and triggered a recession in the early 1980s that seriously eroded the industrial base on which Hobart depended.

In contrast to Hobart Brothers, the postwar decades at Hobart Cabinet were marked by continuity rather than change. Charles continued to run the company much as he always had. Though assisted by his eldest son Charles Jr., he did not give his son much responsibility and rarely listened to his advice.[47] Hobart Cabinet survived but did not prosper. Not surprisingly, his younger sons, Edward, Edmund, and Jon, found employment and a broader field for their ambitions at Hobart Brothers. Edward became a designer of welding power sources.[48] Edmund became the sales engineering services manager.[49] Jon began work with the maintenance department, then built wire drawing and winding machines for the Filler Metals Division, and eventually worked in Experimental.[50]

One new field Hobart Cabinet entered in the 1960s was producing cabinetry for drugstores. Charles redesigned his standard twenty-seven-drawer cabinet for flat files so that it could hold bottles of pills and painted the metal cabinet white. Card cabinets and check files could be used to keep records on prescriptions. The Revco Drugstore chain became a big customer, buying fifty units a month for nearly a decade. Preassembled shelving also sold well to busy pharmacists.[51]

Liquid natural gas tanker

Interior of the LNG tanker Technigas system

A severe winter in the late 1960s killed a number of Charles' fruit trees and he sold one of his farms to Fulton Farms, the largest fruit farm in the county.[52] He continued to play tennis until he turned eighty in 1970. After that his health began to falter. Always a bit stubborn and cantankerous, his judgment became more erratic and his distrust of conventional medicine kept him from seeking treatment. Employment at Hobart Cabinet dwindled to about fifteen full-time workers.[53] By 1972 Charles' business was in financial crisis, and his four sons rallied together to save the company. Along with their mother, they made the difficult decision that Charles Jr. should

A successful marketing approach that began with a hobby

Scott D. Trostle, marketing analyst of Hobart Brothers Company, had an avid interest in trains. He blended his hobby with his work by developing a series of welding fabrication manuals to help the railcar industry reduce manufacturing costs, improve quality and increase production. Contents included cost-saving tips on the best welding power sources and electrodes to be used with the metals to be joined, and comprehensive welding illustrations. The series was very well received by the railcar industry, making it a highly successful marketing approach from the 1970s through the 1990s.

Scott went on to become a succesful author of several books about railway history.

Charles Hobart

obtain power of attorney for his father so they could attend to his medical care and get a handle on the finances of Hobart Cabinet.[54] Charles Hobart, Sr., passed away on November 18, 1973, at the age of eighty-three.

The four brothers decided to formally incorporate the company with each family member receiving an equal share of stock. Their sister was now living at home in the care of their mother who was her legal guardian. Consulting lawyers told them that Elizabeth B., as her brothers called her to distinguish from their mother, had to have her stock shares cashed out and put into a trust since her guardianship prevented her from controlling stock. In order to do so, they sold one of Charles' farms and the old family home on Staunton Road, which the Troy Schools purchased and remodeled for its new administrative offices. The four brothers, who by now were all married and had families of their own, decided that the best way to provide for their mother and sister as well as to preserve the nearly seventy-year-old tradition of cabinet-making established by their father and grandfather was to make Hobart Cabinet a viable business once again.

Edward decided to leave Hobart Brothers to help his brother Charles run Hobart Cabinet. Edward knew the cabinet company could use an experienced electrical engineer and he had not been entirely happy with recent changes at Hobart Brothers. Edward felt that as long as E. A. had been at the helm engineering was in the driver's seat, but that now it was the marketing and financial people who were starting to dominate the company. E. A. opposed Edward's move and told his nephew he was making a mistake, but Edward believed that in the long run he had made the right choice.[55] Edmund and Jon stayed on at Hobart Brothers, but, as shareholders and officers at Hobart Cabinet, they contributed advice and participated in major decisions.

Charles Sr. had never been a great believer in insurance and, beyond a small policy to cover his funeral expenses, had kept no other insurance for himself, his business, or his employees. Although he often helped workers who found themselves in financial straits, he firmly believed it was the individual's responsibility to purchase life or health insurance. As soon as company finances permitted, Charles Jr. and Edward moved to modernize their employees' benefits, adding a paid vacation as well as life and health insurance. They brightened the plant with fluorescent area lighting to replace the dingy incandescent fixtures over individual workstations. Worker morale improved along with the company's balance sheet. Charles Sr. had run a tight ship with a long list of paternalistic work rules that prohibited smoking or the playing of radios. His sons relaxed those rules but later came to believe that their father may have been ahead of his time on some things.[56] Charles Jr. made a more dramatic break with the past when he learned the computer language BASIC and wrote his own programs to handle the company's accounting, invoicing, and inventory. He also noticed that his dentist was using the company's one-hundred-drawer universal cabinet for storing orthodontic molds and began to successfully market cabinets for this purpose.[57]

The same day that Charles Hobart died Don Karnes turned in his resignation at Hobart Brothers. Resigning with him were Dale Stager and Bob Schnabel. The trio had decided to pool their resources and take out a loan in order to go into business together in Piqua to make flux-cored welding wire. Rumors of this defection had been rife for some time, and their resignation forestalled William who had planned to discharge those three men the next day. People at Hobart Brothers felt betrayed. They believed that Karnes and his partners had stolen Hobart formulas and processes and would seek to lure away their customers. The unfortunate coincidence of timing made the episode all the more bitter. E. A. was upset by the personal loss of his last sibling and the professional loss of a man who had been his close confidante for the past decade, but he eventually rose above it all like a cork bobbing atop a seething ocean. Later he phoned Karnes and upbraided him for not moving in a more open and ethical manner. "You should've told me," he said. "I'd have given you the money to get started."[58]

In 1970 Hobart was the first company to offer a semiautomatic welding package for under $1,000.

◭ TRI-MARK ®

Karnes, Schnabel, and Stager decided to call their company Tri-Mark and built a small sixteen-thousand-square-foot plant in Piqua. Their company specialized in the manufacture of flux-cored electrodes for automatic and semiautomatic processes. Starting from square one with that narrowly focused intent gave them several advantages beginning with plant layout. By the summer of 1974 Tri-Mark was shipping its first products and, within a year, was expanding its factory for the first time. Eventually, Tri-Mark occupied 140,000 square feet in Piqua and acquired a national reputation for quality products.[59]

A number of years after Tri-Mark had been in business, E. A. accepted Karnes' standing offer to visit their factory in Piqua. Riding in a chair, E. A. was wheeled around the plant, asking questions at every turn. He was the first outsider ever given a plant tour. "I'm proud of what you boys have done here," he finally said.[60] Untainted by jealousy no matter what the circumstance, E. A. enjoyed seeing any entrepreneur succeed. However, the final chapter in the story of Tri-Mark and Hobart had yet to be written. ❧

CHAPTER 22

The Tumultuous Eighties

Sometime between the faltering of the postwar economic boom and the onset of the so-called Reagan Recession of the early 1980's, America's Industrial Heartland was transformed in the popular imagination into the "Rust Belt." The Rust Belt conjured up images of aging factories, contentious unions, and hidebound management turning out products that could no longer stand up to international competition. Small and medium-sized companies that were still profitable found themselves targeted for takeover by industrial giants trying to either improve their balance sheet, diversify to survive the next recession or, at the very least, stave off being swallowed by a rival corporation. In the latter half of the 1980s Hobart Brothers too attempted to grow through acquisition.

At first Troy seemed immune from this grim competition where local plants and the jobs they provided were pawns in a game played in the boardrooms of a distant city. For decades Troy's two largest employers, Hobart Corporation and Hobart Brothers, were locally owned companies whose shareholders and employees still identified with the Troy community. Hobart Brothers remained family owned as it moved into the 1980s, but the ownership picture at Hobart Corporation had undergone some recent changes. Hobart Corporation had expanded dramatically in the postwar decades as demand for its top quality commercial food handling and restaurant equipment and KitchenAid home appliances soared in both domestic and international markets. Up to 1964 Hobart Corporation had remained a relatively closely held company controlled primarily by the families of the partners who had bought out C. C. Hobart back in 1904. In 1964 its team of executives, headed by President Guy S. Frisbie, decided to list Hobart Corporation on the New York Stock Exchange. The resulting infusion of capital enabled them to purchase Corley-Miller, a Chicago producer of food wrapping and labeling

Two timeless designs by Egmont Arens

Hobart meat slicer
Model K5-A mixer

systems. By 1969 when Hobart Corporation dedicated its new world headquarters on Ridge Avenue in Troy, the firm controlled thirty-two separate manufacturing facilities and distributed products to more than one hundred countries. Expansion continued during the 1970s through both acquisitions and innovations, such as the universal product bar code (UPC), which was first tested at a Troy supermarket in 1974.[1]

With annual sales over $500 million Hobart Corporation had become a Fortune 500 company, but it also became the target of a bitter takeover bid. In December 1980 Canadian Pacific, a transportation, energy, and hotel conglomerate, tendered an offer for the Troy food equipment maker. Hobart management blocked the sale with a series of lawsuits, but by February it became obvious that

David B. Meeker
President of Hobart
(Manufacturing)
Corporation, 1968–1981
(Photo courtesy of George Meeker)

Model D-300 mixer
(Photos courtesy of Hobart Manufacturing)

Canadian Pacific would soon clear legal hurdles preventing the sale.[2] Hobart President David B. Meeker found a "White Knight" in the form of Dart and Kraft, a recently merged American food industry giant that beat the Canadian offer by $7.50 a share.[3] Dart and Kraft completed its acquisition by May 1981.[4] Now Troy's largest employer was a wholly owned subsidiary of a multibillion dollar Chicago-based corporation, which had just recently been put together itself. Trojans sensed that their own community could experience the uncertainty that gripped cities throughout the industrial Midwest.

In the past, the welding business had been countercyclical to national economic trends because maintenance and repair increase when manufacturing declines. However, the metalworking industry relied more and more upon welding, in construction, shipbuilding, and automobile manufacturing, sectors that were now in precipitous decline. The accident at Three Mile Island in March 1979 produced fallout in the form of cancelled nuclear plant construction projects, a key market for Hobart Brothers, or their conversion to conventional fuel sources. Another jump in oil prices that year left Detroit reeling, and Chrysler, another important customer of Hobart Brothers, was forced to seek a bailout from the federal government in the form of $1.5 billion in loan guarantees. Chrysler's turnaround was slow and painful. The company set a record for American firms in 1980 by running up a $1.7 billion loss.[5] Ford and General Motors fared only marginally better. Two other important Midwestern customers of Hobart welding systems, International Harvester and Caterpillar, staggered through the early 1980s. For a while Caterpillar lost a million dollars a day, and in 1986 International Harvester had to reorganize and changed its name to Navistar in an effort to reshape its battered image.[6] Cutbacks in production and employment sent ripples through the companies that supplied parts, machine tools, and raw materials to these major firms. By 1982 unemployment in the United States had climbed above 10 percent for the first time since the Great Depression.[7]

For the first time in its history Hobart Brothers could not avoid layoffs. Other expenses had been cut first, from suspending publication of the *Hobart Brothers Reporter* to cutting support for the Welding Procedure Lab and reducing research and development.[8] Layoffs and callbacks in the early 1980s were made on the basis of seniority within departments, and Human Resources distributed sacks of groceries to soften the blow.[9] Nevertheless, the special sense of security that had come with a job at Hobart was beginning to slip away. An oasis of relative prosperity throughout the 1970s, Miami County posted an unprecedented unemployment rate of 14.4 percent by January 1983.[10] Internationally, the picture was much the same. Despite some gains in Asia and Latin America, the dramatic drop in sales to the major market of Europe caused a 26.4 percent decline in net sales for Hobart Brothers International between 1980 and 1983.[11] Speaking in England in November

David A. Meeker
President of Hobart
(Manufacturing)
Corporation, 1945–1963
(Photo courtesy of Keith Bader)

C. C. Hobart's signature was the basis for
The Hobart Electric Manufacturing Company
logo and nameplate.

Hobart Manufacturing Ridge Avenue complex
(Photo courtesy of Hobart Manufacturing)

1982, Peter Hobart noted the strong voice European unions had on the boards of many companies. "Business decisions are no longer made for pure business reasons, but the multiple bottom line is applied, and political, social, and ecological considerations come into effect, more perhaps than anywhere in the world." The emphasis on preserving jobs meant that Europe was more reluctant than America or Japan to embrace new technologies and new applications in automatic welding and robotics.[12]

International sales registered a modest gain in 1983–84, but higher taxes, exchange problems, and tariff duties, forestalled a return to profitability.[13] Now that its manufacturing operation in Amsterdam had been curtailed, Hobart International was hurt by the resurgence of the U.S. dollar. The tight money policies of the Federal Reserve combined with a sharp recession had slain the dragon of inflation. The shift in exchange rates made exports from the United States more expensive and threatened to price Hobart products out of some foreign markets. Peter began to shop around for a facility Hobart could use to revive the manufacturing of power sources in Europe.[14]

The stormy economic tides Hobart Brothers had to weather were complicated by an accelerated turnover in management. In 1975 Robert F. Kelley had been hired as executive vice president for operations.[15] Although he impressed colleagues as bright and perceptive, he did not share information in the literally open-door manner that prevailed within the Hobart Brothers Headquarters. His fellow executive vice president for sales, Bill Howell, was angered when he returned from a sales trip to see that Kelley had erected a partition that separated Kelley's office as well as William Hobart's from the rest of the executives. Howell insisted that the partition be taken down.[16] Kelley wanted to make certain changes in operations that the rest of top management would not go along with.[17] William told his brother Peter that he had to let Kelley go because he was not the right man for the job. The company did not continue the position of executive vice president for operations. Shortly afterwards Paul Whaley shifted his position to manage a new real estate division for Hobart Brothers and was replaced as head of the Welding Equipment Division by Chet Woodman who was hired through an executive search firm.[18]

The executive management team built around the third generation of Hobarts that came to the fore in the early 1970s only survived intact for about a decade. In the early

Martha Hobart, E. A. Hobart's wife, 1956

1980s various health problems began to make it difficult for both Bob Bravo and Bill Howell to continue in their day-to-day management functions, although both brothers-in-law remained on the Board of Directors until well into the 1980s. Some believed that Bravo would have been happier with a diplomatic career, but others appreciated his personal manner and discretion. Longtime power systems engineer Larry Atterholt said, "Bravo was a good boss. He had a fine sense of when to step back and when to intervene."[19] Nearly everyone who worked with Bill Howell saw him as a "driving force" within the company and a man who made decisions. Distributors appreciated his frankness and the personal attention he provided in his journeys across the country.[20] Those who worked for Howell respected his ability to play the devil's advocate to pick apart a poorly conceived idea. Although he had a temper that could provoke him to bellow across the cubicles of the sales office, his staff knew they could count on tremendous loyalty from Howell when it came to dealing with customers and other segments of the company.[21]

As the older members of the third generation entered their sixties and began to retire, the last survivors of E. A. Hobart's generation began to pass away. E. A.'s wife Martha had been in poor health for several years, but she was comforted by the presence of her younger sister Mary. Mary Lantis had cared for their elderly parents in Cincinnati and had never married. She moved to Troy after her parents died, and E. A. built a home for her behind where he and Martha lived. Martha died on November 7, 1979. After fifty-eight years of marriage, E. A. was now alone in his steel home above Ridge Avenue.

Rachel Hobart, the widow of E. A.'s brother W. H. remained the matriarch of the Hobart family in Troy. She had always played an active role in the lives of her nineteen grandchildren. By the early 1980s she had twelve great-grandchildren as well. The Howell great-grandchildren called her "Little Grammy" to distinguish her from her taller daughter Marcia who was "Big Grammy."[22] Grammy Hobart always showed great interest in the lives of her grandchildren and great-grandchildren and made each one feel like the center of attention when she sat down to talk, never failing to extol the virtues of obtaining a good education and upholding the Hobart tradition embodied in the company to "be at your best," a phrase later engraved on her tombstone. Rachel Cahill Hobart passed away in her home on Plum Street on December 7,

1984. Three days later Rachel's four children: Marcia, Lucia, William, and Peter, sat in their overcoats in the front row during graveside services on a raw, gray morning when a brilliant orange and black Monarch butterfly fluttered under the awning. It flitted among the funeral flowers and landed for a moment atop the covered mound of dirt before it took wing and meandered out of the tent. Marcia and Lucia exchanged a look of wonderment. "That's her," Marcia thought to herself. "I guess Mother had to check things out."[23]

E. A. continued to drop by the office and plants as often as his health permitted in his wheelchair or his electric battery charged vehicle. He always attended Milestone meetings and award ceremonies. However, the company events he enjoyed most were rollouts for new pieces of equipment. E. A. was ninety-six years of age when assistants wheeled him up to the Engineering Lab to see the new CT150 power unit. Naturally, E. A. insisted on donning a helmet and welding with the new machine. When he raised the visor he was beaming and "looked like a kid with a new toy."[24] E. A. remained an engineer's engineer to the end. By July 1985 he was confined to his bed at home and hooked up to various monitors. One day a monitor suddenly began beeping wildly. A nurse rushed into the room, but saw E. A. was awake and resting. She quickly ascertained that there was no medical emergency and began fiddling with the malfunctioning monitor. Calmly, E. A. sat up in bed. "Wait a minute," he said. "I know how to fix that." And, of course, he did.[25]

Edward Alvah Hobart died at the age of ninety-six at his welded-steel home in Troy on July 26, 1985. His life had spanned nearly one century of dizzying change. When E. A. was born his father C. C. was nursing a three-year-old company that made electric generators to power incandescent lights, a form of technology still struggling for survival against several alternatives. When E. A. died he left to his heirs a company that employed over two thousand people worldwide and sold more than $250 million a year of welding power sources, filler metals, aircraft ground power units, and, yes, battery chargers that descended from the first units he built in the basement of his parents' home after graduating from Ohio State more than seventy years earlier. Few men in the twentieth cen-

Chairman E. A. Hobart, 1980 (Photo by Edward Woody)

tury have had as great an impact on their hometown as E. A. Hobart and his brothers had on Troy. The *Troy Daily News* devoted most of its front-page and two other pages to words and photographs that celebrated E. A. Hobart's and his brother's achievements in Troy, from dozens of patents to the Overfield Tavern restoration and the Hobart Arena.[26] But perhaps the greatest legacy E. A. Hobart left to his family, his employees, and his community, were his generosity, his entrepreneurial spirit, and his love of innovation and his fellow man.

In September 1985 Hobart Brothers broke with tradition and announced that Kim Packard, the forty-six-year-old former president of Cleveland machine toolmaker Warner-Swasey, would become the company's first non-family president and COO. Packard arrived with a mandate for change. Hobart would begin "looking at acquisitions that were semi-diversified."[27] William, who now assumed E. A.'s former position as chairman of the Board and CEO, called this a strategy of "edging out" from the company's core products.[28] When asked about possible cuts in employment, Packard said that "minor adjustments" had to be made. "Our hope is to achieve that by attrition. But we haven't guaranteed it." Packard was impressed by the company's "incredible concern for people," its customers, its employees, and for those in the community.[29] During the next year Hobart Brothers would undergo the most sweeping changes it had seen since the company had geared up for World War II.

The inevitable ax fell on December 13, 1985, a day Hobart Brothers employees later referred to as "Black Tuesday." The company experienced its first widespread permanent layoffs. Supervisors in most departments had to let people go based on their value to the company without regard to seniority.[30] Employment Manager Trenton Bell, who had to fire six people in his department, called it "the saddest day of my life."[31] Many employees later admitted that the move was necessary but objected to the way it was done. The lack of warning with an opportunity to improve and the inclusion of employees with many years of experience were in sharp contrast to Hobart tradition. "We had to bite the bullet to survive," said Bell. "It was a bitter bullet."[32] Black Tuesday was a clear signal that business as usual could no longer be the norm, and that Hobart Brothers could not both prosper and shelter its workforce from the harsh dictates of an increasingly competitive world market.

Another change Packard accelerated was decentralization. Divisionalization of the company had begun in the late 1960s and proceeded gradually as manufacturing, marketing, and engineering personnel were assigned to the following divisions: Welding Equipment, Filler Metals, Power Systems, and Advanced Welding Systems, but always as one company.[33] Packard decentralized purchasing and accounting to make the divisions into individual profit centers, although facilities and even machine tools continued to be shared by some divisions.[34] At this time Hobart International, A.G. ceased its independent existence and its foreign subsidiaries and joint ventures were brought under the direct control of Hobart Brothers in Troy.[35]

Decentralization created both advantages and disadvantages for Hobart Brothers, like so many American companies. For those still charged with functions that served the company as a whole, the disadvantages were more apparent. "When the divisions were put on their own budgets, the elbows went up," said Communications Director Glenn Nally. Cooperation needed to create live welding demonstration exhibits at trade shows in the United States and around the world became much harder to obtain. Fear that an unprofitable division could be sold made executives reluctant to incur expenses charged against their own division's bottom line.[36] Howard Cary, now vice president and general manager of the Advanced Welding Systems Division, blamed decentralization for drying up support for the Welding Procedure Laboratory. "We were unable to host customers with demonstrations and procedure development work, and as a result got much criticism from the field from our customers, distributors and sales reps."[37] Some quantity discounts were lost by dividing the purchasing of equipment and supplies.[38] Although one purpose behind the creation of divisions was to encourage competition for higher profits, it also fostered a more petty kind of competition. "If their office got a laser printer, our department should get one too."[39] Often this internal rivalry delayed the resolution of employee complaints because people in another division could end up clamoring for the same change.[40] Packard admitted that he sometimes found people pulling apart instead of together.[41]

Despite those problems, decentralization created solid benefits as well. Accounting by division enabled Hobart Brothers to get a much clearer picture of where it was making and where it was losing money and gave executives the perspective they needed to map out a long term plan to both expand the business and to balance its portfolio. As early as 1977 there were indications that the Power Systems Division was becoming the most profitable part of the company when that two-year-old division exceeded its ambitious sales goal by 7 percent while the Welding Equipment and Filler Metals Divisions increased sales but fell slightly short of their respective goals.[42]

By the time Packard became president in the fall of 1985, the Power Systems Division had established itself along with the Filler Metals Division as one of the leading profit centers of the company. What had once been the old Motor Generator Corporation had emerged from the shadow of the welding divisions thanks to the strong sales of its high quality aircraft ground power systems and electrical battery chargers.

Within the Power Systems division, Hobart Brothers' oldest product line, battery chargers, had become its most profitable. Due to the onset of the energy crisis and an increasing concern for protecting the environment, the 1970s witnessed a resurgence of interest in clean, efficient electrically powered vehicles, especially in the materials handling industry. Don Bercaw, "a creative, get-it-done guy" and son of the late Bob Bercaw, managed the Bat-

Within the Power Systems Division, Hobart Brothers' oldest product line, battery chargers, had become its most profitable.

Hobart International, A.G. ceased its independent existence and its foreign subsidiaries and joint ventures were brought under the direct control of Hobart Brothers in Troy.

tery Charger Department.[43] Larry Heisey, a University of Cincinnati engineer who had co-oped at Hobart Brothers, directed battery charger engineering and focused redesign "toward highly-efficient 'intelligent' fail-safe chargers that could 'read' a battery's discharge" and recharge it accordingly.[44] Besides charging up forklift trucks, Hobart battery chargers were at work at a wide variety of jobs: some of the chargers monitored battery temperature and some monitored battery usage, rugged low-profile models kept diggers humming as they chewed into veins of coal in mines deep below the earth, others recharged postal vehicles and powered the Nautilus ride and the electric light parade at Disney World in Florida. Still others powered uninterruptible power systems (UPS) for computers and other critical load applications at hospitals and utility companies.[45]

A key factor behind the growth of the domestic market for ground power units was the Airline Deregulation Act of 1978. The federal government stepped away from regulating fares and service, and the ensuing upheavals in the airline industry created two strong trends that emerged from the tumult of start-ups and bankruptcies: lower fares and more passengers. In the twenty-five years between 1975 and 1990, fares, adjusted for inflation, fell by nearly one-third, while in the same period passenger miles nearly tripled.[46]

Roger Frantz, a World War II veteran who had been with Hobart since 1946 and a former director of engineering, was chosen to head the new Power Systems Division in 1976. A respected engineer, Frantz kept Hobart's industry-leading ground power units abreast of the latest innovations in technology. Roger Williams transferred from materials management to succeed Frantz as Vice President and General Manager in 1982 and brought a more aggressive style to managing the division. Williams learned that Hobart had acquired a reputation as the "Rolls Royce" of the ground power industry but still sold its products at "Chevy" prices. He realized that he could institute incremental price increases while demand for ground power was high and his costs were low due to the recession. Profits jumped sharply. More effort was made to increase foreign sales as well.[47] William Hobart pegged Williams as a key executive in the Board's plan to grow the business and in 1985 sent him to a seventeen-week advanced management class at Harvard.[48] The challenging course gave Williams the confidence that he could hold his own alongside executives from some of the top companies in America. Williams developed a simple philosophy of business.

Roger Frantz, vice president of engineering, and later managing director of the Power Systems Division

"Push for sales in the short term, engineer for the long term, and watch finances all the time."[49]

Seeing the strong profits in ground power and recognizing that spending by the airlines was closely tied to the ongoing rise in passenger miles, the company developed a "surround the airplane" concept to guide acquisitions for the Power Systems Division. However, the first acquisition opportunity to present itself was close to home and to the company's core business. Tri-Mark, the manufacturer of flux-cored welding wire in Piqua, had enjoyed excellent growth since its inception in 1973. In 1984 it had acquired Airco's line of flux-cored wire and was now producing and marketing it under the brand name Corex.[50] By 1986 the company employed 120 people and was at a crossroads where it required a major infusion of capital in order to reach the next level, but its three founders now had considerable assets they did not want to risk in a new set of loans.[51] Several American and international welding companies had already shown interest in buying Tri-Mark. The best offers came from Hobart Brothers and National Standard, a wire manufacturer based in Niles, Michigan.

Despite the fact that all three Tri-Mark partners, Karnes, Schnabel, and Stager, were former Hobart employees, they decided to request sealed bids and make their choice based purely on economics. Hard feelings at Hobart were such that several executives balked at delivering the offer, so Jeanne Sargent, Packard's executive assistant, brought it to Piqua. The partners opened the sealed bids. Hobart's was highest. All three Tri-Mark executives came back to Hobart Brothers for a period of time. The Tri-Mark acquisition strengthened the overall profitability and product offering of the Filler Metals Division.[52]

Terry Lefever had been vice president and general manager of Filler Metals since 1977 and had instituted a number of innovations during his tenure. In 1980 Andre Odermatt, head of engineering for Hobart International arrived from Amsterdam and became plant manager. Since filler metal production was a new field for him, he donned overalls and spent time at each station in the plant and was dismayed to find that the factory had a scrap rate of 8 percent. Changes reduced the rate to 3.5 percent. Odermatt challenged one of the production workers to see if he could operate three machines at once. When Odermatt found that he could, he created the Multi-Machine Operator (MMO) program, a monetary incentive for employees who met qualification standards. The system was extended to Tri-Mark after its acquisition.[53]

In the late 1980s Lefever's division did away with time clocks and shifted to alternating forty-four-hour four-day weeks and thirty-six-hour three-day weeks, a change that cut absenteeism. Lefever pursued contracts to supply brand-name welding wire to Matsushita Panasonic in Japan and Honda, in the northern Miami Valley. "We nearly choked on the specs," said Packard, "But our team said we could do it." Through retraining and the use of quality circles, Hobart Filler Metals met the exacting Japanese standards and became the only approved domestic source for solid wire.[54] Packard saw Lefever and Josh Kurd as two of the best people for communicating changes at the floor level.[55] Kurd, like Odermatt, had worked for Hobart International in Europe and exuded an optimistic can-do spirit. He worked closely

with his brother-in-law Robb Howell who became plant manager for the Welding Equipment Division while Kurd served as materials manager. Since he and Howell were fourth-generation members of the Hobart family, hourly workers tended to trust them as people who had a long-term stake in the company and often came to them with problems.[56]

Wollard luggage loader

Surround the airplane moved into full swing in 1987 with the acquisition of Wollard Airport Equipment located near Miami, Florida. Wollard produced a variety of equipment that serviced commercial planes on the tarmac, including mobile passenger stairs, portable baggage loaders, passenger bridges, carts, mobile work platforms, commissary trucks, and lavatory service trucks, affectionately known as "honey wagons."[57] Now that Hobart had a range of ground service equipment to offer along with its ground power units, it sought to improve its technology by purchasing Nova Electric, a small firm in New Jersey manufacturing uninterrupted power systems (UPS). Nova repackaged their UPS units to make a solid state ground power unit that converted 60 Hertz power to 400 Hertz power. Later Hobart engineers designed new units that were more rugged for all weather use and led to a series of successful ground power units.[58]

According to Packard, there was still one crucial gap to close in the effort to surround the airplane, passenger bridges. Passenger boarding bridges are the climate-controlled walkways, which allow passengers to enter planes directly from the second story of a terminal. They are also a means for reducing clutter on the tarmac by replacing a ground power vehicle with a small converter box attached to the bottom of the passenger bridge and wired to a central station unit inside the terminal. A Utah-based company called Jetway had captured such a large market share of air-

ways sold in the United States that, like Frigidaire for refrigerators or Hobart for ground power units, "Jetway" became the common term for a passenger bridge. Recently, Jetway had begun packaging a ground power unit with its popular airways and threatened to cut into Hobart's market. The only real competition to Jetway was Hobart's own Wollard and a company called Stearns in Fort Worth, Texas, which produced passenger bridges and indoor baggage sorting units. Stearns had been purchased by Phillips Industries, a Dayton-based company. Robert H. Brethen, an executive at Phillips who had sat on Hobart Brothers' Board for several years as part of William Hobart's plan to introduce more objectivity and perspectives from outside the family, indicated that Stearns was for sale.[59]

Roger Williams was chosen to head a team to go to Fort Worth to evaluate Stearns. Williams brought Jim Rasbach, Bill Bliss, John Lang, Frank Tracy, and Paul Whaley and instructed them to write separate reports and compare them in a meeting three days later. Each man on the team thought the purchase was highly questionable. Stearns had a long history of problems and used an unfamiliar system of accounting called "percentage of completion" that allowed the company to take credit in percentages for sales not yet made. Williams suspected that games could be played with the system. What might be standard in Texas made Midwesterners suspicious. Packard refused to believe the negative report he received from this team and insisted that Stearns had cleaned up its act. Packard overrode the report and took his recommendation to buy Stearns to the Board and got approval, but in nego-

Stearns passenger bridge

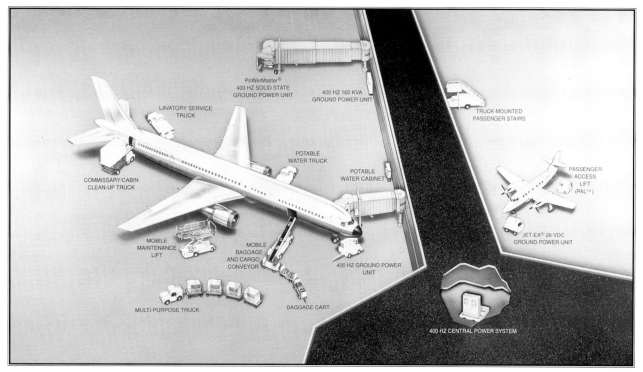

Surround the airplane marketing strategy

tiation with the mercurial Jesse Phillips the company ended up paying $2 million more for Stearns than it had planned.[60]

In 1989 Hobart renamed its Power Systems Division as Hobart Airport Systems and its advertising proudly displayed how it could now surround the airplane with its ground service equipment. Total sales for Hobart Brothers jumped to over $350 million in 1990, with its Airport Systems providing over a quarter of gross sales and a much larger portion of its profits.[61] Despite those glowing numbers, the purchase of Stearns proved disastrous. The purchase of ground power units and equipment that serviced planes on the tarmac was in the hands of the airlines, whereas the decision to buy passenger bridges and indoor baggage handling equipment was up to the municipalities that owned the airports. "It was a very different business from what Hobart was used to," said Conrad Schwab, a former general manager at Piper that Williams had hired to manage ground power.[62] When Stearns' president had to be absent for two weeks in late June 1990 for his annual service as a reserve officer, Williams came to Fort Worth to pinch hit for him. After enduring a good deal of stonewalling, Williams finally got a look at the true financial picture at Stearns.[63] It was appalling. A major passenger bridge order from Belgium had to be cancelled because Stearns could have fulfilled the contract only by incurring a huge loss. This problem was uncovered at the very last minute by a thorough analysis by a Hobart

finance team composed of Frank Tracy, Harrison Hobart, and Greg Schaffer.[64]

Following close on the heels of the financial problems at Stearns was a major debacle for welding equipment and filler metals in Europe. Peter Hobart had for a time hoped that Hobart Brothers' reorganization in the mid-1980s would enable it to recapture the market share it had held in the heady days of the 1970s. In 1985, Pat Gonzalez, a native of Santiago, Chile, had been promoted to director of international marketing for Hobart Brothers as the parent company took control of the network of distributors, subsidiaries, joint ventures and licensees created by Hobart International.[65] Hobart's Board decided that it may have been hasty in curtailing the manufacture of power sources in Europe, since American-made machines were no longer competitive internationally and even losing market share in the United States. Hobart acquired Wemi, headed by Ermanno Barocco, a producer of welding equipment in Vicenza, Italy. Wemi would be branded together with Hobart, producing its own models as well as Hobart designs, and serve as a distributor and center for service and training for Hobart equipment in Italy.[66]

Peter Hobart and the International Division, most importantly, had also decided to form a strategic alliance with Oerlikon Industries, a major Swiss diversified manufacturing company (machine tools, armaments, airplanes, and welding) which was also struggling. Internationally,

Hobart was known for its high-quality equipment line while the consumables of Oerlikon's welding division had an equally fine reputation. A marriage of these two firms could create the fourth- or fifth-largest welding group in the world. Oerlikon owned a subsidiary in Houston that produced fine quality stainless steel electrodes but was losing money because it lacked the distributor network needed to make large sales in the American market. Hobart first agreed to market Oerlikon's electrodes and then began producing them under license in Troy. Within three years it had 20 percent of the domestic market for stainless steel electrodes. Troy thought that Oerlikon could return the favor and streamline Hobart's overseas operations by becoming the master distributor for Hobart equipment in Europe and elsewhere. Oerlikon also specialized in establishing turnkey electrode plants, ideal for licensing arrangements.[67] Odermatt was apprehensive about breaking the ties with European distributors, some of whom had sold Hobart Brothers products for decades. Nevertheless, an alliance was made with Oerlikon in 1987 at Packard's insistence. Odermatt was sent to Europe to cancel the distributorships and sell Hobart's filler metal plant in Bellegarde, France because Oerlikon would now manufacture Hobart flux-cored wire under license.[68] Back in Troy, Welding Equipment engineers under Ralph Barhorst embarked on an ambitious project to design a line of modular inverter welders for the European market, based on British Welding Institute research and patents. Hobart introduced these "Ultra-Tek" power sources at the 1989 Welding Show in Essen, but Oerlikon's distributors proved to be unable to promote the equipment of Hobart, a longtime competitor.[69] Filler metal distributors were not effective at selling machines, just as machine distributors were not effective at selling filler metals.

Disaster struck Oerlikon in August 1990, barely a month after Hobart had learned about trouble at Stearns. Armament manufacturing was the largest portion of Oerlikon's business, and it was just about to ship a billion dollar integrated air defense system to Kuwait when Saddam Hussein invaded that Persian Gulf nation. Naturally, the order was never delivered and had to be written off as a loss at which point the banks stepped in. As the international recession deepened in 1991, Oerlikon encountered more financial difficulties and sold its entire welding division to Air Liquide, the French welding and industrial gases giant. This effectively left Hobart Brothers high and dry in Europe.

Kim Packard had precious little capital in the form of goodwill to draw upon when the balance sheet turned against him in 1991. Along with being bright and ambitious, he had an abrasive style, an explosive temper, and a tendency to take personal credit for success rather than building a team. As the first nonfamily president of Hobart Brothers, he felt more pressure and less security than previous generations of executives. He was not a people person as was the tradition at Hobart Brothers. By now the fourth generation of Hobarts had grown into adulthood, but only a few of the nineteen grandchildren of W. H. and Rachel Hobart had chosen to forge their careers within the company. Those who did not saw it only as a source of investment income, and that meant the Hobart Board was beginning to resemble that of a publicly held company, where the size of the annual dividend loomed larger as a factor in decision making than investment for research and development.

Packard's often-expressed ambition was that a future edition of Tom Peter's *In Search of Excellence* would contain a chapter or two on Hobart Brothers, but years later he could not shake the residue of resentment from "Black Tuesday." "Some still think of me as Genghis Khan," he said.[70] His personal style could be intimidating at times. Packard did not react well to criticism or disagreement. He once told a vice president that he had ten minutes to decide if he wanted a future with the company. When Packard unveiled an advertising campaign that featured the slogan "In Order to Form a More Perfect Union," Glenn Nally objected that some people might be offended by the glib reference to the Constitution or see it as sarcasm in view of the company's anti-union stance.

The easiest way to deal with Packard was to produce steady profits.[71] That was more easily said than done, especially for the Welding Equipment Division, which endured high turnover among top management in the 1980s, including Chet Woodman who left the company and soon

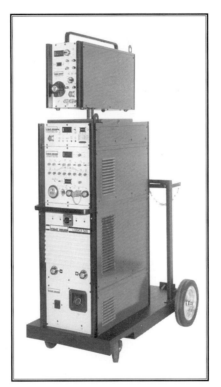

Ultra-Tek modular inverter welding power source for distribution in the European market by Oerlikon, Hobart's strategic partner

Hobart Brothers of Canada located outside Woodstock, Ontario

got hired by Lincoln Electric.[72] One reliable source of profits during this period was Hobart Brothers Canada, which Peter Hobart liked to call "the crown jewel of Hobart's international operations." In 1989 the Woodstock, Ontario, subsidiary enjoyed its best year to date with $32 million in sales and $4 million in profits. Its General Manager Chic Bartlett believed that "hiring the right people to do the right jobs" was the key to profitability. Bartlett and his loyal team of Dave Fink and Gordon Stoll made their profits with a workforce that had been unionized since 1973.[73] An important step in improving distribution in Canada was setting up thirty-four Linde distributors to sell Hobart products in 1983–84.[74] Key customers for HB Canada included pipeline builders, Hydro-Quebec, which had several massive hydroelectric projects underway in northern Quebec, Canadian automobile plants, Accuride in London, Ontario, which produced steel wheels for vehicles, and two large manufacturers of railroad cars, the Trenton Car Works in Nova Scotia, and National Steel Car in Hamilton, Ontario.[75]

Bartlett suffered a heart attack in 1988. After three months off to recover, he returned as president of Hobart Brothers Canada but planned to reduce his hours and become chairman while Gordon Stoll prepared to step up to the presidency of the subsidiary. Late in Packard's

Chic Bartlett was president and general manager of Hobart Brothers of Canada.

tenure as president of Hobart Brothers, Bartlett attended a corporate retreat in Ponte Vedra Beach, Florida. After a couple days of alternating rounds of meetings, golf, and meals, all the Hobart executives were seated at a table for a final round robin discussion of what the retreat had accomplished. Bartlett was seated just to the left of William Hobart and found that he would be the next to last person to speak. As the discussion proceeded Bartlett's frustration grew and, perhaps emboldened by his recent heart attack, he resolved to speak frankly. When his turn came up he said, "I guess the meeting was ok, but we never talked about *people*—who did what, and who was doing well, and who was having problems. Isn't this company *about* people? All we ever talked about was money." Bartlett glanced across the table. Packard was staring at him livid. There was a long, tense pause before William spoke. "You know what?" he said. "Chic's right." At that point one of the corporate lawyers invited Bartlett out for a walk on the beach.[76] Bartlett never felt any repercussions from his frank remarks, but it had been a telling moment. Throughout the past decade Hobart Brothers had found it increasingly difficult to both earn steady profits and remain true to its traditions. By the spring of 1991 the Board had lost faith in Kim Packard's ability to achieve either of those goals and asked for his resignation.[77] ❧

CHAPTER 23

Hobart Hones the Cutting Edge
of High Technology

NASA had a big problem. To be more accurate, NASA had a myriad of problems to overcome in designing and building the space shuttle, the world's first reusable spacecraft. One of its biggest hurdles was how to reduce the cost and speed the manufacture of the huge aluminum external fuel tank. This tank would not only carry the liquid oxygen and hydrogen that would fuel the shuttle's main engines and power it into orbit; "it was the structural backbone of the entire space shuttle. It mounted both the orbiter and the solid rocket boosters (SRBs), with a strong beam running across its internal diameter to take the thrust of those boosters."[1] Unlike the astronaut-carrying orbiter and the SRBs, the external tank (ET in NASA-speak) would burn up upon reentering the atmosphere. In order to meet an ambitious launch schedule, NASA would need a new ET for each mission, and that meant it had to strive to save both time and money in its construction while still meeting demanding safety standards that required each part of the shuttle to tolerate flight conditions 40 percent worse than predicted.[2]

Aluminum had always been a difficult metal to weld, but in the mid-1970s Hobart Brothers had achieved some major improvements in response to a request from Boeing. Ralph Barhorst, an Air Force veteran who had joined Hobart Brothers in 1969 after earning an electrical engineering degree at the University of Dayton, received a patent for a plasma arc welding system he designed for high current welding of aluminum alloys from 3/16 to 3/8 of an inch thick in a single pass.[3] The novel feature of this power source was its variable polarity "square wave" output. Welding aluminum with straight polarity produces aluminum oxide, which contaminates the weld. Reverse polarity strips off the aluminum oxide and purifies the weld.[4] The power source Barhorst designed "was,

Ralph Barhorst was director of Engineering for the Welding Equipment Division.

in effect, two machines, one with straight polarity and one with reverse polarity connected by means of a high-speed electronic switch."[5] The prototype, a rather unwieldy machine, was delivered to Boeing in September 1975.[6]

While Hobart Brothers worked to produce a smaller, more practical version of the power source, Bill Chaisson, who marketed special products and had contacts within the aerospace industry, visited the Martin Marietta plant at Michoud outside New Orleans and watched as one of the first external tanks for the shuttle was manufactured. The time-consuming and labor-intensive effort to weld the tank required three passes with a DC TIG machine, one to melt the metal and two to fill, and much scraping of aluminum oxide to prepare the surface. There were three miles of welds in every tank. Concerned about meeting production schedules, Martin Marietta's Art Lang came to Troy to look at the unit Barhorst had designed for Boeing.[7] The Product Development engineers at Hobart were eager to tackle the problem, but many doubted there would be enough customers to justify developing such a system. William Hobart decided that contributing to the country's aerospace effort would prove rewarding.[8]

A team headed by Barhorst spent nearly two years perfecting a variable polarity power source custom-designed to weld the space shuttle's external fuel tank. Dick Reeves adapted the computers needed to control every aspect of the fully automated machine. The 300-amp system could weld aluminum over 3/8 of an inch thick in a single pass.[9] Gas, forced out at high velocity around a recessed tungsten electrode, is transformed into a concentrated high-temperature plasma arc that penetrates the aluminum creating what is called a keyhole. The arc also melts an aluminum electrode fed in electronically from the side, and the high temperature makes the entire process much faster than gas tungsten

NASA Space Shuttle external fuel tank

arc (TIG) welding.[10] The toughest problem to solve was switching the polarity of the circuit fast enough to prevent the arc from shutting off. Two power supplies were employed to switch the current in less than one hundred microseconds, creating the "square" wave. Welding procedures developed at the Marshall Space Center in Huntsville, Alabama, under Joe Sexton determined that a ratio of nineteen milliseconds of electrode-negative cycle to create the weld to three milliseconds of electrode- positive cycle for ionic stripping of aluminum oxide was the best ratio for the job. By late 1979 the new system was installed at Martin Marietta's Michoud plant. An excited NASA official predicted it would save the space agency $200 million over the course of the shuttle program.[11]

NASA's James Odom, ET program manager at the Marshall Space Center, explained to a reporter from *Aviation Week* in 1984:

We have, as best we can tell, the largest weld tool in the world. We put the whole hydrogen tank together; it's

Hobart variable polarity system for welding aluminum

just like a great big lathe. We start off with a dome, and then we drop an approximately 20-foot cylinder in and just keep dropping these cylinders in until you get to the end and then you put another dome on the other end."[12]

It took eleven days to transport the external tanks by barge from the Michoud plant up the Mississippi and Tennessee Rivers for testing at Huntsville. The delivery journey from New Orleans to Cape Canaveral itself usually took about a week.[13] The first shuttle was launched on April 12, 1981, but it was not until the sixth mission almost two years later that the new lightweight external tanks welded by the Hobart Brothers VP300 power source began to fly.[14]

The achievement garnered a good deal of recognition for Barhorst and Hobart Brothers. A flurry of articles in technical journals described the remarkable new power source developed for NASA. *Design News* magazine gave Barhorst an Apple Computer for winning its annual contest, and

Barhorst was invited to give talks in the United States and around the world. Despite the hefty quarter of a million dollar price tag for the first complete systems, Hobart Brothers eventually sold almost fifty of the units to customers ranging from the European Space Agency's Arian program to the CSX railroad.[15] The Challenger disaster occurred January 28, 1986, when a failure of the o-rings in one of the solid rocket boosters caused the entire shuttle to explode killing all seven crew members. The investigation that followed did not recommend any redesign of the external fuel tank, but in 1991 NASA awarded Martin Marietta a contract to further reduce the weight of the ET in order to increase the shuttle's payload.[16]

By this time Barhorst had become director of engineering for the Welding Equipment Division, so Larry

Larry Atterholt,
senior power system
engineer

Atterholt undertook the redesign of the variable polarity power source to weld the new lithium-aluminum alloy employed in the super lightweight tank (SLWT). The new 500-amp power source could weld aluminum up to one-inch thick, but new welding procedures had to be developed to weld the alloy, which was very sensitive to contamination. Eventually, the redesign resulted in a weight savings of seventy-three hundred pounds. The first SLWT flew on shuttle mission No. 91 in August 1998. Hobart Brothers' variable polarity power sources have welded over one hundred external tanks for the shuttle program.[17]

Commercially, a key development for welding in the 1980s was the introduction of inverter power sources. Acting on behalf of the shipbuilding industry, the U.S. Maritime Administration had requested a portable welding power source that could be carried through small hatches to any part of a ship. Taking power from a utility line at standard 60hz frequency, the inverter uses solid-state electronic components to convert power to very high frequency, which is then transformed into smooth DC current for welding. Thanks to the high frequency,

Cyber-Wave® multiple programmed,
pulsed Tig welding power source

inverter power sources are only about 25 percent the size and weight of conventional rectifier welders.[18] Both Hobart Brothers and Miller Electric competed to be the first to bring inverter welders of various capacities to the U.S. market following earlier machines already on the Japanese and European markets. Performance of early inverters tended to be uneven because of two factors: a lack of thorough debugging of the new technology and human error by welders who were either unaware or forgetful of the need for new procedures.[19]

Atterholt, Barhorst, and Bryce Muter collaborated on the design of a particularly versatile power source, the Cyber-Wave® 300. This machine used three-phase power to create a stable arc with precise control through square wave AC output. When welding nonferrous metals, the adjustable square wave output eliminated the need for high frequency, which often interfered with other electronic equipment. The Cyber-Wave® 300 could be used in applications ranging from DC welding with stick electrodes to AC plasma keyhole welding. This power source was the first of its kind when it reached the market in 1984.[20]

Hobart Brothers cooperated with General Electric at their jet engine plant in Evendale just north of Cincinnati to develop a welding system that could repair knife-edge rotary seals in jet engines. Conventional MIG and TIG welding had been tried but lacked the precise control to produce bead sizes small enough to create deposits from 0.4 mm to 2.0 mm in size. Lab work at GE and the Hobart Institute discovered that oscillating the wire feed and pulsing the electrical arc on a programmed Cyber-Tig® power source could produce the minute beads needed. GE patented the "Dabber System" and designated Hobart to develop and supply Dabber System equipment. Eventually, Howard Cary's Advanced Welding Division created eight different systems for the repair of various jet engine parts, end mill cutters, and other machine tools that required hard surfacing or repair of sophisticated alloys.[21] With deregulation, jet engines on commercial airliners racked up miles quickly, and the Dabber System produced excellent cost savings permitting airlines to repair rather than replace engines. In the early 1990s Russia's Ministry of Civil Aviation expressed interest in Dabber technology, but cash-strapped Moscow never put in an order.[22] Worldwide many airlines and national air forces did purchase these systems and continue to employ them today.

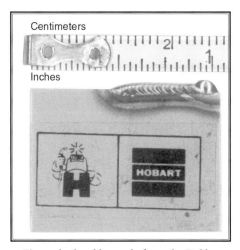

Fine pulsed weld sample from the Dabber

Dabber welding of a GE jet engine rotor

Despite some promising advances in technology, standard Hobart power sources experienced a decline in market share during the 1980s. Leo Wildenthaler, senior product manager for welding equipment in the early 1980s and later the division's general sales manager, believed that Hobart's marketing may have been too technical.[23] To hard-pressed American CEO's whose eyes were focused on their quarterly earnings, price took precedence over most other considerations in their purchasing of equipment. This was as true for airlines as for the major buyers of welding equipment. "Listen," an American Airlines executive told Hobart's Roger Williams, "I spend $3 million a year on *peanuts.*" By implication, ground power units would be replaced only when needed and would go to the lowest bid.[24]

Another burden on Hobart engineers was the need to design power sources for both the domestic and export markets. Designers who "did not get their noses sunburned enough" by welding alongside those who would end up using their machines were not fully aware of the very real differences.[25] In general, European and Asian welders wanted a gentle arc with little spatter. Workers took care of their equipment and energy costs were high. Consequently, companies in those markets wanted lighter, energy efficient machines and were quick to adopt new technologies except for those, like robots, that would anger unions by lowering employment. In contrast, American and Latin American welders favored a driving arc and rugged equipment that could tolerate abuse, and most companies were leery of new technology that entailed retraining its workforce, unless that technology involved robots that could reduce labor costs.[26]

To complicate matters, ESAB, a multinational from Sweden that was at the moment the world's largest welding company, entered the U.S. market and purchased a plant in South Carolina.[27] Lincoln Electric remained a tough competitor and a low cost producer, but it was Miller Electric whose market share in welding power sources surged in the 1980s.[28] While Lincoln relied mainly on direct sales and Miller sold primarily through independent distributors, Hobart had a foot in each camp selling through both independents and its own branch offices. That strategy had worked well as long as the market for power sources was growing, but it led to friction once Hobart and its distributors found themselves dividing a shrinking pie.[29] At a Distributor Advisory Council meeting in January 1983, two distributors pointed out that Hobart tended to complain about distributor sales of competitive products, while the distributors tended to object to Hobart's direct sales to customers in their territory. Both parties needed to "focus their efforts instead on the large market segment where *potential*

Howard Cary, president of the Hobart Institute of Welding Technology

sales offer Hobart and the distributors *mutually* profitable opportunities." Council members "agreed emphatically" that this doctrine should be adopted.[30]

This was more easily said than done. A series of recent Supreme Court decisions had changed the rules of the game between manufacturers and distributors. Distributors had more independence now to set their own prices, including prices lower than the manufacturer's minimum.[31] While the sales of Hobart power sources stagnated, its share of filler metal sales, bolstered by the acquisition of the Tri-Mark and Corex lines, was growing. This allowed distributors to play one division off against the other, requiring a discount on power sources in order to sell the full line of Hobart filler metals.[32] Miller did not manufacture filler metals, so it was not unusual in the 1980s for a company to buy Miller machines and supply

them with Hobart welding wire. Several people in the welding industry, among them William Hobart, began to think that at some point it would make sense to bring these two family-owned companies together.[33]

Naturally, the innovations in welding technology meant the Hobart Institute had to grow and change to meet the educational needs of its diverse clientele. In 1978 a thirty-three-thousand-square-foot addition and a modernization of another seventeen thousand square feet provided a total of two hundred welding training stations and five sound-proofed, air-conditioned classrooms. The Programmed Audio-Visual Training (PAT) system was made available on videotape as well as film.[34] Training programs became more flexible as the Institute adopted a "school cafeteria system," allowing students to take courses in four-week increments up to thirty-six weeks to meet national qualification standards. Students or companies training employees could pay by the week and set up their own preferred sequence of courses, ranging from a two-hour refresher class to qualification for nuclear welding concluded by an x-ray examination of welds. To help house students, the Institute maintained a list of Troy residents who took boarders or had rental units. Increasingly, instructors came to their students, whether they were at the GE plant outside Cincinnati or around the world in Taiwan, Saudi Arabia, or Gabon. Apart from teaching and traveling, key instructors even found time to write basic textbooks in the field, such as Rudy Mohler's *Practical Welding Technology* and Hoobaser Rampaul's *Pipe Welding Procedures*. Chief Instructor Ron Scott began the traveling school concept that reduced training expenses for participating companies. By the mid-1990s any given week

Programmed Audi-visual Training (PAT)

*An early Hobart
Motoman robotic
arc welding system*

would find two to four instructors from the Institute's Field Training Department on the road teaching courses on-site.[35]

After more than thirty years at its helm, Howard Cary stepped aside as president of the Hobart Institute of Welding Technology in 1989. Jon Lang became its new president while Cary chaired its Board and continued to serve the company as senior advisor of special projects. Cary had served a term as president of the American Welding Society in 1980–81. He remained an active member and continued to revise editions of *Modern Welding Technology*, the textbook he had first published in 1979.[36] Don Karnes was placed in charge of Advanced Systems following its reorganization.[37]

Interviewed at a welding show in South Africa in 1984, Peter Hobart waved a hand at the equipment on display and said:

Five years ago 80 percent of this wasn't here. In another five years 80 percent won't be here either. Once welding equipment had a life expectancy of thirty to fifty years. With electronics that's all changed. . . . Exotic materials, which are expensive, are one justification for robotic use. . . . You inevitably need robots for dangerous environments such as the nuclear industries and the mining industry. Automation through robots means steady repeatable quality. . . .[38]

By 1978 robots had begun to appear on assembly lines in Detroit to do spot welding on automobiles, a function they soon came to dominate.[39] At about the same time, Cincinnati Milacron approached Hobart Brothers to see if its newly developed hydraulic robot could be used for welding. Hobart installed a welding head and torch and found that it could. Milacron began using its welding robot and asked Hobart to help market its new apparatus. Although they worked with both Milacron and Unimation robots, Hobart engineers soon discovered that hydraulic robots were too heavy and slow-moving to enable arc welding robots to reach their potential.

Hobart Brothers was one of the harbingers of automation, along with other key worldwide positioning manufacturers: Ransome, Panjiris, and F. Bode and Sons of Great Britain, Langepin of France, Nimak and Uniweld of Germany, and Ansaldo and Comau of Italy. Hobart's advanced motion devices established its position as a leader in welding, cutting, and coating applications for robots. Due to union resistance and management reluctance to integrate robots into American production lines, American robot manufacturers, like the Unimation models developed by Joe Engleberger, soon lost their competitive edge. Europeans too were slow to enter the field, while Japan charged ahead when its Ministry of Industry (MITI) established robotics as a national priority. Hobart had no choice but to work with the world's leader. At the direction of Peter Hobart and the International Division, Howard Cary journeyed to Japan to examine robots manufactured by Hitachi, Necci, Panasonic, and Yaskawa and decided that Yaskawa Electric made the robotic arm best suited for arc welding.[40]

Phil Monnin, president of Motoman,
with teaching module and robot

Hobart mated its welding equipment with Yaskawa's robots and achieved success marketing them in the United States under the brand name Motoman. In 1983 Hobart Brothers and Yaskawa purchased a controlling interest in a Swedish company called Torsteknik. Under the leadership of Berndt Siegfridsson, Torsteknik had become a leading European manufacturer of positioning equipment for automatic welding. Since 1978 it had been integrating its multi-axes servo-positioners with Motoman robots and marketing these robotic welding systems throughout Eastern and Western Europe.[41] This business alliance proved to be quite a success. Over five thousand Motoman robotic welders had been installed worldwide by 1985. In fact, more than half of all arc welding robots then in use were Motomans.[42]

The market for robotic welders in North America developed to the point where Hobart Brothers and Yaskawa decided to invest $3 million each in 1989 to form Motoman, Inc., to manufacture robotic welding systems. Philip Monnin was chosen to become president of the new company, which would be headquartered in Troy with additional facilities in Cincinnati and Detroit.[43] Monnin had begun his career in the machine tools industry in the Miami Valley before spending time in Silicon Valley, Japan, and Georgia before becoming vice president of General Motors' robot group.[44] Edmund Hobart, who was adept at solving customer problems that cropped up during the selling and early installation process, became Chief Technical Manager for Welding Equipment and Weld Technologies for Motoman.[45]

Shortly before the inception of Motoman, Hobart had purchased Multicon, a Cincinnati company that integrated video cameras with control software so that robots could "see" the task at hand.[46] The robotic systems Motoman developed demanded built in safety devices, sophisticated computer interfaces for control, and careful training of those who would program and operate the robots. Monnin was given the freedom to "edge out" and take Motoman robots beyond welding functions to solve problems for customers in the areas of gluing, coating, packaging, loading, and unloading. In order to undertake these tasks, Monnin tried to continually upgrade the educational level of his workforce. "I'm looking to step up each time an employee leaves or retires: replace a worker with a technician, a technician with an engineer, an engineer with an engineer with a master's degree."[47] In August 1990 Motoman

Representatives of Hobart, Yaskawa, and Motoman
join to officially sign the joint venture agreement, 1989.

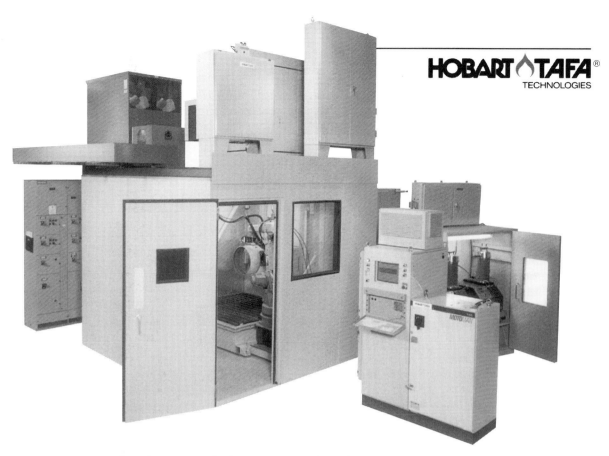

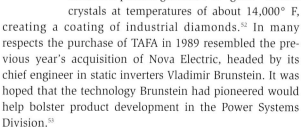

The Hobart TAFA Technologies HAWCS II advanced robotic motion and process control

consolidated its Troy and Cincinnati operations in a large new facility that faced Interstate 75 in West Carrollton, Ohio.[48] By 1992 the robot maker earned $2.6 million in profits on $28.3 million in sales.[49]

During that same year the company introduced the Hobart Advanced Welding Control Systems or HAWCS for short. This sophisticated software enabled a controller to program and monitor up to sixteen different outputs, from voltage and wire feed speed to gas flow, pulsing, and magnetic oscillation, in order to bring unprecedented precision to plasma and gas tungsten arc welding. An operator controlled the process through a color-coded touch screen monitor that eliminated the need for knobs or switches. HAWCS could program parameters to ensure that welds be made within a set range on a time period as short as one hundred microseconds.[50] Clearly, welders of the twenty-first century would need a very different set of skills from those of the men and women who welded Liberty ships in World War II.

One of the new systems Monnin sought to integrate into Motoman robots was brought into the picture by yet

Edmund Hobart

another acquisition. TAFA, headquartered in Concord, New Hampshire, was the world's leading supplier of arc spraying equipment and thermal surfacing technology. In the tradition of C. C. and E. A. Hobart, TAFA's founder and president, Merle L. Thorpe, was an engineer-entrepreneur who continued to guide its technological development. TAFA had created new thermal coating processes that ranged from corrosion resistance to decorative surface treatments, and the company also conducted advanced research "in areas such as inert atmosphere and low pressure arc spray, and induction plasma applications."[51] One of the cutting edge projects pursued by Hobart/TAFA was the use of an induction plasma generator to "grow" carbon crystals at temperatures of about 14,000° F, creating a coating of industrial diamonds.[52] In many respects the purchase of TAFA in 1989 resembled the previous year's acquisition of Nova Electric, headed by its chief engineer in static inverters Vladimir Brunstein. It was hoped that the technology Brunstein had pioneered would help bolster product development in the Power Systems Division.[53]

The strategy of purchasing new technology rather than relying solely on innovation from within was continued by Packard's successor, Michael Wolf. In May 1992 Hobart purchased Martek Lasers in Livermore, California, and renamed it Hobart Laser Products (HLP).[54] Don Karnes coordinated the purchase of Martek and the integration of its technology and personnel into Hobart's Advanced Systems.[55] HLP manufactured lasers for advanced cutting, welding, and surfacing that used the Nd:YAG type of laser beam. Lasers are devices that produce "a concentrated coherent light beam [a stream of photons] by stimulating electronic or molecular transitions to lower energy levels."[56] While gas lasers use a mixture of helium, nitrogen and CO_2 gases, the Nd:YAG is a solid state laser that uses a crystal rod made of yttrium, aluminum, and garnet (YAG) that is doped with neodymium (Nd) and emits photons when its electrons are excited. The intense short wavelength light produced by solid-state lasers requires special eye protection.[57] Naturally, that factor and the sophisticated applications for which lasers were intended made them ideal for integration with Motoman robots. Hobart lasers employed a fiber optic delivery system that projected welding and cutting up to 150 meters from the power and laser source, thus permitting modification or repair in inaccessible or hazardous areas, such as heat exchanger tubes in nuclear power plants.[58]

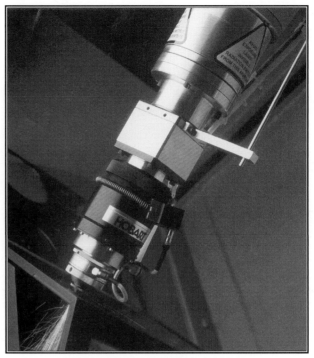

A Hobart 3.0-kilowatt Nd:YAG laser makes a high-speed cut on sheet metal.

Hobart Plasma Transferred Arc/K-10 robot system

Integrated systems developed by Motoman and Hobart Laser Products enjoyed great success in the automotive market. At one point over 90 percent of this market had purchased their systems from Hobart.[59]

For any company that manufactures potentially dangerous equipment it is sometimes the sales that are not made which can be among the most important. Hobart Brothers had been acutely aware of that fact ever since it began selling welders to the U.S. Navy in the 1930s. Over the decades many of its sophisticated power conversion machines have had military or defense industry capabilities, and precautions had to be taken to prevent their misuse or acquisition by the wrong parties. In March 1995 representatives from Aum USA, a religious nonprofit organization, approached Hobart Laser Products to purchase a $450,000 three-kilowatt laser designed to operate within a glove box for projects that produced nuclear emissions. Hobart

Hobart made an impressive impact on trade show audiences. Up to seventeen continuous live welding demonstrations were made in many of the annual American Welding Society Shows. Hobart enjoyed an inside the main entrance location for years throughout the United States as shown in the above 1991 Detroit exhibition. Hobart's sales policy was to participate in major trade shows worldwide.

representatives were puzzled by Aum's stated plans for the device and suspicious of the hurry-up nature of the order and the claim that payment would be in cash. The deal fell through. Days later members of the Aum Shinrikyo cult released Sarin gas in the Tokyo subway, killing twelve and injuring thousands. Subsequent investigations revealed the cult had labs for making chemical and biological weapons and plans for acquiring nuclear capabilities.[60]

E. A. Hobart would have been proud of how his family-owned company had carried on his "hobby shop" tradition of pursuing cutting edge technology. He would have been less comfortable with how that new technology was pursued. In contrast with the decision he and his brother W. H. made to expand organically during World War II without recourse to government loans, management in the late 1980s and early 1990s had incurred

Hobart products regularly earned cover recognition in the AWS Welding Journal as well as in other major industry trade and business publications.

$64 million in debt in making its acquisitions.[61] The focus on acquiring new technology and absorbing subsidiaries did have some negative effect on innovation within the company itself. The underfunding of the Procedure Lab temporarily shorted out the circuit between customer feedback and creative problem solving. Between 1987 and 1993 Hobart Brothers went nearly six years without being granted a U.S. patent, its longest drought since E. A. Hobart had received his first in 1930.[62] There was little doubt within the company that pursuing new technologies was the right path to take for the future. What was less certain was whether a privately owned company like Hobart Brothers had the resources it needed, in capital and personnel, to develop these new technologies and the patience to wait for demand to rise to the level where steady profits could be earned.[63]

CHAPTER 24

The Family Finds a Suitable Suitor

illiam Hobart Jr. was relaxing at home on a Sunday night when at about 10:30 the phone rang. "Hey, we've got a fire over here." The caller was an employee at the filler metals plant.[1] It was May 13, 1990, exactly two weeks past the one-hundredth anniversary of the fire that destroyed C. C. Hobart's first factory. As his grandfather had in 1890, William hurried to the plant two miles away and off the same road as his home. When he arrived heavy smoke and flames were still pouring from the northeast corner of the filler metals building. The Troy Fire Department fought the blaze and declared victory about 4:45 in the morning. Four firefighters were treated for heat exhaustion. The next day investigators discovered the cause was a heater turned on in an empty plastic rinse tank. Someone had missed a note that the tank was slated for repair. Damage was estimated at a quarter of a million dollars.[2] More troubling was the disruption the fire would cause to production of cash generating welding consumables. "Throughout the plant, machinery and equipment were covered with deposits of greasy film and corrosive material. 'It looked like we'd be out of business for some time,' William recalled."[3]

Hobart Brothers, however, was not the fledgling enterprise of one hundred years ago. It had about two thousand employees worldwide and sales of close to $350 million a year. More importantly, its people were imbued with the company philosophy that had been formally composed in 1987 but practiced for over a century:

We recognize that only by efficiently serving our customers do we reach true security for our employees, shareholders, and surrounding community.

We believe in treating others as we would like to be treated and we take pride in our tradition of being people oriented.

Heavy smoke and flames were pouring from the northeast corner of the filler metals building.

We understand the value of teamwork and actively seek the support of our co-workers in the pursuit of our goals.[4]

Consequently, the first people contacted in the wake of the fire were customers who were informed of the mishap and assured the company, with the help of its Canadian subsidiary, would do its best to meet their needs. By 5 p.m. of the day after the fire Terry Lefever and his team had devised a plan to get the damaged plant operational. Employees put in twelve-hour days as work went forward seven days a week, cleaning, rebuilding, and installing new equipment. Just eight weeks after the fire the plant was back in business.[5] News of the financial trouble at the Stearns subsidiary in Texas made this quick turnaround all the more crucial.

Despite the difficult business climate of the 1980s, the company had strengthened its commitment to its people by increasing the percentage of pre-tax profits allocated to the employee's retirement fund from 15 percent to 20 percent and made half that amount available as cash or for investment in a 401(k) plan. Quarterly meetings kept employees better informed about how the company was doing. ". . . fourteen years ago we'd tell them how we did, percentage wise, against our plan. . . ." Lefever explained. "Today we tell them how much money we make. Because of the profit-sharing plan that's important to them."[6] Another example of the family-like cohesion of the company came in the spring of 1991 when management instituted an austerity program due to the recession that followed the Persian Gulf War and to recoup losses from Stearns, which had just been sold. Hobart planned to send a much smaller delegation than usual to the annual American Welding Society Show held in Detroit that year but learned that many employees planned to attend anyway to see what the competition was up to. The company rewarded this dedication by purchasing entry tickets for all Hobart people traveling at their own expense.[7]

The third generation of industrial Hobarts was also encouraged to see several members of the next generation taking up the challenge of carrying the company forward. Shortly after the Board of Directors was broadened and professionalized in the early 1980s by the addition of two Miami Valley business-men, Bob Brethen, the executive vice president of Phillips Industries, and Leo Ladehoff, CEO of Amcast Industrial Cor-poration, the Board adopted a policy regarding the employment of sharehold-ers and their relatives. ". . . the individ-ual under consideration must be qualified." Those seeking a management position had to be college graduates "with a major that is applicable to the business or have equivalent training or experience for the position." Also, working for a non-Hobart company "for several years" to gain an outside perspective was deemed a desirable experience for future managers at Hobart Brothers.[8] Whereas William and Peter Hobart firmly endorsed this policy, Bill Howell did not want barriers placed in the way of family members who wanted to work for the company. Robert Bravo, plagued by the return of polio symptoms, had retired from the Board and been replaced by his wife Lucia. Lucia felt her two brothers were uncomfortable with the presence of a woman on the Board, but their differences were philo-sophical as well. Lucia wanted the Board made into a democracy where all shareholders had a vote on all mat-ters. This was quite different from William's vision of a board that represented shareholders' interests and resem-bled the way a publicly held company works.[9]

Family members who had decided to make their career within the company had a very different perspec-tive from those who had worked at Hobart briefly or not at all. Third-generation cousins, Edmund and Jonathan Hobart, had worked their entire adult lives at Hobart Brothers. Among the fourth generation, Robb Howell, his younger brother David, and their brother-in-law Jos Kurd had been working for the company for years and clearly saw a future for themselves at Hobart. Each had risen to responsible positions. After being plant manager for weld-ing equipment, Robb Howell was promoted to vice presi-dent for sales and marketing of battery chargers.[10] Jos Kurd became director of manufacturing systems for the reor-ganized Welding Products Group that combined equipment and filler metals.[11] David Howell had worked for the sales branch in Cincinnati, managed the Atlanta office, and then

became international sales administrator.[12] William's son Harrison graduated from Yale in 1988, served two years at Citibank, helped to do strategic planning at Hobart, and then was sent to California as vice president for operations of Hobart lasers.[13] For three generations, Hobart Brothers had been owned and managed by individuals like these, family members and shareholders who also forged their professional careers within the company. However, there were many more individ-uals in the fourth generation who were family members and shareholders who did not envision a career with the com-pany. The Board tried to address their needs and provide liquidity by allowing them to sell shares back to the company.[14]

In 1987 two members of the fourth generation joined the Board of Directors when Robb Howell replaced his father Bill Howell and Larry Hard, a Seattle lawyer married to the Bravo's oldest daughter Hylton, replaced his mother-in-law Lucia Bravo.[15] Besides representing the younger generation and the Howell and Bravo clans, Howell and Hard could also speak for shareholders working within and outside the company respectively.

Bob Brethen left the Hobart board in 1990.[16] Dan Duvall, the CEO of Robbins and Meyers, a Dayton-based company that manufactured industrial pumps and equip-ment, took his place and his input soon earned him the respect of company officials at Hobart.[17] The reorganized board undertook a nearly six-month executive search to find a new president to replace Kim Packard. The board chose Michael A. Wolf, a forty-nine-year-old former vice-president and general manager of the Agriculture Division of Case Corporation, a producer of earth-moving and con-struction equipment. He also had international experience from serving as a vice president at Firestone. Wolf took office in February 1992 as Hobart Brothers prepared to cel-ebrate the seventy-fifth anniversary of the company's for-mal incorporation.[18]

Vice Chairman Peter Hobart sent Wolf an eight-page memo to introduce him to the company and give his per-spective on the future. Peter noted that a dropping mar-ket share in power sources had been a problem for the past ten years and that this had led to "a tendency to change the whole nature of the company from what was originally a machine oriented business to a filler metal ori-ented business. . . ." He emphasized his desire to develop high technology and a total systems approach. "What we desperately need in the company is sales and marketing expertise. . . . Right now the company is being run by the financial and engineering people. . . ."[19] Peter endorsed

Family members who had decided to make their career within the company had a very different perspective from those who worked elsewhere.

the proposed acquisition of McKay, a nonferrous filler metal company based in York, Pennsylvania, "if we can do it in an intelligently financed way," but advocated a return to one of Hobart Brothers' core values. "Your predecessor's idea of growing was to buy companies and market share, let the other people do it for us, and this did not work. You will have to re-instill in the company a feeling of self-reliance. . . ."[20]

Peter went on to state that the North American Free Trade Agreement (NAFTA) meant that the domestic market now had to be viewed together with Canada and Mexico and enclosed a separate memo on Hobart Brothers Canada as an operation "we should take a lesson from" because of its effective marketing.[21] In discussing Wolf's planned trip to Europe in May he warned, "Europe is in a terrible condition right now," due to the recession and the collapse of the strategic alliance with Oerlikon. He hoped for the time and support to rebuild but sensed the ax would be out. "You can well imagine that after thirty years in the European team it is tragic for me to see it dying. . . ."[22]

Weightier concerns were set aside to celebrate the seventy-fifth anniversary of Hobart Brothers' 1917 incorporation. Festivities began April 15 with the opening of the Hobart Institute of Welding Technology Auditorium and a display on the company's history hosted by the institute. The centerpiece of the celebration came ten days later with the dedication of a commemorative sound chamber sculpture by Dayton musician-sculptor Michael Bashaw. Undeterred by a cold rain, the ceremony also marked the formal dedication of the Hobart sculpture park, which had

already grown to fifteen pieces of welded sculpture on the grounds of the Hobart Institute. In his remarks William Hobart reaffirmed the family's desire "to stay private as a company" but acknowledged the challenge to "be selective and prioritize" in making choices in a time of accelerating change. His brother Peter decried America's recent "orgy of importing everything, buying everything, let somebody else do it. . . . That's not what we're about. We're creative, industrious, inventive. . . . That's why we like to put the artistic creativity next to the industrial and technical creativity." Bashaw followed his remarks by leading his group "The Bridge" in a concert of original works performed on the welded steel sound chamber.[23] The anniversary celebration continued through May with an employee luncheon at Hobart Arena, a vendor's day, and an open house for the community. In addition, the C. C. Hobart Foundation sponsored an exhibition at the Troy-Hayner Cultural Center put together by Christina O'Neil on the company's welded steel houses from the 1930s.[24]

Although the celebration sparked reflections on the past, two recent developments demonstrated the impact the Hobart family and Hobart Brothers Company would continue to have on the future of the Troy community. In 1960 William Hobart's wife Julia had founded the Overfield Early Childhood Program, a nursery school that met in two rooms of the restored Overfield Tavern Museum. Parents who felt the need for a quality nursery school program in the community enrolled the first class of twelve students. By 1988, Overfield, which operated five days a week and had received accreditation from the National Association for the Education of Young Children (NAEYC), had sixty-five students attending and had outgrown its namesake facility. The Hobart family suggested that E. A.'s and Martha's welded-steel house at 172 Ridge Avenue become the next home for Overfield with the surrounding two acres for outdoor play. The refurbished house opened its yellow doors to one hundred students and nine teachers in September 1989 and soon proved to be an ideal place for the school. In 1996, William and Julia Hobart purchased the property including all surrounding buildings from the company and gave it to the school. The

"SOUND CHAMBER" sculpture by Michael Bashaw

E. A. and Martha Hobart's welded-steel residence is now the home of the Overfield School. (Photo montage by Kathie Johnson)

school, by 2003, had a faculty of fourteen teachers and 170 children enrolled from the ages of eighteen months to full-day six-year-old kindergarten. It is said to be without peer in southern Ohio. The family thought E. A. and Martha would be delighted with the new life of their former home in which the childless couple had entertained two generations of nieces and nephews.[25]

Another community asset that stemmed from a grass-roots effort by local parents in the 1960s was Riverside, a program for the education and recreation of children with disabilities. As these children grew into adults the lack of employment opportunity became obvious, and RT (Riverside Training) Industries was founded in 1974 as a non-profit corporation that sought partnerships with area businesses to employ adults with disabilities. On land donated by Forrest and Thelma Archer, RT Industries built its own facility on Foss Way in Troy in 1988.[26] That same year Hobart's Larry Heisey, working in his basement with various sample parts, designed and built a prototype battery charger for the low-end market. Don Bercaw had seen the need for an inexpensive light duty industrial battery charger, but the pair believed that if it were developed through the normal channels at Hobart Brothers it would be too expensive and miss the intended market.[27] Though more complicated than anything yet assembled at RT Industries, Heisey and the supervisors at RT devised a process that worked remarkably well. Edward J. Hobart at Hobart Cabinet, another local business that employed people from RT, built test equipment for the chargers. Marketed under the name LTD, for Light, Tough, and Dependable, the line of battery chargers grew to six different models and became a half million-dollar business.[28] By 1991 Hobart-supplied components made up 70 percent of the second-generation LTD chargers assembled at RT under the supervision of Julie Lutz, and plan-

ning was underway for Hobart Brothers to build light-duty chargers under the Deka brand name based on the LTD design to complement the line of industrial chargers Hobart already made.[29] RT Industries expanded its Troy plant in 1997 and employed 180 adults as it entered a new century.[30]

The presidency of Mike Wolf proved to be a difficult time of transition at Hobart Brothers. Some executives felt that Wolf did not have his heart in the job. He continued to live at a bed and breakfast in Troy during the week and often spent weekends with his wife at their home in the Chicago area.[31] Wolf wanted to shut down rather than help the money-losing operations in Europe and considered selling off some recent acquisitions because companies had curtailed their purchases of capital equipment and high technology in response to the recession.[32]

Hobart Brothers had reorganized in 1991, combining the welding equipment and filler metals divisions, advanced systems and training for the entire NAFTA market, the United States, Canada, and Mexico, under Executive Vice President Terry Lefever. A second group, renamed Diversified Products and International, included ground power, battery chargers, the Wollard and TAFA sub-

Conrad Schwab, vice president of Airport Systems

sidiaries as well as all training and marketing outside the NAFTA region. Senior Vice President Conrad Schwab led this group.[33] Roger Williams had hired Schwab to become general manager for ground power in 1988. Schwab became vice president of airport systems two years later when Williams retired. Prior to coming to Hobart, Schwab had served as general manager of Piper Aircraft and had spent most of the two previous decades in Europe. Schwab had always been intrigued by businesses in state of flux and had enjoyed working with a family-owned company in Switzerland. In 1992 the board assigned him the difficult task of scaling back Hobart operations in Europe.[34]

Larry Heisy   *Don Bercaw*

A combination of personal dedication and corporate-community teamwork broadens customer satisfaction

Larry Heisey, a Hobart designer of battery chargers and aircraft ground power units saw a market need for small, efficient battery chargers. He designed three models on his own time at home. Hobart Brothers Co. agreed there was a market but production facilities were at their limit. Larry and Hobart Marketing Manager Don Bercaw developed a plan to assemble the products at RT Industries* in Troy, Ohio. Hobart then marketed the products.

Briefly, in the wake of the collapse of Oerlikon, which was nearly a fatal blow to Hobart's European strategy, there had been hope that the demise of communism in Eastern Europe would create new sales opportunities for Hobart Brothers. In 1990 Hobart found a distributor in Poland, and in October William Hobart, Conrad Schwab, and Andre Odermatt led a delegation to the Soviet Union. Following the fall of the Berlin Wall in 1989, Mikhail Gorbachev sought to accelerate "perestroika,", his restructuring of the Soviet economy, by fostering more trade and technology exchanges with the West. The Hobart delegation exhibited at Moscow Aerospace '90 and visited an aircraft repair plant and the E. O. Paton Welding Institute in Kiev.[35] By the following year Hobart tried two authorized distributors in the USSR, a market which had previously been directly served by Hobart's Austrian subsidiary. That October Hobart hosted Russian delegations from the Paton Institute and the Ministry of Civil Aviation.[36] Ultimately, Soviet interest in Hobart's applied technology, such as the dabber system for repair of jet engines, and Hobart interest in advanced Soviet research, such as welding in space, foundered on the Soviet Union's lack of hard currency for trade or saleable products to barter.[37] The Kremlin maintained an unrealistically high exchange rate for conversion of rubles to western currencies. Once the USSR splintered into fifteen separate nations and the newly elected Russian government reversed this policy, the ruble collapsed in value. Several years of contentious reorganization ensued before Russian industry could afford to make major purchases from the West. Apart from sporadic orders of specialty products, such as power sources to weld Yugos in a Belgrade plant, similar conditions throughout Eastern Europe thwarted Hobart's hopes of major sales to the region.[38]

Generous Dutch labor laws made liquidation of Hobart's Amsterdam facility a lengthy and expensive process.[39] In March 1993 Hobart sold its 51 percent stake in the Italian welding firm Wemi to the Cerso Group, and two months later sold its share of the Swedish robotics firm Torsteknik to Yaskawa, thus ending nearly thirty years of manufacturing in Europe. Some of Hobart's international effort was redirected to its promising Latin American market by changing its sales and distribution centers in Mexico City and Santiago, Chile.[40] Meanwhile, ground power sales to the booming East Asian market through new offices in Singapore and Beijing helped offset another round of retrenching in the American airline industry that witnessed the demise of such giants as Eastern and Pan Am.[41]

Hobart Brothers established its position as a solid number two among domestic producers of welding consumables when it finalized its acquisition of McKay Welding Products in December 1992. McKay was a 111-year-old company in

York, Pennsylvania, that possessed its own network of distributors for its market-leading electrodes for stainless steel and hard surfacing. By the summer of 1993 Hobart had con-**McKAY**® solidated manufacture of the McKay product lines by expanding its Piqua and Troy filler metal plants and adding 105 employees.[42] However, Mike Wolf would not preside over the channeling of this new revenue stream because dissatisfaction had provoked another change of leadership at Hobart Brothers.

Frank O. Anderson had joined the Hobart Board in April 1992. Several board members knew Anderson as the recent CEO of the Roy Smith Company, Hobart's distributor in Detroit. Anderson had spent most of his career in the automobile industry, including twenty-five years at Chrysler. When he was just thirty-five Chrysler put Anderson in charge of a troubled foundry in Indianapolis. From that point he rose in the corporation holding various positions in manufacturing and purchasing until he became group vice president for U.S. Automotive Manufacturing with responsibility for fifty-five Chrysler plants. The federal government tapped Anderson for the nation's Strategic Executive Reserve, a group of business leaders who would be relocated to a secure underground facility in the case of war or disaster to take control of the country's infrastructure and get it up and running once again. Periodically, Anderson went to Chicago to participate in war game exercises. Anderson remained at Chrysler through the early tenure of Lee Iococca and the launch of the K car before taking early retirement at age fifty-six in 1981.[43]

Anderson later told Frank Smith of the Roy Smith Company what he intended to do for the remainder of his career. "I don't need pay. I just want to stay busy and help American companies."[44] Not long after he left Chrysler he was asked to become CEO of the Motor and Machinery Castings Company to shepherd it out of bankruptcy. After consulting for a while, he took the helm at the Roy Smith Company, which was experiencing trouble due to upheavals in the U.S. automobile industry and the transition between second- and third-generation owners. "Anderson brought in a system. He knew what the whole auto plant needed, and he found ways to give successes to others in the company," said Steve Smith who, along with his brother Greg, stood to inherit the Detroit company founded by their grandfather. "Frank Anderson has the biggest brain and the smallest ego of anyone I've ever met."[45]

Anderson brought a customer's view of Hobart Brothers to the board. For decades Chrysler had been one of the world's largest users of Hobart welding systems, and his stint at Roy Smith provided him with a distributor's perspective on the company as well.[46] He was truly a welding man talking to welding people. The interim arrangement where a resident nonfamily director served as acting CEO

Frank O. Anderson, president and CEO, 1993–1997

but had to operate through Mike Wolf was not working.[47] Furthermore, a major shift in the domestic welding business had just occurred. Illinois Tool Works (ITW), a multibillion dollar diversified manufacturing company, had purchased Miller Electric.[48] For several years William Hobart had been trying to interest Margaret Miller Gilson, daughter of company founder Niels Miller, in a merger of the two family-owned welding firms. Several Miller executives had shown interest, but Gilson was opposed. Gilson died in 1991, and her daughters who inherited the company had little interest in running it. William had talked to them several times before, but ITW's acquisition of the Appleton, Wisconsin-based welding firm postponed William's dream of combining the synergistic strengths of Miller Electric and Hobart Brothers.[49] Cleveland-based Lincoln Electric was still the nation's largest welding company, and now Miller would be a better-financed competitor. In 1993 it became the first domestic welding manufacturer to attain ISO 9001 registration, a coveted quality rating from the Swiss-based International Standardization Organization.[50] In effect, Hobart's room to maneuver had been considerably reduced.

In late October 1993, a series of meetings between board members and Hobart family members produced change in the form of a new leadership team. On October 30 the sixty-nine-year-old Anderson became chairman and president of Hobart Brothers. Mike Wolf resigned and William Hobart became chairman emeritus and later retired in 1994 at age seventy.[51]

Anderson approached the company as a doctor would a patient: ask questions, check the vital signs, compose a diagnosis, and begin treatment. In assessing Hobart

Brothers he found many strengths. "About 90 percent of the people there were excellent. William Hobart was a prince of a guy who was sensitive to the fact that Hobart Brothers couldn't continue to go it alone." Peter Hobart "was a big thinker, a good face for the corporation. The Hobart name and history meant a lot to him." Andre Odermatt in Engineering, Carl Hatton in Power Conversion, and Executive Vice President Terry Lefever were other executives he found particularly able. The company had a great name within the industry, and the Hobart Institute was a wonderful asset. However, there were problems in quality control, and manufacturing costs were high. He believed acquisitions had left the company over-diversified in aircraft support equipment and had saddled it with too much debt. Anderson intended to sell off most of Hobart's acquisitions in order to raise money and provide breathing room for the company.[52] In this strategy he concurred with that of William Hobart and the financial people as opposed to Peter Hobart, Bill Howell and those in the company who saw the pursuit of new technologies as the key to future growth.

Vice Chairman and head of Hobart International Peter C. Hobart (photo by Adriana Vitali, 2004)

In reinvigorating the company's traditional core competencies, Anderson sought to focus on selling welds, the total combination of machines, wires, and processes. In a mature industry with modest growth potential, one had to achieve high quality at low cost in order to compete. Anderson was a great believer in what he called "the sting of accountability." Executives had to sign off on the annual business plan and meet with him monthly to assess progress. When targets were missed managers had to explain why and offer a plan of action. Anyone could see him about a problem, but he expected people to come with ideas and not just dump problems on his desk.[53] Although Anderson had high expectations, his management style reminded older employees of the days of E. A. Hobart.[54] After an early morning jog, Anderson spent his first hour at work walking the plant and getting to know workers on a first-name basis just as he had done at Chrysler. This encouraged employees to take advantage of his open door policy. Early in his tenure a female machine operator who had made an appointment to see Anderson delivered a litany of complaints. "When are things going to change at

Hobart Brothers?" she asked in exasperation. "Things have changed," he replied. "You can come here and bitch at the president."[55]

The year 1993 had been a tough one for the company. Although economic recovery had led to an increase in gross sales of over 13 percent compared to 1992, the losses incurred from restructuring European operations, relocating McKay filler metal production, and an environmental cleanup of the former Nova plant site in New Jersey had more than offset the gains. In December Hobart agreed to sell Yaskawa its 50 percent share in Motoman for $3.5 million and identified both Wollard and TAFA as "assets held for sale."[56]

As the American economy surged forward in 1994, the demand for welding products jumped with the automotive, agricultural, and railcar markets leading the way. In April Anderson told a reporter, "We are running twenty-four hours a day, seven days a week at our filler metal factory. I couldn't make another pound if I wanted to."[57] The company had developed a five-year product plan with the intent of creating the best products in the industry for the markets in which it chose to compete. As in the auto industry, new products would be designed on common platforms in an effort to reduce the total number of parts by 80 percent.[58] Underutilized facilities were put to work manufacturing parts for other companies. For example, a new $850,000 state-of-the-art electrostatic powder paint shop was built that summer with enough excess capacity to seek outside contracts.[59]

In October Hobart divested itself of two more subsidiaries. Wollard Airport Equipment was sold to Northwestern Motor Company and TAFA was sold to Eutectic Corporation.[60] The Wollard acquisition, which came shortly before a sharp downturn for domestic airlines, was a victim of poor timing. TAFA represented some promising new technologies, but Hobart lacked the deep pockets needed for research and the time to wait for markets to develop. Hobart Laser Products had spent a great deal of money to develop a reliable new 3.0 kilowatt Nd:YAG laser, which it hoped would allow lasers "to move out of the laboratory environment and into production facilities" by replacing resistance spot welding.[61] With its eye on the automotive industry, Hobart rolled out its new laser at its new service center in the Detroit suburb of Troy in early December.[62]

The coming-out party for the new industrial laser featured high technology and was designed for a global market with its media guide folder in four languages, just the kind of promotion Peter had always favored to market the company's products.[63] The need to right the company's bottom line had forced it to drastically scale back its European operations and its efforts to expand into new technologies. Although, Peter felt those choices would hamper the company's future growth, he was encouraged by the Board's decision to add two directors, one as a technology specialist and a second with expertise in marketing capital goods.[64] He had long advocated these additions to the Board.[65]

Hobart had returned to profitability in 1994. Sales rose 15 percent to $254 million, and the company reduced its outstanding debt by one-sixth.[66] In order to rejuvenate its image and underscore the company's focus on developing its core technologies for the next century, Hobart planned to unveil a new color scheme at the April 1995 American Welding Society Show in Cleveland. The traditional gold and blue employed since the late 1950s would be replaced by a dynamic new trio: electric orange, purple, and platinum. Orange, the color of the weld puddle, stood for the welding industry. Purple symbolized Hobart's rich industrial history, and platinum represented the company's commitment to state-of-the-art technology.[67] Executives soon realized that the pending change of colors could mark a much more far-reaching shift when Illinois Tool Works (ITW) expressed an interest in acquiring Hobart Brothers. First approached by William in 1993 after its acquisition of Miller, ITW now contacted Hobart and said it wanted to talk.

Based in Glenview, Illinois, ITW was a well-run seventy-three-year-old internationally diversified manufacturing company that had grown dramatically in the past fifteen years. It roots, however, were similar to those of Hobart Brothers. For decades ITW had been a closely held medium-sized Midwestern industrial company led by three successive generations of the Smith family. In the 1940s Harold Byron Smith, grandson of the founder, decentralized ITW's operations in order to focus on specific markets. Like Hobart, ITW acquired its first international subsidiaries in the 1960s. In the early 1980s ITW developed its 80/20 approach to business.[68] ". . . 80 percent of a business' sales are derived from the 20 percent of its product offering being sold to key customers."[69] Thanks to simplifying its processes, its product lines, and its customer base to focus on the

Chairman Emeritus William H. Hobart announcing to the press the merger with ITW, which he initiated. February 1996

most profitable market segments, ITW expanded rapidly by acquiring premier name companies in niche industries and was generating over $3 billion a year in revenue by the mid-1990s.[70]

ITW had entered the welding business in 1993 when it acquired the Miller Group, but Miller manufactured only welding power sources, a capital good. ITW discovered that its 80/20 approach demanded that it also possess the capacity to produce filler metals, welding consumables that generated steadier profits than power sources. Just as W. H. Sr. had convinced his brother E. A. back in the 1930s, ITW needed to sell "razor blades" to complement its "razors." As the second-largest domestic producer of welding consumables and a family-owned company in the midst of a generational transition, Hobart Brothers was a perfect fit for what ITW sought.

William Hobart Jr. had approached ITW once before. Now, in the spring of 1995, ITW was contacting him again, and both the board and the family thought William and Frank Anderson had better take a look.[71] On their visit to ITW's headquarters in suburban Chicago, Anderson and

Hobart noted how ITW valued innovation within its corporate culture. The corporation had institutionalized this value in an ITW Patent Society, which held an annual black tie awards dinner at the Museum of Science and Industry in Chicago. ITW prided itself on the thousands of patents held by its subsidiaries worldwide and recognized its top inventors as Distinguished Fellows and inducted a select few into its Hall of Fame.[72] Anderson spent time with the ITW staff selling Hobart for what it was, a trusted name in the welding business whose people had earned 116 patents to date, and for what it could become, a lucrative producer of filler metal formulas to patent.[73]

The offer from ITW came at a time when the company's transition team was searching for the next CEO from among the family's fourth generation. There was no clear agreement as to who that choice should be. A stock trade with ITW would allow the family to sidestep this and other potentially divisive issues and at the same time provide better liquidity for shareholders who had careers outside the company. As William outlined the pros and cons of the proposed merger for family shareholders, he pointed out that most practical considerations favored the move, while the counter-arguments were mainly emotional in nature.[74] Despite the proposed merger, Hobart Brothers would maintain its identity in the marketplace and in the Troy community. Though family control would end, the company and the jobs it provided would be more likely to survive, and ITW could provide the needed capital to modernize production, fund research, and ultimately strengthen the business C. C. Hobart and his sons had created eight decades ago.

Teams from both ITW and Hobart Brothers began doing diligence to provide an accurate accounting of what Hobart was worth. However, each of the three main measures in use, the net worth of its assets, a multiple of its earnings over the past eight to ten years, or the percent of return on capital employed, would result in a figure skewed towards the low end. Peter wanted to offer ITW a higher figure based on gross annual sales minus current indebtedness. The outside directors did not think that would work, but Frank Anderson thought it was worth a try. With a handshake over a desk at the Hobart Brothers office building ITW's CEO John Nichols accepted the offer. The final confirmation meeting was held at the Racquet Club atop

Hobart signs the agreement with ITW on February 2, 1996. Left to right: Peter C. Hobart, vice chairman of Hobart Brothers Company; John Nichols, chairman of ITW; Frank O. Anderson II, chairman and president of Hobart Brothers Company.

the Kettering Tower in Dayton with the Hobart Brothers Board of Directors and several other Hobart family members present. Representing ITW were Chairman John Nichols, President W. James Farrell, and Executive Vice President Robert H. Jenkins, who had been the point man for the ITW acquisitions team that studied Hobart Brothers. Representatives from William Blair and Company, a Chicago investment banking firm, were also present. Hobart shareholders would exchange their stock for ITW stock. Frank Anderson would remain as CEO of ITW's new Troy-based subsidiary whose workforce would still be employed by Hobart Brothers. ITW planned no immediate changes in management or operations.[75]

Hobart and ITW announced the sale on Friday May 19, 1995, in Troy. The Hobart Board issued management and employees a question and answer sheet explaining the merger, which William Hobart elaborated on in an issue of the *Hobart Brothers Reporter*.[76] "You will be part of a large Midwestern manufacturing-oriented parent with a strong track record—one that is in it for the long haul . . . the shareholders will continue to be invested in HB, but as part of a larger entity, ITW. This is not a Sell-and-Walk-Away situation."[77] ITW executives also played a role in reassuring employees and the community. President Farrell promised to retain the Hobart name, "the Hobart name recognition as far as integrity is one of the main drivers for wanting to do this expansion. . . . We think of ourselves as a solid, Midwestern collection of businesses, just like Hobart."[78] Troy Mayor Peter Jenkins, a former personnel director at Hobart Brothers, said he felt better about the sale after talking to executives of both firms.[79]

Though most employees were by no means shocked that the company had been sold, they and the community needed reassuring. Employment across town at Hobart Corporation had declined ever since the company had been acquired. Premark International (PMI), its current owner, had sold the KitchenAid division to Whirlpool and removed the Hobart name from in front of its plant on Ridge Avenue. NCR in Dayton had recently been acquired by AT&T and had reduced its local presence as well. Kermit Vandivier spoke for many in Troy when he wrote in an editorial, "Things will never be the same again." He could not help but be apprehensive that Troy had lost its last major locally owned business. Even so, he stated ITW:

. . . must be first class else the current owners of Hobart Brothers would never have dealt with them. One thing C. C. Hobart's heirs had drilled into them was that anything the company did impacted the community and every move they made was considered in the light of its effect on the city.[80]

After briefly recapping the impact of the Hobart family on the development of public facilities for the community, Vandivier expressed his hope that ITW would also be a good neighbor but warned it had a tough act to follow.

Hobart Brothers had been sold while the company was enjoying an upswing in business. Sales for the first quarter of 1995 rose nearly 20 percent compared to the first quarter of 1994, but profits were twice as high as Hobart began to reap benefits from more efficient use of its facilities and divesting itself of money-losing subsidiaries. This meant that profit-sharing bonuses rose to 4.85 percent of wages, the largest Profit Sharing Plus payout in more than two years.[81] In May 1995 the company achieved two coveted marks of recognition. One was the Governor's "E" Award for Excellence in Exporting for increasing both export sales and the number of export-related jobs. Also, Hobart's Filler Metals operations received ISO 9002 certification, reinforcing its reputation for world-class quality assurance standards for welding consumables.[82] That same year a battery charger developed by a cross-functional team at Hobart won the competition to power the "People Movers" for the 1996 Summer Olympics in Atlanta.[83] However, an unexpected snag in the sale to ITW made the summer and fall of 1995 as full of anxiety as it had been exactly one century earlier for C. C. Hobart when he had first moved the old Hobart Electric Company to Troy.

Lincoln Electric protested to the Federal Trade Commission (FTC) that, in light of ITW's recent acquisition of Miller Electric, it should not be permitted to purchase Hobart Brothers because the proposed merger would give ITW control of too large a share of domestic manufacturing of welding equipment. When ITW's Chairman Nichols first met with the young lawyers from the FTC, he asserted that the deal would go through and that the FTC's concerns would soon be swept aside.[84] Instead, the FTC blocked the sale. "Hobart has been an aggressive competitor on the basis of price in the markets for both industrial power sources and industrial engine drives; allowing these businesses to be swallowed up by Illinois Tool Works presents clear antitrust concerns," said FTC Bureau of Competition Director William J. Baer.[85] News that the sale had been blocked threw Hobart Brothers' employees, customers, suppliers and distributors into a state of uncertainty as to whether the sale would happen and concerned over what might have to be done to complete it.

Seventy years earlier, C. C. Hobart had found it necessary to divide his company in order to preserve family unity. Now his grandchildren and great-grandchildren faced the task of divesting themselves of one portion of Hobart Brothers before they could accept the offer from ITW. Preferably, they could find a buyer for industrial power sources, those rated at 250 amps and higher, who would be willing to keep those manufacturing jobs in Troy. Prestolite Electric of Ann Arbor, Michigan, stepped forward with an offer. Prestolite's CEO was none other than Kim Packard, the former president of Hobart Brothers who had been asked to resign less than five years earlier. In addition to the Industrial Welding Equipment Division, Packard wanted the highly profitable Industrial Battery Charger Division. Conrad Schwab approached Troy city officials to secure tax abatement to help relocate those divisions in a new facility in a developing industrial park west of Interstate 75.[86] This proposed divestment did nothing to cool ITW's interest in acquiring Hobart Brothers. ITW already had the capacity to produce industrial power sources for welding from its purchase of Miller. ITW's desire to add Hobart Brothers' production of filler metals was its main impetus for the deal. Battery chargers were a valuable segment of the business, but so were Hobart's ground power units, which would remain a part of the company ITW planned to acquire. The FTC announced its approval of this arrangement on February 2, 1996. Following the customary sixty days for public comment, the merger of ITW and Hobart Brothers and the sale of two Hobart divisions to Prestolite would be final.[87]

Though simple enough on paper, separating the manufacture of industrial power sources and battery chargers from other products would prove difficult to achieve on the factory floor. Both personnel and machine tools were shared among divisions that used the old Main Street plant. Before the deal had been finalized, Andre Odermatt had taken prospective buyers through the plant at night trying to determine who should get which tool.[88] Ralph Barhorst, who was unit manager for Welding Equipment at the Main Street plant, found that deciding which employee would be assigned to either stay with Hobart or go with Prestolite was an even more difficult task.[89] These were the same issues that had bedeviled C. C. Hobart and his three sons seven decades ago when Hobart Cabinet had been split off from Hobart Brothers. By November 1996 the transition had been completed, and the former employees of Hobart's Battery Charger and Industrial Welder Divisions moved into the new Prestolite facility on Corporate Way in Troy. That same month Frank Anderson retired as head of ITW's welding group.[90] The story of the companies C. C. Hobart had founded in Troy was by no means over, but it had certainly entered a new phase. ❧

Epilogue

Over four generations many members of the Hobart family have enjoyed the experience of paddling a canoe down the Miami River or one of its tributaries that helped form the Miami Valley. While gliding downstream with the gentle current one often sees a wedge of land that appears to divide the river into separate branches. Willows and sycamores obscure the view of the other channel, but after a minute or so pass by one sees the piece of land is but an island, and the reunified current propels the canoe forward at a more insistent pace. Very gradually, mile upon mile, the river deepens and widens as new streams add their current. Yet some parts of the river look so like stretches upstream that it seems one's canoe has passed by them before. The story of the companies C. C. Hobart founded resembles such a journey.

A major confluence of currents occurred in 2000 when ITW purchased PMI, the parent company of Hobart Manufacturing Corporation. Thus, the companies C. C. Hobart founded two decades apart, Hobart Manufacturing (1897) and Hobart Brothers (1917), were brought into the same fold one hundred and three years after the birth of the first. Troy residents believe the nature of their community and the work ethic of its people had something to do with ITW's decision. The Hobart name still stands for quality and integrity and is a valuable asset in the marketplace. Although Miller power sources for welding are manufactured in Troy today, a wide variety of products still bear the Hobart name: a diverse array of filler metals for welding, ground power units for aircraft, commercial food processing equipment, scales, labeling systems, metal cabinets for offices and shops, and many more. Briefly, Hobart Brothers Canada became ITW Welding but soon returned to the Hobart name customers and distributors knew so well.[1] Prestolite did not hold onto its two former Hobart divisions for long. Thermadyne, based in St. Louis, purchased the Industrial Welder Division and renamed it Thermal-Arc. In 2000 Prestolite sold the Battery Charger Division to Ametek. The modern descendants of Hobart Brothers' original product line are still built in Troy but marketed under the name Ametek Prestolite Power.[2] Motoman, the former Hobart joint venture in robotic welding with Yaskawa, has expanded its facilities in Troy and West Carrollton, Ohio, and has installed more than seventeen thousand robots in the Americas.[3] The Hobart Institute of Welding Technology remains one of the world's premier educational centers for welding. More than eighty thousand people have graduated from its training programs in its seven decades.[4]

The Hobart Cabinet Company is the only business founded by C. C. Hobart that is still entirely owned by the Hobart family. Martin Hobart, the son of Charles Hobart Jr., majored in history and political science in college but returned after graduation to work at Hobart Cabinet in sales. In contrast to his own experience, Charles Jr. resolved to bring his son along in the business by consulting him and gradually giving him more responsibility. Martin was sales manager by the time Charles retired and Thomas Boyer became president. As sales manager Martin added distributors, put the firm's products in more mail order catalogs, and set up a website. In February 2001 Martin Hobart took the helm as president of Hobart Cabinet, the sole member of the fourth generation to direct a business founded by his great-grandfather.[5] Martin also inherited the tall, lanky build of C. C. Hobart and, like C. C., runs a small company whose brick factory sits near the banks of the Miami River. History never repeats itself exactly, but some of its currents run in similar channels.

Edward J. Hobart still does engineering for Hobart Cabinet, carrying on the family tradition of designing and tinkering with electrical equipment. In the basement of a warehouse across the street from the cabinet company he maintains quite a collection of old power sources and other electrical machinery from past decades of the Hobart companies. "A bad habit I picked up from my uncle," he explains, but the big grin on his face betrays that he is proud to have inherited that habit from E. A. Hobart. One of the final jobs Edward's younger brother Jon performed at Hobart Brothers was to convert some of the company's last engineering drawings to computer

. . . some parts of the river look so like stretches upstream that it seems one's canoe has passed by them before. The story of the companies C. C. Hobart founded resembles such a journey.

The Great Miami River flows through Troy, past First Island and the Hobart boathouse.

files. Jon took early retirement from Hobart Brothers shortly after the ITW purchase.[6]

Starting in the 1970s Edmund Hobart set out on his own journey paddling upstream to explore the far reaches of his family history, seeking sites and branches that lay beyond the memory of any living relatives in Troy. For a time he served as president of the Troy Historical Society and wrote entries on C. C. Hobart and his three sons for a history of Miami County. He corresponded with fellow Hobart genealogists across America and in England and compiled books, documents, and photographs on his family and the companies it founded that eventually filled more than two-dozen boxes in the office of the warehouse on Water Street. On vacations from his job at Motoman Edmund visited the ancestral roots of the Hobart and Jones clans in New England. Outside Westford, Vermont, he found the home built by his great-grandfather Charles Hobart still occupied by distant cousins. Edmund catalogued scores of photographs and used them to illustrate a videotape history of the Hobart companies and their various product lines which he narrated himself.[7] He also wrote a family history that he continually added to and modified as his research progressed.

Edmund was diagnosed with Amyloidosis, a condition where abnormal proteins accumulate in internal organs, and, characteristically, he took to the internet to research it, eventually contacting the world's leading experts on the disorder. He underwent an experimental procedure in Columbus to treat it, but died shortly after on October 27, 1998. Edmund left a valuable legacy of information for his family, and his cousin Peter carried forward their shared dream of composing a comprehensive history of the industrial Hobarts.

In retirement Bill and Marcia Howell divided their time between homes in Vero Beach, Florida, and Walloon Lake, Michigan, migrating with the seasons. Marcia continued to golf while Bill swam almost daily while they kept in touch with their five children, seven grandchildren, and two great-grandchildren. Marcia was an active supporter of the Vero Beach Fine Arts Center, while Bill was a sponsor of Harbor Hall, a halfway house for men in Michigan. The Howells were among the chief sponsors of Troy's new YMCA south of town. Marcia passed away in Walloon Lake on September 21, 1999, at the age of seventy-nine. Eighty-three-year-old Bill Howell had just brought his wife to Troy for her funeral when he suddenly died at his son's home three days later. Neither had been ill, so their deaths were a shock to the family. This pair who had been so close throughout their fifty-eight years of married life were laid to rest following a joint funeral.[8]

While she and her husband Robert raised six children and saw twelve grandchildren added to their family, Lucia

The newly renovated Hobart Arena aglow in evening lights

Bravo played an active role in several civic and cultural organizations. She served on boards for the Troy–Miami County Public Library, the Dayton Ballet, Miami County Mental Health, the Dayton Museum of Natural History, Miss Hall's School, the Bruckner Nature Center and Trinity Episcopal Church. Lucia was president of the Dayton Garden Club for several terms and served four one-year terms on the Board of the Garden Club of America. She chaired the Great Miami River Corridor Committee for Shelby and Miami Counties to protect the river and develop its recreational potential. Lucia was also an advocate for historic preservation.[9] The Bravos were instrumental in the effort to beautify and improve downtown Troy. Robert Bravo had founded Troy's Human Relations Committee and served as president of Troy Housing Opportunity United, which built the community's first low-income housing in addition to his work on the Pan American Development Board that brought surplus industrial equipment to serve the needs of Latin America. Declining health confined Bravo to a wheelchair and he spent most of his later years in Vero Beach.[10]

During a visit to Hobart Arena in 1995 their son Alexandre Bravo noted the declining condition of the arena and suggested a renovation project to coincide with the upcoming fiftieth anniversary of its dedication. The Bravos contributed more than a million dollars as seed money toward the complete renovation of the arena. Work began in April 1997, but Robert Bravo passed away at eighty years of age in Vero Beach on July 4, 2001, just as the renovation neared completion. Lucia continues to live in Hobart Landing on Lucia Drive, the Vero Beach housing community built by her father and uncle.[11]

Upon retiring as chairman of the Board at Hobart Brothers, William Hobart Jr. moved his office several blocks east to quarters overlooking Public Square in downtown Troy. William felt that sale of the company to ITW "freed the prisoners," giving shareholders the liquidity and independence needed to make their own choices. He and his wife Julia now had more time to devote to their family of six children and many grandchildren and a wide range of cultural and community interests. Like his uncle, E. A. Hobart, William had become a director of the Miami Conservancy District, the entity that controls the network of dams and levees built following the 1913 flood to manage the area's rivers. Combined, E. A. and William Hobart provided a half-century of continuous service. William also sat on boards for the Upper Valley Medical Center, Greater Dayton Public Television, the Ohio Chapter of the Nature Conservancy, the Aullwood Audubon Center, and the Miami Valley School in addition to the C. C. Hobart Foundation and the Hobart Institute of Welding. As the founding director of the Overfield Early Childhood Program, Julia Hobart continues to visit the school and advise its directors. In 2000 the Upper Valley Association for the Education of Young Children honored her as their Educator of the Year. Along with serving on several boards with her husband, Julia also is a member of Culture Works, the Dayton Philharmonic, the Dayton Ballet, and the Miami Valley School.

In 1996 William was inducted into the Troy Hall of Fame along with his father, grandfather, and two uncles. The American Welding Society recognized his many contributions to the welding industry and his efforts to advance welding education by naming him an AWS Counselor in 2003.

Peter Hobart continued to live in Rome where he established Amaranta Productions, a company that makes films and videos to document contemporary art and culture. From 1993 to 1999 Peter chaired the International Sculpture Center of Hamilton, New Jersey, and continues to promote sculpture as its chairman emeritus. He returns to Troy several times a year to participate on the Board of the Hobart Institute and do consulting for ITW's Welding Division. Writing a complete history of the industrial Hobarts was the major goal he pursued since the summer of 1999. While at work on those projects he saw his daughter marry and give birth to a granddaughter and two grandchildren born to his son and daughter-in-law. Peter achieved a globe-trotting milestone in 2001 when he traveled to Antarctica, the only continent he had not yet visited. He had discovered that the river C. C. Hobart had embarked on over a century ago was capable of carrying him anywhere in the world.

Americans were shocked by the tragic loss of life on September 11, 2001. Hobart family members and employees who had participated in the construction of the twin towers of the World Trade Center felt a painfully personal connection to the tragedy. The towers had been built to withstand the impact of a Boeing 707, the largest passenger jet in service when the Trade Center was designed. Of course, at the time no one had envisioned a terrorist attack. The idea was for the towers to survive a strike by a jet that had lost its way in bad weather en route to Kennedy or LaGuardia Airports. The 767s that struck the towers on September 11 were slightly larger than 707s and traveling at more than 350 miles per hour, but ultimately the most destructive factor was the tons of aviation fuel they carried. Structurally, the towers possessed the resilience to absorb the massive shock and snap back to vertical within seconds after impact. In the words of the official performance study conducted by the Federal Emergency Management Agency (FEMA), "The fact that the structures were able to sustain this level of damage and remain standing for an extended period of time is remarkable and is the reason that most building occupants were able to evacuate safely."[12] Although most of the jet fuel was consumed in the initial fireballs, the uncontrollable secondary fires begun by the fuel provided the second loading factor which eventually brought the towers down.[13]

Like many Americans, the Hobart family and the Troy Community demonstrated that 2001 would not be a year marked solely by destruction. In May of that year air conditioning was installed in Hobart Arena, enhancing its ability to serve as a year-round facility and ending a fifty-year tradition of sweaty commencements.[14] In June Robb Howell returned to his family's entrepreneurial roots by starting his own business in Piqua. MCD Plastics and Manufacturing would do machining, fabricating, die cutting, and assembly in its ten-thousand-square-foot facility.[15] That summer the C. C. Hobart Foundation made a donation to begin development of the Hobart Urban Nature Preserve and Sculpture Park, an eighty-acre island of farmland and woods surrounded by Troy's expansion that the family had donated to the Miami County Park District in 1999.[16]

November 4, 2001, was a cool but sunlit day as Trojans gathered inside the fifty-one-year old Hobart Arena to celebrate its renovation and rededication. The $3.2 million renovation was a truly community effort with the Troy City Council, the park and recreation boards, the Troy Foundation, the C. C. Hobart Foundation, the architectural firm of Lorenz and Williams, and the arena staff under Charles Sharrett all making valuable contributions of time, money, and talent to the initial contribution of the Bravos. The arena emerged with new windows, repairs to the roof and exterior, an upgraded lobby, rubberized skate-proof flooring, room for the Troy Hall of Fame, new concession stands, revamped locker rooms and restrooms, new seating, an enlarged ice surface, new sound and electrical systems, and walls that shined with a fresh coat of paint in Troy's red, gray, and white colors.[17]

Among those inducted into the Troy Hall of Fame that day was someone with a connection to the Hobart Brothers family. Megan Williams, daughter of Gladys and the late Glyn Williams, was honored for her work as an Academy Award-nominated documentary filmmaker and for founding TRIPOD, a model school program for deaf children and their families.[18] Among those from the fourth generation who spoke at the rededication were Lucia's son Alexandre and her daughter Liz Benson along with Peter's daughter Michelle Peyser. Lucia Bravo and William Hobart Jr. represented the third generation along with Mayor Peter

Jenkins, a former Hobart executive whose father had worked alongside the second generation Hobarts. Near the entrance to the refurbished arena is a large photograph of the three Hobart brothers of that generation: Edward, Charles, and William cutting a figure together on the ice on the arena's opening night over a half century ago.

It is a short walk from the Hobart Arena to the bank of the same stretch of the Miami River those three Hobarts had skated across as boys. On this late autumn day the river looked serene as it flowed below the grass-covered levee. The brisk wind had stripped away most of the fiery-colored leaves that had recently obscured the landmarks across the river to the south in Troy. To the east just beyond the railroad bridge sat the Hobart Cabinet Company. To the west, between the Market Street and Adams Street bridges, stood the old Brewery, the first plant occupied by the Hobart Brothers Company. Above them all floated the pale rose stone cupola of the same Miami County Courthouse that had greeted C. C. Hobart when he had arrived in Troy 106 years ago. Continuity was visible that day. Though the activities of future generations may be more diverse and geographically scattered, the industrial Hobarts had established a tradition of building something positive, contributing to the community, and embracing the creativity of people.

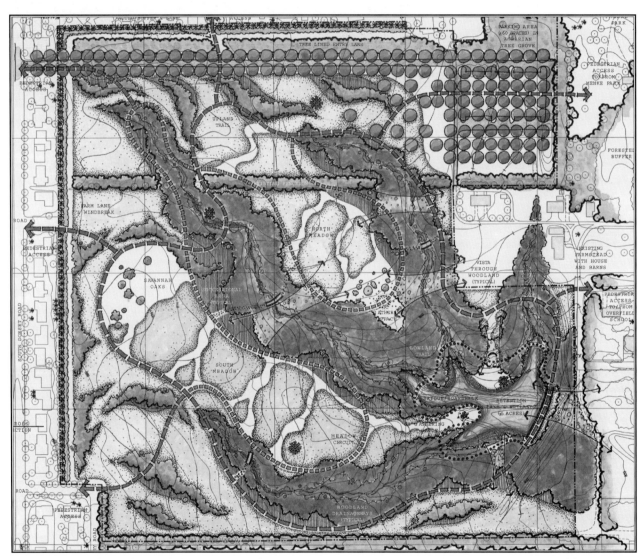

A unique project for the future of the area is the Hobart Nature Preserve and Sculpture Park, an eighty-acre island of farmland and woods surrounded by Troy's expansion. The family donated this to the Miami County Park District in 1999. It is to be a passive green space area and will contain a lake, wetlands, grasslands, and prairie, as well as fine examples of modern sculpture. It is to encourage an interest in and appreciation for the natural environment and its preservation, nature's work and man's work that will be a long-lasting treasure and inspiration for Troy and Miami County.

This has been the drama of a family and a century-old company in the American Midwest. Free market capitalism under just laws coupled with a Protestant, even Puritanical work ethic and strong religious beliefs was the answer then. The question is: have these values remained valid today?

One value, almost an obsession, was self-reliance, self-sufficiency, freedom, and independence. Obviously there had to be justice, strong education, hard work, fairness, and honesty, where people are responsible for themselves and their actions. The quality of these values is essential and, whether they are Hobart values, Ohio values, Midwestern values, or American values, they are the same.

These values made America the superpower it is today with its leading technology that is being challenged day by day and is no longer supreme. However, the social and human values are suffering under the pressure of the times and are deteriorating rather than progressing as profit reigns under the guise of the market economy, allowing this to be the final judge. A nation without its own industry is in danger and vulnerable in both war and peace. Technology is universal, with measurable progress, whereas political ideology and social progress is much more transient. Under constant assault, the new American dream seems to be drawn in Hollywood, in an urban environment and appears hostile to the values of Midwestern family companies. Government too is usurping many of the initiatives of the individual and must constantly be reminded that it is the servant of the people. Government for and by the people must endure. After the solid material reality of the last century, the virtual reality of the Information Age pales by comparison. It remains to be seen whether the values of the Industrial Age of the past century shall persevere both individually and embodied in companies into the next millennium.

C. C. Hobart, *Homo Faber* and *Homo Sapiens*, personified these values and provided a vision for the family and his companies. A true Midwestern pioneer, he and other men and women around him were inventive, self-reliant, and responsible religious people who understood the dignity of work, accepted the burden of sacrifice, and dedicated themselves with fervor, individually and as a team, to the task of constructing a better life.

The dedication of the Michael Bashaw sound chamber to the City of Troy on November 17, 2003. From left to right: Marty Baker, Mike Beamish, Ron Scott, Peter Jenkins, Dave Anderson, Jeanne Sargent, William Hobart, Allen Kappers, Andre Odermatt, Peter Hobart, Joe Reardon, and our former treasurer, Dick Cultice.

The pride of belonging to a close family group and to a strong community without the tempting mobility or distractions of modern society was an essential ingredient to building a sound technical company for America and the world, and, it is hoped, the future. The pride of invention and creation was essential in this world of technology. Loyalty and close interaction among manufacturers, suppliers, and customers, not the present-day distant outsourcing, was another key to strength. Globalization, always seeking the lowest global cost, has it advantages, but decidedly has its disadvantages as well. We should be fully aware of both.

ITW, who is now running the major Hobart companies with its strong 80/20 strategy, will inevitably change Hobart Brothers, which was basically a 20/80 company, where the next technological challenge was king.

These issues are typical of many companies and families in the mainstream of American life, and this book is intended to provide important teachings to future generations to help avoid the mistakes of the past, and to document what was a Golden Age for American industry, a very happy and rewarding period for all those who lived it. Such knowledge permits us to reinvest the great wealth of America in all our tomorrows.

❧

"De tous les actes le plus complet est celui de construire."
"Of all action the most complete is that of building."
(French Poet Paul Valery)

❧

ENDNOTES

Introduction

1. Donald M. Herbert. *The Ancestors and Descendants of John Sullivan Hobart.* (Bryn Mawr, Pa., 1951) 1–2.

2. Lorena Haing Hart and Francis Russell Hart. *Not All is Changed: A Life History of Hingham.* (Hingham, Mass.: Hingham Historical Commission, 1993) 23.

3. The cause of Peter's death on January 8, 1679, is not given in the journal he kept until the end of 1678 and was continued by his son David. However, all five of the other Hingham residents who died that winter have smallpox listed as the cause. *Journal of Peter Hobart and Descendants, 1635–1735.* (Hingham, Mass.: New England Historical and Genealogical Registry, 1967) 200.

4. Herbert, pp. 2–3; Edmund Faxon Garret Hobart, "Clarence Charles Hobart" in *History of Miami County, Ohio.* (Tipp City, Ohio: Miami County Historical Society, 1982) 476.

5. Herbert, 3–4; EFG Hobart, "Clarence Charles Hobart," 476.

6. Edmund Faxon Garret Hobart Papers, correspondence.

7. Mary Griffith, *The Descendants of Edmund Hobart of Hingham, Massachusetts.* (San Francisco: California Genealogical Society, 1952) 35; Herbert, 4; Edmund Faxon Garret Hobart Papers, copy of pages from genealogy compiled by Alvah Sabin Hobart, 1897.

CHAPTER 1: A Young Man Reinvents Himself

1. George C. Crout. *Middletown Diary, Vol. 1,* (Middletown, Ohio: 1968) 270, 341–2; Crout, Vol. 2, 138–40, 312; *Middletown Signal,* May 1, 1890; EFG Hobart Papers, Family History-CCH Factory; Don Karnes, personal interview 24 November, 1999.

2. Quoted in Neil Baldwin, *Edison: Inventing the Century.* (New York: Hyperion Books, 1995) 22–3.

3. EFG Hobart Papers, Alvah Sabin Hobart Genealogy.

4. *The C. C. Hobart Foundation.* (Troy, Ohio: C. C. Hobart Foundation, 1942) 7.

5. Lilian Baker Carlisle, ed. *A Look Around Chittenden County, Vermont.* (Burlington, Vt.: Chittenden County Historical Society, 1976) 39; EFG Hobart Papers.

6. EFG Hobart Papers, Alvah Sabin Hobart Genealogy, New Hampton Institute Diploma of Clarence Charles Hobart.

7. Howard D. Williams, *A History of Colgate University, 1819–1969.* (New York: Van Nostrand Reinhold Co., 1969) 199–204; Colgate University Alumni Records.

8. Williams, 190–91.

9. Williams, 175, 192, 211.

10. John C. Gerber, *A Pictorial History of the University of Iowa.* (Iowa City: University of Iowa Press, 1988) 41–2.

11. Edmund Faxon Garret Hobart, "Timeline History of Hobart Companies in Troy, Ohio," (1 February 1997) 1; Donovan Karnes, personal interview, 24 November 1999.

12. EFG Hobart Papers, Alvah Sabin Hobart Genealogy.

13. Ted Jefferson, *First Hundred Years of Hobart.* (Troy, Ohio: Hobart Brothers Company, 1986) 5; Donovan Karnes.

14. Crout, 1: 366; 2: 223–4; Benjamin F. Hartwitz, *Historical Sketches of Middletown* (Middletown, Ohio: 1978) 127–8; *Historical and Biographical Cyclopedia of Butler County, Ohio.* (Cincinnati: Western Biographical Publishing Co, 1882) 634–5.

15. Crout 223–4, 475; *Butler County Democrat,* March 8, 1883; La Favre, "The Brush Arc Lamp," Charles F. Brush. www.ameritech.net/users/jeff_lafavre/lamparc.htm.

16. Crout, 1: 361–2; Crout 2: 475–6; Hartwitz, 129–30.

17. Edmund Faxon Garret Hobart, "Clarence Charles Hobart," 477; Jefferson, 5.

18. Hartwitz, 129–30.

19. Crout, 2: 476.

20. Crout, 2: 475; Hartwitz, 130.

21. Crout, 1: 5, 47; 2: 40, 132; *Historical Cyclopedia of Butler County,* 635; EFG Hobart Papers, Jones Family of Middletown.

22. EFG Hobart, "Clarence Charles Hobart," 477; Papers, Jones Family of Middletown; *Middletown Signal,* 26 January, 2 February, 9 February, 1884.

23. *C. C. Hobart Foundation,* (Troy, Ohio: C. C. Hobart Foundation, 1942) 8.

24. Crout, 2: 138–40; Jefferson, 7; Karnes interview.

25. Hartwitz, 2: 155; *Historical Cyclopedia of Butler County,* 632–3; *Middletown Signal,* August 9, 1883.

26. Jefferson, 7.

27. Crout, "C. C. Hobart Got His Start Here," (*Middletown Signal,* 7 October 1946).

28. Jefferson, 11.

29. EFG Hobart, "Timeline," 1.

30. EFG Hobart Papers.

31. Jefferson, 8; Karnes interview.

CHAPTER 2: A Businessman Moves to Troy

1. C. C. Hobart, letter to Alvah Hobart, EFG Hobart Papers.

2. EFG Hobart, *History of the Hobart Companies,* (video, 1992).

3. Charles S. Barkelew, letter to the C. C. Hobart Foundation, 25 September 1947, EFG Hobart Papers, Troy, Ohio.

4. *1891 Middletown City Directory,* 90.

5. Barkelew.

6. Barkelew.

7. Barkelew.

8. Edward Armstrong Ince, *Miscellany, First Baptist Church Middletown, Ohio,* (Cincinnati: Press of George P. Houston, 1889) 11.

9. Crout, 2: 299–300.

10. Karnes.

11. EFG Hobart Papers.

12. Barkelew.

13. Crout, 2: 137–8.

14. James West Davidson, William E. Gienapp, Christine Leigh Heyrman, Mark H. Lytle, and Michael B. Stoff, *Nation of Nations,* Vol. 2, (Boston: McGraw Hill, 1998) 728.

15. EFG Hobart, "Timeline History," 1; Jefferson, 8.

16. Barkelew.

17. *Miami Union,* 17 October 1895.

18. Thomas Bemis Wheeler, *Troy: The Nineteenth Century,* (Troy, Ohio: Troy Historical Society, 1970) 201–2.

19. Wheeler, 154–5.

20. Bert S. Bartlow et al., eds., *Centennial History of Butler County, Ohio,* (New York: B. B. Bowen & Co., 1905) 304; Crout, 1: 216–7; Hartwitz, 161; Wheeler, 155.

21. Donovan Karnes.
22. Jefferson, 10; EFG Hobart, *History of the Hobart Companies*; *Troy Daily News*, 4 December 1924.
23. Barkelew.
24. Wheeler, 173–8.
25. Buckeye, 10 October 1895; *Miami Union*, 10 October 1895; Wheeler, 203–4.
26. Barkelew.
27. EFG Hobart Papers, Family History-Grandfather, 4; Jefferson, 10.
28. Wheeler, 204.
29. Wheeler, 209.
30. *Troy Daily News*, 4 December 1924.
31. Wheeler, 204.
32. *Troy Daily News*, 22 January 1938.
33. C. C. Hobart, Proposition to H. L. Johnston, 14 July 1897, EFG Hobart Papers.
34. Three Articles of Incorporation of the Hobart Electric Mfg. Co., EFG Hobart Papers.
35. J. Don Mason, "Biography of Herbert L. Johnston," Hobart Manufacturing Corporation; *Troy Daily News*, 22 January 1938.
36. *Troy Daily News*, 4 December 1924; 22 January 1938.
37. *Troy Daily News*, 4 December 1924.
38. Wheeler, 243.

CHAPTER 3: The Entrepreneur Tackles New Problems

1. Wheeler, 264–5.
2. *Miami Union*, 4 December 1924; *C. C. Hobart Foundation*, 19.
3. EFG Hobart Papers, Hobart Electric Mfg. Co. Brochure, Price List and Data.
4. David A. Meeker, *Better Eating . . . From Start to Finish*, (New York: Newcomen Society, 1960) 12; *C. C. Hobart Foundation*, 19; Jefferson, 11.
5. Leonard S. Reich, *The Making of American Industrial Research: Science and Business at GE and Bell, 1876–1926*, (Cambridge: Cambridge University Press, 1985) 46.
6. Sales Brochure, Hobart Electric Manufacturing Company, Troy, Ohio, EFG Hobart Papers.
7. Meeker, 12.
8. Harold C. Passer, *The Electrical Manufacturers, 1875–1900*, (Cambridge: Harvard University Press, 1953) 1.
9. Donovan Karnes.
10. Meeker, 12.
11. *Miami Union*, 4 January 1904.
12. *Miami Union*, 4 December 1924.
13. No. 786,293, e-mail to authors from John Graham, Public Documents & Patent Dept., 4 April 2000.
14. Nancy Bowman, "A Troy Corporation Marks First 100 Years," (*Troy Daily News*) 20 July 1997.
15. *Seventy-Five Years of Kitchenaid: 7th Annual Recipe Book*, (St. Joseph, Mich.: Whirlpool Corporation, 1993) 2; Yount, 18.
16. Bowman.
17. *Miami Union*, 13 August 1914.
18. Bowman; Meeker, 13; Irene E. Miller, ed., *A Hobart Corporation, History of Miami County, Ohio*, (Tipp City, Ohio: Miami County Historical Society, 1982) 104.
19. Jefferson, 13.
20. *Miami Union*, September 1904.
21. Jefferson, 13.
22. *Troy City Directory, 1905*.
23. *C. C. Hobart Foundation*, 21; Edmund Hobart, *History of the Hobart Companies*, (video).
24. *Miami Union*, September, 1904; *Troy City Directory, 1905*; The Troy Historical Society 1989 Calendar, (January).
25. *C. C. Hobart Foundation*, 22; Jefferson, 14.
26. Williams, 23–25.
27. Estella Baird Broomhall, *The Story of the Altrurian Club, 1894–1934*, (Troy, Ohio: Altrurian Club, 1936) 13–5.
28. Broomhall, 25.
29. Broomhall, 20.
30. Broomhall, 199.
31. Location was the southwest corner of Ash and Wayne Streets, *Piqua City Directory, 1913–14*.
32. *Troy Daily News*, 31 July 1914.

CHAPTER 4: A Progressive Runs for Congress

1. *Troy Daily News*, 3 June 1932.
2. Davidson, 785.
3. *Miami Union*, 29 August 1912.
4. *Miami Union*, 26 September 1912.
5. *Miami Union*, 26 September, 17 October 1912.
6. *Miami Union*, 17, 24 October 1912.
7. *Miami Union*, 6 November 1912.
8. Hoyt Landon Warner, *Progressivism in Ohio, 1897–1917*, (Columbus, Ohio: Ohio State University Press, 1964) 471.
9. *Miami Union*, 27 August 1914.
10. *Shelby County Democrat*, 16 August 1914.
11. *Miami Union*, 29 October 1914; Michael W. Williams, "Profits from Prohibition: Walter Kidder and the Hayner Distillery," *Timeline*, (March/April, 1999) 27.
12. *Miami Union*, 10 September 1914.
13. *Miami Union*, 29 October 1914.
14. *Miami Union*, 29 October 1914; *Shelby County Democrat*, 30 October 1914.
15. *Miami Union*, 22 October 1914; *Shelby County Democrat*, 23 October 1914.
16. Michael J. Durbin, ed., *U.S. Congressional Elections, 1788–1997*, (Jefferson, N.C.: McFarland & Co., Inc., 1998) 402–04; Miami Union, 5 November 1914; *Shelby County Democrat*, 6 November 1914.
17. *Miami Union*, 5 November 1914.
18. Elting E. Morison, ed., *Letters of Theodore Roosevelt*, Vol. 8, (Boston: Harvard University Press, 1954) 836.
19. Morison, 1060–1.
20. C. C. Hobart, letter to Theodore Roosevelt, 19 June 1916, EFG Hobart Papers.

21. C. C. Hobart, letter to Frank M. Sterrett, n.d., Peter C. Hobart Papers.

22. C. C. Hobart, letter to Frank M. Sterrett, n.d.

CHAPTER 5: Three Sons Come of Age

1. William Harrison Hobart, "Edward," Biographical Poem, 8 May 1948, Peter C. Hobart Papers, Troy, Ohio; 1–2.

2. William H. Hobart, "Edward," 3–4; Lucia (Hobart) Bravo, personal interview, 19 April 2000.

3. Thomas B. Wheeler, "This and That," *Troy Daily News*, 23 February 1965.

4. Edward Alvah Hobart, letter to Charles Hobart, 22 January 1898, EFG Hobart Papers.

5. Edward Alvah Hobart, letter to Charles Hobart, n.d., EFG Hobart Papers.

6. Edward Alvah Hobart, letter to Margaret Hobart, n.d., EFG Hobart Papers.

7. William H. Hobart, "Edward," 5.

8. Charles Berka, "From Battery Chargers to Arc Welders: 53 Years of Pioneering Pay Off," (*The Welding Distributor*, Mar.–Apr. 1978) 60.

9. Berka, 58–9; Jefferson, 16.

10. Jefferson, 16.

11. Lucia (Hobart) Bravo, personal interview.

12. Rob Doughty, "Edward Alvah Hobart," *History of Miami County, Ohio*, (Tipp City, Ohio: Miami County Historical Society, 1982) 479; Jefferson, 16–7.

13. Thomas C. Mendenhall, ed. *History of the Ohio State University, Vol.2, 1870–1925*, (Columbus: Ohio State University Press, 1926) 54–5, 91, 97.

14. Jefferson, 17.

15. Tamar Chute, Asst. Archivist, Ohio State University Archives, personal e-mail to authors, 11 November 1999; Jefferson, 17.

16. Tamar Chute, personal e-mail to authors, 11 November 1999.

17. Jefferson, 17.

18. Berka, 60; Jefferson, 17.

19. William H. Hobart, "Edward," 3.

20. EFG Hobart, "Charles Clarence Hobart Family," *History of Miami County, Ohio*, 475; Jefferson, 17.

21. *Miami Union*, 12 September 1912.

22. EFG Hobart, "Charles Clarence Hobart Family," 475.

23. *Pratt Institute Catalog, 1911–12*, 89.

24. *Pratt Institute Catalog, 1911–12*, 85.

25. EFG Hobart, "William Harrison Hobart Family," *History of Miami County, Ohio*, 480.

26. William H. Hobart, "Edward," 33.

27. Lucia (Hobart) Bravo, personal interview, 19 April 2000; P.C. Hobart, 16 November 1999.

28. Cara Gilgenbach, Denison University Archives, personal e-mail to authors, 1 December 1999; Martin J. Hackett, University of Pennsylvania Archives, personal e-mail to authors, 1 December 1999.

29. Edward Alvah Hobart, letter to Lou Ella Hobart, 3 April 1913, EFG Hobart Papers, 1.

30. E. A. Hobart, letter to Lou Ella Hobart, 3 April 1913, 2; Lois S. Davies, "The 1913 Flood in Troy," *History of Miami County, Ohio*, 44–5.

31. E. A. Hobart, letter to Lou Ella Hobart, 3 April 1913, 2.

32. Davies, 41, 46.

33. E. A. Hobart, letter to Lou Ella Hobart, 3 April 1913, 3.

34. E. A. Hobart, letter to Lou Ella Hobart, 3 April 1913, 1.

35. David Halberstam, *The Reckoning*. (New York: William Morrow, 1986) 801.

36. Stuart W. Leslie, *Boss Kettering: Wizard of General Motors*. (New York: Columbia University Press, 1983) 46–7.

37. Jefferson, 18; E. John De Waard and Aaron E. Klein, *Electric Cars*. (New York: Doubleday, 1977) 32–3.

38. Jefferson, 18.

39. EFG Hobart, "History of the Hobart Companies," (video, 1992).

40. EFG Hobart, "History of the Hobart Companies"; Jefferson, 18.

41. Thomas B. Wheeler, "This and That," *Troy Daily News*, 24 June 1967.

42. *Miami Union*, 29 March 1917.

43. Newspaper clipping, n.d., Papers of Hobart Brothers Company, Troy, Ohio.

44. *Troy Daily News*, 2 April 1918.

45. *Troy Daily News*, 18 February 1918.

46. *Seventy-Five Years of Kitchenaid*, 2; "Hobart Corporation," *History of Miami County, Ohio*, 104.

47. *Troy Daily News*, 1, 2 April 1918.

48. EFG Hobart, Chapter 2: Dad, *Family History*, 2.

49. *Piqua Directory, 1887–88*, 51, 75.

50. *Forest Hill Cemetery, 1868–1982*, Piqua, Ohio: Flesh Public Library, 1983.

51. *Piqua Daily Call*, 22 August 1903.

52. *Piqua Daily Call*, 26 February 1934; James C. Oda and Linda Grimes, *Piqua and Miami County: A Primer of Community History*, (Piqua, Ohio: Flesh Public Library, 1991) 79.

53. *Piqua Daily Call*, 26 February 1934.

54. *The Piquonian*, 1912, 17.

55. *The Official Roster of Ohio Soldiers and Sailors in the World War, 1917–18*, Vol.8, (Columbus, Ohio: F. J. Heer Printing Company, 1926) 7671.

56. *Troy Daily News*, 12 November 1918.

CHAPTER 6: Hobart Brothers Charges into the Twenties

1. James M. Flammung, *100 Years of the American Auto*, Lincolnwood, Ill.: Publications International, 1999, 73, 89.

2. Flammung, 87.

3. Davidson, 838.

4. Jefferson, 18–19.

5. E. A. Hobart, Patent No. 1,750,713: Voltage-Regulation Winding for Electric Generators. U.S. Patent Office, filed June 18, 1923, patented Mar. 18, 1930.

6. Jefferson, 18; "Living Pioneers: E. A. Hobart," *Welding Engineer*, September, 1966, 66.

7. Mail Order Brochure, Hobart Brothers Company, Troy, Ohio, n.d., EFG Hobart Papers.

8. Hobart Brothers ad, *Popular Mechanics*, 148; Jefferson, 19; Mail Order Brochure, Hobart Brothers Company, Troy, Ohio, n.d., EFG Hobart Papers.

9. William H. Hobart, Direct Mail Cover Letter, n.d., EFG Hobart Papers.

10. Hobart Brothers ad, *Popular Mechanics*, 148; Jefferson, 19.

11. William H. Hobart, Sales Incentive Letter, EFG Hobart Papers.

12. Patent Nos. 82,889; 1,771,889; 1,786,242; 1,802,175; 1,813,998; 1,842,173; 1,907,110; listed in "Honoring Hobart Brothers Company Inventors," Troy, Ohio: Hobart Institute Library, 1995.

13. Marion Centliver, personal interview, 18 April, 2000; Don Karnes, personal interview, 24 November, 1999; Fax on Milestone Meeting, 13 August 1990, William H. Hobart Jr. to Peter C. Hobart.

14. Chaffee, W. J., "The Hobart Bros. Company," 36–7, excerpt from 1933 Troy History, Peter C. Hobart Papers.

15. Chaffee, 37.

16. Chaffee, 37.

17. Chaffee, 37.

18. Jefferson, 21; dated photograph of construction, EFG Hobart Papers.

19. Jefferson, 20.

20. "Dixie Highway & Interstate 75," www2.kenyon.edu/people/people/slomanj/roads.htm.

21. William H. Hobart, "Edward," a biographical poem. Peter C. Hobart Papers, Troy, Ohio., 3.

22. *Troy Daily News*, 12 October 1921.

23. *Troy City Directory*, 1927, 1929.

24. Lucia (Hobart) Bravo, personal interview, 19 April 2000; Marion Centliver, personal interview, 18 April 2000; *Troy City Directory*, 1927, 1929.

25. C. C. Hobart, letter, 9 June 1924, Peter C. Hobart Papers, Troy, Ohio; slightly edited version in *Troy Daily News*, 9 June 1924.

26. *Troy Daily News*, 9 June 1924.

27. *Troy Daily News*, 9 June 1924.

28. C. C. Hobart to William H. Hobart, II, 28 July 1924, Peter C. Hobart Papers.

CHAPTER 7: The Maverick Charts His Own Course

1. Harry A. Toulmin Jr. to C. C. Hobart Foundation, 22 October 1946, EFG Hobart Papers.

2. Charles C. Hobart Jr., personal interview, 21 February; Edmund Hobart, *Family History*, "Dad": 3; on the deductions available at the time, Gerald Carson, *The Golden Egg*, 87..

3. Edmund Hobart, *Family History*, "Dad": 7.

4. Clarence C. Hobart to Charles C. Hobart, 30 September 1924, Peter C. Hobart Papers.

5. Edmund Hobart, "Timeline History of Hobart Companies in Troy,"; Ben Sutherly, "Hobarts Remain the Boys from Troy," *Dayton Daily News*, Neighbors Section, 1.

6. Don Karnes, personal interview, 2

7. Edmund Hobart, *Family History*, "Dad": 3.

8. Hobart Cabinet Sales Catalog, circa 1926, EFG Hobart Papers; Edmund Hobart, *Family History*, "Hobart Cabinet Products": 1.

9. Hobart Cabinet Sales Catalog, circa 1926, EFG Hobart Papers.

10. Edmund Hobart, *Family History*, "Hobart Cabinet Products": 2.

11. Edmund Hobart, *Family History*, "Hobart Cabinet Products": 2.

12. Edmund Hobart, *Family History*, "Mom": 2–3.

13. *Troy Daily News*, 29, 31 May 1934.

14. *Troy Daily News*, 31 May 1934.

15. "Interview with Bus Sewell, 7 August 1994," EFG Hobart Papers.

16. Charles C. Hobart Jr., personal interview, 21 February 2000; Ben Sutherly, "Hobarts Remain the Boys from Troy," 10.

17. "Interview with Bus Sewell, 7 August 1994," EFG Hobart Papers.

18. "Crystal Frost" ad, Hobart Cabinet Company, EFG Hobart Papers.

19. "Interview with Bus Sewell, 7 August 1994," EFG Hobart Papers.

20. Edmund Hobart, "Charles Clarence Hobart Family," *History of Miami County, Ohio*: 476.

21. Edmund Hobart, "Charles Clarence Hobart Family": 475; Jefferson, 24.

22. Charles C. Hobart Jr., personal interview, 18 April 2000; Edmund Hobart, *Family History*, "Dad": 5–6, "Early Life—Up to Grade School": 11; Edmund Hobart, "Charles Clarence Hobart Family," *History of Miami County, Ohio*: 476; Hobart Fruit Farms ads, EFG Hobart Papers.

23. Charles C. Hobart Jr., personal interview, 21 February 2000.

24. Robert Bravo, audiotape interview with Lucia Howell, July 1990.

25. Edmund Hobart, *Family History*, "Dad": 7–8.

26. "Tennis," Encarta. www.encarta/msn.com.

27. Edmund Hobart, *Family History*, "Dad": 7–8, "Early Years—To Grade School": 9–10; "Fred Perry," "Tony Trabert," International Tennis Hall of Fame. www.tennisfame.com.

28. Charles C. Hobart Jr., personal interview, 21 February 2000; Edmund Hobart, "The Family of Charles Clarence Hobart": 476.

CHAPTER 8: Welding Generates a New Future

1. Don Karnes, personal interview, 24 November 1999.

2. Edward A. Hobart—Biographical Sketch": 1; Julie Petersen (OSU assistant archivist), e-mail to Michael W. Williams, 1 February 2001.

3. Raymond Moley. *The American Century of John C. Lincoln*. New York: Duell, Sloan and Pierce, 1962: 68–70; Corporate Information: Our History. Lincoln Electric. www.lincolnelectric.com.corporate/profile/history.asp.

4. Jefferson, 21–22; Don Karnes, personal interview, 24 November 1999.

5. Chafee, "The Hobart Bros. Company": 37.

6. Howard B. Cary, *Modern Welding Technology*, 4th ed. Upper Saddle River, N.J.: Prentice-Hall, 1998: 6–7; Richard D. Simonson, *The History of Welding*, Morton Grove, Ill.: Monticello Books, 1969: 1–11.

7. Cary, *Modern Welding Technology*, 7; Simonson, 18.

8. Moley, 69.

9. Cary, *Modern Welding Technology*, 7–8.

10. Chaffee, "The Hobart Bros. Company": 37; Simonson, 22.

11. Simonson, 22.

12. Correcting this problem was one of the stated goals of the American Welding Society, founded in 1919, Andrew Cullison and Christine Tarafa, "Welding and Society": 48; Simonson, 103.

14. Jefferson, 22.

15. Simonson, 89.

16. Simonson, 102.

17. Cullison and Tarafa, 48.

18. Jefferson, 21; Don Karnes, personal interview, 24 November 1999.

19. Jefferson, 22.

20. Cary, *Modern Welding Technology*, 8; Simonson, 24.

21. Berka, 60; E. A. Hobart, Patent No. 1,825,064 "Electric Welder," U.S. Government Patent Office, filed 19 July 1929, patented 29 September 1931; Jefferson, 23; "Outstanding Features of the Hobart 'Constant Arc' Welder", Hobart Brothers Brochure, circa 1928, Peter C. Hobart Papers.

22. "H.B. Welder—Extra Equipment," memo, Hobart Brothers Company, 27 June 1927, Peter C. Hobart Papers.

23. "Outstanding Features of the Hobart 'Constant Arc' Welder."

24. Lucia (Hobart) Bravo, personal interview, 2 August 2001; Marcia (Hobart) Howell, audiotape interview with Lucia Howell, 9 July 1990; *Troy Daily News*, 29, 30 December 1925.

25. *Troy Daily News*, 29 December 1925.

26. *Troy Daily News*, 29 October 1929.

27. *Troy Daily News*, 2 November 1929.

CHAPTER 9: A Sales Pitch Creates a Trade School

1. Ads and brochures, Hobart Brothers Company, circa 1935, Peter C. Hobart Papers.

2. Jefferson, 25.

3. Chaffee, "The Hobart Bros. Company": 38; Jefferson, 25.

4. *Troy Daily News*, 1 July 1965.

5. Chafee, "The Hobart Bros. Company": 38.

6. *Troy Daily News*, 1 July 1965.

7. "Christmas Greeting from Hobart Brothers," 1940 promotional sheet, Hobart Brothers Company Records.

8. Don Karnes, personal interview, 24 November 1999.

9. "Hobart School of Welding Technology," *History of Miami County, Ohio*. Tipp City, Ohio: Miami County Historical Society, 1982: 186; Jefferson, 26.

10. Jefferson, 49.

11. "Hobart School of Welding Technology": 187.

12. W. J. Chaffee, Foreword, *Electrical Arc Welding Manual*, 2nd ed. Troy, Ohio: Hobart Brothers Company.

13. *Troy Daily News*, 22 July 1974.

14. Quoted in Hobart Brothers Brochure, circa 1940, Peter C. Hobart Papers, Troy, Ohio: 34.

15. Jefferson, 26.

16. *Troy Daily News*, June 3, 1932.

17. *Troy City Directory*, 1933.

18. Marion Centliver, Don Kendall, Jean (Collmorgan) Mochida, 18 April 2000.

19. Jean (Collmorgan) Mochida, 18 April 2000.

20. Minutes of Milestone Meeting, 13 August 1990, Peter C. Hobart Papers.

21. *Troy Daily News*, 1 March 1933.

22. *Troy Daily News*, 1 March 1933.

23. *Troy Daily News*, 15 March 1933.

24. Jefferson, 26-7.

25. Glenn Nally, personal interview, 19 April 2001; *Welding Engineer*, March 1934: 1.

26. Glenn Nally, personal interview, 19 April 2001.

27. Quoted in Jefferson, 26.

28. Edward Alvah Hobart, Assets 1935, EFG Hobart Papers.

CHAPTER 10: The Brothers Build Welded-Steel Houses

1. Quoted in H. A. Toulmin Jr., *Patents and the Public Interest*, New York: Harper & Brothers, 1939: 201.

2. "Edward A. Hobart—Biographical Sketch."

3. Michelle Hobart, "Steel Welded Houses in Troy, Ohio. Prefabrication: the Impossible Compromise, 1936–1943," New York University, 1998: 6–11.

4. "Edward A. Hobart—Biographical Sketch."

5. Lucia (Hobart) Bravo, personal interview, 2 August 2001; Michelle Hobart, 13.

6. Frank Chouteau Brown, "Chicago and Tomorrow's House?," *Pencil Points*, June 1933: 248.

7. $3,500 for a 4-room model and $4,000 for a 5-room version, Brown, 249-50.

8. Michelle Hobart, 14; Jefferson, 31; William R. Turner to Christina O'Neal, 22 February 1987: 1–2.

9. Michelle Hobart, 19.

10. Michelle Hobart, 16; Turner, 2.

11. Michelle Hobart, 6–10.

12. Edward A. Hobart, Photo Scrapbook, circa 1935, Hobart Brothers Company Archives, Troy, Ohio.

13. Michelle Hobart, 20–21.

14. Pencil Points, February 1936: 67–69.

15. Quoted in Michelle Hobart, 22.

16. Michelle Hobart, 20–22.

17. *Troy Daily News*, 9 April 1937.

18. Michelle Hobart, 18.

19. Quoted in Michelle Hobart, 17.

20. *Troy Daily News*, 9 April 1937.

21. Turner, 1.

22. *Troy Daily News*, 9 April 1937.

23. Turner, 1.

24. Michelle Hobart, 15.

25. Christina O'Neal, *Steel Houses Troy, Ohio: Case Study of a Dream*. Exhibition Catalogue for the Dayton Visual Arts Center, Dayton, Ohio, 1992.

26. Turner, 2.

27. Howard B. Cary, personal interview, 10 August 1999; Marion Centliver, personal interview, 18 April 2000; Larry Heisey, personal interview, 9 September 2000; Don Karnes, personal interview, 24 November 1999; Glenn Nally, personal interview, 15 July 1999.

28. Turner, 4.

29. Turner, 3.

30. Marion Centliver, interview; Don Karnes, interview, *Troy Daily News*, 1 March 1965.

31. *Troy Daily News*, 13 October 1975.

32. Jefferson, 32.

33. Jefferson, 32.

34. Michelle Hobart, 25; Jefferson, 32; Hobart Brothers Company Archives.

35. Michelle Hobart, 25–26.

36. Michelle Hobart, 26.

37. Marion Centliver, interview.

38. Janet Pansing, quoted in O'Neal.

39. Michelle Hobart, 26–27.

40. Turner, 1.

CHAPTER 11:

New Products Blaze a Path Through the Depression

1. Don Karnes, personal interview, 24 November 1999.

2. Marion Centliver, personal interview, 18 April 2000; Edward A. Hobart, Deposition for Patent Interference Case No. 53,690, 15 April 1926, Patent Box 1, Hobart Brothers Company Archives, Troy, Ohio.

3. Harry A. Toulmin Jr. became one of the nation's leading authorities on patent law and wrote several books on the subject. David C. Greer, *Sluff of History's Boot Soles: An Anecdotal History of Dayton's Bench and Bar*. Wilmington, Ohio: Orange Frazer Press, 1996: 199.

4. The term *interference* is used rather than *infringement* since the issue was a prior application rather than an approved patent. Edward A. Hobart, letter to Rochester Electric, 2 February 1928, U.S. Patent Office Appeals Board Ruling, 13 February 1929, Patent Box 1, Hobart Brothers Company Archives.

5. Karnes, interview.

6. James Lincoln to Edward A. Hobart, 17 August 1934, HBC Archives.

7. Edward A. Hobart to James Lincoln, 21 August 1934, HBC Archives.

8. Hobart "Simplified" Arc Welding, Hobart Brothers Company sales brochure, circa 1940, Peter C. Hobart Papers: 8–9.

9. Hobart "Simplified" Arc Welding, 6–7.

10. Hobart "Simplified" Arc Welding, 5, 13.

11. *Seventy-Five Years of Kitchenaid: 7th Annual Recipe Book*. St. Joseph, Mich.: Whirlpool Corporation, 1993: 5.

12. Hobart "Simplified" Arc Welding, 20–22.

13. Hobart "Simplified" Arc Welding, 25; Jefferson, 25.

14. Hobart "Simplified" Arc Welding, 5; John D. Sampson, personal interview, 7 August 2001.

15. Hobart "Simplified" Arc Welding, 15.

16. *The Gas and Welding Distributor Staff, A History of the National Welding Supply Association*, Cleveland, Ohio: Penton Publishing, 1994: 35; Simonson, 123.

17. Jefferson, 27; Simonson, 124.

18. Cary, *Modern Welding*, 308–309; Simonson, 124.

19. Hobart "Simplified" Arc Welding, 23; Jefferson, 27–28.

20. Edward A. Hobart, Patent Number 1,956,864: Weldrod, U.S. Patent Office, filed 5 October 1931, patented 1 May 1934.

21. Edward A. Hobart, Patent Number 1,956,864.

22. Simonson, 112.

23. Simonson, 113.

24. Lucia (Hobart) Bravo, personal interview, 2 August 2001; Jefferson, 27.

25. *Dayton Daily News*, 8 August 1942.

26. Keith Aufhauser, e-mail to Michael W. Williams, 22 August 2001.

27. *Dayton Daily News*, 8 August 1942.

28. Keith Aufhauser, e-mail to Michael W. Williams, 22 August 2001.

29. Hobart "Simplified" Arc Welding, 30–31.

30. Quoted in *Teacher's Guide to New York: A Documentary Film*, Thirteen WNET: New York, 1999.

CHAPTER 12: Hobart Goes to War

1. *Troy Daily News*, 10 October 1939.

2. *Troy Daily News*, 12 September 1939.

3. *Miami Union*, 17 October 1940.

4. Thomas A. Bailey, *A Diplomatic History of the American People*, 9th ed. Englewood Cliffs, N.J.: Prentice-Hall, 1974: 714–15.

5. Lucia (Hobart) Bravo, personal interview, 19 April 2000.

6. www.deddington.org.uk/history/generalhobart.html.

7. Bailey, 717.

8. *Troy Daily News*, 12 June 1940.

9. *Troy Daily News*, 12 June 1940.

10. *Troy Daily News*, 11 May 1940.

11. "Hobart School of Welding Technology," in *History of Miami County*: 187.

12. *Troy Daily News*, 11 May 1940.

13. *Troy Daily News*, 24 June 1940.

14. Lucia (Hobart) Bravo, 19 April 2000.

15. Don Karnes, personal interview, 24 November 1999.

16. Don Karnes, 24 November 1999.

17. *Troy Daily News*, 12 December 1940.

18. Jefferson, 34.

19. Kenneth S. Davis, *FDR: The War President, 1940–43*. New York: Random House, 2000: 289–90.

20. Charles C. Hobart Jr., personal interview, 18 April 2000.

21. Charles C. Hobart Jr., 18 April 2000.

22. Edmund Hobart, *Family History*, "Dad": 5–6.

23. Edmund Hobart, *Family History*, "Mom": 3–4.

24. Hobart Brothers Company Records, Box 2000-1-1067-2, Troy, Ohio.

25. Gladys Williams, personal interview, 15 August 2001.

26. John Sampson, personal interview, 8 August 2001.

27. Hobart Brothers Company, "Merry Christmas to You!" promotional sheet, December 1940, Peter C. Hobart Papers.

28. Evelyn Finnegan quoted by Gladys Williams, personal interview, 15 August 2001.

29. Franklin D. Roosevelt, "The Arsenal of Democracy," 29 December 1940, www.tamu.edu/scom/pres/speeches/fdrarsenal.html.

30. *Miami Union*, 23 February 1941.

31. *Miami Union*, 2 January 1941.

32. Lowell Mott, personal interview, 21 November 2001.

33. John Sampson, personal interview, 8 August 2001.

34. Cliff Priest, *Edward A. Hobart: Biographical Sketch*, Troy, Ohio: Hobart Brothers Company, 1965: 8.

35. William H. Hobart Jr., personal interview, 17 October 2000; Jefferson, 35; *Troy Daily News*, 27 November 1941.

36. *Troy Daily News*, 27 November 1941.

37. Don Karnes, 24 November 1999.

38. *Troy Daily News*, 27 November 1941.

39. Boxes of I.D. buttons and their matching file cards still exist, Hobart Brothers Company Records, Troy, Ohio.

40. The New Hobart Arc Welders, Hobart Brothers sales brochure, circa 1947, Peter C. Hobart papers: 21–23.

41. John Sampson, 8 August 2001.

42. Bob Irving, "What Welding Accomplished 'Way Back When'," *Welding Journal*, January 1994:59; Jefferson, 36.

43. Quoted in Andrew Cullison and Christine Tarafa, "Welding and Society," *Welding Journal*, June 1999: 51.

44. Howard B. Cary, personal interview, 10 August 1999. Cary's first job after graduating from Ohio State with a degree in Industrial Engineering was at the Fisher Body Plant in Flint, Michigan, building tanks; *Troy Daily News*, 10 December 1941.

45. Tom Noftle, personal interview, 22 November 2000.

46. Jefferson, 36; The New Hobart Arc Welders, 24.

47. Jefferson, 36; Priest, 5.

48. John Sampson, 8 August 2001.

49. Priest, 5–6.

50. John Sampson, 8 August 2001.

51. John Sampson, 8 August 2001.

52. Don Karnes, personal interview, 24 November 1999; John Sampson, 8 August 2001.

53. *Troy Daily News*, 7 October 1942.

54. Ibid.

55. Ibid.

56. Hobart Manufacturing Company Training Programs, Entry 283, War Manpower Commission, Region 5, Manpower Utilization Surveys & Case Histories, 1943–45, Ohio, Chicago: National Archives, Great Lakes Region.

57. Susan P. Pauly, "Clayton J. Brukner," in *Miami County, Ohio*: 435.

58. See *Troy Daily News*, 5 May 1944, 6 June 1944, 5 October 1944 for examples.

59. *Troy Daily News*, 1 September 1944.

60. Cincinnati Ordnance District 1944 Report, RG 158, U.S. Army Ordnance Department, Region 5, Ohio, Chicago: National Archives, Great Lakes Region: 37. Hobart Brothers factories were among the 141 plants that composed the Cincinnati Ordnance district, which reported a manpower shortage of 7.3 percent in December 1944; *Troy Daily News*, 16 December 1944.

61. John Sampson, 8 August 2001.

62. Jefferson, 34.

63. The Cincinnati Ordnance District reported 31 price adjustments up and 94 price adjustments down for Fiscal Year 1945, a net savings of almost $5.2 million, Cincinnati Ordnance District 1945 Report, RG 158, U.S. Army Ordnance Department, Region 5, Ohio, Chicago: National Archives, Great Lakes Region: 26.

64. Hobart Brothers Company Records, Box R-142.188, Troy, Ohio.

65. Jefferson, 35.

66. Carson, 122; James West Davidson, et al., *Nation of Nations, A Narrative History of the American People, Vol. 2 Since 1865*, 3rd ed., Boston: McGraw-Hill, 1998: 957–58; Jefferson, 35;

67. Marion Centliver, personal interview, 18 April 2000; Don Karnes, 24 November 1999.

68. John Sampson, 8 August 2001.

69. Marion Centliver, 18 April 2000.

70. Records of the Committee on Fair Employment Practice, RG 228, Region 5; Records of the National War Labor Board, RG 202, Region 5, Chicago: National Archives, Great Lakes Region.

71. *Troy Daily News*, 6 June 1944.

72. www.deddington.org.uk/history/generalhobart.html.

73. *Troy Daily News*, 8 May 1945.

74. *Troy Daily News*, 13 May 1945.

75. *Troy Daily News*, 6–10 August 1945.

76. *Troy Daily News*, 15 August 1945.

77. *Troy Daily News*, 10 August 1945.

78. Charles Berka, "From Battery Chargers to Arc Welders: 53 Years of Pioneering Pays Off," *The Welding Distributor*, March/April 1978: 60; Jefferson, 35–6.

79. Wilbur J. Chaffee to William H. Hobart, 3-page report, 13 April 1943, Peter C. Hobart Papers.

80. *Troy Daily News*, 15 August 1945.

CHAPTER 13: Civic Pride Renews the Face of Troy

1. Hobart Brothers Company Records, Box 2000-1-1067-2, Troy, Ohio.

2. E. A. Hobart, "History of the C. C. Hobart Foundation," 5 December 1974, EFG Hobart Papers: 1.

3. C. C. Hobart Foundation Articles of Incorporation, reproduced in *The C. C. Hobart Foundation*, Troy, Ohio: circa 1946: 31.

4. *The C. C. Hobart Foundation*, 34–35.

5. E. A. Hobart, "History of the C. C. Hobart Foundation": 1.

6. "Hersheypark Arena, 1936–2001." www.hersheyarena.com/65th season.html

7. *Troy Daily News*, 29 October 1946.

8. *Troy Daily News*, 6 November 1946.

9. E. A. Hobart, "History of the C. C. Hobart Foundation": 1.

10. *Troy Daily News*, 25 November 1946.

11. *Troy Daily News*, 26 November 1946.

12. *Troy Daily News*, 27 November 1946.

13. Editorial endorsing the Hobart recreational plan for Troy, *Troy Daily News*, 30 November 1946.

14. *Troy Daily News*, 25, 26, 30 November 1946.

15. Jefferson, 46.

16. Lucia (Hobart) Bravo, personal interview, 24 April 2000.

17. Jefferson, 46.

18. Arthur E. Morgan, *The Miami Conservancy District*, New York: McGraw-Hill, 1953: 453–68.

19. Cliff Priest, *Edward A. Hobart: Biographical Sketch*, Troy, Ohio: Hobart Brothers Company, 1965: 14.

20. *Troy Daily News*, 3 March 1947.

21. *Troy Daily News*, 1 March 1947.

22. Lois Schilling Davis, "Sequel to the 1913 Flood," in *History of Miami County, Ohio*: 48; *Troy Daily News*, 1 March 1965.

23. *Troy Daily News*, 5 March 1947.

24. Jefferson, 43.

25. *The C. C. Hobart Foundation*. Troy, Ohio: C. C. Hobart Foundation, circa 1946.

26. *Troy Daily News*, 26 November 1946.

27. *Troy: Yesterday, Today, and Tomorrow*. Troy, Ohio: "Many Friends," Historical Societies of Troy and Miami County, P.R. Dept. of Hobart Brothers Company, 1950: 7–8.

28. Jefferson, 43.

29. In 1969 the Overfield Tavern restoration received an Achievement Award from the Ohio Association of Historical Societies. Virginia G. Boese, "Overfield Tavern," in *History of Miami County, Ohio*: 182–3; Jefferson, 43; "Overfield Tavern, Troy, Ohio," www.tdn-net.com/overfield.html; Priest, 12.

30. Priest, 7.

31. Jefferson, 32.

32. Davis, 46; *Troy Daily News*, 6 September 1950.

33. *Troy Daily News*, 6 September 1950.

34. *Troy Daily News*, 6 September 1950.

35. *Troy Daily News*, 8 September 1950.

36. *Troy Daily News*, 8 September 1950.

37. Kelly Isaacs Baker, "Troy's Hobart Arena Nears 50; It's Still Nifty," *Dayton Daily News*, 1 May 2000.

38. *Troy Daily News*, 21 April, 2003.

39. *Hobart Arena Rededication Program, 1950–2001*: November 4, 2001. Troy, Ohio: Peters Printing, 2001: 12.

CHAPTER 14: A Third Generation Joins the Company

1. Broomhall, 199; Lucia Hobart Bravo, personal interview, 24 April 2000.

2. Peter Clayton, personal interview, 15 August 2000.

3. Lucia Hobart Bravo, 24 April 2000.

4. Lucia Hobart Bravo, Marcia Hobart Howell, audiotape interviews with Lucia Howell, Summer 1990.

5. Lucia Hobart Bravo, 24 April 2000; William Hobart, phone interview, 6 March 2002.

6. Robb Howell, personal interview, 1 March 2002.

7. Marcia Hobart Howell, audiotape interview with Lucia Howell, June 1990.

8. Wilbur J. Chaffee, "The Hobart Brothers Story: From Bike to Jet in Three Generations," Hobart Brother Company Records, Troy, Ohio: 37.

9. Robb Howell, personal interview, 1 March 2002.

10. Michelle Drobik, Ohio State University Archives, e-mail to Michael W. Williams, 28 December 2001.

11. Robb Howell, 1 March 2002.

12. Deborah Howell Kurd, phone interview, 25 March 2002.

13. Robb Howell, 1 March 2002.

14. William H. Hobart Jr., personal interview, 17 October 2000.

15. Robb Howell, 1 March 2002; Deborah Howell Kurd, 25 March 2002.

16. Marcia Hobart Howell, audiotape interview with Lucia Howell, June 1990.

17. Lucia Hobart Bravo, phone interview, 24 March 2002.

18. Official Release, Naval Reserve Base, Squantum, Mass., 27 November 1942, Amherst College Alumni Records.

19. "Consolidated OA-10 'Catalina'," United States Air Force Museum. Aircraft Index. www.wpafb.af.mil/museum/modern_flight/mf20.htm.

20. Lucia Hobart Bravo, 19 April 2000, 24 March 2002.

21. Lucia Hobart Bravo, 19 April 2000, 24 March 2002.

22. William H. Hobart Jr., personal interview, 17 October 2000.

23. William H. Hobart Jr., 17 October 2000.

24. Stephen J. Ambrose, *Citizen Soldiers: the U.S. Army from the Normandy Beaches to the Bulge to the Surrender of Germany, June 6, 1944–May 8, 1945*. New York: Simon & Schuster, 1997: ?.

25. William H. Hobart Jr., 17 October 2000.

26. William H. Hobart Jr., 17 October 2000.

27. *1949 Class Book*, Yale University, 1949: 296; www.yale.edu/library/divinity/073-3D-F.

28. William H. Hobart Jr., 17 October 2000.

29. William H. Hobart Jr., 17 October 2000.

30. Officers and Directors, the Hobart Brothers Company, 31 December 1954, EFG Hobart Papers.

31. William H. Hobart Jr., 17 October 2000.

32. Charles C. Hobart Jr., personal interview, 21 February 2000.

33. Charles C. Hobart Jr., 21 February 2000.

34. Charles C. Hobart Jr., 21 February 2000.

35. Norman Willard Schul, "The Development of a Midwestern City: Troy, Ohio (Master's Thesis)," Miami University, 1957: 56.

36. Lowell Mott, personal interview, 21 November 2001; Ben Sutherly, "Hobart Mainstay of Troy History," *Dayton Daily News*, ? 2000.

37. Charles C. Hobart Jr., 21 February 2000.

38. Edmund Hobart, *Family History*, "Teen Years": 1–5.

39. Edmund Hobart, *Family History*, "Teen Years": 6–7.

40. Edward J. Hobart, personal interview, 18 April 2000.

41. Glenn Nally, personal interview, 17 July 1999.

42. Jonifer A. Hobart, personal interview, 18 April 2000.

43. Charles C. Hobart Jr., 21 February 2000; Robb Howell, 1 March 2002.

44. Deborah Howell Kurd, 25 March 2002.

45. Robb Howell, 1 March 2002.

46. *Troy Daily News*, 26 July 1986.

47. Robb Howell, 1 March 2002.

48. Don Karnes, personal interview, 24 November 1999.

49. Marcia Hobart Howell, audiotape interview with Lucia Gray Howell, date?

50. W. H. Hobart, "Edward," 8 May 1948.

51. Lucia Hobart Bravo, 24 April 2000.

CHAPTER 15: Ground Power Takes Off

1. Edward A Hobart, "What's Ahead for 1946," 5 December 1945, Peter C. Hobart Papers.

2. Wilbur J. Chaffee to William H. Hobart, 3-page report, 13 April 1943, Peter C. Hobart Papers.

3. Jefferson, 38–9.

4. B-29 "Superfortress," United States Air Force Museum, Aircraft Index. www.wpafb.mil/museum/modern flight/mf20.htm.

5. Jefferson, 39; Glenn Nally, personal interview, 17 July 1999.

6. Jefferson, 39.

7. Don Bedwell, *Silverbird: the American Airlines Story*. Sandpoint, Idaho: Airways International, 1999: 71; Rene' Francillon, *McDonald Douglas Aircraft Since 1920: Vol.I*. Arnays, Md.: Naval Institute Press, 1988: 314-16. A DC-4 fitted with an electric wheelchair lift and nicknamed "Sacred Cow" by FDR served as the first aircraft set aside for regular use by a U.S. president.

8. Motor Generator Corporation, Auxiliary Ground Power Unit Specification Sheet, 12 September 1946, John Sampson Papers; John Sampson, Report on Trip to American Airlines, 21 January 1947, John Sampson Papers.

9. John Sampson, e-mail to Michael W. Williams, 6 May 2002.

10. Jefferson, 40.

11. Bedwell, 92–3; Serling, Robert, *Eagle: The Story of American Airlines*. New York: St. Martin's/Marek, 1985: 196.

12. Jefferson, 40.

13. Lucia Hobart Bravo, personal interview, 24 April 1999.

14. www.discovery.com/exp/epidemic/polio/polio.html.

15. Lucia Hobart Bravo, phone interview, 24 March 2002.

16. Lucia Hobart Bravo, phone interview, 1 December 2002.

17. Larry Heisey, personal interview, 20 December 2002.

18. Serling, 187.

19. Jefferson, 40.

20. Larry Atterholt, personal interview, 25 July 2002.

21. Larry Atterholt, 25 July 2002.

22. AXA Power, Mission/History, www.axapower.dynamicweb.dk/Default.asp?ID = 6.; Guinault. Ground Support Equipment, www.guinault.com/cadre_English.htm.; Stewart & Stevenson. Stewart & Stevenson Company History, www.ssss.com/ssss/co_history.asp.

23. Hobart Brothers Company. Power Systems Division, Hobart Corporate Brochure. Troy, Ohio: circa 1978: 13.

24. Super 70s.Com. "The Jumbo Jet-747," www.super70s.com/Science/Transportation/Aviation/747.asp; Jefferson, 40–1.

25. Roger Williams, personal interview, 20 April 2002.

26. Moeller, Col. Stephen P., "Vigilant and Invincible," *ADA (Air Defense Artillery) Magazine*, May–June 1995, www.fas.org/nuke/guide/usa/airdef/chap2.html.

27. Jefferson, 41.

28. "The Pinetree Line," www.pinetreeline.org.

29. Charles Buderi, *The Invention That Changed the World*. New York: Simon & Schuster, 1996: 404; "The DEW Line," www2.magmacom.com/~1wilson/dewline.htm.; Moeller; John Sampson, personal interview, 7 August 2001.

30. Buderi, 395; "The Mid-Canada Line," www.magma.ca/~1wilson/mcl.htm.

31. "The DEW Line."

CHAPTER 16: The Quest for Rutile Leads to Florida

1. Marcia Hobart Howell, audiotape interview with Lucia Howell, 15 July 1990.

2. Don Karnes, personal interview, 24 November 1999.

3. Harry Aubrey Toulmin, *Diary of Democracy: The Senate War Investigating Committee*. New York: R. R. Smith, circa 1947.

4. William H. Hobart Sr., "Excerpt from Toulmin's Letter on What to Do," 19 March 1951, Peter C. Hobart Papers.

5. Jefferson, 44.

6. Simonson, 56.

7. Frederick A. Hauck, "Sands of the Sea," *Yale Scientific Magazine*. January 1957: 32–35.

8. Jefferson, 44.

9. Don Karnes, "History of Mining Operation: Winter Beach, Florida": 2.

10. Priscilla Petty (who compiled an oral history of Frederick A. Hauck), quoted in *Cincinnati Post*, 5 May 1997. www.cincy-post.com/news.

11. "Entrepreneur Cases: Dr. Frederick Hauck." www.entre-ed.org/cs.hauck.htm.; Greater Cincinnati Chamber of Commerce, Great Living Cincinnatians: Frederick A. Hauck. www.gccc.com/about_cincinnati/awards/glc/1979/hauck.asp; Barry M. Horstman, "Frederick Hauck: 'Mr. Cincinnati' Loved his Hometown." www.cincypost.com/living/1999/hauck050399.htm.

12. Hauck, 4–5?

13. Hauck, 1?.

14. Don Bercaw, phone interview, 1 June 2002.

15. Henry Arrowood, "Titanium Operation Produces Many New Waterfront Homesites," *Vero Beach Press-Journal*, 4 September 1958.

16. Edmund Hobart, *History of the Hobart Companies*, video, 1992; "Major Welding Manufacturer Recovers Rutile in Florida," *Engineering and Mining Journal*, December 1957, Vol. 158, No. 12: 98.

17. Peter C. Hobart, "Better Welding from the Sands of Florida," 1960: 2?; William H. Hobart Jr. "From Sea Sand to Better Welding: From Raw Material to Finished Electrode," script to accompany film on Florida Mining Operations, 4 June 1958: 8.

18. Lowell Mott, personal interview, 21 November 2001.

19. Lowell Mott.

20. John Sampson, personal interview, 7 August 2001.

21. Edward A. Hobart, "Apparattus for Separating Minerals from Sand," Patent No. 2,780, 356, granted 5 February 1957, filed 20 July 1953. U.S. Patent Office, Donald Bercaw papers, Vero Beach, Florida.

22. "Major Welding Manufacturer Recovers Rutile in Florida," *Engineering and Mining Journal*, Vol. 158, No. 12: 99.

23. "Major Welding Manufacturer," 98; Peter C. Hobart, "Better Welding," 2?; William H. Hobart Jr., "From Sea Sand," 9.

24. Don Karnes, personal interview, 24 November 1999.

25. Henry Arrowood, "Titanium Operation Produces Many New Waterfront Homesites," *Vero Beach Press-Journal*, 4 September 1958.

26. Jefferson, 45.

27. Arrowood.

28. "Hauck Was Prominent Name in Cincinnati," www.cincy-post.com/news/1997/hauck51297.htm.

29. "Edward A. Hobart—Biographical Sketch," Troy, Ohio: Hobart Brothers Company, 1965: 2.

30. Charles C. Hobart Jr., personal interview, 21 February 2000; Edmund Hobart, audiotape interview with Lucia Howell, summer, 1990.

31. William H. Hobart Jr., "From Sea Sand": 10–11.

32. U.S. Patent Nos. 2,938,627; 2,966,262; 3,000,502 all issued in 1960–61. "Honoring Hobart Brothers Company Inventors," Hobart Institute Library, 21 January 2000: 2.

33. Don Bercaw, phone interview, 1 June 2002.

34. Arrowood.

35. U.S. Census Bureau, Indian River County, Florida, 1950: 11,872; 1960: 25,309. www.census.gov/index.html.

36. "A New Domestic Source of Electrode Coating for Hobart Bros. Company of Troy, Ohio and a New Industry for Indian River County, Florida," Don Bercaw Papers: 3.

37. Don Bercaw, phone interview; Don Karnes, "History of Mining Operation": 4–5.

38 Rutile Mineral Commodity Summary for 2001. www.miner-als.usgs.gov/minerals/pubs/commodity/titanium/pdf.

CHAPTER 17: The Technical Center Expands Its Reach

1. "Hobart Begins Work on a New Welding Institute," *Welding Engineer*, October 1957: 64.

2. Marty Baker and Al Lesnewich, "Tribute to a True Professional," *World of Welding*, Summer 2002: 1; Howard B. Cary, personal interview, 10 August 1999.

3. Howard B. Cary, "A Brief History of the Hobart Brothers Technical Center Building," 10 December 1990: 1.

4. "Hobart Begins Work": 64; Howard B. Cary, "A Brief History,": 1–2.

5. Howard B. Cary, "A Brief History": 2; Cary, personal interview.

6. Howard B. Cary, "A Brief History": 2; Cary, personal interview.

7. *Troy Daily News*, 27 March 1947.

8. William H. Hobart Jr. to Peter C. Hobart, Minutes of Milestone Meeting, 13 August 1990, Peter C. Hobart Papers.

9. Carolyn Hinel, audiotape interview with Lucia Howell, 8 August 1990.

10. Nan Kidder, audiotape interview with Lucia Howell, Summer 1990.

11. Jefferson, 55.

12. Howard B. Cary, "A Brief History": 2.

13. Wilbur J. Chaffee, "The Hobart Brothers Story: From Bike to Jet in Three Generations," Hobart Brothers Company Records, Troy, Ohio: 39.

14. U.S. Patent Nos. 2,457,372 and 2,490,871, "Honoring Hobart Brothers Company Inventors," Hobart Institute Library, 21 January 2000: 1.

15. Howard B. Cary, *Modern Welding Technology*, 4th ed. Upper Saddle River, New Jersey: Prentice Hall, 1998: 74; Edmund Hobart, "Chronology of Products: Hobart Brothers Company," EFG Hobart Papers.

16. U.S. Patent No. 2,802,981, "Honoring Hobart Brothers Company Inventors": 1.

17. Cary, *Modern Welding Technology*: 313–14.

18. Cary, interview.

19. Cary, "A Brief History": 2; interview.

20. Chaffee, "The Hobart Brothers Story": 39 (number of products), 35 (sales growth).

21. Jefferson, 51–52.

22. Cary, "A Brief History": 3.

23. Library Services, pamphlet, Hobart Institute of Welding Technology, 2001.

24. Cary, "A Brief History": 2.

25. Cary, "A Brief History": 4–5.

26. *Troy Daily News*, 29 June 1961.

27. "Edward A. Hobart—Biographical Sketch," Troy, Ohio: Hobart Brothers Company, 1965; Edward A. Hobart, "History of the C. C. Hobart Foundation," 5 December 1974, EFG Hobart Papers: 3.

28. Larry Heisey, personal interview, 9 September 2000.

29. Edward A. Hobart, "History of the C. C. Hobart Foundation": 4.

30. *Troy Daily News*, 20 June 1964.

31. Titan Museum Background and History. www.pimair.org/titan_01htm#history.

32. Gladys Williams, personal interview, 15 August 2001.

33. Peter C. Hobart, "Welded Sculpture: A Truly American Art Form," *Welding Journal*, January 1996: 32–34.

34. Jefferson, 52–53.

35. Jefferson, 52.

36. *Troy Daily News*, 20 June 1967.

37. *Troy Daily News*, 23 June 1967.

38. *Troy Daily News*, 22 July 1967.

39. Jeanne Sargent, personal interview, 10 April 2001.

CHAPTER 18: Hobart Creates the Complete Package

1. Wilbur J. Chaffee, "The Hobart Brothers Story: From Bike to Jet in Three Generations," Hobart Brothers Company Records, Troy, Ohio: 27.

2. Chaffee, "The Hobart Brothers Story": 28.

3. Carolyn Hinel, audiotape interview with Lucia Howell, 8 August 1990.

4. Gladys Williams, personal interview, 15 August 2001.

5. Chaffee, "The Hobart Brothers Story": 27.

6. Robert Bravo, audiotape interview with Lucia Howell, 11 July 1990.

7. Lucia (Hobart) Bravo, personal interview, 24 April 2000.

8. Robert Bravo, audiotape interview.

9. William H. Hobart Jr. to Peter C. Hobart, Minutes of Milestone Meeting, 13 August 1990, Peter C. Hobart Papers.

10. Robert Bravo, audiotape interview.

11. Wilbur J. Chaffee, "The Hobart Brothers Story": 35–36.

12. Chaffee, "The Hobart Brothers Story": 38–39.

13. Chaffee, "The Hobart Brothers Story": 40.

14. Chaffee, "The Hobart Brothers Story": 50–51; Jefferson, 55–56.

15. Various issues of the *Hobart Arc Welding News* and *Hobart Welding News*, 1942–1967. The Blankenbuehler Library in the Hobart Institute of Welding Technology has a complete collection.

16. Glenn Nally, personal interview, 15 July 1999.

17. Jefferson, 56.

18. Hobart Brothers Company, "Hobart Micro-wire Automatic Wire Feed Welding Process," advertising brochure, circa 1961: 2.

19. Chaffee, "The Hobart Brothers Story": 41; Jefferson, 56.

20. Larry Atterholt, personal interview, 25 July 2002; *Troy Daily News*, 8 April 1965.

21. Robert Bravo, audiotape interview with Lucia Howell, 11 July 1990.

22. Jefferson, 57.

23. Howard B. Cary, personal interview, 10 August 1999.

24. Nan Kidder, audiotape interview with Lucia Howell, Summer 1990.

25. John Sampson, personal interview, 7 August 2001.

26. Debbie Howell Kurd, phone interview, 25 March 2002; Lucia Howell, audiotape interview with Robert Bravo; Robb Howell, personal interview, 1 March 2002.

27. Robb Howell, 1 March 2002.

28. Thomas B. Wheeler, "This and That," *Troy Daily News*, 23 February 1965.

29. William H. Hobart, untitled poem from 1939, Peter C. Hobart Papers.

30. Gladys Williams, 15 August 2001.

31. Tom Noftle, personal interview, 22 November 2000; *Troy Daily News*, 25 February 1965; Gladys Williams, 15 August 2001.

32. *Troy Daily News*, 25 February 1965; Gladys Williams, 15 August 2001.

33. *Troy Daily News*, 1 March 1965.

34. American Welding Society. Past Presidents. www.aws.org/about/past_prezi.htm; Marty Baker, e-mail to Mike Williams, 15 July 2002.

35. *Troy Daily News*, 1 July 1965.

36. *Troy Daily News*, 13 October 1975, 24 February 1977.

37. Edward J. Hobart, audiotape interview with Lucia Howell, summer 1990.

38. Don Karnes, audiotape interview with Lucia Howell, 22 August 1990.

39. Don Karnes, personal interview, 24 November 1999.

40. Don Karnes, 24 November 1999.

41. Wilbur J. Chaffee, "The Hobart Brothers Story": 35–36.

42. Wilbur J. Chaffee, "The Hobart Brothers Story": 59.

43. Christmas Letter from E. A. and W. H. Hobart to Bravo, Hobart, and Howell children, December 1964, Robb Howell Papers, Troy, Ohio.

CHAPTER 19:

Hobart International: "The Beginning of Globalization"

1. Jozef Kormornik, Slovakia (1939–1945) www.adc.sk/english/slovakia/index.htm.

2. Wilbur J. Chaffee, "The Hobart Brothers Story: From Bicycle to Jet in Three Generations," Hobart Brothers Company Records, Troy, Ohio: 23.

3. Chaffee, "The Hobart Brothers Story": 24.

4. Peter C. Hobart, "The Saga of Hobart Brothers International A.G." Peter C. Hobart Papers; Jefferson, 58.

5. Peter C. Hobart, "The New Frontier in the Welding Industry," *Welding Engineer*, January 1958: 64.

6. Jon R. Bauman, *Pioneering a Global Vision: The Story of Baker & McKenzie*. Chicago: Baker & McKenzie, 1999: 85–6.

7. Robert Bravo, "Hobart Brothers, A.G. History," 10 January 1966. Peter C. Hobart Papers: 1–2.

8. Peter C. Hobart, Hobart Brothers, A.G.—Business Report, 1961, Peter C. Hobart Papers: 2.

9. Andre Odermatt, personal interview, 30 May 2001.

10. Odermatt, 30 May 2001.

11. Robert Bravo, "Hobart Brothers, A.G. History": 4; Odermatt, 30 May 2001.

12. Robert Bravo, "Hobart Brothers, A.G. History": 5; *Troy Daily News*, 26 June 1964.

13. Wilbur J. Chaffee, "The Hobart Brothers Story": 38; *Troy Daily News*, 26 June 1964.

14. Peter C. Hobart, Hobart Brothers, A.G.—Business Reports, 1963: 1, 1964: 1.

15. David Howell, audiotape interview with Lucia Howell, Summer 1990.

16. Robb Howell, personal interview, 1 March 2002.

17. Debbie Howell Kurd, phone interview, 25 March 2002.

18. Peter C. Hobart, Hobart Brothers, A.G.—Business Report, 1970: 3.

19. Peter C. Hobart, Hobart Brothers, A.G.—Business Report, 1965: 1–2.

20. Peter C. Hobart, Hobart Brothers, A.G.—Business Report, 1971: 7; 1972: 3.

21. Odermatt, 30 May 2001.

22. Peter C. Hobart, Hobart Brothers, A.G.—Business Report, 1969: 2.

23. Peter C. Hobart, Hobart Brothers, A.G.—Business Report, 1969: 1.

24. Peter C. Hobart, "Hobart Brothers, A.G.—Business Report, 1971: 4.

25. Richard J. Barnet, *The Alliance: America, Europe, Japan: Makers of the Postwar World*. New York: Simon and Schuster, 1983: 326–27.

26. Hobart Brothers Company. Informational Brochure. Circa 1978: 16–18; Peter C. Hobart, Hobart Brothers, A.G.—Business Report, 1971: 6–7; 1973: 4–5.

27. Hobart Brothers Company. *Hobart Weldworld*. AWN 195-202, 1973–77.

28. Peter C. Hobart, Hobart Brothers International, A.G.—Business Report, 1973–76.

29. Odermatt, 30 May 2001.

30. Clayton C. Bartlett, personal interview, 20 June 2002; Peter C. Hobart, Hobart Brothers, A.G.—Business Report, 1965: 2–3; 1973: 7–8.

31. Peter C. Hobart, Hobart Brothers International, A.G.—Business Report, 1974: 6.

32. Ib Rasmussen, "Arabian Pipelines," *Hobart Weldworld*. AWN 195, 1973: 18–19.

33. Peter C. Hobart, Hobart Brothers International, A.G.—Business Report, 1978: 7.

34. Peter C. Hobart, Hobart Brothers International, A.G.—Business Report, 1979: 8; Robb Howell, personal interview, 1 March 2002.

35. Peter C. Hobart, The Saga of Hobart Brothers International, A.G., Index: 1.

36. "Hobart Joint Venture Company in Mexico Sees Bright Future," *Hobart Weldworld*. AWN 202, 1977: 8–9.

37. "Mexico Builds Largest, Most Modern CO2 Pipeline in the World," *Hobart Weldworld*. AWN 205, 1978: 5–9.

38. *Troy Daily News*, 21 February 1968, 6 March 1983; Jeanne Sargent, personal interview, 10 April 2001.

39. Peter C. Hobart, Hobart Brothers, A.G.—Business Report, 1967: 3.

40. Peter C. Hobart, Hobart Brothers, A.G.—Business Report, 1975: 6.

41. Peter C. Hobart, Hobart Brothers, A.G.—Business Report, 1971: 9.

42. David Halberstam, *The Reckoning*: 535.

43. Peter C. Hobart, Hobart Brothers International, A.G.—Business Report, 1976: 15, 1977: 5–6.

44. Larry Atterholt, personal interview, 25 July 2002; Odermatt, 30 May 2001.

45. Hobart Brothers International, A.G.—Business Report, 1976: 2.

46. Peter C. Hobart, Hobart Brothers International, A.G.—Business Report, 1978: 2, 1979: 1.

47. Odermatt, 30 May 2001.

48. Peter C. Hobart, Hobart Brothers International, A.G.—Business Report, 1978: 3–6, 1979: 5–7.

49. Peter C. Hobart, Hobart Brothers International, A.G.—Business Report, 1978: 4, 1979: 2.

50. *Woodstock News Sentinel*, 17 August 1979.

51. Clayton C. Bartlett, personal interview, 20 June 2002; "Hobart Brothers of Canada Expands Plant," *Hobart Weldworld*. AWN 205: 24.

52. Clayton C. Bartlett, personal interview, 20 June 2002.

53. Peter C. Hobart, Hobart Brothers International, A.G.—Business Report, 1979: 3, 6.

CHAPTER 20: Employees Achieve Many Milestones

1. Audiotape interview with Lucia Howell, Summer 1990.

2. Marion Centliver, personal interview, 18 April 2000; Wilbur J. Chaffee, "From Bike to Jet: The Hobart Brothers Story": 2.

3. Chaffee, "The Hobart Brothers Story": 9.

4. Chaffee, "The Hobart Brothers Story": 25.

5. Tom Noftle, personal interview, 22 November 2000.

6. Marion Centliver, personal interview, 18 April 2000; Charles C. Hobart, personal interview, 21 February 2000; Don Karnes, personal interview, 24 November 1999; Don Kendall, personal interview, 18 April 2000.

7. Don Karnes, personal interview, 24 November 1999.

8. Louise Rex, transcript of audiotape interview with Lucia Howell, Summer 1990.

9. Nan Kidder, audiotape interview with Lucia Howell, Summer 1990.

10. Frank Smith, personal interview, 16 June 2002.

11. Personal interview, 16 June 2002.

12. Robb Howell, personal interview, 1 March 2002.

13. Steve Smith, personal interview, 16 June 2002.

14. Opel Donnelson, audiotape interview with Lucia Howell, Summer 1990.

15. Gift letters, E. A. and W. H. Hobart to W. H. Hobart's grandchildren, various years, Robb Howell Papers, Troy, Ohio.

16. Quotation is from Leo Wildenthaler, personal interview, 15 January 2001; Larry Atterholt, personal interview, 25 July 2002; John Sampson, 7 August 2001.

17. Chaffee, "The Hobart Brothers Story": 25; Lowell Mott, personal interview, 23 November 2001.

18. Chaffee, "The Hobart Brothers Story": 26; Jefferson, 46.

19. Hobart Brothers Company, Hobart Brothers Reporter, Vol. 3 No. 4. Winter 1966.

20. Chaffee, "The Hobart Brothers Story": 27.

21. Larry Bohlender, "Hobart Brothers First-Aid Training Stresses Prevention, Quick Action," *Troy Daily News*. 24 June 1965.

22. *Hobart Brothers Reporter*, Vol. 1, No. 1. Summer 1964.

23. *Hobart Brothers Reporter*, Vol.13, No. 1. January–February 1976.

24. The Blankenbuehler Library in the Hobart Institute of Welding has a complete collection of the *Hobart Reporter*.

25. Chaffee, "The Hobart Brothers Story": 29.

26. *Troy Daily News*, 12 January 1967.

27. Hobart Brothers Company, Milestone Program, 1967, 1971, 1987; *Hobart Brothers Reporter*, Vol. 8, No. 2; Vol. 8, No. 3, 1971; Vol. 9, No. 3, 1972.

28. Tom Noftle, personal interview, 22 November 2000.

29. Peter Jenkins, personal interview, 15 August 2000.

30. Peter Jenkins, 15 August 2000; Don Kendall, personal interview, 18 April 2000.

31. *Troy Daily News*, 4 November 1968.

32. Hobart Brothers Company, IUE Campaign Time Table, 22 November 1968. Hobart Brothers Company Records, Troy, Ohio.

33. Hobart Brothers Company, "Seniority Simply Means Who Gets Laid Off Last" flyer. Hobart Brothers Company Records.

34. Hobart Brothers Company, "Unions Mean Strikes" flyer. Hobart Brothers Company Records.

35. Hobart Brothers Company, "Face It . . . Unions and Strikes Go Together" flyer. Hobart Brothers Company Records.

36. *IUE Hobart Report*, issues for 29 November, 11 December 1968, 14 January 1969. Hobart Brothers Company Records.

37. Jonathan Miller, "Hobart 2-1 Winner; Union Will Try Again," *Troy Daily News*, 17 January 1969.

38. William H. Hobart Jr., Progress Report to Employees, 7 March 1969. Hobart Brothers Company Records.

39. *Hobart Brothers Reporter*, Vol. 6 No. 5, 1969.

40. William H. Hobart Jr., personal interview, 17 October 2000.

41. William H. Hobart Jr., To All HB Employees and Your Families, 28 June 1978. Hobart Brothers Company Records.

42. International Molders and Allied Workers later changed to Glass, Molders, Pottery, Plastic, and Allied Workers was the union at Hobart Brothers of Canada. Clayton C. Bartlett, personal interview, 20 June 2002.

43. Don Karnes, personal interview, 24 November 1999.

44. Don Karnes, audiotape interview with Lucia Howell, 22 August 1990.

45. *Hobart Brothers Reporter*, Vol. 8, No. 3. 1971.

46. Robb Howell, personal interview, 1 March 2002.

47. Nan Kidder, audiotape interview with Lucia Howell, Summer 1990; Louise Rex, transcript of audiotape interview with Lucia Howell, Summer 1990.

48. Personal interview, 25 July 2002.

49. *Troy Daily News*, 17 January 1969.

50. *Hobart Brothers Reporter*, Vol. 9, No. 3. 1972.

51. *Hobart Brothers Reporter*, Vol. 10, No. 6. 1973: 9.

52. Nan Kidder, audiotape interview with Lucia Howell, Summer 1990.

53. Howard Cary, personal interview, 10 August 1999.

54. Jeanne Sargent, personal interview, 10 April 2001.

55. Personal interview, 15 January 2001.

56. William H. Hobart Jr., personal interview, 17 October 2000.

CHAPTER 21:

A New Team Reorganizes for the Seventies

1. Personal interview, 17 October 2000.

2. Keith Aufauser, e-mail to Michael W. Williams, 17 August 2001.

3. *Troy Daily News*, 13 January 1972.

4. *Hobart Brothers Reporter*, Vol. 3 No. 4., 1966.

5. Roger Williams, personal interview, 20 April 2002.

6. Larry Atterholt, personal interview, 25 July 2002.

7. Roger Williams, phone interview, 31 March 2003.

8. *Troy Daily News*, 13 January 1972.

9. *Hobart Brothers Reporter*, Vol. 5, No. 2, 1969.

10. Glenn Nally, personal interview, 17 July 1999.

11. Cary, *Modern Welding Technology*: 10.

12. Cary, "A Brief History of the Hobart Brothers Technical Center Building": 3.

13. "Porta-slag . . . the Giant Filler!" *Hobart Weldworld*, AWN-186: 2.

14. "Hobart Welds the World Trade Center," *Hobart Weldworld*, AWN-189: 2–3.

15. "Hobart Welds. . . .": 4, 6.

16. Angus Kress Gillespie, *Twin Towers: The Life of New York City's World Trade Center*. New Brunswick, N.J.: Rutgers University Press, 1999: 83.

17. "Porta-slag for the Tallest Buildings in the World," *Hobart Weldworld*, AWN-188: 2–3.

18. "Porta-slag, the Giant Filler!": 4–5.

19. "Hobart Welds . . .": 6.

20. For example, Hobart Brothers Company, "When the Three Millionth Weld Depends on the First, One Name Leaps to Mind." Advertising Brochure, circa 1986, Peter C. Hobart Papers.

21. Glenn Nally, personal interview, 17 July, 1999; Gillespie, 117.

22. "Welding at Work on World's Tallest Building," *Hobart Weldworld*, AWN-195: 5-7.

23. Canada's National Tower. www.cntower.ca/information/13_info_aboutus.htm.

24. "Strict Quality Standards Make CN Tower Steel Fabrication Demanding Welding Task," *Hobart Weldworld*, AWN-199: 5–7.

25. Cary, *Modern Welding Technology*: 9.

26. Cary, *Modern Welding Technology*: 164.

27. "Rapid Transit in San Francisco," *Hobart Weldworld*, AWN-188: 15.

28. History of BART (1946–1972). www.bart.gov/about/history/history_1.asp.

29. Bill Howell, "Trans Alaska Pipeline," *Hobart Reporter* Vol. 11, No. 4, 1975: 1; *800 Miles to Valdez*: 109.

30. *800 Miles to Valdez*: 110–111.

31. William H. Hobart Jr., phone interview, 19 August 2002.

32. Don Bercaw, personal interview, 7 September 2002; "Welders Specially Equipped for Alaska," *Hobart Reporter*, Vol. 11, No. 4, 1975: 11.

33. Howard C. Cary, *Modern Welding Technology*: 290–91.

34. *800 Miles to Valdez*: 110, 118.

35. "Construction of World's Largest Gas Pipeline Gets Underway in Canada," *Hobart Weldworld* AWN-209: 5.

36. "Construction of World's Largest Gas Pipeline. . . .": 7.

37. Lowell Mott, personal interview, 21 November 2001.

38. *Hobart Brothers Reporter*, Vol. 15, No. 1: 10.

39. Peter C. Hobart, "Ecological Considerations in Modern Arc Welding," reprinted from *FWP Journal*, February 1973: 5–6.

40. Charles Babcock, "Foreign Welding Engineers and Scientists Attend Hobart Center," *Troy Daily News* 20 July 1972; U.S. Patent No. 3,798,409, issued 19 March 1974, "Honoring Hobart Brothers Company Inventors," Hobart Institute of Welding Library, 21 January 2000: 2.

41. Peter C. Hobart, "Ecological Considerations. . . .": 5; "Towmotor Adopts Smoke Exhaust System," *Hobart Weldworld* AWN-194, 1973: 12–13.

42. "Cyber-Tig®!" *Hobart Weldworld* AWN-192, 1972: 12–13.

43. "Welded Valve Guarantees Zero Leakage," *Hobart Weldworld* AWN-198, 1975: 4; "Meeting Nuclear Codes With GTAW," *Hobart Weldworld* AWN-198, 1975: 11; "Hydrofoils Bring Jet Age to Water," *Hobart Weldworld* AWN-203: 14.

44. "Linear Aids Large Weldment Fabrication," *Hobart Weldworld* AWN-198, 1975: 21.

45. "Hobart Cyber-Tig® Seals Oscilloscopes," *Hobart Weldworld* AWN-207, 1979: 9–10.

46. "Hobart Cyber-Tig® Meets Rigid Standards for Construction of LNG Membranes," *Hobart Weldworld* AWN-204, 1978: 5–7.

47. Charles C. Hobart Jr., personal interview, 21 February 2000.

48. Edward J. Hobart, personal interview, 18 April 2000.

49. *Hobart Reporter*, Vol. 12, No. 2: 4.

50. Jonifer A. Hobart, personal interview, 18 April 2000.

51. Charles C. Hobart Jr., phone interview, 8 December 2002.

52. Charles C. Hobart Jr., phone interview, 8 December 2002.

53. Charles C. Hobart Jr., 21 February 2000.

54. Charles C. Hobart Jr., audiotape interview with Lucia Howell, summer 1990.

55. Edward J. Hobart, personal interview, 18 April 2000.

56. Charles C. Hobart, Jr., audiotape interview with Lucia Howell, summer 1990.

57. Charles C. Hobart Jr., phone interview, 8 December 2002.

58. William Hobart, Jr., personal interview, 30 May 2003; Don Karnes, personal interview, 24 November 1999.

59. "Trimark," *A History of the National Welding Supply Association*. Cleveland, Ohio: Penton Publishing, 1994.

60. Don Karnes, personal interview, 24 November 1999.

CHAPTER 22: The Tumultuous Eighties

1. Nancy Bowman, "Troy Corporation Marks First 100 Years," *Troy Daily News*, 20 July 1997.

2. *Troy Daily News*, 14 February 1981.

3. Dart made plastic containers, most notably Tupperware products, West Bend appliances, and Duracell batteries. Kraft controlled several popular brands of food products. *Troy Daily News*, 17 February 1981.

4. Jill Gearhart, Food Service Sales, Hobart Corporation, e-mail to Michael W. Williams, 14 October 2002.

5. *Troy Daily News*, 27 February 1981.

6. International Truck and Engine. "Our Story," www.careers-international.com/history_main.html; Caterpillar. "Company History," www.caterpillar.com/about_cat/company_information/_history/history.html.

7. James West Davidson, et al. *Nation of Nations*: 1176.

8. Howard Cary, "A Brief History of the Hobart Brothers Technical Center Building": 3.

9. Peter Jenkins, personal interview, 15 August 2000.

10. Bureau of Labor Statistics, U.S. Department of Labor. Local Area Unemployment Statistics, www.state.oh.us/ASP/LAUS/VULAUS.asp.

11. Peter C. Hobart, Hobart Brothers International, A.G.—Annual Report, 1983: 1.

12. Peter C. Hobart, "The Future of the European Welding Industry," *Metal Construction*, January 1983: 11–12.

13. Peter C. Hobart, Hobart Brothers International, A.G.—Annual Report, 1984: 1.

14. Andre Odermatt, personal interview, 30 May 2001.

15. *Hobart Brothers Reporter*, Vol. 13, No. 1, January–February 1976: 3.

16. Lucia Hobart Bravo, personal interview, 19 April 2000.

17. Leo Wildenthaler, personal interview, 15 January 2001.

18. William Hobart Jr., personal interview, 30 May, 2003; *Troy Daily News*, 6 April 1978.

19. Personal interview, 25 July 2002.

20. Frank and Steven Smith, personal interview, 16 June 2002.

21. Leo Wildenthaler, personal interview, 15 January 2001.

22. Robb Howell, personal interview, 1 March 2002.

23. Marcia Hobart Howell, audiotape interview with Lucia Howell, 9 July 1990.

24. Larry Atterholt, personal interview, 25 July 2002.

25. E. A.'s doctor, Bob Buchan as told to Larry Atterholt, personal interview, 25 July 2002.

26. 26 July 1985.

27. *Troy Daily News*, September 1985.

28. William Hobart Jr., personal interview, 17 October 2000.

29. *Troy Daily News*, September 1985.

30. Leo Wildenthaler, personal interview, 15 January 2001.

31. Trenton Bell, audiotape interview with Lucia Howell, Fall 1990.

32. Trenton Bell, audiotape interview with Lucia Howell, Fall 1990.

33. *Troy Daily News*, 10 December 1985.

34. Conrad Schwab, personal interview, 19 October 2002.

35. Peter C. Hobart, Hobart Brothers International, A.G.—Business Report 1985, Peter C. Hobart Papers: 1.

36. Glenn Nally, personal interview, 15 July 1999.

37. Howard Cary, "A Brief History of the Hobart Brothers Technical Center Building," 10 December 1990: 3.

38. Ralph Ehlers, audiotape interview with Lucia Howell, Fall 1990.

39. Opal Donnelson, audiotape interview with Lucia Howell, Summer 1990.

40. Trenton Bell, audiotape interview with Lucia Howell, Fall 1990.

41. Kim Packard, audiotape interview with Lucia Howell, Fall 1990.

42. *Hobart Brothers Reporter*, Vol. 15, No. 1. 1977 Report to Employees: 8, 10, 12.

43. Roger Williams, personal interview, 20 April 2002.

44. Dan Plow, quoted in *Hobart Brothers World Reporter*, Vol. 1, No. 6, November/December 1981: 3.

45. Larry Heisey, personal interview, 9 September 2000.

46. Morison, *Evolution of the Airline Industry*: 7, 12.

47. Roger Williams, personal interview, 20 April 2002.

48. William Hobart, phone interview, 19 August 2002.

49. Roger Williams, 20 April 2002.

50. *Troy Daily News*, 10 December 1986.

51. Don Karnes, audiotape interview with Lucia Howell, 22 August 1990; *Piqua Daily Call*, 10 December 1986.

52. Don Karnes, personal interview, 24 November 1999; Jeanne Sargent, personal interview, 10 April 2001.

53. Andre Odermatt, personal interview, 30 May 2001.

54. *Troy Daily News*, 15 November 1988; *Miami Valley News*, 12 November 1989.

55. Kim Packard, audiotape interview with Lucia Howell, Fall 1990.

56. *Hobart Brothers Reporter*, January/February, 1988; Trenton Bell, audiotape interview with Lucia Howell, Fall 1990; Robb Howell, personal interview 30 March 2002; Josh Kurd, audio-tape interview with Lucia Howell, Summer 1990.

57. *Hobart Brothers Reporter*, January/February 1989; Hobart Brothers Company, "Taking a World View," advertising brochure, 1989, Peter C. Hobart Papers.

58. Larry Atterholt, personal interview, 25 July 2002; Larry Heisey, e-mail to Michael W. Williams, 3 December 2002; Roger Williams, personal interview, 20 April 2002.

59. Robb Howell, personal interview, 1 March 2002; Roger Williams, personal interview, 20 April 2002.

60. Roger Williams, personal interview, 20 April 2002.

61. *Dayton Daily News*, 23 December 1990.

62. Personal interview, 19 October 2002.

63. Roger Williams, personal interview, 20 April 2002.

64. William Hobart, phone interview, 19 August 2002.

65. *Hobarteering*, International Edition, No. 85-02.

66. *Hobarteering*, International Edition, No. 87-03; Andre Odermatt, personal interview, 30 May 2001.

67. *Hobart Brothers Reporter*, January/February 1988; Andre Odermatt, personal interview, 30 May 2001.

68. *Hobart Brothers Reporter*, January/February 1988; Andre Odermatt, personal interview, 30 May 2001.

69. Ralph Barhorst, personal interview, 27 November 2002; *Hobart Brothers Reporter*, June–September 1989.

70. Tom Peters reference-*Dayton Daily News*, 23 December 1990; Genghis Khan quote-*Miami Valley News*, 12 November 1989.

71. Chic Bartlett, personal interview, 20 June 2002; Roger Williams, personal interview, 20 April 2002.

72. Leo Wildenthaler, personal interview, 15 January 2001.

73. Chic Bartlett, personal interview, 20 June 2002.

74. "Welding in Canada," *A History of the National Welding Supply Association*: 22.

75. Chic Bartlett, personal interview, 20 June 2002.

76. Chic Bartlett, personal interview, 20 June 2002.

77. Announced 10 May, 1991, *Troy Daily News*.

CHAPTER 23:
Hobart Hones the Cutting Edge of High Technology

1. T. A. Heppenheimer, *History of the Space Shuttle, Vol.2: Development of the Space Shuttle, 1972–1981*. Washington, D.C.: Smithsonian Institution Press, 2002: 190.

2. Dennis R. Jenkins, *Space Shuttle: the History of the National Space Transportation System*. 3rd ed. Dennis R. Jenkins: Cape Canaveral, Fla., 2001: 230; Heppenheimer, 192.

3. Ralph Barhorst, personal interview, 27 November 2002; U.S. Patent No. 3,999,034 21 December 1976, "Honoring Hobart Brothers Company Inventors," Hobart Institute Library: 2.

4. Ralph Barhorst, personal interview, 27 November 2002.

5. Howard B. Cary, *Modern Welding Technology*: 324.

6. Ralph Barhorst, personal interview, 27 November 2002.

7. Larry Atterholt, personal interview, 25 July 2002; Ralph Barhorst, personal interview, 27 November.

8. Larry Atterholt, personal interview, 25 July 2002.

9. Ralph Barhorst, personal interview, 27 November 2002.

10. Howard B. Cary, *Modern Arc Welding*: 86.

11. Ralph Barhorst, personal interview, 27 November 2002.

12. Quoted in Heppenheimer: 193.

13. Heppenheimer: 194, 198.

14. Larry Atterholt, personal interview, 25 July 2002; Jenkins: 266, 422.

15. Ralph Barhorst, personal interview, 27 November 2002.

16. Jenkins: 423.

17. Larry Atterholt, personal interview, 25 July 2002; Ralph Barhorst, personal interview, 27 November 2002; Jenkins: 423–24.

18. Cary, *Modern Welding Technology*: 318–19.

19. Larry Atterholt, personal interview, 25 July 2002; Ralph Barhorst, personal interview, 27 November 2002; Robb Howell, personal interview, 1 March 2002; Leo Wildenthaler, personal interview, 15 January 2001.

20. Larry Atterholt, personal interview, 25 July 2002; Ralph Barhorst, personal interview 27 November 2002; Hobart Brothers Company, Cyber-Wave® Sales Brochure, 1986; *Hobarteering*, International Edition, July 1984.

21. Cary, "A Brief History of the Hobart Brothers Technical Center Building": 4; " Technology Developments from Troy," Hobart Supplement to *Welding Review*, February 1986.

22. *Hobart Brothers Reporter*, October–December 1990: 4–5; Andre Odermatt, personal interview, 30 May 2001.

23. Leo Wildenthaler, personal interview, 15 January 2001.

24. Roger Williams, personal interview, 20 April 2002.

25. Larry Atterholt, personal interview, 25 July 2002.

26. Larry Atterholt, personal interview, 25 July 2002; Ralph Barhorst, personal interview, 27 November 2002; Andre Odermatt, personal interview, 30 May 2001.

27. ESAB History. www.esabna.com/html/esabna01.html.

28. Howard B. Cary, personal interview, 10 August 1999; William Hobart Jr., phone interview, 19 August 2002.

29. Frank and Steve Smith, personal interview, 16 June 2002.

30. Greg Smith of the Roy Smith Company in Detroit and Gary Blake of Colony, Inc. in Hingham, Mass., made the presentation, *Hobarteering Marketing Newsletter*, 1 February 1983: 9–10.

31. Leo Wildenthaler, personal interview, 15 January 2001.

32. Ralph Barhorst, personal interview, 27 November 2002.

33. William H. Hobart Jr., phone interview, 19 August 2002.

34. Cary, "A Short History. . . .": 4; "Hobart's Technical Support Capabilities," Hobart Supplement to *Welding Review*, February 1986.

35. Howard B. Cary, personal interview, 10 August 1999.

36. Marty Baker and Al Lesnewich, "Tribute to a True Professional," World of Welding, Summer 2002: 1; *Hobart Brothers Reporter*, October-December 1989.

37. *Hobart Brothers Reporter*, June–September 1989.

38. Quoted in "A Third Generation Welding View," *Industrial Management*, Vol. 1, No. 12, April 1984: 31.

39. Frank Anderson, phone interview, 19 August 2002; Cary, *Modern Welding Technology*: 384.

40. Howard B. Cary, "A Short History. . . .": 4.

41. Torsteknik Company Brochure, "Torsteknik + Motoman = Greater Productivity": 2–3.

42. "Technology Developments from Troy," Hobart Supplement to *Welding Review*, February 1986.

43. *Hobart Brothers Reporter*, June–September 1989.

44. Philip Monnin, audiotape interview with Lucia Howell, Fall 1990.

45. Philip Monnin to Michael W. Williams, e-mail, 23 April 2004.

46. *Hobart Brothers Reporter*, January/February 1989.

47. Philip Monnin, audiotape interview with Lucia Howell, Fall 1990.

48. *Dayton Daily News*, 20 July 1990.

49. Hobart Brothers Company, *1992 Annual Report*: 8.

50. Hobart Brothers Company, Hobart Welding Technology: Hobart in Europe, brochure, 1992.

51. *Hobart Brothers Reporter*, June–September 1989.

52. *Hobart Brothers Reporter*, October–December 1990: 11.

53. Larry Atterholt, personal interview, 25 July 2002; Roger Williams, personal interview, 20 April 2002.

54. Hobart Brothers Company, *1992 Annual Report*: 5.

55. Philip Monnin to Glen Nally, e-mail, 22 April 2004.

56. Cary, *Modern Welding Technology*: 255.

57. Cary, *Modern Welding Technology*: 256.

58. Hobart Laser Products, "Lasers" Brochure, 1994.

59. Philip Monnin to Glen Nally, e-mail, 22 April 2004.

60. Renamed Aleph, the cult has been disrupted by arrests and confiscations, but is still in existence and remains on the U.S. State Department list of international terrorist organizations. Aum Shinrikyo. www.religiousmovements.virginia.edu/nrms/Aums.html; David Ballingrud, "An Unheeded Warning," *St. Petersburg Times*, 14 October 2001. www.sptimes.com/News/101401/An_unheeded-warning.shtml; Melissa Chiric, "Changing Preconceptions of the Nuclear Terrorist Threat: A Case Study of the Aum Shinrikyo Cult," www.georgetown.edu/sfs/program/stia/students/vol.02/chiricom.htm.

61. Hobart Brothers Company, *1994 Annual Report*: 6.

62. "Honoring Hobart Brothers Company Inventors," Hobart Institute Library, 21 January 2000.

63. Howard B. Cary, personal interview, 10 August 1999; William H. Hobart Jr., personal interview, 17 October 2000.

CHAPTER 24: The Family Finds a Suitable Suitor

1. Quoted in John H. Sheridan, "Managing by the 'Golden Rule'," *Industry Week*, 18 November 1991.

2. *Troy Daily News*, 14, 15 May 1990.

3. Sheridan, "Managing by the 'Golden Rule'."

4. *Hobart Brothers Reporter*, January–February 1988.

5. Sheridan, "Managing by the 'Golden Rule'."

6. Quoted in Sheridan, "Managing by the 'Golden Rule'."

7. Sheridan, "Managing by the 'Golden Rule'."

8. Hobart Brothers Company Board of Directors, Policy Concerning the Hiring of Hobart Brothers Company Shareholders or Their Relatives, 22 April 1982, Hobart Brothers Policy Manual.

9. Lucia (Hobart) Bravo, personal interview, 19 April 2000; William Hobart Jr., personal interview, 9 November 2002.

10. Hobart Brothers Company, *Annual Report for 1992*: 13.

11. *Hobart Brothers Reporter*, August–October 1991: 14.

12. *Hobart Brothers Reporter*, January–February 1989.

13. Hobart Lasers & Advanced Systems, Harrison Hobart-Biographical Information, Media Packet for Demonstration of the New 3000 Watt Nd:YAG Laser, 6 December 1994, Hobart Application and Service Center, Troy, Michigan.

14. Sheridan, "Managing by the 'Golden Rule'."

15. *Hobart Brothers Reporter*, May–June 1987.

16. *Dayton Daily News*, 16 October, 30 November, 5 December 1990.

17. Conrad Schwab, personal interview, 19 October 2002; Hobart Brothers Company, *Annual Report for 1992*: 13.

18. Hobart Brothers Company, *Annual Report for 1992*: 14; Bob Irving, "Michael Wolf Charts New Courses for Hobart," *Welding Journal*, April 1993: 85–6.

19. Peter C. Hobart to Michael A. Wolf, 4 March 1992: 2, Peter C. Hobart Papers.

20. Peter C. Hobart to Michael A. Wolf, 4 March 1992: 5.

21. Peter C. Hobart to Michael A. Wolf, 4 March 1992: 2.

22. Peter C. Hobart to Michael A. Wolf, 4 March 1992: 4.

23. Hobart Seventy-fifth Anniversary "Sound Chamber" Dedication, audiotape, 25 April 1992.

24. Response to *Troy Daily News* Questions on Hobart Brothers Company Seventy-fifth Anniversary, Fax from Peter C. Hobart to Nancy Bowman, 4 March 1992, Peter C. Hobart Papers.

25. *Hobart Brothers Reporter*, October–December 1990: 12; Overfield Early Childhood Program History, www.overearly-childhoodprogram.com; William H. Hobart Jr., personal interview, 9 November 2002.

26. "Non-Profit Helps Communities Help Themselves," www.tdn-net.com/special/industryguide_2002/ articles/rt.htm.

27. Larry Heisey, e-mail to Glenn Nally, 20 December 2003.

28. Larry Heisey, personal interview, 9 September 2000.

29. *Hobart Brothers Reporter*, January–April 1991: 9.

30. "Non-Profit Helps Communities Help Themselves," www.ten-net.com/special/industryguide_2002/ articles/rt.htm.

31. Frank Anderson, phone interview, 19 August 2002; Robb Howell, personal interview, 1 March 2002; Jeanne Sargent, personal interview, 10 April 2001; Conrad Schwab, personal interview, 19 October 2002; Steve Smith, personal interview, 16 June 2002.

32. William H. Hobart Jr., phone interview, 19 August 2002.

33. Hobart Brothers Company, *Annual Report for 1992*: 4–5.

34. Hobart Brothers Company, *Annual Report for 1992*: 14; Conrad Schwab, personal interview, 19 October 2002; Roger Williams, personal interview, 20 April 2002.

35. *Hobart Brothers Reporter*, October–November 1990: 1, 4–5.

36. *Hobart Brothers Reporter*, August–October 1991: 6–7.

37. William H. Hobart Jr., personal interview, 9 November 2002; Andre Odermatt, personal interview, 30 May 2001.

38. Andre Odermatt, personal interview, 30 May 2001.

39. Conrad Schwab, personal interview, 19 October 2002.

40. Hobart Brothers Company, *Annual Report for 1993*: 4.

41. Petzinger, *Hard Landing*: xix, 343; Conrad Schwab, personal interview, 19 October 2002.

42. *Dayton Daily News*, 17 December 1992, 27 July 1993; Hobart Brothers Company, *Annual Report for 1992*: 5; *A History of the American Welding Supply Association*: 28.

43. Frank O. Anderson, phone interview, 19 August 2002; Frank O. Anderson, II, Edcor Consulting, www.edcor.com/consulting/Anderson.html; Steve Smith, personal interview, 16 June 2002.

44. Frank Smith, personal interview, 16 June 2002.

45. Steve Smith, personal interview, 16 June 2002.

46. Robb Howell, personal interview, 1 March 2002.

47. Frank Anderson, phone interview, 19 August 2002.

48. ITW History, www.itwinc.com/itw_history.html.

49. William H. Hobart Jr., phone interview, 19 August 2002, personal interview 5 June 2003.

50. 1993: Alliance with ITW, 1993: ISO 9001 Registration, Miller Electric Mfg. Co. 1929–Present. www.millerwelds.com/main/about/history/1993.phtml.

51. *Dayton Daily News*, 30 October 1993.

52. Frank O. Anderson, phone interview, 19 August 2002.

53. Frank O. Anderson, phone interview, 19 August 2002.

54. Jeanne Sargent, personal interview, 10 April 2001.

55. Frank O. Anderson, phone interview, 19 August 2002.

56. Hobart Brothers Company, *Annual Report for 1993*: 4–9.

57. *Dayton Daily News*, 3 April 1994.

58. *Dayton Daily News*, 3 April 1994.

59. *Dayton Daily News*, 7 August 1994.

60. Hobart Brothers Company, *Annual Report for 1994*: 2.

61. Hobart Brothers Company, *Annual Report for 1994*: 4.

62. Hobart Brothers Company, Media Packet for Hobart Lasers & Advanced Systems: The New 3000 Watt Nd:YAG Laser, 1994, Peter C. Hobart Papers.

63. Hobart Brothers Company, Media Packet for Hobart Lasers & Advanced Systems: The New 3000 Watt Nd:YAG Laser, 1994.

64. Hobart Brothers Company, *Annual Report for 1994*: 5.

65. Peter C. Hobart to Michael A. Wolf, 4 March 1992: 2–6.

66. Hobart Brothers Company, *Annual Report for 1994*: 6.

67. *Hobart Brothers Reporter*, November 1994–May 1995: 1.

68. ITW History, www.itw.com/itw_history.html

69. About 80/20, www.itw.com/itw_about80/20.html

70. *Hobart Brothers Reporter*, November 1994–May 1995: 1.

71. Frank O. Anderson, phone interview, 19 August 2002; William H. Hobart Jr., phone interview, 19 August 2002.

72. Frank O. Anderson, phone interview, 19 August 2002; ITW Innovation, www.itw.com/itw_innovation.html; Conrad Schwab, personal interview, 19 October 2002.

73. Frank O. Anderson, phone interview, 19 August 2002.

74. William Hobart Jr., Pros and Cons Memo, 18 April 1995.

75. Frank O. Anderson, phone interview, 19 August 2002; Conrad Schwab, personal interview, 19 October 2002; *Troy Daily News*, 19, 20 May 2002.

76. *Troy Daily News*, 19, 20 May 2002.

77. *Hobart Brothers Reporter*, November 1994–May 1995: 2.

78. Quoted in *Troy Daily News*, 19 May 2002.

79. *Troy Daily News*, 19 May 2002.

80. *Miami Valley Sunday News*, 28 May 2002.

81. *Hobart Brothers Reporter*, November 1994–May 1995: 3.

82. *Hobart Brothers Reporter*, November 1994–May 1995: 6–7.

83. Robb Howell, personal interview, 1 March 2002.

84. Conrad Schwab, personal interview, 19 October 2002.

85. Quoted in *Dayton Daily News*, 3 February 1996.

86. *Dayton Daily News*, 3, 6 February 1996; Conrad Schwab, personal interview, 19 October 2002; *Troy Daily News*, 5 February 1996.

87. *Dayton Daily News*, 3 February 1996.

88. Andre Odermatt, personal interview, 30 May 2001.

89. Ralph Barhorst, personal interview, 27 November 2002.

90. Frank O. Anderson, phone interview, 19 August 2002; Ralph Barhorst, personal interview, 27 November 2002; Conrad Schwab, personal interview, 19 October 2002.

Epilogue

1. Clayton C. Bartlett, personal interview, 20 June 2002.

2. www.ametek.com; www.prestolite.com; www.thermadyne.com.

3. www.motoman.com.

4. Marty Baker, e-mail to Michael W. Williams, 3 June 2002.

5. Ben Sutherly, "Hobarts Remain the Boys from Troy," *Daily Dayton News*, 8 March 2001; Charles Hobart Jr., phone interview, 8 December 2002; www.hobartcabinet.com.

6. Edward J. Hobart, Jonathon A. Hobart, personal interview, 18 April 2000.

7. Edmund Hobart, letter to stockholders/relatives, 25 April 1994, Peter C. Hobart papers.

8. *Dayton Daily News*, 1 October 1999; Robb Howell, personal interview, 1 March 2002.

9. Lucia (Hobart) Bravo, personal interview, 19 April 2000; *Troy Daily News*, 19 January 1975.

10. Lucia (Hobart) Bravo, phone interview, 1 December 2002; *Dayton Daily News*, 6 July 2001.

11. Lucia (Hobart) Bravo, phone interview, 4 June 2003; *Dayton Daily News*, 6 July 2001. *Hobart Arena Rededication*, 1950–2001: November 4, 2001. Troy, Ohio: Peters Printing, 2001.

12. FEMA, Therese McAllister, ed. *World Trade Center Building Performance Study: Data Collection, Preliminary Observations and Records*. Washington, D.C., 2002: 82.

13. FEMA, McAllister: 82–84.

14. *Dayton Daily News*, 26 May 2001.

15. Robb Howell, personal interview, 1 March 2002.

16. *Dayton Daily News*, 26 June 2001.

17. *Hobart Arena Rededication*.

18. *Hobart Arena Rededication*.

BIBLIOGRAPHY

Articles

Baker, Marty and Al Lesnewich. "Tribute to a True Professional," *World of Welding* (summer 2001): 1–2.

Berka, Charles. "From Battery Chargers to Arc Welders: 53 Years of Pioneering Pays Off," *The Welding Distributor* (March/April 1978): 58–61.

Chaffee, W. J. "The Hobart Bros. Company," 36–38.

Crout, George. "C. C. Hobart Got His Start Here," *Middletown Signal* (7 October 1946).

Cullison, Andrew, and Christine Tarafa. "Welding and Society," *Welding Journal* (June 1999): 48–53.

Hauck, Frederick A. "Sands of the Sea," *Yale Scientific Magazine* (January 1957).

"Hobart Begins Work on New Welding Institute," *Welding Engineer* (October 1957): 64.

"Hobart Move into Advanced Welding Systems," *Metal Construction* (February 1984): 71–3.

Hobart, Peter C. "Ecological Considerations in Modern Arc Welding," reprinted from *F.W.P. Journal* (February 1973): 1–11.

____. "The New Frontier in the Welding Industry," *Welding Engineer* (January 1958): 64.

____. "The Future of the European Welding Industry," *Metal Construction* (January 1983): 11–13.

____. "Welded Sculpture: A Truly American Art Form," *Welding Journal*. January 1996: 31–8.

Irving, Bob. "What Welding Accomplished—Way Back When," *Welding Journal* (January 1994): 59–70.

"Living Pioneers: E. A. Hobart," *Welding Engineer* (September 1966): 65–6.

O'Neal, Christina. "The Homes That Hobart Built," *Dayton Monthly* (May/June 1995): 62–7.

Sheridan, John H. "Managing by the 'Golden Rule'," *Industry Week* (18 November 1991).

Sutherly, Ben. "Hobart Mainstay of Troy History," *Dayton Daily News* (n.d., 2000): 1F, 4F.

____. "Hobarts Remain the Boys from Troy," *Dayton Daily News*, Neighbors Section (8 March 2001): 1, 10.

Books

Ambrose, Stephen J. *Citizen Soldiers: The U.S. Army from the Normandy Invasion to the Surrender of Germany, June 6, 1944–May 7, 1945.* New York: Simon and Schuster, 1997.

Baldwin, Neil. *Edison: Inventing the Century.* New York: Hyperion, 1995.

Barnet, Richard J. *The Alliance: America, Europe, Japan, Makers of the Postwar World.* New York: Simon and Schuster, 1983.

Bartlow, Bert S., et al., eds. *Centennial History of Butler County, Ohio.* New York: B. F. Bowen and Co., 1905.

Bedwell, Don. *Silverbird: The American Airlines Story.* Sandpoint, Idaho: Airways International, 1999.

Bicentennial Committee, *Fairfax, Vermont: Its Creation and Development.* Fairfax, Vt.: Town of Fairfax, 1980.

Buderi, Charles. *The Invention That Changed the World: How a Small Group of Radar Pioneers Won the Second World War and Launched a Technological Revolution.* New York: Simon and Schuster, 1996.

The C. C. Hobart Foundation. Troy, Ohio: C. C. Hobart Foundation, circa 1946.

Carlisle, Lilian Baker, ed. *A Look Around Chittenden County, Vermont.* Burlington, Vt.: Chittenden County Historical Society, 1976.

Carson, Gerald. *The Golden Egg: The Personal Income Tax, Where It Came From, How It Grew.* Boston: Houghton Mifflin, 1977.

Cary, Howard B. *Modern Welding Technology,* 4th ed. Upper Saddle River, N.J.: Prentice Hall, 1998.

Catton, Bruce. *The War Lords of Washington.* New York: Harcourt Brace Jovanovich, 1948.

Cauffield, Joyce V. B, and Carolyn E. Banfield, eds. *The River Book: Cincinnati and the Ohio.* Cincinnati, Ohio: The Program for Cincinnati, 1981.

Chaffee, W. J. *Electric Arc Welding Manual,* 2nd ed. Troy, Ohio: Hobart Brothers Company, 1935.

Cheney, Sheldon and Martha Candler Cheney. *Art and the Machine: An Account of Industrial Design in 20 Century America.* New York: Acanthus Press, 1992.

Crout, George C. *Industrial Middletown.* Middletown, Ohio: 1958.

____. *Middletown Diary,* 2 Vols. Middletown, Ohio: 1968.

Davidson, James West, et. al. *Nation of Nations: A Narrative History of the American Republic, Vol.2: Since 1865,* 3rd ed. Boston: McGraw-Hill, 1998.

Davis, Kenneth S. *FDR: The War President, 1940–1943.* New York: Random House, 2000.

Dowd, J. W., and C. L. Van Cleve. *A Historical Sketch of the Schools of Troy.* Troy, Ohio: 1945.

Dubin, Michael J. *U.S. Congressional Elections, 1788–1997.* Jefferson, N.C.: McFarland and Co., Inc., 1998.

Flammang, James M. *100 Years of the American Auto.* Lincolnwood, Ill.: Publications International, 1999.

Francillon, René. *McDonald Douglas Aircraft Since 1920: Volume 1.* Arnays, Md.: Naval Institute Press, 1988.

Gable, John Allen. *The Bull Moose Years: Theodore Roosevelt and the Progressive Party.* Port Washington, N.Y.: Kennikat Press, 1978.

The Gases & Welding Distributor Staff. *A History of the National Welding Supply Association.* Cleveland: Penton Publishing, 1994.

Gerber, John C. *A Pictorial History of the University of Iowa.* Iowa City: University of Iowa Press, 1988.

Gersick, Kelin E., et. al. *Generation to Generation: Life Cycles of the Family Business.* Boston: Harvard Business School Press, 1997.

Gillespie, Angus Kress. *Twin Towers: The Life of New York City's World Trade Center.* New Brunswick, N.J.: Rutgers University Press, 1999.

Goodrich, John E. *Vermont Revolutionary War Rolls.* Rutland, Vt.: Tittle Company, 1904.

Griffith, Mary, from the records of Edgar Hobart. *The Descendants of Edmund Hobart of Hingham, Mass.* San Francisco: California Genealogical Society, 1952.

Greer, David C. *Sluff of History's Boot Soles: An Anecdotal History of Dayton's Bench and Bar.* Wilmington, Ohio: Orange Frazer Press, 1996.

Hart, Lorena Laing, and Francis Russell Hart. *Not All is Changed: A Life History of Hingham.* Hingham, Mass.: Hingham Historical Commission, 1993.

Hartwitz, Benjamin F. *Historical Sketches of Middletown,* 2 vols. Middletown, Ohio: 1978.

Hass, Ed. *Fire Equipment.* San Diego: Thunder Bay Press, 1998.

Heppenheimer, T. A. *Turbulent Skies: The History of Commercial Aviation.* New York: John Wiley and Sons, 1995.

_____. *History of the Space Shuttle, Vol.2: Development of the Space Shuttle, 1972–1981.* Washington, D.C.: Smithsonian Institution Press, 2002.

Herbert, Donald M. *The Ancestors and Descendants of John Sullivan Hobart.* Bryn Mawr, Pa., 1951.

Historical and Biographical Cyclopedia of Butler County, Ohio. Cincinnati: Western Biographical Publishing Co., 1882.

Hobart, L. Smith. *William Hobart: His Ancestors and Descendants.* Springfield, Mass., 1886.

Huffman, Dale, and Andy Snow. *Dayton: The Cradle of Creativity.* Memphis, Tenn.: Towery Publishing, 1998.

Ince, Edward Armstrong. *Miscellany: First Baptist Church of Middletown, Ohio.* Cincinnati: Press of George P. Houston, 1889.

Jefferson, Ted. *First 100 Years of Hobart.* Troy, Ohio: Hobart Brothers Company, 1986.

Jenkins, Dennis R. *Space Shuttle: The History of the National Space Transportation System,* 3rd ed. Dennis R. Jenkins: Cape Canaveral, Fla., 2001.

Journal of Peter Hobart and Descendants, 1635–1732. Hingham, Mass.: New England Historical and Genealogical Registry, 1967.

Knepper, George W. *Ohio and Its People.* Kent, Ohio: Kent State University Press, 1989.

Koch, Karl, III, with Richard Firstman. *Men of Steel: The Story of the Family That Built the World Trade Center.* New York: Crown Publishers, 2002.

Lane, Frederick C. *Ships for Victory: A History of Shipbuilding Under the U.S. Maritime Commission in World War II.* Baltimore: Johns Hopkins Press, 1951.

Maciarello, Joseph A. *Lasting Value: Lessons From a Century of Agility at Lincoln Electric.* New York: John Wiley and Sons, 2000.

McDonald, Forest. *Insull.* Chicago: University of Chicago Press, 1962.

McCoy, Alan H., ed. *Middletown Memories: A Bicentennial Year.* Middletown, Ohio: Middletown Area Bicentennial Commission, 1991.

Meeker, David A. *Better Eating . . . From Start to Finish: The Story of the Hobart Manufacturing Company.* New York: Newcomen Society, 1960.

Mendenhall, Thomas C. *History of the Ohio State University,* vols. 1 and 2. Columbus: Ohio State University Press, 1920, 1926.

Miller, E. Irene, ed. *History of Miami County, Ohio.* Tipp City, Ohio: Miami County Historical Society, 1982.

Miller, Roger L. and George C. Crout. *Middletown, Ohio.* Images of America Series. Charleston, S.C.: Arcadia, 1998.

Moley, Raymond. *The American Century of John C. Lincoln.* New York: Duell, Sloan and Pierce, 1962.

Morgan, Arthur E. *The Miami Conservancy District.* New York: McGraw-Hill, 1953.

Morris, John V. *Fires and Firefighters.* Boston: Little, Brown and Company, 1955.

Morrison, Steven and Clifford Winston. *The Evolution of the Airline Industry.* Washington, D.C.: Brookings Institute, 1995.

Nelson, Donald M. *Arsenal of Democracy: The Story of American War Production.* New York: Harcourt, Brace and Company, 1946.

Noble, Winona S. *The History of Cambridge, Vermont.* Cambridge, Vt.: Crescendo Club Library Association, 1976.

Novick, David, Melvin Anshen, W. C. Truppner. *Wartime Production Controls.* New York: Columbia University Press, 1949.

Oda, James C. *A Diversity of Piqua Industry, 1800–1900.* Piqua, Ohio: Piqua Historical Society, 1985.

_____, Linda Grimes. *Piqua and Miami County: A Primer of Community History.* Piqua, Ohio: Flesh Public Library, 1991.

The Official Roster of Ohio Soldiers, Sailors and Marines in the World War, 1917–18, vol. 8. Columbus, Ohio: F. J. Heer Printing Co., 1926.

Passer, Harold C. *The Electrical Manufacturers, 1875–1900.* Cambridge: Harvard University Press, 1953.

Petzinger, Thomas, Jr. *Hard Landing: The Epic Contest for Power and Profits That Plunged the Airlines into Chaos.* New York: Random House, 1995.

Porcher, Connie M. *History Preserved: Piqua-Caldwell National Register Historical District.* Piqua, Ohio: Piqua Historical Society, 1985.

Priest, Cliff. *Edward A. Hobart: Biographical Sketch.* Troy, Ohio: Hobart Brothers Company, 1965.

Pusey, Merlo J. *Charles Evans Hughes,* 2 vols. New York: Macmillan, 1951.

Ravner, John A. *The First Century of Piqua, Ohio.* Piqua, Ohio: Magee Brothers Company, 1916.

Roscow, James P. *800 Miles to Valdez: The Building of the Alaskan Pipeline.* Englewood Cliffs, N.J.: Prentice-Hall, 1977.

Serling, Robert. *Eagle: The Story of American Airlines.* New York: St. Martins/Marek, 1985.

Seventy-Five Years of Kitchenaid: 7th Annual Recipe Book. St. Joseph, Mich.: Whirlpool Corporation, 1993.

Silverberg, Robert. *Light for the World: Edison and the Power Industry.* Princeton, N.J.: D. Van Nostrand Co., 1967.

Simonson, Richard D. *The History of Welding.* Morton Grove, Ill.: Monticello Books, 1969.

Sims, Harry. *Middletown in Black and White.* Middletown, Ohio: Journal Publishing Co., 1906.

Toulmin, Harry A., Jr. *Patents and the Public Interest.* New York: Harper and Brothers, 1939.

Troy: Yesterday, Today, and Tomorrow. Troy, Ohio: "Many Friends," Historical Societies of Troy and Miami County, P.R. Dept. of Hobart Brothers. Company, 1950.

Michael Wallis. *Oil Man: The Story of Frank Phillips and the Birth of Phillips Petroleum.* New York: Doubleday, 1988.

Warner, Hoyt Landon. *Progressivism in Ohio, 1897–1917.* Columbus: Ohio State University Press, 1964.

Wheeler, Thomas Bemis. *Troy: The Nineteenth Century.* Troy, Ohio: Troy Historical Society, 1970.

Williams, Howard D. *A History of Colgate University, 1819–1969.* New York: Van Nostrand Reinhold Co., 1969.

Census Records

First Census of the United States. *1790: Vermont.* Washington, D.C.: Government Printing Office, 1907.

City Directories

Middletown, Ohio, 1891.

Piqua, Ohio, 1887–8, 1897, 1902, 1906–7, 1909–10, 1911, 1913–14.

Piqua and Troy, Ohio, 1916.

Troy, Ohio, 1927, 1929, 1933, 1935, 1938, 1940, 1942, 1946.

Internet

Accu Oerlikon, Ltd. Accu Oerlikon Company History. www.accuoerlikon.com.

American Welding Society. Past Presidents. www.aws.org/about/past_prezi.htm.

AXA Power. Mission/History. www.axapower.dynamicweb.dk/Default.asp?ID = 6.

Bay Area Rapid Transit. "History of BART (1946–1972)." www.bart.gov/about/history/history_1.asp

International Tennis Hall of Fame. www.tennisfame.com.

D.C. Roberts Aircraft Co. Jet Start Ground Power Units. www.dcaircraft.com.au/jetstart.htm.

"Hersheypark Arena, 1936–2001." www.hersheyarena.com/65th season.html

Irving, Bob, and Linda Hart. "Welding—As Time Goes By," About AWS: The Society's Past Present and Future. www.amweld.org/about/time_by.html.

"Jumbo Jet—The 747," Super 70s.com. www.super70s.com/Super70s/Science/Transportation/Aviation/747.asp

La Favre, Jeffrey. "The Brush Arc Lamp," Charles Francis Brush. www.ameritech.net/users/jeff_lafavre/lamparc.htm.

_____. "Charles Brush and the Arc Light," Charles Francis Brush. www.ameritech.net/users/jeff lafavre/brushbio.htm.

Lincoln Electric. "Corporate Information: Our History." www.lincolnelectric.com/corporate/profile/history.asp.

"Tennis," Encarta. www.encarta/msn.com.

Trilectron Industries, Inc. "About Us." www.trilectron.com/abtus.asp.

Troy Hall of Fame. Aka Bohumyla Klym-Pereyma. www.tdn-net.com/troyhalloffame/pereyma_aka.html.

United States Air Force Museum. Aircraft Index. www.wpafb.af.mil/museum/modern_flight/mf20.htm.

Interviews

Frank O. Anderson, 19 August 2002.

Larry Atterholt, 25 July 2002.

Clayton C. Bartlett, 20 June 2002.

Donald Bercaw, 10 September 2002.

Lucia (Hobart) Bravo, 19 April 2000; 2 August 2001; and 24 March and 1 December 2002.

Howard B. Cary, 10 August 1999.

Marion Centliver, 18 April 2000.

Larry E. Heisey, 9 September 2000.

Charles C. Hobart Jr., 21 February and 18 April 2000; and 8 December 2002.

Edward J. Hobart, 18 April 2000.

Jonifer A. Hobart, 18 April 2000.

William H. Hobart Jr., 17 October 2000, and 6 March, 19 August, and 9 November 2002.

Robb Howell, 1 March 2002.

Peter Jenkins, 15 August 2000.

Don Karnes, 24 November 1999.

Don Kendall, 18 April 2000.

Deborah Howell Kurd, 25 March 2002.

Jean Mochida, 18 April 2000.

Lowell Mott, 21 November 2001.

Glenn Nally, 15 July 1999, and 19 April 2001.

Tom Noftle, 22 November 2000.

Andre Odermatt, 30 May 2001.

John Sampson, 7 August 2001.

Jeanne Sargent, 10 April 2001.

Conrad Schwab, 19 October 2002.

Frank Smith, 16 June 2002.

Steven Smith, 16 June 2002.

Leo Wildenthaler, 15 January 2001.

Gladys Williams, 15 August 2001.

Roger Williams, 20 April 2002.

Newspapers

Buckeye (Troy, Ohio)

Butler County Democrat

Dayton Daily News

Miami Union (Troy, Ohio)

Middletown Signal

Shelby County Democrat

Sidney Daily Journal

Troy Daily News

School Yearbooks

The Piquonian, 1912

Unpublished Sources

Amherst College Alumni Records.

Bravo, Robert B. "Hobart Brothers, A.G. History." 10 January 1966. Peter C. Hobart Papers. Troy, Ohio.

Cary, Howard. "A Brief History of the Hobart Brothers Technical Center Building," 10 December 1990.

Chaffee, Wilbur J. "The Hobart Brothers Story: From Bike to Jet in Three Generations," Hobart Brothers Company Records. Troy, Ohio.

Colgate University Alumni Records.

Denison University Alumni Records.

"Edward A. Hobart—Biographical Sketch," Troy, Ohio: Hobart Brothers Company, 1965.

Electric Light—Thomas A. Edison Construction Department—Stations—Ohio—Middletown (D83-054), 1883.

Hobart Arena Rededication Program, 1950–2001: November 4, 2001. Troy, Ohio: Peters Printing, 2001.

Hobart Brothers Company Records. Troy, Ohio.

Hobart, Edmund. "Time Line History of Hobart Companies in Troy, Ohio," 1 February 1997.

____. "History of the Hobart Companies," video, 1992.

____. "Family History," 1997.

Hobart, Michelle. "Steel Welded Houses in Troy, Ohio. Prefabrication: the Impossible Compromise, 1936–1943," Institute of Fine Arts, New York University, 1998.

Hobart, Peter C. Hobart Brothers, A.G.—Business Reports, 1961–1985. Peter C. Hobart Papers. Troy, Ohio.

____. "The Hobart Story: From Man to Industry," 1967.

____. "The Saga of Hobart Brothers International, A.G." December 1994.

"Honoring Hobart Brothers Company Inventors," Hobart Institute Library. 20 January 2000.

Howell, Lucia. Audiotape Interviews with Hobart Family Members and Hobart Brothers Employees, summer 1990.

Ohio State University Alumni Records.

Pratt Institute Alumni Records.

Schul, Norman Williard. "The Development of a Midwestern City: Troy, Ohio," (Master's Thesis). Oxford, Ohio: Miami University, 1957.

Smith College Alumni Records.

University of Cincinnati Alumni Records.

University of Pennsylvania Alumni Records.

Yale University Alumni Records.

Acknowledgments

Contacted by phone at his home in Florida, one former Hobart Brothers official responded to a request for an interview with, "Aww . . . go jump in a lake!" That moment was a source of amusement to the authors because it was the sole request for help that was not met with the utmost generosity. The enthusiastic responses and commitment of time and effort from former and current employees, family members, and the greater Troy Community deepened the authors' sense of mission and redoubled their efforts to make this book worthy of the contributions they received. Any errors or shortcomings that remain are the responsibility of the authors alone.

Our list of heartfelt thank-you's begins with Glenn Nally. A retired communications director for Hobart Brothers, Mr. Nally was part of this project from the start and served as the photo editor for the book. With a fine memory for names and an eye for photographs that would reproduce well, he pulled together the best pictures from the hundreds available from family members, company archives, in-house publications, and a host of other sources. In addition, he provided sage counsel on publishing and marketing the book. We also wish to give a special thanks to Bob Hora who scanned photographs and converted program files as he designed the layouts and formatted the book you hold today. We deeply appreciate the professionalism of his contribution.

We owe a special debt of gratitude to Jeanne Sargent. Her post at the Hobart offices overlooking Public Square in Troy served as the communications center for work on this book. Ms. Sargent printed and copied faxes, forwarding countless pieces of mail and e-mail, and always seemed to have at her finger tips the phone number or mailing address of any person we needed to contact. She also read several drafts, pointing out errors and providing suggestions. Her organization, her patience, and her cheerfulness are equally appreciated. The same role

in Rome was played by Charmion Carroll, Peter's administrative assistant and friend for more than thirty years. During that time her efforts contributed to several earlier versions of this history.

Among the many Hobart family members who assisted with the book, several merit special mention. Peter's siblings, William H. Hobart Jr. and Lucia (Hobart) Bravo, made themselves available for multiple interviews and carefully read several drafts of the book. William's insights as a key executive at Hobart Brothers since the 1950s were of course invaluable in composing the last several chapters of the book. Apart from telling her own story, Lucia also provided information on the work of her husband, Robert Bravo who passed away while research for the book was getting underway. "Steel Welded Houses in Troy, Ohio. Prefabrication: The Impossible Compromise 1936–1943," an unpublished 1998 research paper by Peter's daughter Michelle (Hobart) Peyser for the Institute of Fine Arts, New York University, was a key source for Chapter 10 on the efforts of E. A. and W. H. Hobart to build steel homes. Mrs. Peyser's paper places the Hobart effort within the broader context of attempts to construct prefabricated housing throughout the western world. Lucia Howell generously gave the authors access to a set of audiotape interviews she had conducted in the summer and fall of 1990 with family members and Hobart Brothers executives and employees. These interviews were most valuable in providing thoughts and insights from people who had died before the book project began, especially the interview with her mother, Marcia (Hobart) Howell.

Another family member who merits special thanks is Peter's cousin, Edmund Hobart. In the course of pursuing his avocation as a genealogist and writing his autobiography, Edmund traveled and researched extensively, corresponded with other genealogists from the Hobart and related families across America and in England, and collected a wide array of photographs, local histories, and documents and advertising from the various Hobart companies. Sadly, Edmund died in 1998 before the project to create a comprehensive history came to fruition. However, Edmund's brothers, Charles Jr., Edward, and Jonifer, placed the two-dozen boxes of materials Edmund had compiled in an office of a warehouse across the street from the Hobart Cabinet Company and provided access for the authors. Many rewarding hours were spent among the "Edmund Archives," an invaluable source for the early generations of the Hobart family in America, C. C. Hobart and his Jones family in-laws from Middletown, the early decades of the Hobart companies in Troy, the family of Charles Hobart Sr., and the Hobart Cabinet Company. In addition, we offer our thanks to Christopher Hobart, Peter's English cousin, who provided information on the Hobart family in England, past and present.

This book also benefited from the assistance of several professional librarians and achivists. Chief among these was Marty Baker of the Blankenbuehler Memorial Library at the Hobart Institute of Welding Technology. Her mastery of that library's outstanding collection of journals, books, Hobart Brothers publications, and company patents was most helpful. We would also like to thank Juda Moyer at the History Room of the Troy-Hayner Center for help in navigating its local history archives. Employees at the Troy Public Library and the Flesh Public Library in Piqua assisted with many requests for local newspapers on microfilm. The Dayton Metro Library cheerfully handled many interlibrary loans for this project, particularly the employees at the Vandalia branch who often asked about the book's progress when requests were picked up. Thanks to Martin J. Tuohy and Glenn Longacre, a visit to the National Archives–Great Lakes Region in Chicago provided a valuable glimpse into the war production efforts of Hobart Brothers, Hobart Cor-

poration and other Miami Valley companies during World War II. Tamar Chute, an archivist at the Ohio State University, responded to requests for records for the many Hobart family members and company executives and engineers who were OSU alumni.

Among the many current and retired Hobart Brothers employees who granted interviews, contributed documents, and shared their expertise, several deserve special mention. Don Bercaw, Larry Heisey, and John Sampson read our manuscript and used over 150 combined years of engineering and managerial experience to save us from several errors and provide useful suggestions as well. In addition, Larry Heisey led a large team of Hobart people who are still in the process of organizing an extensive collection of Hobart Brothers company records, files, artifacts, and photographs. Those who have contributed to this effort include: Don Adams, Larry Atterholt, Joe Balmer, Ralph Barhorst, Jerry Besecker, Cal Bitner, Al Blackburn, Catherine Bohm, John Brubaker, Arthur Catey, Marjorie Chestnut, Waldo Fine, Merlin Flory, Joyce Heisey, Ron Hufford, Jim Hunt, Bob Lamme, Joel Leavelle, Jim Lyman, Bob Miller, Glenn Nally, Andre Odermatt, Carl Phillis, and Paul Stover.

We would also like to thank the C. C. Hobart Foundation for its financial support of this project.

Peter C. Hobart would like to thank his wife-to-be, Adriana Vitali, and his two administrative assistants, Jeanne Sargent and Charmion Carroll.

Mike Williams would like to thank his family, especially his wife Mary.

Index

England, 6, 63, 75, 77, 102, 142

Engleberger, Joseph, 189

Episcopal Church, 100

Erenyi, Geza, 146

ESAB, 123, 187

Essen Welding Exhibition, 138, 142, 182

Esther Parker, 6

Eta Kappa Nu (Electrical Engineering Fraternity), 30

Europe, 63, 69, 71, 77, 81, 100, 102, 108, 138, 141, 144, 175, 181, 197, 198

European Economic Community, 139

Eutectic Corporation, 200

Evans, Dale, 99

Evendale, Ohio, 186

Exide Battery Company, 36

external tanks (ET), 184–86

F

F. Bode and Sons, 189

F. Gray Company, 34

FabCO® flux-cored wire, 164, 166

Fabick Tractor Company, 168

FabLoy®, 169

Fair Employments Practices Commission, 90

Fair Labor Standards Act (1938), 49

Fairfax, Vermont, 10

Fairgrounds Coliseum, 97

Farrell, W. James, 202

Favelle Industries, 163

Faxon, Sarah, 7

Federal Emergency Management Agency (FEMA), 207

Federal Government, U.S., 175

Federal Housing Authority (FHA), 66

Federal Trade Commission, 203

Filbrun, Perry, 115

Filler Metals Division, 169–70, 178, 179, 197

Fink, David, 183

Firestone, 195

First Baptist Church (Troy), 26

First Baptist Church of Middletown, 13, 16

First Presbyterian Church of Troy, 19, 105

First Troy National Bank, 60

Fisher Body, 119

Fiumicino Airport, 108

Flagler, Henry, 112

Flood of 1913, 31

Flora, Russell, 51, 73, 121, 158

Florida East Coast Railroad, 115

Florida Minerals Company, 113–116, 160–61

Florida, 6, 76, 80, 102, 111–13, 118, 132

Fogelman, Harry, 49

food mixers, 22

Ford Motor Company, 55, 175

Ford, Henry, 32, 36

Fort Worth, Texas, 180

Fortune 500, 174

400 Hertz generator, 110

400 Hertz motors, 107

401(k) plan for employees, 194

409 grade stainless steel, 169

Forty-fourth Infantry Division, 81

Fourth Congressional District (Ohio), 26

France, 69, 77–78, 142, 189

Frankfurt, West Germany, 140

Frantz, Roger, 110, 162, 179

French Lick, Indiana, 16

Frigidaire, 53

Frisbie, Guy S., 174

Frobisher Bay, 110

Fulton Farms, 172

G

G.I. Bill, 120

Galbreath, Earl, 68, 74, 78, 95, 134, 147, 153

Garden Club of America, 206

Garfield, James R., 26

H

K

K Car (Chrysler), 199

Kaiser, Henry, 83

Kangaroo Cranes, 163

Kansas City, Missouri, 46

Karnes, Donald, 135, 173, 179, 189

Kelley, Robert F., 176

Kelvinator, 53

Kennedy Space Center, 124

Kerr, Paul W., 99

Kettering Tower, 202

Kettering, Charles F., 19, 24, 32, 62

Khrushchev, Nikita, 121

Kidder, Nan, 152–53, 159

Kiev, Ukraine, 140, 162

KitchenAid, 65, 93, 174, 202

Kiwanis Club, 93

Kjellberg, Oscar, 54

Knapp, Ed, 31

Knoop, John, 95

Kokomo, Indiana, 101

Korea, 147

Korean War, 110, 112

Kurd, Jos, 140, 180, 195

Kuwait, 143, 182

L

L'Air Liquide, 136

La Soudure Exotherme, 142, 151

Labrador, 110

Ladehoff, Leo, 195

LaGuardia Airport, 107

Lake Champlain, 10

Lakeville, Connecticut, 101

Lanaud, Yves, 142

Lang, Arthur, 184

Lang, Jon, 180, 189

Langepin, 189

Lantis, Mary, 176

Lasers, 192

Latin America, 138, 140, 143–44, 175, 206

Lawrence, Massachusetts, 34

Lea, Dan, 164

Leach, William, 47

Lebanese Civil War, 143

Leclerc, Guy, 99

Leeds, United Kingdom, 140

Lefever, Terence, 179–80, 194, 197, 200

Leibee Block, 16

Leipzig Industrial Fair, 136

Leipzig Trade Fair, 75

Lemoille River, 10

Lend Lease Act, 80, 91, 162

Liberty Bonds, 55

Liberty ships, 83

Life magazine, 125

Lincoln Electric Company, 50, 71, 74–75, 123, 132, 161, 183, 187, 199, 203

Lincoln family, 6

Lincoln, James F., 50, 71, 132–133

Lincoln, John C., 50

Linde, 71, 122

Liquid Natural Gas (LNG) Tankers, 170

Little Sandy (dredge), 113–115

Livermore, California, 192

Lockheed Constellation, 108

London, England, 22

London, Ontario, 183

Long, G. S., 17

Lorenz and Williams, 207

Lorimer, George, 20

Los Angeles, California, 132

Lost Creek, 48

LTD Battery Chargers, 197

Luftwaffe, 78

Lustron Corporation, 69

Lutz, Byron, 61, 90, 117, 153, 162

Lutz, Julie, 197

M

M-2 Stuart tank, 83

M-3 Grant tank, 83

M-4 Sherman Tank, 119

M-4 Sherman tank, 83

M-5 37 millimeter anti-aircraft gun, 83

Macy, Lieutenant Commander R. L., 88

Madison (Colgate) University, 10

magnetic particle testing, 166

Main Street Office Building, 81

Manhattan Island, 163

Manhattan Project, 113

Manila, Philippines, 147

Marines, U.S., 68

Marion Power Shovel, 119

Marshall Space Center, 185

Martek Lasers, 192

Martin Marietta, 184, 185–86

Massachusetts Bay Colony, 6

Matsushita (Panasonic), 180

McCauley, Roy B., 123

MCD Plastics, 207

McKaig, J. W., 17

McKay® Welding Products, 196, 198–99, 200

McKee, Arthur, 117

McKenna, Hillary, 49

McKinnon Dash Company, 18

McKinsey and Company, 150

McKnight, E. H., 17, 18

McLeod, Gordon, 146

Means, J. W., 25

Meeker, David B., 174

Melbourne, Florida, 115

Memorial Stadium, Troy, 96

Menke Park, 134

Menke, Orval H., 30, 68, 70, 78, 80, 94, 134, 159–60

Metallogen, 140, 151

Metcalf, David C., 91

Mexico City, Mexico, 75, 198

Mexico, 57, 78, 113, 136, 140, 144, 196–97

Miami Conservancy District, 35, 93–94, 206

Miami County Commission, 92

Miami County Courthouse, 18, 25, 208

Miami County Fairgrounds, 92

Miami County Mental Heath, 206

Miami County Park District, 207

Miami County Progressive Party, 35

Miami County, 6, 77, 89, 95

Miami County, unemployment, 175

Miami East High School, 80

Miami Queen, 155

Miami River, Great, 17, 23, 31, 48, 93, 96, 99, 102, 113, 115, 117, 204, 208

Miami Shores Golf Course, 96

Miami Specialty Company, 79, 89, 160

Miami Union, 26, 31, 33–34

Miami Valley School, 207

Miami Valley, 16, 93, 99, 100, 132, 159, 190, 204

Miami Valley, paper mills, 17

Miami, Florida, 143, 180

Miami-Erie Canal, 31, 40

Michoud, 184

"Microwire®," 130–31, 138, 167

Mid-Canada Line, 111

Middle Ages, 51

Middle East, 138, 144

Middletown City Council, 13

Middletown Edison, 12–13

Middletown Signal, 8, 13

Middletown, Ohio, 8, 11, 16–17, 25, 28, 66, 95; paper mills, 13; public lighting controversy, 12

Midway, Battle of, 88

Midwest, 7, 58, 76–78, 152, 175, 209

Milanados, Konstantine, 125

Milestone Club, 156

Miller Electric, 123, 187–88, 199, 201, 203

Miller, Glenn, 102

Miller, Niels C., 73, 199

remote control patent, 71

Renegotiation, 89

Republican Party, 25

Republicans, 25–27

Revco Drug Stores, 170

Rex, Louise, 153

Rich, Major Carl, 88

Ridge Avenue, 69

Ritchie, Colonel Scott, 83

Robbins and Meyers, 195

Roberts, Mervyn, 140

Rochester Electric Products Corporation, 70

Rockefeller, John D., 10, 63

Rockwell International, 170

Rogers, Roy, 99

Rome, Italy, 139

Roosevelt, Franklin Delano, 60, 69, 77, 79, 80

Roosevelt, Theodore, 25–26

"Rosie the Riveter," 89

Ross, Donald, 94

Ross, Roy, 47

Rotary Club, 19, 93

Roy Smith Company, 153, 199

RT (Riverside Training) Industries, 197–98

Ruhr, 138

Russell, J. Edward, 26

Russia, 84

Russian Ministry of Civil Aviation, 186

Rust Belt, 174

Rutile, 112–13, 117–18, 132

S

Sabin, Alvah, 10

Sales Department, Hobart Brothers, 58

Salesian Order, 145

Sampson, John, 81, 107

San Francisco Bay, 166

Sand Ridge (Florida), 113, 118

Santiago, Chile, 143, 198

Saratoga Springs, New York, 100

Sargent, Jeanne, 159, 179

Saudi Arabia, 140, 143, 153

Schaffer, Gregory, 181

Schauer, Joseph, 17

Schmidt, Lajos, 138

Schmueker, Richard, 158

Schnabel, Robert, 173, 179

Schober, William, 121

Schreiber, J. J. Servan, 139

Schwab, Conrad, 181, 197, 198

Scott, George W., 17

Scott, Gerry, 168

Scott, Ron, 188

Scully, Vincent, 103

Sea Island, Georgia, 100

Sears Tower, 164

Sears, Roebuck and Company, 23

Seattle, Washington, 101, 132

Sebastian Inlet, 118

Seiko Denki, 110

Semi-automatic welding packages, 130–131

September 11, 2001, 207

Seventy-ninth Armored Division, 90

Shah of Iran, 143

Sharrett, Charles, 207

Shay, Harry, 156–57

Sherwood, Dick, 101, 121, 129

Shinney, 28

Shipman, L. H., Sr., 92

Sidwell Friends School (Washington, D.C.), 101

Sigfridsson, Berndt, 190

Signal Corps, U.S. Army, 78, 84

Sikorsky Skycrane Helicopter, 166

Silicon Valley, 190

Singapore, 147, 198

Skoda Works, 136

Skypod, 164

Sloan, Alfred, 39

Smith College, 35, 101

West, Johnson, 78

Westbrook, 96, 115, 119

Western Europe, 142, 190

Westford, Vermont, 6, 8, 10, 205

Westinghouse, 16, 30, 33, 71, 122, 134

Weston, Massachusetts, 13

Westover Prep School, 100

wet mill separation (of minerals), 115

Weybridge, Vermont, 8

Whalen, Joe, 49

Whaley, Paul, 160, 162, 176, 180

Wharton School of Business, 31, 102

Whidby Island, 101

Whippany, New Jersey, 16

Whirlpool, 202

Whitlow, Dick, 137

Wichita State University, 46

Wildenthaler, Leo, 159, 169, 187

William Blair and Company, 202

Williams, Gladys, 134, 207

Williams, Glyn, 80, 121, 124, 130, 134, 207

Williams, Megan, 207

Williams, Roger, 161–62, 179–81, 187, 197

Williamsburg, Virginia, 63

Willys, 82, 84

Wilson, Woodrow, 26, 33, 52

Wimbledon, 49

WING radio station, 88

Winter Beach, Florida, 113

Winter Olympics, 1988, Calgary, 99

Wogoman, Keith, 168

Wolf, Michael A., 192, 195, 197, 199

Wollard Airport Equipment, 180, 200

Women's Christian Temperance Union, 26

Women's League of Voters, 100

women's suffrage, 26

Woodman, Chet, 176, 182

Woodstock, Ontario, 143, 151, 158, 183

Works Progress Administration (WPA), 60, 77

World Trade Center, 162–64, 207

World War I, 27, 33–34, 51–52. 77, 92, 136

World War II, 6, 58, 69–70, 77, 91–92, 102, 104, 110, 112, 120, 134, 136, 160, 162

World's Fair in Brussels (1958), 162

worldwide sourcing, 161

Worman, Frank T., 17

Wright Cycle Shop, 16

Wright, Frank Lloyd, 81

Wright, Orville, 20

Wright, Wilbur, 20

Wright-Patterson Air Force Base, 49, 104, 111

X

x-rays, 75, 78

Y

Yale University, 80, 101-02, 195

Yamasaki, Minoru, 163

Yaskawa Electric, 146, 189, 198, 200, 204

York, Pennsylvania, 196, 199

Young Business Men's Club, 92

Yugo, 198

Yugoslavia, 103

Z

Zambon, Anna, 103, 137

Zeifkovits, Anton, 140

Zircon, 113, 117

Zirconium, 113

Zug, Switzerland, 138

Zundapp motorcycle, 75

Zurich, Switzerland, 182

About the Authors

Peter C. Hobart is the youngest member of the third generation of "Industrial Hobarts. "He spent over thirty-five years with Hobart Brothers Company traveling the world as a Board member, shareholder, and spokesman for the firm. During most of those years he served as executive vice president in charge of the International Division. Today he is a consultant for ITW, which bought the company in 1996. His experience, his contacts, and his international perspective were essential in composing a balanced history of Hobart Brothers and its founding family.

Hobart has written extensively on a variety of topics, such as technology, international business, and art. Many of his articles have appeared in the *Welding Journal* as well as other international and American trade publications. These articles include "Some Significant Aspects of Welding in Europe," "Welded Sculpture: A Truly American Art Form, Ecological Consideration in Modern Arc Welding."

Hobart was educated in Ohio and Connecticut and graduated with honors from Yale in 1957, earning a bachelor of fine arts with minors in business and engineering. He was an active member of the International Institute of Welding, a fellow of the British Welding Institute and an American delegate to the International Standards Organization. From 1990 to 1996 Hobart chaired the International Sculpture Center and continues to represent the center as chairman emeritus. From 1998 to 2002 Hobart produced some seventy documentary films on modern art and sculpture. Recently, Hobart served as president of Amaranta Productions, a company in Rome that documents contemporary art and modern culture through film and video.

Peter Hobart is an accomplished public speaker and a fluent linguist who has given talks, lectures, and presentations around the world in several languages for the organizations he represents. He is the recipient of many awards in the fields of business, art, and civic service. Peter Hobart lives in Rome with his wife-to-be, Adriana Vitali. He has a daughter, Michelle; a son, Peter John; and three grandchildren.

Michael W. Williams is a writer of local history who teaches social studies and English at the Miami Valley Career Technology Center. For the past four years Williams has researched family and company records and interviewed Hobart family members, business associates, and longtime employees to help compose a picture of the "Industrial Hobarts" of Troy, Ohio, and the companies they created.

Williams writes articles on Ohio businesses in the early twentieth century for *Timeline*, the magazine of the Ohio Historical Society, such as "Profits from Prohibition: Walter Kidder and the Hayner Distillery's Mail Order Alcohol" in the March/April 1999 issue of *Timeline*. This article tells the story of a Dayton-based company which legally earned millions selling liquor by mail order to customers in dry states and counties in the years leading up to national prohibition.

Williams earned a master's degree in history from the University of Dayton where most of his graduate work was in the field of Cold War diplomacy, which provided good background for understanding the defense-related work and international business of Hobart Brothers Company. Since 1987, he has devoted summers to writing projects and teaching history at the University of Dayton and Sinclair Community College.

In 1990 Williams received a Teacher Initiative Grant for "History in Your Own Back Yard," which encourages students to conduct interviews and do other primary research in order to compose a report on family or local history. Williams enjoys presenting his research projects to educational conferences and groups with an interest in local history. He lives in Vandalia, Ohio, with his wife, Mary, and his daughters, Shannon and Emily.

The Industria

1850 1860 1870 1880   1890   1900   1910   1920

...began with Clarence Charles Hobart

Clarence Charles
"C.C." Hobart
b. 20 Sept. 1854,
Westford, VT

Admitted to
Bar 1881

Meets Edison
1885

Marries **Lou Ella Jones**
June 16, 1886

Colgate University
1873-1876

Iowa Law School
1876-1879

Edward Alvah Hobart
b. December 25, 1888

Charles Clarence Hobart
b. September 22, 1890

William Harrison Hobart
b. December 31, 1892

Moves family
to Troy, Ohio
September 1895

Helps found
Miami County
Progressive party
1912

Progressive
candidate
for Congress
1914

Hobart Trade
first conducted
Hobart factory

C.C. Hobart president
E.A. Hobart engineer
Charles Hobart finance
William Hobart sales
Incorporated
March 24, 1917

C.C. Hobart sells off
part of the business
to his partners
July 30, 1914

Separate
business
formed f
cabinet
making
1926

First arc
welder
built
1925

C.C. Hobart president
founded Sept. 1904

...and the five companies he founded

**The American Fixture
& Manufacturing Co.**

The Hobart Brothers Company

Charles Hobart
president

C.C. Hobart president
J. Ambrose Johnston vice-president
H.L. Johnston secretary/treasurer
Edward S. Johnston director
Lou E. Hobart director
incorporated July 20, 1897

Owners Ben Gibbs
and Forrest Stephens

**The American Fixture
& Manufacturing Co.**

C.C. Hobart's business ventures

**The Hobart Electric
Manufacturing Company**

**The Hobart Manufacturing
Company, 1913**

**The Hobart Electric
Company
Middletown, OH**
founded 1886.
Destroyed by fire
April 30, 1890

C.C. Hobart sells his interest
in the company to
A.G. Stouder, E.E. Edgar
and W.E. Bowyer
December 1903

A.G. Stouder president
H.L. Johnston vp/gen mgr
W.H. Coles secretary
E.F. Edgar treasurer
W.E. Bowyer director
January 1904

KitchenAid
trade name
first used for
household products
1918

...during an era of change

Thomas Edison invents the
incandescent electric light 1879

Albert Einstein publishes
Theory of Relativity 1905

First
electric
welding
machine
1907

Charles Kettering invents the
automotive ignition system 1911

Stock market crash

Penicillin discovere
192

First practical four-stroke internal
combustion engine invented 1876

Thomas Edison is granted
the first of over 100
dynamo-electric machine
patents 1880

C.L. Coffin patents first
welding process using
a metal electrode 1890

Strohmenger's
first coated
electrode 1900

Henry Ford creates the
assembly line 1913

TIG welding
invented 1926

A.G. Bell
patents the
telephone
1876

Carbon arc welding
patented by Benardos
& Olszewski 1885

Ford
Model T
introduced
1908

Stainless
steel
invented
1916

U.S. enters
WWI 1917

First
liquid-fueled
rocket 1926

Henry Bessemer
patents his steelmaking
process 1855

U.S.
Civil War
1861-1865

Spanish-American
War 1898

Wright
Brothers
flight 1903

AWS founded 1919

1850 1860 1870 1880   1890   1900   1910   1920

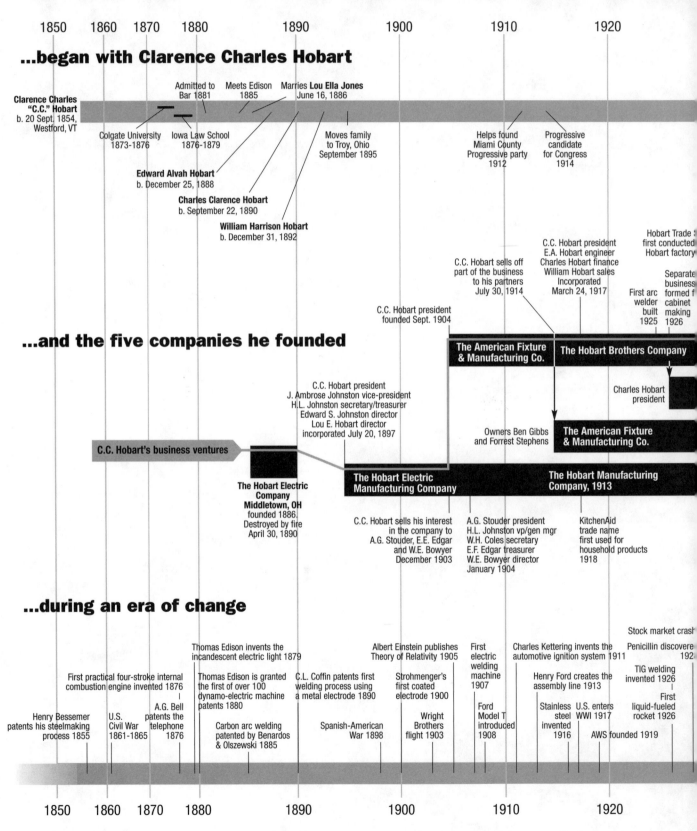